£ 60-00 ONyt
_10006

D1134710

LEEDS BECKETT

Leeds Metropolitan University

17 0467470 9

In the Secret Theatre of Home
Wilkie Collins, sensation narrative, and nineteenth-century psychology

Jenny Bourne Taylor

Routledge
London and New York

LEEDS METROPOLITAN
UNIVERSITY
LIBRARY
1704674709
KV-B
CC-68586
27.10.2006
823.8 Col

First published in 1988 by
Routledge
11 New Fetter Lane
London EC4P 4EE

29 West 35th Street, New York NY 10001

© 1988 Jenny Bourne Taylor

Set in 10/12 pt Plantin, Compugraphic by
Mayhew Typesetting, Bristol, England
Printed in Great Britain by
T.J. Press (Padstow), Cornwall

All rights reserved. No part of this book may be reprinted or reproduced or
utilized in any form or by any electronic, mechanical or other means, now
known or hereafter invented, including photocopying and recording, or in any
information storage or retrieval system, without permission in writing from the
publishers.

British Library Cataloguing in Publication Data

Taylor, Jenny Bourne
In the secret theatre of home: Wilkie
Collins, sensation narrative, and
nineteenth century psychology.
1. Fiction in English. Collins, Wilkie,
1824–1889. Critical studies
I. Title
823'.8
ISBN 0-415-00707-0

Library of Congress Cataloging in Publication Data

Taylor, Jenny, 1949–
In the secret theatre of home: Wilkie Collins, sensation narrative, and
nineteenth-century psychology / by Jenny Bourne Taylor.
p. cm.
Bibliography: p.
Includes index.
ISBN 0-415-00707-0
1. Collins, Wilkie, 1824-1889–Knowledge–Psychology
2. Psychology in literature. 3. Sensationalism in literature.
4. Detective and mystery stories, English–History and criticism.
5. Domestic fiction, English–History and criticism. I. Title.
PR4498.P8T39 1988
823'.8–dc19 87–37623

To my mother, Joan Bourne,
and to John Goode

Her pale, sickly, moist-looking skin; her large, mild, watery, light-blue eyes; the restless, vigilant timidity of her expression; the mixture of useless hesitation and nervous, involuntary activity in every one of her actions, all furnished the same significant betrayal of a life of fear and restraint; of a disposition full of modest generosities and meek sympathies that had been crushed down past rousing to self-assertion, past ever seeing the light. There, in that mild wan face of hers – in those painful startings and hurryings when she moved, in that tremulous faint utterance when she spoke – *there* I could see one of those ghastly heart-tragedies laid open before me, which are not to be written, but which are acted and re-acted, scene by scene, year by year, in the secret theatre of home.

Wilkie Collins, *Basil, A Story of Modern Life*

CONTENTS

ACKNOWLEDGEMENTS

Thanks to the staff of the Leeds Library, the London Library, and the Wellcome Medical Library for their helpful assistance during the course of researching this book, and to Ele Hay and Beverley Toulson for typing the manuscript. Helpful comments and criticisms were offered at various stages of this project by Gillian Beer, Peter Fozzard, Heather Glen, Bill Greenslade, Malcolm Hardman, Cora Kaplan, Tom Kitwood, Roy Porter, Lorna Sage, Simon Schaffer, Ann Scott, Sally Shuttleworth, and Sheila Smith: thanks, too, to them. I'm particularly grateful to Diana Coole, Gill Frith and Simon Frith for providing much needed support at various crucial stages, and above all to John Goode for his unstinting and sustained encouragement, advice, and friendship.

Collins as a sensation novelist

> To Mr Collins belongs the credit of having
> introduced into fiction those most mysterious of
> mysteries, the mysteries that are at our own doors.
> This innovation gave a new impetus to the literature
> of horrors. It was fatal to Mrs Radcliffe and her
> everlasting castle in the Appenines. What are the
> Appenines to us or we to the Appenines? Instead of
> the terrors of Udolpho, we were treated to the terrors
> of the cheerful country house, or the busy London
> lodgings. And there is no doubt that these were
> infinitely the more terrible.
>
> Henry James, *'Miss Braddon'*[1]

Wilkie Collins was an enormously popular nineteenth-century writer
whose career ranged from 1848 to 1889, peaking in the 1860s with
The Woman in White, No Name, Armadale, and *The Moonstone.*
Collins now reads as one of the most 'modern' (even post-modern)
of nineteenth-century novelists. He emphasizes play, doubling, and
duplicity. His labyrinthine narratives are dialogic and self-reflexive.
His heroines can be transgressive and his villains engaging. He
breaks down stable boundaries between wildness and domesticity,
self and other, masculinity and femininity, 'black' and 'white'.
Moreover, his stories involve not only complex explorations of forms
of perception, of consciousness and cognition, but also of the shaping of social identity, above all within that simultaneously psychic
and economic institution the family; they investigate the relationship
between ways of seeing and forms of power. Collins's writing, it
seems, probes 'those most mysterious of mysteries, the mysteries
that are at our own doors' by transposing the disruptive and disturbing elements of Gothic fiction into the homely setting of the family
and the everyday, recognizable world, thus generating suspense and
exploiting undercurrents of anxiety that lie behind the doors of the
solid, recognizable, middle-class home. Closer investigation reveals
that Collins undercuts the familiarity and stability of that world, not
by reaching 'outside' the immediate framework of his culture, but

by assimilating and resisting a contradictory set of contemporary discourses. Discourses about consciousness and identity, about the social formation of the self, about the workings of the unconscious and the interlinking of the mind and the body, about the problematic boundaries between sanity and madness – the concerns of nineteenth-century psychology.

This book considers the connections between stories and theories in popular narratives by exploring the ways in which nineteenth-century ideas about the workings of the mind transform and are transformed in Collins's fiction. It investigates the links between 'literature' and 'psychology': an intricate set of interrelationships whose meanings continually feed into and change each other. It explores how Collins's fiction works at the uneven limits of Victorian ideology by manipulating and interweaving an extraordinarily wide range of contemporary psychological writings, drawing on aspects of those theories to explore social and psychic contradictions, but also transposing them into other keys, pressing them into service as sources of narrative closure or resolution. These theories shape possible meanings within the novels; they also helped to create the cultural context within which Collins's fiction was read. For Collins was read first and foremost as a *sensation* novelist, whose work often, as he put it, 'overstepped in more than one direction, the narrow limits within which [critics] are disposed to restrict the development of modern fiction'.[2] It emerged out of what was perceived as the hardening boundary between popular and serious fiction, and placed within a cultural hierarchy that was in turn framed within particular psychological and physiological terms, terms which provided the context that made sense of the narratives themselves.

'Sensation' was one of the keywords of the 1860s. It encapsulated the particular ways in which the middle-class sense of cultural crisis was experienced during that decade, and its overlapping multiple meanings were conflated in one of its most discussed manifestations, the sensation novel. In one sense this wasn't so much a coherent literary tendency or genre, more a critical term held together by the word 'sensation' itself, and anxieties about what it might signify. Thus *The Woman in White*, initially serialized in *All the Year Round* between 1859 and 1860, was the first novel to be accorded the title, but it was then discussed as both a typical and a superior species of the genre; other chief representatives besides Collins were very different novelists – Mary Braddon, Charles Reade, Mrs Henry Wood – while Dickens, Le Fanu, and Rhoda Broughton, for example, regularly slid in and out of the 'sensation' category.[3] When critics self-consciously referred to the 1860s as the 'age of sensation', they meant, in an obvious way, that the word encapsulated the experience of modernity itself – the sense of continuous and rapid change, of shocks, thrills, intensity, excitement. This was the immediate sense in which Margaret Oliphant used the word in her discussion, in *Blackwood's Edinburgh Magazine* in 1862, of three sensation novels, Collins's *The Woman in White*, Dickens's *Great Expectations*, and Mrs Wood's *East Lynne*. The fictional phenomenon, she argued, is product and expression of a prosaic and secularized culture, in which 'we recognise the influence of a system which has paralysed all the wholesome wonders and nobler mysteries of human existence', which has encountered the shocks of rapid social change, and which, ten years after the expansionist optimism expressed by the Great Exhibition, now feels a sense of anticlimax, of decline:

> We, who once did, and made, and declared ourselves masters of all things, have relapsed into the natural size of humanity before the events that have given a new character to the age. . . . It is a changed world in which we are now standing. . . . It is only natural, in an age that has turned out to be one of event, that art and literature should attempt a kindred depth of effect and shock of incident.[4]

But equally important, the fashionable obsession with the idea of sensation soon became as significant as the ubiquity of 'sensation' itself. 'Not a new sensation' in *All the Year Round* remarked:

> It is much the fashion now to dwell with severity on certain morbid failings and cravings of the grand outside Public – the universal customer – the splendid bespeaker, who goes round every market, purse in hand, and orders plays, poems, novels, pictures, concerts and operas. Yet this taste for fiery sauces and strongly-seasoned meats and drinks is of very ancient date, nay, with the public – so long as it has been a public – it has been a constant taste.[5]

The 'new sensation' was chiefly the newly defined importance of the notion, the journal argued, and it was this that gave the form its status as 'something novel and significant of degeneration'.

Writers have not been slow to perceive that the columns of the daily papers were becoming formidable rivals to quiet novels; and

> it is probably only as a result of the admirable organisation of the
> literary market, that a supply of acceptable fiction has so closely
> followed, or has even to some degree anticipated and created the
> demand

argued an article on the causes and effects of the form in the *Medical
Critic and Psychological Journal,* and the sensation *novel* became a
particularly redolent symptom of cultural, moral, and social crisis
precisely because responses to it formed a chain of associations
which linked its specific conventions, its effect on the reader, its
method of production, and its narrative technique.[6] These connections were forged in the first place through physiological metaphors,
as symptoms which themselves had, principally, physiological
effects. And they thus helped to articulate anxiety about imminent
cultural decline by referring to an image of an implicitly 'feminine'
body that was at once its product and metonymic model, and by
assuming a set of nervous responses that had become pathological by
their very susceptibility to intense excitement and reaction; which
suggested in a single figure the most primitive and atavistic of
human responses and the most advanced signs of civilization, of
frenetic modern life.[7]

The sensation novel was seen as a collective cultural nervous
disorder, a morbid addiction within the middle class that worked
directly on the body of the reader and as an infection from outside,
continually threatening to pollute and undermine its boundaries
through this process of metaphoric transference and analogy. For
the form encapsulated at least two of the slippery meanings of
'popular fiction' – the 'light reading' of a middle-class and
predominantly female public on the one hand, the 'mass entertainment' of a relatively newly formed lower-middle- and upper-
working-class readership on the other – and blurred any possible
distinction between them. 'A class of literature has grown up around
us', Henry Mansel argued in the *Quarterly Review* in 1862,

> usurping in many respects, intentionally, or unintentionally, a
> portion of the preacher's office, playing no inconsiderable part in
> moulding the minds and forming the tastes and habits of its
> generation, and doing so principally, we had almost said
> exclusively, by preaching to the nerves . . . . Excitement, and
> excitement alone seems to be the great end to which they aim. . . .
> And as excitement, even when harmless in kind, cannot be
> continually reproduced without becoming morbid in degree,
> works of this class manifest themselves as belonging, some more,

some less, but all to some extent, to the morbid phenomenon of literature, indications of a widespread corruption, of which they are in part both the effect and the cause; called into existence to supply the cravings of a diseased appetite, and contributing themselves to foster the disease, and to stimulate the want that they supply. . . . A commercial atmosphere hangs around works of this class, redolent of the manufactory or the shop.[8]

It was the form's cynical position as commodity that contributed to its druglike qualities, and three factors were principally responsible for this: circulating libraries, railway bookstalls, and weekly serialization, he argued. Margaret Oliphant stressed that

> the violent stimulus of serial publication – of *weekly* publication – with its necessity for frequent and rapid recurrence of piquant incident and startling situation – is the thing above all others most likely to develop the germ, and bring it to fuller and darker bearing.[9]

The *Westminster Review* too compared the phenomenon with medieval lycanthropy and other forms of both collective insanity and plague: 'Now we have sensational mania. . . . Its virus is spreading in all directions, from the penny journal to the shilling magazine and from the shilling magazine to the thirty-shillings volume.[10]

So the panic generated by the sensation novel as much as the mode itself provided a focus for a range of distinct, though interrelated, tensions about wider and longer-term transformations that were taking place in middle-range middle-class publishing and literary culture. As with responses to the Minerva Press, the establishment and expansion of the circulating libraries, and the rise of Gothic romance in the eighteenth century, worries about the effects on the public's nervous systems, particularly those of 'vulnerable' women readers, were connected with anxieties that class-based cultural boundaries were breaking down with the expansion of new methods of production and circulation: 'She may boast without fear of contradiction, of having temporally succeeded in making the literature of the kitchen the favourite reading of the Drawing Room', the *North British Review* remarked of Mary Braddon.[11] But this anxiety was now specifically connected with worries about the longer-term *evolution* of generic conventions and cultural forms, and here the most important question was whether the sensation novel represented a modern adaptation of earlier Gothic or romance forms or a degenerated sub-species of them – and thus a morbid deviation from a dominant mode. 'Sensation' was now posed against 'sensibility', retrospectively elevating the latter; unlike the quivering reaction generated by the very fantastic and exotic intensity of Gothic romance in which the finely tuned nerves operated as delicate moral mediators, the immediate nervous reaction elicited by sensation fiction apparently short-circuited morality, and thus became morbid by becoming more directly sensualized. 'The faults of the French school are creeping into our literature and threaten to flourish there', maintained *Fraser's Magazine*. 'The morbid analysation of feeling, which we have already reprobated, bids fair to be succeeded by an equally morbid analysation of mere sensation.'[12] 'The progress of fiction as an art', the *Westminster Review*'s article on the evolution of narrative forms, had begun to discuss this process in 1853, arguing firstly that fictional forms became more complex as they came to correspond more closely with the conceptual and scientific models of their culture; secondly, that cultural progress itself was marked by an increasingly hierarchic division between 'higher' and 'lower' forms – divisions that were thus its inevitable concomitant. In this analysis there was a class of novel (represented here by Collins's *Basil*) which occupied an uneasy liminal, or threshold, realm as a form of naturalistic fantasy. This new type was based in recognizable everyday reality rather than the purely marvellous setting of romance proper; it drew on subjective sense experience in a way that correspond with contemporary scientific models, but as it attempted to achieve the intensity of supernatural terror by these means, the stress on subjectivity now meant that the real itself was pathologized. 'It was the fashion then to construct a story out of strange and unnatural *circumstances*, it is the fashion now to elaborate it out of morbid *feelings* and overwrought *sensibilities*.'[13]

Yet this shift towards a materialist supernaturalism, in which 'terror' grew out of realistic psychological and physiological devices and processes used to achieve 'Gothic' effects, was not new either. Actually it had taken place many years before, and in both *Basil* and his early short stories Collins was accentuating a shift in fictional conventions that had begun at the end of the eighteenth century and was developed in the work of Godwin, of Mary Shelley, of Hogg, of the writers of the 'Tales' whose tensions were based primarily in physiological sensation published in *Blackwood's Edinburgh Magazine* and above all in Edgar Allen Poe's intricate, obsessive exploration of the interconnections between physiological and psychological states.[14] George Eliot had approvingly noted the influence of Poe in her review of the collection of stories *After Dark* in the *Westminster Review* in 1856:

> The great interest lies in the excitement either of curiosity or of terror. . . . Instead of turning pale at a ghost we knit our brows and construct hypotheses to account for it. Edgar Poe's tales were an effort of genius to reconcile the two tendencies – to appal the imagination yet satisfy the intellect, and Mr Wilkie Collins in this respect often follows in Poe's tracks.[15]

And while the fictional assimilation of 'sensationist' psychological references only culminated fully with the sensation novel of the 1860s, it contributed to the mode's morbid cultural status primarily in becoming a link in a new chain of cultural and psychological associations, creating meanings which were linked in turn with the other characteristics of the form – above all, though not exclusively, its fascination with various forms of transgressive sexuality. Sensation fiction certainly shared a common pool of narrative tropes, but these were not stable; they drew on and broke down distinct methods of generating strangeness within familiarity, of creating the sense of a weird and different world within the ordinary, everyday one: the tale of terror, high melodrama, the 'Newgate' novel, the domestic story. And it was through these intricate interactions that its appeal to sensation, to 'nerves', had both such psychological resonance and social complexity, providing it with the means that enabled it to explore 'those most mysterious of mysteries, the mysteries that are at our own doors' by bringing into play the possibilities offered by its central narrative features – *secrecy* and *disguise*.

These features were brought into play above all by narrative intricacy, by the plotting itself, the vital characteristic by which sensation fiction was at once distinguished and condemned. The *Spectator* identified 'a host of cleverly complicated stories, the whole interest of which consists in the gradual unravelling of some carefully prepared enigma'.[16] That enigma often involved the disclosure of transgression or villainy – the tearing off of a mask, the lifting of a veil. But what was particularly exciting was that the pleasurable process of unravelling itself involved revealing a secret identity which in turn disclosed not a truth, but another set of questions and dissemblances which hinged on the transgressor's position within the family. In Mary Braddon's *Lady Audley's Secret*, Lady Audley's ostensible secret – that she is a bigamist – both conceals and reveals a further one – that she is mad. As with melodrama, tension hinges on things not being what they seem, but here identity is not simply dissembled through a masquerade. People assume false selves in order to steal a position and a property or to retrieve a place that they had lost: the fallen, outcast heroine of Mrs Henry Wood's *East Lynne*, her face rendered unrecognizable by a railway accident, steals back to her lost home, disguised as the governess to her own children, playing a role that is essentially a lower pitch of her earlier one. In sensation fiction masks are rarely stripped off to reveal an inner truth, for the mask is both the transformed expression of the 'true' self and the means of disclosing its incoherence. In the process identity itself emerges as a set of elements that are actively constructed within a dominant framework of social interests, perceptions, and values. These novels thus focused on the ambiguity of social and psychological codes to insinuate that seeming, too, is not always what it seems to be.

The novels' deviant critical status as a form of morbid naturalism thus depended simultaneously on the two aspects of the way that they explored the instability of social and psychic identity: their focus on plotting, the complex unravelling of incident hinging on improbable coincidence and chance, combined with an unhealthy interest in deviant or abnormal figures, above all, transgressive women. The *Westminster Review* attacked *Armadale* for exhibiting its pathological characters as specimens like freaks at a fairground, stressing at the same time: 'To admire the plot and forget the characters is like admiring the frame instead of enjoying the picture. . . . The sight of having our dinners cooked takes away our appetite.'[17] Yet such hostility was by no means ubiquitous – in 1866, for example, the eminent psychologist Alexander Bain emphasized that plotting, above all, 'that peculiar attitude of suspense while on the gaze of some approaching, and as yet uncertain end, is a powerful fascination', and that it was a characteristic of both poetry and prose even though it was developed most fully in the novel.[18] Also in 1866 E.S. Dallas, one of the most interesting critics of the 1860s, explored the interconnections between the demands of the narrative and the construction of identity within it. In his fascinating attempt to develop a 'science of the laws of pleasure', *The Gay Science* (1866), he maintained that there was nothing inherently inferior, either epistemologically or ontologically, in 'plot centred' novels, and that

the difference between the two lies solely in the relation of the character portrayed to the actions described. . . . The art of fiction, which makes character succumb to the exigencies of plot, is just as defensible as that which breaks down incident before the weight of character.[19]

He noted, too, that while 'plotting' novels apparently

represent circumstance and incident as all important, and characters amid the current of events as corks upon the waves, they generally introduce one character who, in violent contrast to all the others, is superior to the plot, plans the events, guides the storm. . . . He predominates over the plot and the plot predominates over all else.[20]

And as he had acknowledged in his review of *Lady Audley's Secret* in *The Times*, the demands of the narrative itself posed a challenge to conventional representations of femininity which sensation fiction boldly took up, for 'if the heroines have the first place, it will scarcely do to represent them as passive and quite angelic, or insipid – which heroines usually are. They have to be high-strung women, full of passion, purpose, and movement.'[21] At its best, sensation fiction did much more than exploit the narrative possibility of female transgression while finally punishing or assimilating it. It deployed intricate narrative structures to turn deviance itself into a relative and complex term, scrutinizing how it was perceived and defined. It displayed villainy as the mimicking inversion of respectability, feminine anomaly as the masquerading of the codes of femininity. It did not so much exploit difference as explore the structures and relations which produced it, and the pivot or the culmination of this process was often the explicit portrayal of *insanity*.

The repeated use of madness as a crucial narrative convention was often seen as the culmination of the form's pathologized fascination with the pathological. But it also, paradoxically, legitimized the kind of naturalistic fantasy that the sensation novel represented by making it explicit and linking it with a widespread fascination with derangement as a vital clue to the workings of the mind. 'Madness in novels', a short piece in the *Spectator* which discussed Braddon's *Lady Audley's Secret*, Mrs Henry Wood's *St Martin's Eve*, and the anonymous *The Clyffords of Clyffe*, ambivantly defined 'madness' as both the fantastic suspension of the real and as a naturalized legitimation of the supernatural; but beyond this, the article stressed that 'madness' might signal an unassimilable 'wildness', yet acknowledged that there was no one formula or set of conventions for assessing how this process worked. 'The nineteenth century believes in love and jealousy, and in a feeble way, even in hate, but it is aware that the mental concentrativeness out of which these passions spring is in this age rare', the article opened. It went on:

> One does not tumble down wells, but in the murder one might, if only it is artistically told, recognise the undeveloped wild beast in one's own heart. Miss Braddon perceived this, and it is to her credit that she discerned a mode of restoring the lost sensational effect to character. Madness may intensify any quality, courage, or hate, or jealousy, or wickedness, and she made Lady Audley mad. Thenceforward she was released from the irksome regime of the probable. . . . Probability becomes unnecessary, *vraisemblance* a burden, naturalness a mistake in art, everything was possible, and the less possible the emotion, the greater the surprise and pleasure. . . . We say it is natural, but in all events the unnaturalness disappears, for no-one except Dr Forbes Winslow knows what is natural in a patient with intermittent lunacy. . . . We do not deny that there is art in depicting the unnatural, an art shown in conceptions like Fuseli's, an art which rivets the spectator, not in what it sees, but in the thought of what it would see were all the conditions of art reversed.[22]

How did madness focus and manipulate such diverse fictional and ideological tensions? Collins's use of insanity as a narrative strategy is more complex than that of any of his contemporaries, but he wrote in a context in which the fictional mediation of madness helped to shape its cultural meaning, just as sensation fiction itself was positioned through reference to particular psychological paradigms. Mary Braddon's *Lady Audley's Secret* (1862), Charles Reade's *Hard Cash* (1863), and Mrs Henry Wood's *St Martin's Eve* (1866) all illustrate this. *Lady Audley's Secret*, for example, took up and inverted some of the patterns of *The Woman in White* in the figure of its heroine Lucy Graham, the bewitching young governess with golden curls and a secret past, who gains wealth and power by substituting a dead woman for herself; takes on a new identity by marrying the ageing Lord Audley; attempts to dispose of her former husband by pushing him down a well and of other adversaries by burning a village inn. In *The Woman in White* Laura's 'whiteness' allows her identity to be obliterated once its social signs have been removed; Braddon's penniless deserted wife, Helen Talboys, turns herself into Lucy Graham, a governess with an empty past, and gambles on the power of her projected image to become 'Lady

Audley'. Collins and Braddon are each in different ways challenging the blonde child-wife stereotype, both probing the links between the confining contemporary constructions of femininity and of insanity. In *The Woman in White* derangement is the product of the way that Laura is manipulated as the result of her situation; in *Lady Audley's Secret* Lucy's 'latent insanity' is given as an explanation of her behaviour – she is bad because she is mad – but also, more tacitly, it means that her pathologization grows out of her position as object of contemplation.

So both novels revolve around the problem of how to see and how to interpret, each using the expectation generated by the idea of insanity as a means of setting up modes of perception, and undercutting them. In each, this generates a more pervasive cognitive uncertainty, which affects not only how the victim or villainess might be seen, but also how the detective consciousness reads reality, how he interprets the evidence of his own senses. In each, too, the amateur detective's ability to resolve doubt and act on his interpretation of evidence is bound up with consolidating his own masculinity through transforming his class position – overcoming a stagnant, quasi-feudal order with resolute middle-class professional drive. But while in *The Woman in White* this transformation actively hinges on the production and reconstruction of evidence, the perspective of the omniscient narrator of *Lady Audley* progressively shifts from Lucy to Robert Audley, her nephew by marriage and self-appointed private investigator. She becomes the object of disclosure as he becomes the investigating subject; discovering her secret becomes his passage out of aristocratic ennui and into middle-class fortitude as he assimilates legal codes and procedures and makes them work for him. Within this framework though, a double process is at work, one which forms an impossible figure. For in becoming a detective, Robert Audley not only reconstructs Lucy Graham's identity, but engages with her in a battle over who defines sanity. Lucy's fight to reclaim her place culminates in *her* attempt to label Robert mad and have *him* incarcerated. Thus the final resolution – establishing puerperal insanity in Lucy, consigning her to a Belgian asylum, and firmly establishing Robert's social identity – is a re-enactment, in another key, of the plot by which Lucy attempted to secure her own identity.

So the absence of any stable reference point for defining insanity becomes the fulcrum of the novel's more diffuse ideological ambiguity. Lucy's 'insanity' is both the revelation of a truth and an extension of her ability to continually transform herself, confound

11

the distinction between appearance and reality. Robert's role as detective is to write an alternative story of her past out of a tissue of the insubstantial clues of circumstantial evidence; the suspense hinges on *how* the alternative story of the past might be anchored in the present through the detective work. And just as Lucy's cunning is displayed by her skill in manipulating her own appearance, so the signs of her shifting identity first appear in her literal representation. The first clue to Lady Audley's secret emerges through the obsessional, fetishistic projections of her Pre-Raphaelite *portrait*: 'No-one but a Pre-Raphaelite would have so exaggerated every detail of that delicate face as to give a lurid lightness to the blonde complexion, and a strange, sinister light to the deep-blue eyes.' Appearances are deceitful not so much because what seems to be true is false but because the apparently artificial is in fact the natural, the real. And the means of seeing the painting, too, suggests a complicated truth – transformation, projection, revelation – just as the image both can and cannot be identified with its objectified subject:

> It was so like and so unlike; it was as if you had burnt strange-coloured fires before my lady's face, and by their influence brought out new lines and new expressions never seen in it before. The perfection of feature, the brilliancy of colouring were there; but I suppose the painter had copied quaint medieval monstrosities until his brain had grown bewildered, for my lady, in his portrait of her, had something of the aspect of a beautiful fiend.[23]

Robert Audley's learning of detective skills extrapolates from this: he too finally succeeds in building up a chain of circumstantial evidence by projecting meaning into events, but this process initially makes him doubt his own sanity. 'Why was it I saw some strange mystery in my friend's disappearance?' he asks himself:

> Was it monition or a monomania? What if I am wrong after all? What if this chain that I have constructed link by link, is woven out of my own folly? What if this edifice of horror and suspicion is a mere collection of crotchets – the nervous fancies of a hypochondriacal bachelor? Mr Harcourt Talboys sees no meaning in the events out of which I have created a horrible mystery. I lay the separate links of the chain before him and he cannot recognise their fitness. He is unable to fit them together. Oh my God, if it should be in myself all this time that the misery lies![24]

His vacillation is finally overcome by the reaffirmation of an objective reality, which solidifies the links of apparently arbitrary associations; but this in turn depends on deciphering the associative patterns that underlie the apparent delusion. And the truth, when discovered, underlines the deceptiveness of the 'orderly outward world'. The novel finally incarcerates Lucy; but this incarceration has particular, and horrific undertones – the relevant chapter is entitled 'Buried alive'. What is left is a narrative monologue acknowledging the fragility of the order that Lucy's oscillating identity challenged, making the very rigidity of external reality a pathological sign:

> Who has not felt, in the first madness of sorrow, an unreasoning rage against the mute propriety of chairs and tables, the stiff squareness of Turkey carpets, the unbending obstinacy of the outward apparatus of existence? We want to root up gigantic trees in a primeval forest, and to tear their huge branches asunder in our convulsive grasp; and the utmost we can do for the relief of our passion is to knock over an easy chair, or smash a few shillings worth of Mr Copeland's manufacture.
>
> Madhouses are large, and only too numerous; yet surely it is strange they are not larger, when we think of how many hopeless wretches must beat their brains against this hopeless persistency of the orderly outward world, as compared to the storm and tempest, the riot and confusion within: when we think of how many minds must tremble on the narrow boundary between reason and unreason, mad today and sane tomorrow, mad yesterday and sane today.[25]

In *St Martin's Eve*, too, the links between madness and deviant femininity are primarily a means of explaining the heroine's 'unnatural' manipulation of her sexuality to gain a legitimate place; but now the family itself, a psychic as well as a genealogical structure, manifests and reproduces these pathological forms. The lower-middle-class Charlotte Norris, unknowing inheritor of her father's 'taint', marries the gentrified George St John, becoming stepmother to his heir; she and their second son lead a marginalized existence within the family and their displaced relationship to the patrilineal line is compounded by her husband's premature death. Her own 'inheritance' from her father becomes a threat to the pattern of inheritance from which she and her son are both excluded as one genealogy mimics the other. Charlotte's madness, like Lady Audley's, is both 'outside' and 'inside' her, though here her envy and acquisitiveness are on behalf of her son; she suffers from an excess of maternal solicitude, unlike Lady Audley who abandoned her son in a fit of puerperal insanity to seek her own advancement. Charlotte's insanity is half-suggested, half-concealed; one moment an underlying evil nature, the next an incipient propensity which she comes to recognize and struggle against: 'She deliberately intended to do right, but passion and prejudices are strong, unusually strong they were in her, and her mind was ill-regulated.'[26] She is presented as 'striving against her evil nature', at the same time as being driven mad by remorse for the murder of her stepson committed in a fit of madness. Clashing codes of insanity both assimilate and express the 'secret' of Charlotte's nature here, rather than being the truth consolidating the narrative's resolution.

But in Charles Reade's *Hard Cash* the secret and the 'thrill of terror' spring not from madness but from the image of the madhouse, and the stresses it put on the sensibility of the sane subject; the asylum is the 'dark place' where everything is possible – the receptacle of conspiracy and crime. *Hard Cash*, moreover, is an explicitly campaigning novel, which aimed to expose real conditions in actual institutions, and which formed part of a spate of public debate on the confinement of lunatics when it was published in 1863. 'When a writer of sensation romances makes a heroine push a superfluous husband down a well', wrote J.S. Bushman, a physician at Laverstock House asylum in a letter to the *Daily News* during the serialization of the novel as *Very Hard Cash* in *All the Year Round*:

> We smile over the highly seasoned dish, but we do not think to apply the warning to ourselves and for the future avoid sitting on the edge of a draw-well. But when we read, as in the novel *Very Hard Cash* . . . that any man may, at a moment, be consigned to a fate which to a sane man is worse than death, and that not by a single act of any of our Lady Audley's . . . but as part of a regular organised system, with all the compliance of the laws of the land – when we read this, a thrill of terror goes through the public mind. If what Mr Charles Reade says is possible, who is safe?[27]

To which Reade rejoins, 'I . . . desire it to be known that this great question did not begin with me in the pages of this novel, neither shall it end there.'[28] *Hard Cash*, like *The Woman in White*, employs a key sensation convention – one person's wrongful confinement in a private asylum for another's financial gain – and its effects are quite historically specific: they depend on merging the fears elicited by the image of the eighteenth-century madhouse with the particular debates on the nature of confinement and insanity in the late 1850s and early 1860s. Alfred Hardie, the hero, is duped and imprisoned in an asylum by a scheming father because of his knowledge of the latter's fraud. Here the attribution of madness is explicitly seen as a form of social control, re-enacting a family drama of rivalry and retribution between father and son in which the hero is not simply consigned to an unspeakable 'other' place, but to a place where social identity itself is obliterated with the collusion of the most progressive branches of the medical profession. Yet finally the hero reasserts his sanity by reclaiming that social recognition, and the tension revolves around juxtaposing his fundamental coherence with the interpretations of modern psychological medicine, which reads all signs as morbid symptoms. Thus all three novels depend on asserting, ambivalently, that madness may represent absolute difference – 'the wild beast in one's own heart' – *and* that its boundaries are always problematic.

Collins's fiction was part of this cultural context. But, more than any of these contempoary writings, his work raises an intricate set of questions about how to historicize the formation of psychological and fictional conventions, about how to interpret their significance in the light of our own theoretical concerns. For its fantastic and uncanny elements are what seem most 'modern' about Collins's fiction. His novels embody many of the features that Todorov identified as belonging to the 'fantastic-uncanny' mode: they occupy that borderland state between the mimetic and the marvellous in which the boundaries of the real are forever breaking down; they articulate their culture's ambivalence towards the nature of knowledge and identity, they disrupt any fixed relation between the sign and its referent.[29] And beyond this, Collins's fiction is *uncanny* in the specific sense that Freud developed the term in his essay on the phenomenon. Freud argued that weird, or *unheimlich*, elements in a story could not be defined in an obvious way as meaning 'unfamiliar', the opposite of 'homely' – that 'something has to be added to what is novel and unfamiliar' in order to make it 'uncanny', and that something is precisely the *familiar*, as embodied in that ambivalent word, the 'canny'. 'Heimlich' and 'unheimlich', homely and uncanny, should be seen not simply as opposites, but also as replications of each other 'which develop in the direction of ambivalence', he argued; 'heimlich' means cosy, knowable, domesticated, but also hidden, *secret*. 'Uncanny' effects in fiction – the undefinable sense of horror, dread, or haunting, figures returning from the dead, obsessively repeated figures, double selves, madness, somnambulism, or epilepsy – enact the process of projection of the self whereby that ambiguous homeliness is rendered strange, and it is this *strangeness* or wildness that represents the transformation of the familiar that is central to the process of repression itself.[30] In Collins's fiction 'others', split and double selves, are obsessively repeated figures, figures who threaten and move beyond the boundaries of the 'orderly outward world'; they are perceived as anomalous, deviant, or insane, and continually come back in a way that challenges the boundaries that were founded on their exclusion. Strangeness is generated within the perceiving, rational consciousness which is pushed into a state of cognitive uncertainty or an alternative 'visionary' consciousness, recounted through a shifting narrative focus, a struggle over narrative authority, over who defines truth and reality.

Collins's novels are certainly uncanny texts in this respect, and this makes it tempting to apply the kind of analysis of fantasy to his work that extrapolates from Freud's model – to see it as subverting or disrupting 'realist' fictional forms even though it might be ultimately dependent on them. This is the kind of interpretation of transformations within the fantastic mode that is offered, for example, in Rosemary Jackson's *Fantasy: The Literature of Subversion* (1981), and while it develops an important analysis of fantasy, one that expands Todorov's formal distinctions, it leaves open important questions about how to interpret the historical transformation of fictional modes in the light of the psychoanalytic paradigm. For while Rosemary Jackson's analysis of the changing conventions and significance of fantasy aknowledges a process of historical transform-ation in tracing its development from late eighteenth-century Gothic forms in response to an increasingly secularized culture, it none the less still posits the fundamental coherence of the mode itself as the primary criteria of relevance by placing it against its opposite, 'realism'.[31] And while this suggests convincingly that nineteenth-century fantasy was a transformation of the earlier mode in response to cognitive and epistemological changes within the culture, its concomitant, that in the process it was driven 'underneath' a stable set of representational conventions, extrapolates from Freud's notion of psychic repression to explain it in a way that is fraught with problems. For in arguing that these kinds of fantastic motifs always exist in some relation to the real, yet remain the 'wild card' which 'reality' cannot contain, this approach blurs the more contradictory implications of Freud's notion of uncanniness by privileging madness and 'otherness', making them the bearers of a more authentic truth. It also depends on a notion of a stable mimetic realism and a closed scientific system that has to be set up in order to be broken down, so that even though 'realistic' texts contain these subversive elements, a binary opposition within 'realism' as a concomitant of the distinction between realism and fantasy still needs to be sustained if the fantastic mode is to remain unproblematically 'subversive'.

But in Collins's novels 'fantastic' motifs are not simply subjectivized by being given the naturalized setting of domestic realism and thus 'driven underground', so that they return as a repressed 'unconscious' of the text. The narrative conventions themselves draw on the conceptual models of their culture mimetically, and it is this reflexive realism that shifts their cognitive status in the self-conscious use of uncanny, and its ambivalent concomitant, 'canny' motifs. Collins, as will be seen, clearly saw himself as a realist, in a way that paradoxically reinforced, even as it undermined, the complex contempoary sense of the term as being rooted both in and 'beyond' empirical sense experience and incorporating the subjective transformation of external reality; in addition, his development of specific conventions has an implicitly cognitive function in their reworking of contemporary notions of cognition and in their correspondence with their culture's complex heuristic modes. More specifically, madness itself often operates as the bleached-out echo as much as the transgressive underside of the dominant order; it is as likely to be the sign of ultimate powerlessness as 'the unrecognised wild beast in one's own heart'. 'Everything is legitimate, natural and possible, all the exaggerations of excitement have been carefully eschewed', commented Margaret Oliphant, comparing *The Woman in White* to the majority of sensation novels. 'There is almost as little that is objectionable in this highly-wrought sensation novel, as if it had been a domestic history of the most gentle and unexciting kind.'[32] Collins does 'tinge the daylight with morbid shadows', but he does so by exploring the complex interplay between resemblance and difference, and this transforms the significance of his figures of 'otherness', for it is often precisely their homeliness that is most weird. This suggests that while Freud's model of the uncanny is what seems most strikingly meaningful now, Collins's fiction draws out the 'strange' connotations of the *homely*, its point of contact with the weird that Freud himself emphasized, by its association with images that stress the familiarity, the domestication, and through this the social and historical as well as the psychic meaning, of both madness and the unconscious itself.

Beneath this paradox lies the thorny question of how we conceptualize the relationship between contemporary and historical interpretative paradigms – of how we weigh each to assess a story's ideological significance. Inevitably, we now read a novelist like Collins in the light of our own theoretical and political concerns – his writing would be unreadable if we could not. His novels certainly do explore the transgression of psychic and social boundaries; and their present significance is bound to be shaped particularly by our contemporary theoretical appropriation of post-Freudian psychoanalytic paradigms in their exploration of processes of projection and displacement, in their ambiguous gender identities, in their conjuring with the relationship between self and other. With their labyrinthine narratives too, and their concern not only with generating mystery, but also with resolving it, with excavating the hidden traces of the past, reaching a stable interpretation of a range of shifting and contradictory evidence, Collins's novels have been read as prototypical detective fiction, with *The Moonstone* installed as 'the first and greatest of English detective novels' and Collins as the 'father' of the English branch in genealogical histories of the form.[33] It has often been stressed that detective fiction can be read as a prototypical expression of the mechanisms that underlie all narrative – that keep the reader always engaged, suspenseful. Detective stories are structured around absence and the initial disruption of order; the detecting consciousness selects signs, threads its way through labyrinths to follow clues, learns to crack codes, deciphers the shifting traces of the past, then presents that history as a reconstruction written from the vantage-point of the order which the initial absence questioned. They provide the means of linking social and psychic tensions, of investigating the disruptive forces in enclosed, apparently stable communities where everything becomes potentially significant and everyone potentially guilty, or of extending and exploiting the absence of stable identities or signs in the maelstrom of modern urban life.[34]

More precisely, a substantial body of analysis on the ways in which detective stories work as different kinds of symptomatic transformation has been developed; indeed this is one of the clearest examples of the interconnection between fictional and psychological narratives within an explicitly psychoanalytic framework. At its most simple it has been argued that narrative pleasure is generated by replaying the symbolic Oedipal drama embodied in the loss or murder and at the same time disavowing it by displacing the crime on to a deviant other – thus simultaneously transforming and negotiating the central dilemma that Oedipus's own piece of detective work made clear, that as difference is tranformed back into unity the other is revealed to be the self. Geraldine Pederson-Krag's 'Detective stories and the primal scene', is an early example of this kind of approach; it was developed by Charles Rycroft's analysis of *The Moonstone* and has since been elaborated in more sophisticated versions.[35] Again, these meanings stick – and again, a particular interpretative framework cannot only be applied to narratives that emerged out of the culture in which those concepts were in current use. But here I want to explore some different questions from those posed by the dominant use of psychology in contemporary literary theory, beginning with the question of how to shift between different analytical paradigms when one is reconstructuring a history in the light of a cognitive framework that itself is the subject of a process of historical change. Psychoanalytic approaches to literature have stressed the process of transformation whereby psychic tensions are explored. But what of the process of historical transformation through which notions of subjectivity are constructed themselves? How does engaging with this process of historical transformation help us as readers to grapple with the radical historical difference, the *strangeness* as much as the familiarity, of a text?

In Chapter 1, I explore a range of ways in which consciousness and social identity were understood in nineteenth-century psychological writings, discourses which shape the cognitive parameters of Collins's fiction by being appropriated and transformed as narrative strategies, and which thus both provide overarching models within which the self is formed through coherent patterns of narrative authority, and distinct, often dissonant, means of taking that coherent identity and authority apart. 'Psychology' was not a unified discipline in the mid-nineteenth century. It was more a point of intersection of various fields of knowledge – philosophy, physiology, aesthetic and social theory. And while particular models of identity, sanity, and consciousness were firmly located in specific notions and institutional practices, and were crucial to the formation of cultural and social assumptions, they cannot automatically be pinned down to a single meaning, though dominant patterns might be clear. This ideological shiftiness is crucial to the examination of particular strategies within Collins's fiction, but it has a bearing, too, on the relationship between psychological models and cultural forms – the immediate discursive context in which Collins's fiction emerged. I

19

have emphasized that the sensation novel came to be perceived as the 'bad object' of mid-nineteenth-century culture by being read, *qua* cultural object, through a framework of physiological psychology; thus it linked fears about the effects of 'sensation' on individual readers with longer-term evolutionary anxieties about cultural crisis and collective nervous decline. Thus literary meanings were in a sense 'read off' psychological ones, and these in turn were 'culturally' shaped; but this interpretation can imply that the 'cultural' debates appropriated an already given psychological significance, thus generating a self-fulfilling paradigm.

But while this process of continual transformation and exchange had the overwhelming effect of consolidating cultural divisions in the mid-nineteenth century, contributing to a polarization of 'high' and 'mass' culture, 'seriousness of purpose' and 'pleasure', 'sensational' and 'anti-sensational', a shared set of psychological and aesthetic debates could none the less be brought together to argue for radically different interpretations of cultural change. The contrasting positions of G.H. Lewes and E.S. Dallas, both of whom elaborated contemporary psychological hypotheses in their development of a theory of literature, provide one illustration of this. Lewes's own aesthetic ideas can be far more prescriptive and linear than his subtle and complex psychological and social theory was, and he tended not to extrapolate from its more dynamic, interactive implications to make sense of cultural forms in his development of 'realism' as a critical category. Thus while he acknowledges that the 'ideal' element within representational realism encompasses the diverse and the anomalous, his notion of literature as 'the delicate index of social evolution' still fundamentally elaborates the precepts of 'The progress of fiction as an art', using a linear conception of organic growth as the model of cultural improvement.[36] Although he stresses that literature 'in its widest sense' acts as a collective memory and identity, which 'stores up the accumulated experience of the race', it does so by 'connecting Past and Present into a conscious unity; and with this store it feeds successive generations, to be fed in turn by them', and this soon turns into another expression of the familiar fear of the degrading impact of mass culture, as his notion of collective growth is conceptualized through polarized cultural perceptions. He argued:

If many of the novels of today are considerably better than those of twenty or thirty years ago, because they partake in the general advance in culture and its wider diffusion, the vast increase in novels, mostly worthless, is a serious danger to public culture, a danger which becomes more and more imminent, and which can only be arrested by an energetic resolution on behalf of the critics to do their duty with conscientious rigour.[37]

But in the extraordinary and eclectic *The Gay Science*, E.S. Dallas drew on a vast range of philosophical, psychological, and aesthetic theory, extrapolating from associationist, Romantic, and evolutionary models in his analysis of the social production and function of art and of the way it corresponds to the internal working of the individual consciousness. Dallas was the leading critic on *The Times* during the 1860s, and as such was an influential figure, though *The Gay Science* was not really taken seriously by the critical establishment. He was born in Jamaica, but moved to Scotland as a child and before coming to London had been steeped in the intellectual culture of mid-nineteenth-century Edinburgh: he had been a student of William Hamilton, and an associate of the Aesthetic Society, many of whose precepts emerge in his early *Poetics* (1852). *The Gay Science* is a slippery and elusive text, in which Dallas's development of his own theory of art begins with a lengthy discussion of the epistemological and scientific status of criticism itself. But his central arguments are that 'a science of criticism is possible, and it must of necessity be a science of the laws of pleasure, the joy science the gay science'; that 'pleasure suggests something for which we have as yet no adequate language'; and that any critical theory that attempts to define art by abstracting essential qualities such as 'beauty' and 'truth', and reifying their status in opposition to other kinds of mental activity or aesthetic response, can never reach a coherent analysis of the elusive, mysterious nature of specifically fictive effects.[38]

In developing a new conception of how pleasure works and what it might mean, Dallas moves in two, interrelated, directions. He argues firstly that 'in so far as a science of human nature is possible, it lies not in the actions of the individual but of the race, not in the development of a lifetime, but of ages and cycles', and this, in contrast to Lewes, means defining art as an essentially 'popular' activity, but a 'popular' activity that does not elevate the underside of 'higher' forms (he finally concurs with the general view that modern fiction reflects modern neurosis) so much as challenge the process of selection and differentiation on which both are founded.[39] He begins by refuting the idea of a critical élite, a 'fit audience though few':

Now in art the two seldom go together, the fit are not few and the
few are not fit. The true judges of art are the despised many – the
crowd – and no critic is worth his salt who does not feel with the
many. There are no doubt questions of criticism which only a few
can answer; but the enjoyment of art is for all. . . . Great poetry
was ever meant, and to the end of time must be adapted, not to
the curious student, but for the multitude to read while they run,
for the crowd in the street, for the boards of huge theatres. . . .
In a word, the highest pleasure that the drama can give is a
pleasure within reach of the many, and belongs to them, without
the help and wisdom of the learned few.[40]

But secondly, Dallas analyses the ways in which aesthetic pleasure
corresponds to what he calls the 'play of thought' in the individual
mind. And for this

nothing is so much wanting as a direct psychology. We want first
of all, to know . . . the movement of the mind, the movement of
ideas. Why does the mind move in that way? Whither does it
move? Where does it move? What does it move?[41]

Above all it means analysing the movement of unconscious thought,
the working of the 'hidden soul' – 'a secret flow of thought, which
is not less energetic than the conscious flow, an absent mind that
haunts us like a ghost or like a dream and is an essential part of our
lives'.[42] Dallas's notion of the 'play of thought' is thus much more
than a part of Collins's critical context: it actively provides an interpretative framework within which to read the texts themselves.

In his review of Collins's final completed novel *The Legacy of Cain*
in the *Spectator* in 1889, J.A. Noble debated whether or not its
'intellectual scheme', like that of *Armadale*, 'reads like an implicit
protest against the fatalism which is more or less bound up with the
full acceptance of the modern doctrine of heredity'. 'But perhaps',
he goes on,

we are considering too curiously, and breaking an intellectual
butterfly on a critical wheel. Mr Wilkie Collins may occasionally
have a theory to illustrate, but he always has a story to tell, and
the story is more important both to him and his readers than the
theory.[43]

Collins's theoretical complexity lies above all in the narrative play
of his stories and now, as contemporary interest in popular narrative
forms develops, his work is taken increasingly seriously; he is no

22

longer seen simply as an insignificant minor novelist, whose main claim to fame is proximity to Dickens, nor as a shady, isolated, 'underworld' figure, with a laudanum habit and an unconventional private life.[44] But while there is a growing interest in his work – in its ideological ambiguity, particularly in his representation of women, in its narrative complexity, and in its cultural position – there has been no systematic attempt to analyse the range of his work in its historical and discursive context. This is partly because the 'intellectual butterfly' label has tended to stick. Collins was above all a professional novelist who deliberately cultivated a lightweight authorial persona, just as he played the role of Dickens's unconventional companion. During the latter part of the 1850s and the 1860s and, nominally, into the latter part of his career, he prided himself on never taking a didactic, high, serious tone, aiming to 'address the public with something of the ease of letter-writing and something of the familiarity of friendly talk. The literary pulpit appears to me . . . to be somewhat overcrowded with the preachers of Lay Sermons.'[45] Outside the texts themselves there is scant biographical evidence of his systematic engagement with contemporary intellectual movements and ideas. But even it he seems to have been an entertaining dinner guest more than a serious intellectual, his position within mid-century metropolitan culture is extraordinarly varied, if elusive. He was a professional novelist who never really had to enter metropolitan culture as class, gender, or regional *émigré*, yet who was paradoxically both central and marginal, a liminal figure, who moved between cultural worlds, working at and across their limits.

Collins's reputation as a popular novelist was consolidated by the enormous success of *The Woman in White*, which marked a breakthrough in middle-range mass journalism when it was first serialized in Dickens's journal *All the Year Round* in 1859. But even before he joined the staff of *Household Words* in 1856, Collins had already emerged as an interesting and promising, if *risqué* and rebellious young novelist, who often outraged the critical establishment but who could do so from the more or less licensed space of the young, male, middle-class professional, if somewhat Bohemian, writer. He had to work extraordinarily hard for economic survival as a full-time novelist (for which he abandoned an early career in law), but the constraints on his work – both ideological and economic – also proved to be extraordinarily productive tensions and pressures; and he was able to exploit them, initially by drawing on distinct cultural forms and genres, later by growing adept at negotiating the complex and changing publishing structures of the latter part of the nineteenth century, managing publicity, gauging the response of his audience, balancing the demands of serialization and three-volume publication.[46] Collins had grown up in a metropolitan artistic household affected by shifts in patterns of artistic production and patronage that had been under way since the late eighteenth century. He was named after the well-established landscape painter Sir David Wilkie; and Collins's first published work was an act of filial duty – *Memoirs of the Life of William Collins, R.A.* (1848). A moderately successful domestic landscape painter, member of the Royal Academy, dependent on uncertain patronage and often forced by this into sycophancy, William Collins was himself the son of a fringe member of the radical 'English Jacobin' culture of the 1790s, and had been a student of Fuseli's and a friend of Wordsworth and Coleridge in his youth.

Collins's father had to struggle for economic security and professional recognition on the edge of increasingly bourgeois rather than gentrified patronage; and his dull landscapes represented in an immediate, almost symbolic form, the domestication of his old teacher's intensity. But by the 1850s the Collins household was a centre of a more radical artistic culture – the self-consciously oppositional Pre-Raphaelite Brotherhood. Collins's brother Charles was a close associate though never actually a member of the group, and Collins himself was friendly with Millais, Egg, and Rossetti, and supported many of the group's aesthetic aims (and shared their respect for Ruskin), as well as sharing some of its members' ambivalent fascination with moral and sexual transgression. It was through Egg that he met Dickens and became involved in the amateur dramatic productions that were a feature of London's radical Bohemian world, and which began his lifelong fascination with the theatre.[47] Some of his early journalistic experience, too, may well have been gained through his connection with *The Leader*, the radical liberal weekly founded by Thornton Hunt and George Henry Lewes, to which he briefly became a contributor through his friend Edward Pigott.[48] His writing in the 1850s, too, shifts between and experiments with different genres, and this often involves apparently skipping fictional generations: the historical novel *Antonina, or the Fall of Rome* (1850) was imitative of Scott and Bulwer-Lytton; *Basil, a Story of Modern Life* (1852) adapted the tropes of the terror romance, its confessional form, and framing conventions echoing Godwin's *Caleb Williams* and Mary Shelley's *Frankenstein*; the short stories, framed in the collections *After Dark* (1856) and *The Queen of Hearts* (1859), recall the techniques of the

testing the
                                                            waters
                                                            for later
Blackwood's stories. *Bentley's Miscellany*, reviewing *Basil,* *texts.*
emphasized: 'In truth the author of that work should have been
called Mr Salvator Fuseli. There is nothing of either Wilkie or
Collins about it.'[49] The later novels of the 1850s – *Hide and Seek*
(1854) and *The Dead Secret* (1857) were much less risqué domestic
melodramas, and although Dickens had admired *Basil*, it was with
the extremely unsuspenseful *The Dead Secret* that Collins established
his position as an authored, rather than anonymous, serial novelist
on *Household Words*.   *But uses some sensationalist elements*
   Collins's position on *Household Words* and its successor *All the
Year Round* is the most striking example of the simultaneous
pressures and possibilities that shaped his work. With *The Woman
in White*, he played a key role in helping to launch *All the Year Round*
in its circulation battle with its rival *Once a Week*. During the novel's
serialization, sales of the journal increased to over 100,000 – no
better than Reynold's regular achievement, but a breakthrough
which helped consolidate the revolution in mass middle-range
publishing.[50] But *Household Words*, in which Collins established his
reputation as a serial novelist, was above all Dickens's journal. It was
the vehicle through which as public sage he aimed to address *his*
public, but as a 'private', *domestic* one: 'We aspire to live in the
Household affections and be numbered among the Household
thoughts of our readers.'[51] *Household Words* aimed to bring
together distinct kinds of family readers: the established middle-
class audience of the publishing house journals (*Bentley's Miscellany*,
Fraser's Magazine, the *Cornhill*, *Macmillan's Magazine*) on the one
hand and the expanding lower-middle-class audience of such weekly
publications as the *Family Friend*, *Chamber's Journal*, and *Reynold's
Miscellany* on the other.[52] Moreover *Household Words* aimed to
mediate as much as expand this diverse and fluid readership by
addressing it primarily *as* a family. It proposed to consolidate this
shared cultural identity by combining fiction, social reportage and
popular accounts of the marvels of science, to generate a common
stock of allusions and references: 'To bring the greater and lesser in
degree together . . . and to mutually dispose them to a better
acquaintance and a kinder understanding – is one main object of our
Household Words.'[53] Accounts of the lunacy reform movement and
the development of 'mental science' were a central element of this
shaping of a shared subjectivity, and they thus form one of the
crucial ideological parameters of Collins's fiction – above all, of *The
Woman in White*.
   Concluding her discussion of 'Sensation novels' in *Blackwood's*,

Margaret Oliphant commended Collins's extraordinary skill in narrative rhetoric:

> To combine the higher requirements of art with the lower ones of a popular weekly periodical, and produce something which will be equally perfect in snatches and as a book, is an operation too difficult and delicate for even genius to accomplish without a bold adaptation of the cunning of the mechanism and closest elaboration of workmanship.[54]

It is in the 'bold adaptation of the cunning of the mechanism' that Collins's fiction most fully exploits the narrative possibilities of contemporary theories, shaping them into stories which may challenge or reaffirm their dominant ideological meanings. It is in his continual juggling with narrative authority that these notions of consciousness and cognition can most radically question social perceptions and identities – forms of possession, and self-possession, patterns of propriety, of property, of power – as they become the means of suspense, ambiguity, postponement, resolution. For in Collins's novels the struggle for control of the narrative itself – the struggle over who narrates, who appropriates and represents others' testimony and evidence as history which the story reconstructs as truth – is often bound up with both the undermining and the affirmation of a gendered, middle-class subjectivity. The narrative itself lays bare the patterns that lie behind this formation of a social self in dominant psychological writings even as it finally relies upon them to enable the story to end. And framed within this process, the clues, or threads of the narratives themselves actively engage with contemporary conceptions of consciousness in a more indeterminate way. By generating a sense of mystery and suspense within the individual consciousness, by following apparently arbitrary, unconscious processes of association and tracing the hidden secrets of memory back to their equivocal source, they take these notions of cognition and identity through the developing discipline of mental science, working both at and beyond its hardening boundaries.[55]

1

The psychic and the social
Boundaries of identity in nineteenth-century psychology

> Nothing can be more slightly defined than the line of
> demarcation between sanity and insanity. . . . Make
> the definition too narrow, it becomes meaningless;
> make it too wide, and the whole human race becomes
> involved in the dragnet. In strictness we are all mad
> when we give way to passion, to prejudice, to vice, to
> vanity; but if all the passionate, prejudiced and vain
> people were to be locked up as lunatics, who is to keep
> the key to the asylum?
>
> *The Times*, 22 July 1853[1]

MORAL MANAGEMENT AND *HOUSEHOLD WORDS*

During October 1857 Dickens's and Collins's collaborative short
serial *The Lazy Tour of Two Idle Apprentices* appeared in *Household
Words*. The piece humorously traces the picaresque wanderings of
the serious-minded and curious Francis Goodchild and the
hedonistic Thomas Idle. In the fourth instalment Goodchild gives an
account of his visit to 'a remarkable place', a county lunatic asylum.
He begins his description of the institution, however, by using an
ironic pastoral imagery (which immediately recalls Dickens's earlier
account in the same journal of a tour of another public institution,
'A walk in a workhouse'):

> Long groves of blighted men-and-women-trees; interminable
> avenues of hopeless faces; numbers, without the slightest power
> of really combining for any earthly purpose; a society of human
> creatures who have nothing in common but that they have all lost
> the power of being humanly social with one another.[2]

He goes on to focus on the scene, particularly on one 'poor little
dark-chinned meagre man with a perplexed brow and a pensive face,
stooping low over the matting on the floor, and picking out with his

thumb and forefinger the course of its fibres'. The man is discouraged from this activity by the attendant and goes back to his room, but a minute later shuffles out again and returns to poring over the matting. Goodchild continues:

> I stopped to look at him, and it came into my mind, that the course of those fibres as they plaited in and out, over and under, was the only course of things in the whole wide world which it was left for him to understand – that his darkening intellect had narrowed down to that small cleft of light that showed him, 'This piece was twisted this way, went in here, passed under, came out there, was carried away here to the right where now I put my finger on it, and in this progress of events the thing was made and came to be here.' Then, I wondered whether he looked into the matting, next, to see if it could show him anything of the process through which *he* came to be there, so strangely poring over it. Then I thought how all of us, God help us! are poring over our bits of matting blindly enough, and what confusions and mysteries we make in the pattern. I had a sadder fellow-feeling with the dark-chinned, meagre man by that time, and I came away.[3]

The figure of insanity is set in collusive and contradictory frames here. The observer is detached at first, at once impressed and depressed by what he sees. Though the institution is a model one, its stately-home associations turn into a cruel satire on its inmates; mania, like 'the dragon Pauperism' in 'A walk in a workhouse', 'in a very weak and impotent condition; toothless, fangless, drawing his breath heavily enough, and hardly worth chaining up', has been tamed, but in the process has been turned into the ultimate vision of social isolation and powerlessness.[4] But looking at the 'meagre man' more closely, the perspective suddenly shifts, and now the observer is in the middle of the picture. Projecting meaning into the madman's projections, deciphering it as an explanatory narrative, shocks the tourist out of his philanthropic complacency, for now the madman's intricate tracing of clues in the interwoven fibres echoes his own uncertainty, and it is this identification that radically reshapes his sympathy.

The passage would have presented a familiar picture to readers of *Household Words*: five years earlier Dickens had reported his own visit to St Luke's Hospital for the insane poor. But it may have had disturbing echoes too, emphasizing a different, more internal, image of insanity from the one normally stressed in the journal. *Household Words* reported frequently on the lunacy reform movement and the care and cure of the insane. Dispelling old myths about madness and replacing them with enlightened humanitarianism seemed a particularly suitable focus for the journal's self-appointed mission as entertaining educator of a newly defined lower-middle-class family audience.[5] And the human but helpless mad were a particularly worthy subject for such concern, since wherever madness might be found it struck, above all, in the family. 'There are few household calamities so utterly deplorable as loss of reason in husband, wife, or child', noted 'The cure of sick minds' in 1859, summarizing a mass of material that had appeared over the previous few years:

And there is, perhaps, no household calamity for the lightening of which so much can be done or left undone by friends of the afflicted, according to their knowledge or their ignorance of certain leading truths. The development of this kind of knowledge has been the work of science in our own day, and its diffusion is the duty of journals such as ours. For that reason we have, from time to time, dwelt upon points relating to insanity in England, and we now found, upon the latest reports of our county lunatic asylums, a few more notes of profitable information.[6]

The development of this kind of knowledge was not confined to *Household Words*. Discussions of a wide range of theories about the workings of the mind, including the definition, classification, and treatment of insanity, were a significant feature of Victorian journals and periodicals, an integral part of the contemporary intellectual culture.[7] Collins would have been aware of these debates not only through these journalistic discussions but also through immediate contacts: Dickens (the close friend of Conolly and Elliotson, involved in mesmerism as well as criminal and lunacy reform), Reade (also involved with lunacy reform, though not in the same way as Dickens), Bulwer-Lytton, Edward Pigott, George Eliot, G.H. Lewes, and Herbert Spencer were all friends or acquaintances, and this list is not exhaustive. And though evidence for his awareness comes mainly from within the texts rather than from any external commentary, it is clear that Collins is often appropriating precise sources. For example the most frequently cited source for the wrongful confinement of Laura Fairlie in *The Woman in White* is the 'sensational' late-eighteenth-century case of the Marquise de Douhault, described in Mejan's *Recueil des causes célèbres*, a copy of which Collins bought during a trip to Paris in 1856. But much later he also claimed that he had received a letter asking him to intervene in a contemporary wrongful confinement case as he was planning the novel.[8] *The*

Woman in White was serialized in *All the Year Round* during 1859 and 1860; it thus overlapped with the publication and widespread discussion of the Parliamentary Select Committee Inquiry into the Care and Treatment of Lunatics and Their Property of 1858–9. Members of the committee included two of his acquaintances, John Forster and Richard Monckton Milnes. And the Inquiry itself marked the culmination of a specific set of debates and anxieties about how to establish the boundaries of madness, forming part of a longer-term shift in the cultural meaning of the asylum and ideas about the social formation of identity: the 'kind of knowledge' developed by *Household Words*, and encapsulated in the concept and methods of moral management.

Moral management was first and foremost a method of treating insanity, but it gained its enormous authority and appeal from the precision with which it at once absorbed and expressed the aspirations of early Victorian liberalism, with all its familiar antinomies: its notion of a common subjectivity to which all have equal access; its inscription of that subjectivity through a masculine, propertied norm; its belief that social contradictions could be smoothed away by the application of a benevolence that depended on those contradictions for its own benign impulses. Recent histories of psychiatry broadly shaped by the perspective initiated by Michel Foucault's *Madness and Civilization* have stressed the ways in which the discourse of moral management operated as a means of social control through the early part of the nineteenth century.[9] They have emphasized its contribution to the construction of utilitarian models of containment and regulation by establishing a regime of panoptical-style surveillance and thus prompting the insane to internalize reponsibility for their madness. And the broader impact of Foucault's work has extended this assessment: the rise of psychological medicine and the development of the county asylum system helped to shape a landscape of institutions and a dominant discursive regime, a regime that extended through all aspects of social, sexual, and psychic life; was ubiquitous across medical, psychological, legal, educational, technological, sexual, and familial practices; which established an all-pervasive micro-politics of power. My analysis here is inevitably influenced by this analysis, but it aims to avoid many of its monolithic implications. Instead I want to argue that an ideology always contains a trace of resistance to its dominant meanings; to focus on the more equivocal aspects of moral management; and to see it as articulating those points of dissonance that lurked within that unhelpfully nebulous concept, 'Victorian ideology'. These are ambiguities that can initially be located in the complicated resonances of the word 'moral' itself.

'Moral' was certainly primarily a prescriptive term, concerned with reinforcing a benchmark of values, codes of conduct, and proper living which had roots both in evangelicalism and utilitarianism. But its formation in eighteenth-century associationist psychology and philosophy in conjunction with the notion of sympathy gave it a more flexible range of possible meanings in the very way that it was defined *as* subjectivity, as sentiment and emotional response. It was thus a slippery term, one meaning of which seemed perfectly clear, while another resisted stable definition, just as it stressed the malleability of identity itself. These were diverse meanings to be reshaped during the first half of the nineteenth century, and although they might continually merge and depend on each other they did not always inevitably fuse. While they clearly contributed to a dominant model of containment and control, they also had other, more resistant resonances. 'Self-control' might predominantly mean the internalization of another's regulating gaze, a self-objectification within the subject, but the term could none the less be claimed in a struggle for self-definition and autonomy in the face of established power – it retained a trace of its radical connotations even in the face of its recuperation. And 'moral management' itself, drawing on these interlocking meanings, might promote the belief that a stable, sane identity could be built up by proper training and self-regulation, yet at the same time it could also tacitly suggest the very fragility of the identity that it aimed to sustain. This instability of meaning emerged above all in the way that moral management was built up within the culture around two poles, extremities that were forever meeting, the asylum and the middle-class home. It is in this equivocal sense, too, that it provides the overarching ideological framework for Collins's fiction, supplying a dominant model within which narrative authority and meaningful identity are formed, yet at the same time offering a means of overturning that authority, revealing its mechanisms of manipulation, its sources of power. As a model it was shaped unevenly, extending across a variety of writings and practices, permeating contemporary culture as an overlapping set of hypotheses, narratives, impressions, and anecdotes, in which Utopian visions of ideal asylums merged with visits to real ones and memories of good and bad ones, and where particular perceptions qualified, while being set within, a story of triumphant progress and of philanthropic heroism.[10]

This story opened with two mythologized gestures: the epic image of Pinel opening the gates of the Bicêtre in 1793 and striking the chains from its bound and caged inmates ('Citizen, I am convinced that these madmen are intractable only because they have been deprived of air and liberty'[11]) and its more prosaic English equivalent, the philanthropist William Tuke founding the Retreat, an asylum for insane Quakers, near York, in 1792. It was undoubtedly a significant moment, marking a point where Jacobin radicalism merged with English rational religion.[12] But the gestures took on increasingly mythical connotations as the reform movement gained momentum during the first half of the nineteenth century, a momentum that depended in part on a continual process of self-definition, which was based in turn on a repeated writing of its own history. So although in reality there was no absolute break in the treatment and perception of madness around 1800, the horrific image of the eighteenth-century madhouse needed to be continually invoked to highlight and make sense of nineteenth-century progressive reform. W.A.F. Browne wrote in *What Asylums Were, Are, and Ought to Be* (1837):

> From a blind and hard-hearted policy, which embraced only the affliction of one evil by the affliction of another . . . a sudden transition was made to a system, professing to be based on knowledge of the human mind, and on the common sympathies of our nature, and to have as its object the eradication, or if that appeared Utopian, the amelioration of the evil.[13]

Indeed many of the descriptions of 'old corrupt' eighteenth-century asylums, with their ubiquitous imagery of whips, straw, and chains, both bolstered the self-congratulatory portrayal of contemporary reform and justified a prurient horrified fascination with the images of brutality that was not so very different from the despised voyeurism with which earlier observers had viewed the antics of the mad. Dickens's description of Christmas at St Luke's in *Household Words* in 1852 contrasted the scene with how it might have appeared a century earlier:

> Coercion for the outward man and rabid physicking for the inward man were then the specifics for lunacy. Chains, straw, filthy solitude, darkness and starvation; . . . spinning in whirligigs, corporal punishment, gagging, continual intoxication; nothing was too wildly extravagant, nothing too monstrously cruel to be prescribed by these mad doctors. It was their monomania.[14]

An even more explicit picture of redemption was conjured up in 'The star of Bethlehem', a history of that most redolent symbol of the enforced bestiality of madness, Bethlehem Hospital, or Bedlam: 'The remedy for lunacy which we now find in cheerfulness and hope was sought in gloom and terror', the article going on to describe the recurrent signs of benighted brutality – Norris's cage, Cox's spinning chair, cold baths, threats of drowning and of course, whips, chains, and straw.[15] 'Things within Dr Conolly's rememberance' also charts a progress of gradual enlightenment, marking its beginning with Tuke and Pinel and its culmination with 'the wise and good Dr Conolly'.[16] Weightier journals and reports told the same story. Andrew Wynter's lengthy summary of recent psychological findings and medical reports in the *Quarterly Review* in 1857 emphasized:

> It is not fifty years since the state of things which now exist only in the imagination was both general and approved. The interior of Bethlehem at that date could furnish pictures more terrible than Hogarth ever conceived. . . . Through the instrumentality of the Tukes, Gardiner Hill, Charlesworth, Winslow and Conolly, the old method of treatment, with its whips, chains and manacles, has passed away for ever.

And he continues with a striking image: 'And as a true emblem of the revolution which has taken place, we may mention that some years since, a governor, in passing through the laundry of Bethlehem, perceived a wrist manacle, which had been converted by one of the women into a stand for a flat iron.'[17]

The break was not nearly such a dramatic one of course, although the violent and often punitive practices of many eighteenth-century madhouses were not a figment of the reformers' imaginations either. But, *pace* Foucault, while bestial images were widespread in the eighteenth century, positioning the mad as repositories of unreason, perverse reversions to an untamed state, other, liberal, responses were also emerging, responses which saw madness more ambivalently, lurking at the heart of English culture itself. Nervous disorders, in particular hypochondria, melancholy, and spleen, were felt to be peculiarly English diseases of affluence, the symptoms of the over-indulgence, idleness, and excess of the civilized refinement of the upper class of both sexes; but also the cause for a sneaking national pride, the sign of sensibility on the one hand, of ambition, energy, and progressiveness on the other, and this contrasts with, as well as anticipates, the nervous response associated with 'sensation' in the 1860s.[18] 'We have more nervous diseases', noted George Cheyne in *The English Malady* in 1733, 'since the present Age has made Efforts to go beyond former times, in all the Arts of Ingenuity, Invention,

Study, Learning, and all the Contemplative and Sedentary Professions.'[19] There was, too, increasing pressure for the reform of the
private madhouse system during the eighteenth century, which led to
the establishment of pioneering curative asylums.

The methods practised at the Tukes' Retreat, which became the
model for the development of the techniques of moral management
with the massive expansion of the state asylum system during the first
half of the nineteenth century, grew out of this progressive intellectual
tradition; but Tuke was first and foremost a lay philanthropist rather
than a doctor, and his grandson Samuel argued that the method had
the space to develop primarily because the treatment of insanity was
still a relatively low-grade branch of the medical profession:

> In the present imperfect state of our knowledge, of the very
> interesting branch of the healing art, which relates to the cure of
> insanity; and unable as we are to ascertain its true seat in the
> complicated labyrinths of our frame, the judicious physician is very
> frequently obliged to apply his means, chiefly, to the alleviation and
> suppression of symptoms.[20]

This meant, too, that the Retreat could become a crucial reference
point for the expansion of moral management as a method of treatment and for the growth of the county asylum system precisely
because it preceded the transformation of the institutional landscape
that it helped to shape. It was a private asylum, set up partly to
provide an alternative to the notoriously corrupt York madhouse; and
like other private non-restraint asylums for the wealthy set up at the
beginning of the century (such as Brislington House and Ticehurst
Asylum), it was small enough to look like a modest country house, in
contrast with the vast, almost palatial edifices of the mid-nineteenth-
century model county asylums such as Hanwell or Colney Hatch.[21]
And it was as a Quaker 'home' that the Retreat came to absorb and
express the distinct and by no means coherent facets of early Victorian
ideology. On the one hand, the 'domestication' of madness and the
reshaping of the subjectivity of the mad obviously contributed to the
values of self-control and self-help that can be seen as essentially
compatible with utilitarian values. But equally, that reform could
only be consolidated in a cultural context in which the newly important middle-class family had become the linchpin in the imaginary
shaping of social identity, and where sexual divisions were underpinned by rational religion and a set of moral precepts that might
merge with utilitarianism, but were not subsumed within it.

Thus treatment gained its initial coherence from social relations –

the reciprocal bonds of authority and affection of the family. Patients were fed well, taken on invigorating walks, encouraged to reshape themselves by taking up fitting accomplishments for their gender and station; they were placed back into an imaginary childhood in which learning 'proper feeling' marked their passage back into humanity. 'The principle of fear, which is rarely decreased by insanity, is considered as of great importance in the management of the patients', Tuke wrote. 'But it is not allowed to be excited beyond that degree which naturally arises from the regulation of the family.'[22] Like children, patients 'quickly perceive that their treatment depends in great measure on their conduct', and this 'leads to many struggles to overcome their morbid propensities'.[23] This hidden theatre, where patients enacted a projected version of their proper selves, culminated in the Retreat's famous tea parties, where the inmates, becoming visiting guests, audience, and actors,

> dress in their best clothes and vie with each other in politeness and propriety. The best fare is provided and the visitors are treated with all the attention of strangers. The evening generally passes in the greatest harmony and enjoyment . . . the patients control, to a wonderful degree, their different propensities; and the scene is at once curious and affectingly gratifying.[24]

Moral treatment at the Retreat thus emphasized the 'common sympathies of our nature' while implying that there was no given self outside the social relations of the family, and this would in turn have been tempered by the already formed subjective identity of the predominantly middle-class Quaker inmates, who shared the religious and moral framework that was an essential part of their treatment.

How had the meaning of moral management shifted by the mid-nineteenth century? Dickens's description of Christmas at St Luke's in 1852, 'A curious dance round a curious tree', also focuses on the patients' party as the sign of their newly acquired social identity. But the dance is now seen as a bizarre parody of 'normal' society and of Tuke's earlier model. The family, by implication, is still a central reference point, but here it suggests not so much bonds of affection as gender division; a means of fixing rather than reshaping the self: 'At one end were a number of mad men, at the other, a number of mad women, seated on forms. . . . The ball was proceeding with great spirit but with great decorum.'[25] The narrator here is both well-informed observer and public personality. As in the other articles on insanity in *Household Words* (most of which were written by Henry

Morley), insanity is seen as a primarily working-class phenomenon, the product of poverty and 'grinding parochial parsimony'. But Dickens's optimistic perspective is continually undermined by the passivity, the lack of reciprocity, of the insane themselves, and here the decorum and orderliness of the mad, their learning of useful work and social skills, is paradoxically both a way of resisting insanity's powerlessness and isolation, but also a means of compounding it. Unlike the 'meagre man' in the *Lazy Tour*, the mad are unambiguously 'other' here, but they are strange by virtue of the very decorum with which they go through the motions of social life. Propriety makes sense of them, but *they* make propriety seem weird.

St Luke's was a pauper hospital with none of the resonances of the purpose-built county asylums; Dickens's description makes the place seem like the inverse of the public face of those mid-century stages of moral management, which themselves transformed the earlier connotations of the Retreat. The lunacy reform movement had been able to develop partly because of the absence of any coherent state or private structure. When the Retreat was founded there were various ways in which the insane could be confined: the wealthy at home or in private madhouses; paupers in prisons, in charitable institutions such as Bethlehem and St Luke's, or farmed out by the parish to private madhouses.[26] Following the 1809 County Asylums Act, the reformers' aim had been to encourage the development of the state sector, and to lobby for increased local state inspection of private madhouses and asylums; but the two sectors remained organizationally separate until 1845. This meant that although the development of county asylums encountered considerable resistance from landed interests, it was primarily these institutions, rather than the progressive private establishments set up during the first half of the century, that became primary models for the treatment and thus the definition of insanity.[27]

For insanity now became ambiguously inflected in these new mass institutions. It was associated with the predominantly working- or lower-middle-class inmate of the place, but also with the image of the country house, a private place that is on display as an embodiment of itself. Conolly, outlining the ideal asylum in *The Construction and Government of Lunatic Asylums and Hospitals for the Insane* (1847), stressed the importance of classification through the social organization of space: 'Separate wards and bedrooms for the tranquil, for the sick, for the helpless, for the noisy, the unruly or violent, and the dirty', while emphasizing:

36

There can be no doubt that the best site for an asylum is a
eminence, of which the soil is naturally dry and in a fertile and
agreeable country. . . . Patients of all classes derive advantage
from the circumstances of situation just mentioned; and if it is
intended to receive patients of the educated classes into the house,
it should unquestionably be situated amid scenery calculated to
give pleasure to such persons when of sane mind.[28]

And his *The Treatment of the Insane Without Mechanical Restraints*
(1856) reinforces this social slippage, stressing the importance of
seclusion and repose to lull the patient out of a manic state and
suppress all distressing associations. Madness is here seen as an
irritation, to be smoothed away rather than wrestled with by the sane
self, and through these 'leisured' resonances, the mad are 'reborn'
into a new identity that has already been shaped:

When they are taken out to walk in a quiet garden, or a pleasant
field, among trees, and shrubs, and flowers, they are impressed
with the sensations of a kind of new world. When, sitting down
to comfortable dinners, they find that some of the officers still
come to see that all is conducted properly, a conviction that they
are carefully looked after necessarily arises in their thoughts. . . .
Day after day these influences operate, and day by day mental
irritation subsides, and suspicions die and gloomy thoughts
gradually disperse, and confidence grows and strengthens, and
natural affections re-awake and reason returns.[29]

Of course, gender divisions are the fulcrum of this process; in
becoming culturally assimilated, insanity becomes feminized. The
close links between the cultural construction of femininity and of
insanity had been forged long before the mid-nineteenth century,
but now both draw on and contribute to the ideology of domesticity
in newly pervasive ways.[30] The nervous disorders of upper-class
women of the eighteenth century tended to be associated with their
class; although an excess of feminine sensibility came to be seen as
increasingly pathological, sensibility itself remained an essentially
moralized term.[31] But now an even more complicated process is at
work, one that encapsulates all the ambiguities of moral management. For with the development of the medical and psychiatric
professions, the figure of middle-class feminine domestic virtue
becomes the epitome of rationality and self-management, just as
domesticity acquires new kinds of *homely* connotations; this is set
against the differently pathologized imaginary excesses of upper- or

working-class sexuality, of hysteria or of mania.[32] The madwoman of every class is cured through learning to be a middle-class gentlewoman; yet the key sign of that social identity is now receptivity – self-possession merges into being possessed in 'propriety' itself. If the female inmates of Dickens's St Luke's look more 'humanly social' in the homely surroundings of the workroom in contrast with the bleak and 'utterly vacuous' wards, it is because they enact a tableau of homeliness through silent diligence that the observer actively interprets:

> It was a relief to come into the workroom; with coloured prints over the mantel-shelf, and china shepherdesses upon it; furnished also with tables, a carpet, stuffed chairs, and an open fire. I observed a great difference between the demeanour of the occupants of this apartment and the inmates of the other room. They were neither so listless or so sad. Although they did not, while I was present, speak much, they worked with earnestness and diligence.[33]

Andrew Wynter's 'emblem' of progress (the wrist-iron transformed into an iron-stand) elaborates the same point:

> We find the apartments [in the reformed Bedlam] occupied by a score of busy workers, the majority of whom appear to be gentlewomen. Every conceivable kind of needlework is dividing their attention with the young lady who reads aloud *David Copperfield*;. . . while beside the fire, perhaps, an old lady with silver locks gives a touch of domesticity to the scene.[34]

Yet moral management also turned the codes of femininity itself into the site of a tacit ideological contest. For while the fit between the pliant female asylum inmate and the dutiful wife is apparent, the image existed in a continual tension with the older association between genteel idleness and 'feminine vulnerability', an association resolutely opposed by the more radical aspects of the liberalism that characterized the early reform movement. Conolly, for example, hovers on the threshold of these different meanings in his arguments that inmates be allowed some control over their own appearance as a useful means of re-establishing self-possession: 'A neglect of this really proper feeling is a frequent cause of discontent in asylums and sometimes retards recovery . . . many of the women should indeed be indulged in wearing neat articles of dress.'[35] But equally alienists stressed that it was the 'artificial' nurture and limited education of women that led to a lassitude that might slide into nervous debility, and this was taken up in a series of articles on insanity in the renascent feminist *The English Woman's Journal* between 1859 and 1861.

The first of these, 'Insanity: its cause and cure', is a textbook outline of moral treatment tenets, naming 'the excessive luxury and excessive povery which prevail at the two extremes of the social scale' as insanity's principal causes. 'In what does a healthy mind consist? In the vigor of the reasoning faculties, in the subordination of the passions and emotions, in the supremacy of the judgment, in the balance of all the powers', and it is this which is used as the linchpin of arguments for women's increased independence and education:

> The nurture and education is as enervating as possible . . . a species of hothouse culture is forced upon the mind. . . . Having come out, her life is passed between two extremes, the extreme of excitement in the season devoted to society, the extreme of aimlessness in the season of seclusion. . . . Now we begin, we suppose, to show the cloven foot, to make a demand for strong-minded women. Yes, we own it, while repudiating much that this abused term has been made to include.[36]

Collins's manipulation of these tensions forms one of the crucial sources of suspense in *The Woman in White*, but it is inextricably linked to the sinister role of the benign private asylum as embodiment of seclusion and repose.

John Conolly himself, the good genius of moral management, embodies these ideological shifts and tensions in his mythologized figure and his uneven career; for by the late 1850s the model county institutions were both contrasted with and undermined by the anxieties that surrounded those other places, the private asylums. By the early 1840s Conolly, architect of the non-restraint system at Hanwell (the Middlesex County Asylum), whose work Shaftesbury (Chairman of the Lunacy Commission) described effusively as 'the greatest triumph of skill and humanity the world has ever known', was an ideal candidate for the situation of self-made hero of lunacy reform.[37] From an indigent farming family and after a difficult early career as a physician lacking private means, Conolly took up a teaching post in the newly established medical school of University College, London, and was appointed superintendent of Hanwell in 1839. He was a philanthropic radical in these early days. His first book, *An Enquiry Concerning the Indications of Insanity* (1830), certainly aimed for professional respectability, but it did so by questioning many orthodox presuppositions.[38] Selectively drawing on

phrenological and associationist models, Conolly argued here that
the definition of insanity was unstable; that aberrant states could be
clues to the workings of the mind as a whole, and that its recognition
depended on a range of shifting propensities and signs. Confinement
in an asylum, he maintained, could in many cases precipitate
insanity:

> The crowd of most of our asylums is made up of oddly harmless
> individuals, not much more absurd than the numbers who are at
> large. . . . To these patients, confinement is the very reverse of
> beneficial. It fixes and renders permanent what might have passed
> away, and ripens eccentricity, or temporary excitement or depres-
> sion, into actual insanity.[39]

The first question, he went on, was 'that of considering . . . *whether
or not departure from sound mind be of a nature to justify confinement
of the individual, and the imposition of restraint upon him, as regards the
use and disposal of his property*'.[40] It was this analysis, combined
with his enthusiasm for working-class education and self-
improvement, which lay behind the zeal with which he advocated
the abolition of mechanical restraint. For Conolly, the ideal asylum
was a Utopia of paternalistic self-management, a harmonious
community watched over by kindly guardians. If this focused on the
managerial side of the Owenite ideal, it was none the less inspired
by Owen himself in part – Conolly invited him to Hanwell.

But by the late 1840s Conolly had been transformed into the shadow
side of his earlier self. Forced, partly by financial pressure, into the
dubious position of proprietor of a private asylum for female patients
and expert witness for the prosecution in criminal cases where the
insanity defence was used, and called upon to legally establish
unsoundness of mind in cases of disputed insanity relating to the
control of property, he now reinforced the position he had formally
repudiated.[41] Eliza Nottridge's was one case in point. She was a
wealthy and eccentric spinster, who insisted on living in a millenial
community, the 'Abode of Love', where, it was alleged, 'a mock
religion and a boundless fanaticism sanction modes of worship which
tend to destroy all sense of modesty', and for Conolly, she illustrated
the dangers of 'leaving imbecile, visionary and fanatical women at
large'. Only confinement, he now argued, could protect her reputation and property, and whether she recovered or not, 'her habits
would at least be regulated, all excess avoided, all painful exposure
prevented.' This expressly overturned the defence's case that 'no
lunatic should be confined unless dangerous to himself or others'

that was based on his own earlier argument in *Indications*.[42] And in 1859 he was sued by a patient he had committed to Moorcroft asylum in which he had a financial interest.[43]

Conolly's mythological role underwent a similar transformation as his figure was pressed into service by different elements of the reform movement. For Dickens and Morley he was still the wise genius of professional philanthropy in the late 1850s, but by the early 1860s he had been parodied as the smooth-talking Dr Wycherley in Reade's *Hard Cash*, and Dickens felt obliged to publish a disclaimer dissociating *All the Year Round* from the views expressed in the serial – not only the thinly disguised pastiche of Conolly, but the portrayal of the Lunacy Commissioners as well-meaning incompetents, led by the nose by the medical establishment.[44] The 'sensation' of *Hard Cash* initially depends on the hero's incarceration in an 'old' corrupt madhouse, but the 'thrill of terror' is quickly transposed to contemporary practices as he falls prey to Wycherley's manipulations. For Wycherley is an expert who has become a monomaniac, a 'collector of mad people', so puffed up by his own discourse that he interprets all behaviour as pathological, and the acknowledgement of madness as the only sign of sanity. His book *The Incubation of Insanity* parodies and inverts Conolly's *Indications*, his obsession with the question of Hamlet's madness echoes Conolly's own 'Study of Hamlet', published earlier in 1863.[45] The hero of the novel is an unproblematically sane, middle-class male, but in adapting the genre of scandalized exposure of the private madhouse system that had been appearing since the end of the eighteenth century in order to focus its attack on the power of modern psychological medicine to define its own object, *Hard Cash* contributed to a furore that had been developing in the debates on confinement themselves.[46] The fulcrum of its narrative tension is that 'in lunacy law the extremes of intellects meet', and that legal and medical definitions of madness can be pressed by this institutional power along infinitely expandable limits.[47] Reade himself had been actively involved in the protection of alleged lunatics; he had begun collecting material on asylum conditions in the early 1850s, and in 1859 had protected John Fletcher, an escaped inmate (the case is documented in 'Our dark places').[48] The book thus marked the culmination of a panic about the plight of inmates in private asylums which recalled older fears, but which, like Reade's novel, sprang from anxieties generated by the professionalization of the reform movement itself. These anxieties contributed to the setting up of the 1858 Parliamentary Select

Committee into the Care and Treatment of Lunatics and Their Property.

'The tenacity of a private lunatic asylum is unique', commented the narrator in *Hard Cash*. 'A little push and you slide into one, but to get out again is to scale a precipice with crumbling sides.'[49] The debates on the 'liberty of the subject' prompted by the position of the inmates of private asylums, potential victims of their relatives' manipulations, obviously involved a very different 'subject' from the one to be found in a county asylum, where it was rarely stressed that psychological perceptions could be shaped by social interests. Yet this meant, too, that it was those private institutions that could highlight the tenuousness of the very idea of a coherent social identity. The establishment of the Lunacy Commission in 1845 had formed part of a national structure of inspection and surveillance, but now anxieties about confinement formed a set of overlapping associations: harking back to the 'dark places' of the corrupt asylum, while transposing these fears into a new register as the idea of what it meant to be mad itself shifted.[50] The dominant perception of the insane as repositories of unreason in the eighteenth century meant that the principal fears about wrongful confinement carried into the nineteenth century laid the emphasis on *wrongful*, reserving sympathy primarily for the sane victims of conscious conspiracy. 'What must a rational mind suffer when it is treated in such an irrational manner?' demanded a much-publicized letter to the *Gentlemen's Magazine* in 1763, highlighting the plight of the wrongly committed.[51] And even in Mary Wollstonecraft's *The Wrongs of Women*, where the madhouse is an analogue for women's intellectual confinement and lack of autonomous identity in marriage, the heroine describes herself as 'a wretch condemned to reason on the nature of madness, by having wrecked minds continually under my eye, and almost wish myself mad, to escape the contemplation of it.'[52]

This 'wild' image of the madhouse was kept alive in the early nineteenth century – and not only as a necessary counterpoint to the reform movement: the number of private madhouses in England trebled between 1808 and 1845.[53] But the wrongful confinement cases during the 1850s, while emphasizing this continued malpractice and profiteering, increasingly came to debate the question of confinement itself, developing the points that the early Conolly had made in *Indications*.[54] A crucial figure here is John Perceval, Chairman of the Alleged Lunatics' Friends Society, a body which had been set up in 1845, and which intervened in individual cases as well

LEEDS METROPOLITAN UNIVERSITY LIBRARY

as collecting evidence that was cited to the 1858 Select Committee. He strongly argued against the chairman, Shaftesbury's point that all abuses were the outcome of insufficient state surveillance and control:

> I would first refer to the danger to which the liberty of the subject is exposed through unjust or unnecessary efforts being made to confine him . . . I think patients have sometimes to be protected against medical advice and experiments as well as any other danger.[55]

But Perceval is crucial in another respect, one that goes far beyond even Reade's libertarianism; and Collins, whose manipulation of the image of the asylum far exceeds both Dickens and Reade in its fictional and ideological complexity, made a significant inversion in his naming of the splenetic villain of *The Woman in White*.

For John Perceval, a younger son of the assassinated prime minister Spencer Perceval, published an extraordinary document in 1838 and 1840: *A Narrative of the Treatment Experienced by a Gentleman in a State of Mental Derangement, Designed to Explain the Causes and Nature of Insanity, and to Expose the Injudicious Conduct Pursued Towards Many Unfortunate Sufferers Under that Calamity.* As its ponderous title implies, this is a plea on behalf of the insane and a scandalized exposure of methods of treatment, even in such reportedly enlightened institutions as Fox's asylum.[56] Perceval writes:

> I open my mouth for the dumb, I write in defence of youth and old age, of female delicacy . . . and not only of man and of manhood. . . . In the name of humanity . . . I intreat you to place yourselves in the position of those whose sufferings I describe, before you attempt to discuss what course is to be pursued towards them.[57]

Moreover, Perceval himself had been confined in various asylums, both in Fox's Brislington House and Ticehurst Asylum, and his narrative is not only an account of the conditions he experienced while he considered himself sane, but also, crucially, an exploration of the processes which underlay his own derangement: 'Having lived with Lunatics, observing their manners and reflecting on my own, I deem that alone sufficient excuse for setting forth my grief and theirs'; and to do this he draws on the narrative form of the *confession*.[58]

It is this double exposure, this dual exploration of the treatment and the experience of insanity, that makes Perceval's *Narrative* so compelling. For while he is elaborating an attack on the continuing widespread methods of restraint and coercion, he is also suggesting that these are the extensions of many of the implicit power relations of moral management itself. Like Tuke and Conolly, he argues that nothing is more likely to exacerbate derangement than being strapped down and denied all mental and physical exercise; he stresses that the regaining of a coherent subjectivity depends on reinforcing self-esteem, which here fuses with 'moral sense'. But this immediately leads into a critique of the internalization of responsibility that Tuke, in advocating non-restraint, makes the linchpin of his treatment:

[The patient] is professedly a pitiable object of scrupulous care, the innocent dupe of unintelligible delusion, but he is treated as if responsible, as if his dupery is his fault; yet if he resists the treatment he is then a madman! and if, as in my case, he is agonised and downcast by a continual and unmeasured self-accusation of his great guilt in being insane, he receives no correcting intimation that he has something to say to himself, that he is the appalling witness of the power of disease; no encouragement, no inspiration of self-confidence; but all around tends to keep down his spirits, to depress his energies, to debase and degrade him in his own estimation.[59]

He unpicks the precise workings of that internalized surveillance in attempting to disentangle the structures of religious, social, and psychic authority that are transformed and enacted within his derangement: 'I . . . suffered from an habitual error of mind . . . that of fearing to doubt, and of taking the guilt of doubt upon my conscience.'[60]

To do this involves learning that it is necessary to discover the uses of doubt in order to disentangle himself from a complex network of delusion, in a way that fundamentally upturns the precepts of moral management, yet without ascribing a privileged authenticity to madness. It involves Perceval's acknowledgement that to lay bare the force of the delusion, it is necessary to accept both the subjective logic, the reality that underlies it, and to trace its roots in his own history. Thus he reconstructs the precise way in which his religious obsessions grew out of his own excessive 'moral sense' – his overenthusiastic evangelicalism; he shows how this zeal took the form of a ubiquitous but absent paternal and deified power, a power to which he was continually an inarticulate other; an exaggerated version, in other words, of the position in which he found himself as an inmate in Fox's madhouse, which he first conceived as the house of the friend of his dead father, and where he imagined his keepers were representations of the Trinity.

> I mention these facts to show the reasonableness, if I may so call it, of my lunacy, *if it was entirely lunacy*; to speak more clearly, to show the reality of the *existence of that power*, by the use or abuse of which I became insane. If by the abuse of it, because the Lord confounded me for my disobedience, if by the use of it, because, though real, it was the spirit of delusion.[61]

As both subject and object of this process of analysis, like the spectator at the play of his own derangement, he attempts to trace the process of transformation which underlies its emotional power, and to learn the figurative significance of his physical symptoms:

> I suspect that many of the delusions which I laboured under, and which other insane persons labour under, consist in their mistaking a figurative or poetic form of speech for a literal one; and this observation may be important to those who attend to their cure. The spirit speaks poetically but the man understands it literally . . . and his imagination not being under his own control, he in a manner feels it.[62]

Perceval's *Narrative* is unique as a document tracing the reworking of a psychotic experience in the early nineteenth century. But in its precise use of the conventions of the confession, in which the re-formed narrator is the product of the process that he is narrating, its structure anticipates the complex critique of moral management embodied in Collins's *Basil: A Story of Modern Life*. And in its exploration of the sense of symptoms and the transformative processes involved in the workings of the unconscious, it forms a strand in a complex set of debates on the internal working of the mind, debates that now need to be investigated in more detail.

'IN THE COMPLICATED LABYRINTHS OF OUR FRAME'

How were these shifts in the cultural landscape and the significance of madness shaped by contemporary debates about cognition, consciousness and identity? In *The Indications of Insanity*, Conolly had emphasized the difficulty of laying down fixed criteria for establishing unsoundness of mind, though later he was willing to do so. He had argued, too, that the specific understanding of insanity depended on analysing 'the constitution of the human understanding' – that it was essential to see the relation between 'healthy' and 'morbid' workings of the consciousness before they could be distinguished.[63] Tuke's 'lay' application of the precepts of moral management had implied a dualistic concept of the self, and it was Perceval's 'soul' which 'survived that ruin' of loss of reason.[64] But Conolly's analysis combined an intricate reinterpretation of associationist psychology with a physiologically-based model of the mind, and these strands were more generally interwoven in mid-nineteenth-century psychology. They influenced investigations both of the way that identity might be stamped upon its outward signs and of the internal workings of the mind, manifested in various kinds of 'unconscious cerebration': dreams, somnambulism, spectral illusion.[65] These debates were transformed again by the impact of the 'Development Hypothesis' or evolutionary theory, which emphasized that the individual could only be understood in a collective context, as a moment in a continually unravelling history.[66]

They were not free-floating debates. They too were overdetermined by the institutional context in which they were developed. They display a continual process of correspondence and of slippage between the urge to establish various boundaries (between healthy and morbid forms of consciousness, between a rationalized dominant subject and a pathologized other, been official and unofficial kinds of knowledge, between a masculine medical gaze and a set of feminine signs) in ways which clearly helped to reinforce hierarchies of gender, class and race.[67] But it is too simple to collapse these processes completely into each other, and to characterize them all as fixed oppositions, for what these debates often illustrate above all is how very fragile, how tenuous, the boundaries of a coherent subjectivity really were. For these discussions of consciousness were marked by an extraordinary ambivalence, and mid-century psychology continually wavered between a fascination with the apparently irrational workings of the mind, and the urge to regulate and control them. Collins's narratives continually exploit the tenuousness of this balance, not least in their interweaving of experiments, eye-witness records, legal testimonies, diaries – evidence which displays the truth's subjective construction even as it proves it.

The reader is at the centre of this process, but it is often mediated through the struggle *within* the subjective narrating consciousness to separate thoughts, to distinguish between valid and delusory perceptions, to doubt whether one can trust the evidence of the senses. Robert Audley expressed one aspect of the dilemma in Braddon's *Lady Audley's Secret*: 'Was it monition or a monomania? . . . What if this chain that I have constructed link by link is woven out of my own folly?'[68] In elaborating it Collins, like Braddon, draws on a precise terminology and set of perceptual codes.

A starting-point is that distinction between 'monition' and 'monomania' and (linked with this) between 'monomania' and 'moral insanity', since legal as well as psychological opinion attempted to approach and resolve the vexed questions of criminal responsibility and of how to establish unsoundness of mind by differentiating between these terms.[69] The concept of monomania, a development of the earlier, humoral, melancholia (as distinct from mania), had first been established in France by Esquirol and Pinel. In England it was elaborated by James Cowles Pritchard in *A Treatise on Insanity and Other Disorders Affecting the Mind* (1835) and *On the Different Forms of Insanity in Relation to Jurisprudence* (1842), and by the mid-nineteenth century it had become a widely used term that could be stretched to mean almost any kind of irrational obsession. Pritchard opened his *Treatise on Insanity* by reiterating that it was hard to establish the boundaries of madness, but he quickly attempted to do so by modifying Locke's observation that 'madmen have not lost the faculty of reasoning; but having joined some ideas together very wrongly, they mistake them for truths, and they err, as men do that argue right from wrong principles.'[70] This was only one aspect of madness, Pritchard went on to argue, for insanity itself, as well as the object it applied to, now needed to be divided into two categories, 'intellectual' and 'moral'. It was this conceptual distinction between *irrationality* and *perversion* which had a crucial bearing on the ideological significance of definitions of derangement, even as the terms of one were constantly being smuggled over into the territory of the other. Intellectual insanity could be further subdivided, into monomania ('in which the understanding is partially disordered or under the influence of some particular delusion, referring to one subject and involving one train of ideas, while the intellectual powers appear, when exercised on other subjects, to be altogether unimpaired'), mania ('in which the understanding is generally deranged'), and dementia.[71]

Monomania was essentially compatible with moral management,

and as such was defined as partial insanity.[72] 'The affection of the brain that causes these delusions is not madness', argued John Barlow in *Man's Power Over Himself to Prevent and Control Insanity*, 'but the *want of power or resolution to examine them is*.'[73] But the concept of moral insanity also shifted the cognitive status of 'moral', making the explicitly prescriptive use of the term the central, infinitely expandable, criterion. Moral insanity, Pritchard argued, consisted in 'a morbid perversion of the feelings, affections and active powers, without any illusion or erroneous conviction being impressed upon the understanding'.[74] The concept 'has completely removed all the barriers which separate vice from insanity and thrown the subject of madness into the direst confusion', commented the *Quarterly Review* in 1854, for now according to Pritchard, 'excessive intensity of any passion is disorder in the moral sense'.[75] The concomitant of this process was that crime was pathologized and criminals could not be held responsible for their actions if the moral insanity definition was literally applied. But Pritchard suggested that in practice unrestrained monomania could lead to moral insanity, and that this reinforced the need for rigorous early training. He developed a string of 'sensational' anecdotes to illustrate his point, such as the case of 'an only son of a weak and indulgent mother', the heir to a large estate, who 'gave himself up habitually to the gratification of every caprice and passion of which an untutored and violent temper was susceptible', and who finally threw one of his employees down a well.[76] He noted that the disease often took the form of 'an unusual prevalence of angry or malicious feelings which arise without provocation or any of the ordinary incitements'.[77] Sensation fiction was thus provided with a set of ready-made conventions for villainy, conventions it would both resort to and twist around to turn the assumptions of moral insanity back on to the perceiver who defined it.

In his *Treatise on Insanity* Pritchard stressed the distinction between moral and physical *causes*, defining moral here as everything not immediately traceable to an organic cause, then broke each of these distinctions down into 'predisposing' and 'exciting' categories.[78] But this dichotomy tended to disintegrate in the actual analysis of the relationship between the structure and function of the mind, while the interpretative methods through which these categories were represented drew on conceptual metaphors derived from each other. Moreover, they took place in a particular interpretative context which had come to permeate psychological, aesthetic, and fictional conventions by the mid-nineteenth century, a context shaped by the perceptual codes of *physiognomy* and *phrenology*. These both claimed in different ways that the inner self could be defined and understood through outward appearance, and the process by which consciousness and identity were constructed and understood was crucially mediated through their contrasting hypotheses.

The idea of a semiotic system in which outward signs were the index of latent intellectual and moral traits was already well established by the beginning of the nineteenth century. The tradition of classical physiognomy derived from Aristotle and was based on humoral theory combined in the seventeenth and eighteenth centuries with a model based on animal analogy.[79] But it was the work of Caspar Lavater at the end of the eighteenth century that was to be the main reference point for nineteenth-century applications of the method. Lavater did not fundamentally modify physiognomy's idealist basis, maintaining that the face constituted a *symbolic* system in which each feature, individually and in combination, had a culturally universal meaning. It did not matter that the method was not yet a fully-fledged science, since for Lavater, popular preconceptions about what people look like already constituted a kind of folk science, which physiognomy merely attempted to systematize.

> Let any person, but for two days, remark all that he hears and reads among men, and he will every day hear and read . . . 'You might have read it in his eyes' – 'The look of the man is enough' – 'He has an honest countenance'. . . . The very judgments that seem to militate against the sciences are but exceptions which confirm the universality of physiognomic sensation.[80]

The proliferation of popular treatise on physiognomy none the less implied that his work conferred scientific credibility on already existing preconceptions. And physiognomic representations of insanity followed the same kind of self-fulfilling process in their use of the conventions of portraiture. Pinel and Esquirol (like Lavater) focused on movable expression as well as facial structure in their use of the method for classifying pathological types, as did Alexander Morison in *The Physiognomy of Mental Diseases*, but they all relied on existing techniques of portraiture, and thus helped to 'fix and render permanent that which might have passed away' by shaping the visual expectations that viewers brought to insanity.[81]

Physiognomy was attractive precisely because it could be adapted to so many uses and interpretations: Charles Bell had argued that active projection was necessary to interpret the dynamic meaning of the face, and the flexibility of the significance of the method was emphasized by E.S. Dallas in the *Cornhill* as late as 1861.[82] And while Bell's analysis had echoed 'eighteenth-century' images of madness, stressing its animality, placing the insane half-way up a hierarchical chain of being, in *The Expression of the Emotions*, Darwin was to reinterpret this use of animal analogy to argue that the insane signified a more intense humanity precisely because the most recognizably 'human' of expressions are those which have the closest animal equivalents.[83] Bell's work provided an important reference point for the Pre-Raphaelite interpretation of naturalism too; ironically, his aesthetically shaped conventions conferred an authenticity to their own principles of breaking free of established techniques. Holman Hunt recommended *The Anatomy and Philosophy of Expression as Connected with the Fine Arts* to Millais in 1848, and both employed Bell's methods, which in many respects were directly comparable with Ruskin's argument that 'truth to nature' precisely consisted in the most subtle, complex, even violent emotion.[84] In Collins's fiction physiognomy can have radically different meanings in different narrative contexts. In *The Woman in White* it becomes a crucial means of mediating and compounding Hartright's neoplatonic idealism; much later, in *The Evil Genius* (1886), it is a means of creating a self-ironizing narrative distance:

> The personal appearance of Miss Wigger might have suggested a modest distrust of his own abilities to Lavater, when that self-sufficient man wrote his book on physiognomy. What ever betrayal of her inner self her face might have presented in the distant time when she was young was now overlaid by a surface of flabby fat which, assisted by green spectacles, kept the virtues (or vices) of this woman's nature a profound secret until she opened her lips.[85]

Phrenology, on the other hand, used a completely different set of interpretative devices in its claim to read latent character in manifest physical signs; devices rooted not only in a contrasting theory of meaning, but in a completely different notion of the physiological workings of the consciousness and the constitution of identity. Physiognomy saw the face and body as an expressive mask on which the inner drama of identity was stamped; phrenology was interested in the shape of the skull as an index of different organs which signified particular psychological propensities – localized, but juxtaposed, like the interacting pieces of a mosaic. Franz Joseph Gall first developed this theory of character in Vienna at the end of the eighteenth century; it was based (as Roger Cooter has explained) on certain key tenets: the brain is the organ of the mind, and it is not a homogenous unity but a collection of distinct mental organs; these organs or faculties are topographically localized in particular functions; the relative size of an organ reflects its strength of influence, and since the skull hardens over the brain during infant development, external craniological means can be used to diagnose the internal state of the mental faculties.[86]

In England phrenology was popularized by George Combe, an ambitious Edinburgh lawyer, who drew on the ideas of Gall's student J.G. Spurzheim, and whose *Constitution of Man* became the fourth most popular book of the mid-nineteenth century after the Bible, *The Pilgrim's Progress*, and *Robinson Crusoe*.[87] It too was a kind of moral manual as well as a treatise on the structure and function of the brain, and phrenology gained its immensely powerful popular authority during the first half of the nineteenth century because, like moral management, with which it was closely associated, it represented both a radical, even liberating, form of knowledge of the self that merged with a Utopian social theory, and a more utilitarian model of containment, classification, and control. Combe's topography followed the conventional distinction between 'intellectual faculties' and 'feelings'. The latter category was subdivided into 'propensities', including amativeness, combativeness, acquisitiveness, and secretiveness on the one hand, and 'sentiments', such as self-esteem, pride, veneration, on the other. The former broke down into 'external senses', 'faculties which perceive existence', and 'faculties which perceive the existence of external objects'.[88] Each individual was made up of a combination of these faculties and propensities, and character traits could be explained by the degree of development of particular organs.

It was phrenology's scientific ambitions as well as its more inventive and speculative aspects which came under widespread attack by the mid-nineteenth century. 'It was a strange topography and a still stranger psychology', wrote Dallas. 'There was no doubt or ambiguity about the system. . . . Phrenology makes a pretence of science, affects precision and leaps to conclusions.'[89] But this was one of its main attractions for many of the superintendents of county asylums: William Ellis, John Conolly, W.A.F. Browne, Forbes Winslow, and Daniel Noble were all active members of phrenological societies at some time. For phrenology provided a model that could mediate physical, intellectual, and moral definitions and causes of insanity; that could reconcile and balance biology and environment; that could stress the importance of self-discipline yet facilitate psychological medicine's accelerating move towards the definition and classification of the passive insane in the new state institutions. Andrew Combe, George's brother, argued in *Observations on Mental Derangement* in 1831 that 'mental derangement is always symptomatic of cerebral disease' but this belief tended to be modified in specific applications of the method in arguing for criminal and lunacy reform.[90] Spurzheim had stressed the adaptive powers of the various faculties: 'I am intimately convinced that no faculty itself can be bad, and that all the inmate powers of man have some aim'. Similar sentiments were taken up by *The Zoist*, the main journal to advocate the application of phrenology: 'If all criminals are objects of pity, let us feel it our duty to ameliorate their character and not to strangle them.'[91] Phrenology always held an uneasy relationship to the scientific establishment but many of its presuppositions were to shape the terms of the debate on the relationship between structure, function, and adaptation that would be developed in mid-nineteenth-century social and psychological theory. Certain of its elements contributed to the development of neurophysiology during the century's latter half, to the work of Pierre Broca, J.H. Jackson, and David Ferrier (whom Collins cites in *Heart and Science* in 1883).[92]

Phrenology thus did more than offer the means to interpret the outward manifestations of character. It also claimed to explain internal mental mechanisms, offering a physiological model of how various cognitive faculties were localized which challenged Locke's conception of the association of ideas as the basis of rational thought.[93] In this respect it paradoxically both clashed and interacted with the critical reinterpretation of the associationist tradition as laid down by Locke and modified by Hartley in early-nineteenth-century psychological and aesthetic theory in Britain.[94] This critique is most familiar in Romantic theories of the active, dynamic power of the imagination as shaping all forms of thought, above all Coleridge's development of German Romanticism in his analysis of the ways in which the 'esemplastic power' assimilates and transforms all perception and cognition.[95] A significant feature of the emergent discipline of psychological medicine was the recasting of metaphysical debates in the philosophy of mind in the context of the empirical study of mental mechanisms, as the paradoxical impact of the Edinburgh philosophers Dugald Stewart, Thomas Brown and (in a rather different context) William Hamilton, bear witness.

Brown's *Lectures on the Philosophy of the Human Mind* (1820) was a continual reference point for many later writers and had been through twenty editions by 1860. In it he emphasizes that his aims are not to explore 'That *speculative* and *passive* philosophy only, which enquires into the nature of our intellectual part, and the mysterious connection with the body which it animates, but that *practical* science, which relates to the duties, the hopes, and the great destiny of man, and which, in analysing the powers of his understanding, and tracing all the modifications of which it is individually susceptible, views it chiefly as a general instrument of good.'[96] Brown acknowledges that all mental activity proceeds through a process of assimilation, through which the mind modifies and transforms present and past sensations and impressions to produce new combinations and meanings, but he argues that the notion of *suggestion*, which links visual image and emotional response is preferable to that of association in Locke's sense. 'Rational' and 'imaginative' thought work through essentially similar processes of comparison, projection and metaphoric transference, he maintained, implicitly undercutting Coleridge's distinction between fancy and Imagination. Even in its most prosaic moments the mind essentially proceeds through fantasy, creating stories as intricate as any sensation novel:

> The writer of romance gives secret motives and passions to the characters which he invents, and adds incident to incident in the long series of complicated action which he develops. What *he* does, we, too, are doing every hour; contriving events that are never to happen, – imagining motives and passions, and *thinking* our *little romances*, of which ourselves, as may be supposed, perhaps are the *primary heroes*, but in the plot of which there is a sufficient complication of adventures of those whom we love, and those whom we dislike, *connected* with the *main piece*, or episodically intermingled. Our romances of real life, though founded on facts, are, in their principle circumstances, *fictions still*; and, though the fancy which they display may not be as *brilliant*, it is still the *same in kind* with that which forms and fills the history of imaginary heroes and heroines.[97]

In his posthumous *Lectures on Metaphysics* (1859) Hamilton emphasized even more emphatically that the process of association can only be understood as one of continual unconscious modification. Drawing on Reid, Stewart and Hartley, he identified three 'degrees of latency' to distinguish between various forms of

unconscious activity. The first suggests simply that most of the
mind's possible recollections lie beyond the immediate range of
consciousness; the second degree is seen at work in those forms of
'double consciousness' exemplified by somnambulism – that state of
trance in which the mind seems to have two entirely separate identities. But the third degree of latency 'necessitates the conclusion that
the sphere of our conscious modifications is only a small circle in the
centre of a far wider sphere of action and passion, of which we are only
conscious through its effects'.[98] It determines perception as well as
suggestion or association through the accumulated force of habit, and
here Hamilton argues that the process of association often proceeds
by the mind connecting two impressions by means of a suppressed
link or thread that always remains hidden in its obscure recesses.

Hamilton's complaint that the importance of unconscious thought
had been ignored in British philosophy and psychology (unlike its
German and French counterparts) was considerably exaggerated.
But the interpretation of its significance undoubtedly underwent
particular modification in the context of the development of
mainstream physiological psychology. John Abercrombie's earlier
influential textbook *Inquiries Concerning the Intellectual Powers and
the Investigation of Truth* (1830) together with its companion volume,
The Philosophy of the Moral Feelings (1833) in particular engaged
with 'the deep interest which the philosophy of mind . . . presents
to the medical inquirer', and argued that the principles of such
philosophy could only be of use to the analysis of the internal working of the mind by applying the methods of inductive science.[99] He
combines a detailed epistemological discussion of the nature of scientific knowledge and rationality with a more descriptive investigation
of mental processes themselves. This means that his adaptation of
notions of association, or suggestion, though echoing many of
Brown's points, are always turned around to stress the importance
of the indirect or direct control of the mind over its own associative
mechanisms, in a way that directly feeds into Pritchard's analysis.
Thus Abercrombie, in distinguishing various kinds of 'voluntary
association' ('natural or philosophical', 'local or incidental', and
'arbitary or fictitious') stresses continually that the 'culture and
improvement of the attention and memory' consists in 'learning
habits of correct association', 'associations made on sound principles, or according to the true and important relations of things'.
He notes that this involves continually eschewing an over-active
imagination: 'There is no power of the mind that requires more
cautious management or stern control.'[100]

Abercrombie's distinction between four kinds of states in which 'the ideas or images in the mind follow one another according to associations over which we have no control': dreams, somnambulism and double consciousness, spectral illusion and insanity, was a widespread one.[101] Mid-nineteenth-century analysis of aberrant states proceeded largely through detailed anecdotal case studies, and by reference to such accounts as De Quincey's *Confessions of an English Opium-Eater* to demonstrate the existence of these mental activities, and to describe them in physiological terms rather than to interpret them. But it was widely acknowledged that dreaming was more than simply 'a suspension of the judgment' – that it was 'an active state of memory, imagination, etc.'. The problem lay in how to interpret the bizarre logic of suppressed associations. 'It is undoubtedly owing to the faculty, sometimes possessed by sleep, of renewing long forgotten ideas, that persons have long forgotton facts communicated to them in dreams', noted the phrenologist Robert MacNish, who argued in *The Philosophy of Sleep* (1830) that in general the content of dreams was determined by the localized propensities of the dreamer.[102]

Abercrombie outlined distinct kinds of dream activity: recent events and emotions mixed up with one another and with past ones 'though in other respects they were entirely unconnected'; 'trains of images brought up by association with bodily sensations'; 'dreams consisting in the revival of old associations, repeating things which had entirely passed out of mind, and which seem to have been forgotton', and dreams which embody 'a strong propensity of character or a strong mental emotion', but which are apparently fulfilled by coincidence.[103] This last point was developed by the physician John Addington Symonds (senior), a close friend of Pritchard. He had been a member of the Aesthetic Society in Edinburgh, and like Dallas, was interested in linking psychological and aesthetic theory.[104] His *Sleep and Dreams* (1851) maintains that dreams recall traces of the past, but in a way that seems to be outside history; in sleep 'images do not arise with the stamp of the past upon them, as in our waking hours, and they are combined together in fantastic association without any control of the will.'[105] He indicates that the limits of fantasy are continually shifting in accordance with the different kinds of associative processes at work in dreaming. Dreams, too, can have a cognitive function; they can seem prophetic precisely because they refract the past within the consciousness in a way that can indirectly determine its outcome: 'Some dreams work their own fulfilment. The mind vehemently possessed of an idea this received, instinctively acts up to it.'[106]

Double consciousness or somnambulism, with spectral delusion, or 'ghost seeing', were placed between dreaming and insanity. They suggested even more emphatically the tenuousness of the limits of consciousness and of a single coherent identity. Of these, spectral illusion was the least contentious. Here, as Symonds argued 'individuals turn out to be the subject of a peculiar nervous disorder, that destroys the balance between the perceptive and conceptive faculties.'[107] Materialist explanations of spectral illusion had become widely established by the mid-nineteenth century. 'On Visions and Dreams', an article in *Fraser's Magazine* in 1862 for example, cites Ferriar's *Sketch Towards a Theory of Apparitions*, which had appeared in 1813, along with Abercrombie to differentiate between projection and optical illusion, and notes: 'Any state of excitement, sensibility or irritation may make our mental conceptions take a phantom shape . . . and considering how all our thoughts are visions, it is only a wonder that we are not more haunted by spectres than we are.'[108] However double consciousness, in which the mind might switch between different states or voice suppressed desires, recall long forgotten traces of the past, and otherwise indicate its extraordinary powers, was more contentious, and the phenomenon was often (as in Abercrombie) described rather than explained. For Hamilton it was proof of the latent modification of the consciousness. For Symonds it was only 'the alteration of healthy and morbid conditions of mind, even though in the morbid state there might be achievements of memory and the other mental faculties not attained to in the walking condition'; in phrenological debates it was proof of the physical division of the brain.[109] A.L. Wigan had taken this latter argument even further in *The Duality of Mind* in 1844, arguing that the mind was literally made up of two wills governed by the brain's two hemispheres. But the possible significance of double consciousness and of somnambulism was most hotly contested in debates about its artificial inducement through the practice of *mesmerism*.

Mesmerism, or animal magnetism, had made its original impact in pre-revolutionary France, when Franz Anton Mesmer arrived from Vienna in 1778 and published *Sur la Decoverte du Magnetisme Animal* a year later. This claimed to offer a cure for physical and psychic ills and thus a prescription for complete social and individual harmony – to that extent it was a rearticulation of much older vitalist and transcendentalist concepts.

Mesmer's theory was based on the notion of a universal energy, force, or fluid 'of an incomparably rarified nature', which ebbed and flowed, as tides, according to precise laws, and which formed 'a mutual influence between the Heavenly bodies, the Earth, and Animate Bodies'.[110] And since all material and organic substances were governed by these laws, he alleged, understanding them could form the basis for an all-embracing theory of influence and control. Diseases and nervous disorders were caused by the misdirection of this 'fluid' through the body; massaging the body's 'poles' would induce a crisis involving trance or somnambulism, through which the patient would pass to harmony and health.[111]

Mesmer maintained that the magnetic force was a material power, but the concept itself blurred the boundaries between the material and metaphysical, the literal and the metaphorical. And this was one of the effects of its popular impact in England from the 1830s: it signalled cognitive confusion and could be used to support widely differing theories – of the self, of the nature of derangement, of reality. Debates on mesmerism often entangled discussion of the phenomenon itself with disputes over the validity of its evidence and over the nature of the influence it was thought to manifest – influence of the mesmerizer over the mesmerized as well as of the subjects themselves as it came to be used as an all-embracing term for the exercise of psychic and sexual power. The problem, as 'What is mesmerism?' in *Blackwood*'s maintained in 1851, was how to

> lay down accurately what is claimed for it – not vaguely, as I find it in letters and lectures, where that which is asserted at one time as its power is denied at another; but to speak clearly of its congruent powers or asserted powers, without vacillation; then to follow these powers to their consequences – their necessary conse-quences – if they be powers at all; and draw conclusions arising from the two natures upon which it works – or perhaps is worked upon – materiality or spirituality.[112]

At times it almost functioned as a 'wild' term around which opponents and adherents alike clustered, confirming or refuting it to advance their own positions in different ways and cultural contexts. This cognitive ambiguity contributed and sprang from its increasingly marginalized scientific and medical status in England; yet here mesmerism grew out of mainstream physiology even as it challenged it, and reflected as well as questioned many of its concerns. Dickens's close friend John Elliotson's development of the technique of artificial somnambulism to disclose and cure nervous disorders grew directly out of his phrenological interests. He founded and was president of the Phrenological Society in 1824 and, in 1843, started *The Zoist: A Journal of Cerebral Physiology and Mesmerism and their Application to Human Welfare*, which advocated 'phrenomesmerism' as a new compound science.[113] Like Mesmer's follower Puysegur in France, Elliotson was a strict empiricist, basing his claims on case studies and public displays of mesmeric efficacy. These displays, however, compounded its disreputable status as occult trickery in the eyes of the medical and scientific establishment.[114]

Elliotson had first developed the method of artificial somnambulism in the treatment of nervous disorders in the late 1830s during the course of his work at University College Hospital, basing his treatment on the premiss that the trance could prefigure and precipitate the course of the illness and thus hasten the process of cure. However, it led to his more extravagant claim that the method of induced trance could be a means of divining extraordinary 'psychic' powers, and of controlling the states of mind opened up by the manipulated 'double consciousness' in a way that would culminate in clairvoyance, which Elliotson considered to be magnetism's most highly developed stage. His outline of this hypothesis in *Human Physiology* (which he amended in 1840 to include a defence of mesmerism) follows a summary of conventional conceptions of dreams and double consciousness, but goes on to quote Gall's assertion that 'all the nervous system is an identity and a totality – a pure transparence without cloud, an infinite expansion without bounds or obstacles', and to link this with Dugald Stewart's point that it was the fact that mesmerism did work that was important, not *how* it worked[115] He none the less came under increasing attack from the medical authorities which culminated in the scandal surrounding the Okey sisters whose extraordinary powers under trance were put on public display, and claims of 'ecstatic delirium' merged with charges of sexual manipulation. The *Lancet* took a particular strong line in attacking Elliotson, who resigned his position at University College in 1838.[116]

Mesmerism thus made up an extraordinarily rich and flexible discourse, providing a set of terms and references that could invoke, in a simultaneously realistic and figurative way, processes of dominance and subordination, hidden forces within the self, secret traces of the past, links between the body and the surrounding world and the psychic and the physical, correspondences and modes of transference between self and other; and this contributed to its fascination for so many nineteenth-century novelists.[117] With Collins this fascination culminates in *The Moonstone*, in which mesmeric methods are both exploited and scrutinized in the context of an intricate narrative investigation of the workings of the unconscious and the cognitive processes through which it can be known. The novel was published in 1868, the year Elliotson died, and while Collins was too young to be caught up in the movement to the same extent as Dickens and Bulwer-Lytton, he had accompanied Dickens on a visit to the mesmeric enthusiasts the de la Rues in Genoa in 1853 (Mme de la Rue was magnetized by Dickens for hysterical attacks).[118] During the previous year also Collins had contributed 'Magnetic evenings at home', a short series of reports on mesmerism, to *The Leader*:

> Here was some strange influence working on the intellectual faculties, the nerves and the whole vital principle – the question is – How did it work? I cannot tell . . . I have a thinking machine about me, commonly called a 'brain' – by what process is it set working? What power, when I am asleep, when my will is entirely inactive, sets this thinking machine going, going as I cannot make it go when my will is active and I am awake?[119]

A sceptical G.H. Lewes countered this by arguing that mesmerism could be explained as a kind of autosuggestion, and that 'the fallacy of clairvoyance is, I take it, the interpretation of a *dreaming* power for a *seeing* power', to which Collins replies that he merely wished to 'vindicate the special experiment . . . as a genuine experiment.'[120]

Moreover, Lewes's point that mesmerism worked not through some intangible but material force so much as through the heightened suggestibility of its subjects was taken up by its adherents as much as its detractors. James Braid dismissed the idea of a 'fluid', yet he took up many of Elliotson's hypotheses in developing his own techniques of hypnosis, and his method highlighted the importance of suggestibility in a way which would be taken up by Charcot in Paris in his development of the method as a means of probing the unconscious causes of neurotic symptoms.[121] In England William Carpenter reiterated the explanatory importance of suggestibility in his critique of the theory, *Mesmerism, Spiritualism, etc., Historically and Scientifically Considered* (1877), where he argued that the trance rose from 'a special *rapport* between the 'mesmerizer' and his 'subject'; and that this was clearly explicable by the 'expectancy' under which the subject passed into the state of second consciousness.[122] He saw this as reinforcing Braid's point that there was no essential difference between mesmerism and hypnotism. But this observation developed out of his own theory of 'unconscious cerebration' and its role in the shaping of identity, and by the mid-nineteenth century Carpenter's model of mental activity was regarded as the fullest and most authoritative.[123]

In Carpenter's psychology (as in Bain's and Spencer's) associationist methods directly feed into and are modified by a linear, progressivist evolutionism. The individual subject holds a homologous relationship to collective social and organic development, and the emphasis on continuous links between the historical past and present finds both its source and its reflection in the patterns of the individual mind. Carpenter's model of consciousness differs significantly from Lewes's or Dallas's in this respect; although Lewes's literary criticism is shot through with this linear notion of cultural development, his psychological theory is more dialectical and less prescriptive in its rebuttal of associationism. He argues in *The Foundations of a Creed* that the traces of the past are always present in the self, but they exist unevenly and discontinuously; the mind can neither be seen in isolation from the social organism nor reduced to individual perception and sensation:

> The mind is not a passive recipient of external influences but an active co-operant. . . . It is a variable mechanism which has a *history*. What the senses inscribe on it are not merely changes in the external world but these characters are co-mingled with characters of preceding inscriptions. The sensitive subject is no *tabula rasa* . . . but a palimpsest.[124]

Carpenter also has a concept of the self as layers of past impressions. But in *The Principles of Mental Physiology* (a development of the earlier *Principles of Human Physiology*) he draws a very different inference, citing Abercrombie to underline the importance of memory in forming a continuously coherent self, but extending the point to argue that the principle of association can be extended to include unconscious memory:

> And as our ideas are linked in 'trains' or 'series' which further inosculate with each other like the branch lines of a railway . . . so . . . an idea which has been 'hidden in the obscure recesses of the mind' for years – perhaps for a lifetime – and which seems to have faded completely out of *conscious* memory may be reproduced,

as by the touching of a spring, through a *nexus* of suggestions, which we can sometimes trace out continuously, but of which it does not seem necessary that all the intermediate steps should fall within our cognisance.[125]

Carpenter argued that memory essentially worked automatically, as a set of reflexive gestures, and he went on to emphasize the extraordinary emotional power of 'unconscious cerebration':

> Here again, it would seem as if the material organ of those Feelings tends to *form itself* in accordance to the impressions habitually made upon it; which may be completely unaware of the changes which have taken place in it, as we are by those by which passing events have been registered in our memory, until some circumstance calls forth the unconscious manifestation, which is the 'reflex' of the new condition which the organ has acquired. And it is desirable, in this connection, to recall the fact that the Emotional state seems often to be determined by circumstances of which the individual has no Ideational consciousness, and especially of the emotional states of those by whom he is surrounded: a mode of influence that acts with peculiar potency on the minds of children, and which is most important to their Moral education.[126]

A coherent moral identity was thus dependent on the continual struggle of the conscious mind to reclaim its obscure recesses, to cast a beam on its own secret places. 'There must be in addition a *recognition* of the reproduced state of consciousness', he emphasized; and this 'consciousness of agreement between the present and our past mental experiences, constitutes our sense of personal identity.'[127]

Carpenter's description of a *nexus* of suggestions, some of which may remain unconscious, recalls Hamilton's conception of mental modification. But Hamilton's image of a vast sphere surrounding a small spot of consciousness is developed most fully in E.S. Dallas's witty and eclectic attempt to grasp and explain the elusive yet dynamic and playful power of 'hidden thought'. In *The Gay Science* Dallas reiterates the point that aesthetic effects are essentially an extension of all forms of mental activity. But he goes on to elaborate how this process is expressed in the 'play of thought' that lies behind *pleasure*, a quality which 'in no way stands in opposition to truth'.[128] He claims that only a 'correct psychology . . . of . . . the movement of the mind' can begin to analyse its particular qualities. 'In inviting [my readers] to a psychological discussion', he insists,

'I am luring them not to a study which will break their jaws with hard words and their patience with the husks of logic, but to one which, if not unfairly treated, ought to be as fascinating as romance.'[129] However his analysis of the 'play of thought' starts with the inadequacy of existing attempts to explain the elusive movement of creative thought, theories of the Imagination. 'The first born of the intellectual gifts, it is the last studied and the least understood' – and here Dallas boldly claims that even the most widely different definitions and assessments of imagination, from Locke to Coleridge, slide away from explaining its peculiar power and appeal, its resistance to being set in opposition to any other stable term.[130] They all simply make it mean whatever faculty they want it to be, he argued, and thus it is not so much a name for an indefinable power, more a 'wild term' in itself:

> First it appears as mere memory . . . suddenly it is the mind's eye; sudden again, a second sight; anon, it is known as intuition; then it is apprehension; quickly it passes into a dream; as quickly it resolves itself into sympathy and imitation; in one moment it turns to invention and begins to create; in the next moment it adopts reason and begins to generalise; at length it flies into a passion, and is lost in love. It takes the likeness and apes the style by turns of every faculty, every mood, every motion of thought. . . . Has it . . . a form and character of its own, which . . . we may be able to fix and to define? Is there such a thing as imagination different from the other faculties of the mind? and if so, what is it?[131]

He stressed that imagination's elusive quality could only be grasped by focusing on the continual and slippery process of transformation by which it was defined. For Dallas this was the only way to 'reconcile the philosophical analysis which reduces imagination to a shadow with the popular belief which gives it the empire of the mind. I propose this theory, that the imagination or fantasy is not a special faculty but that it is a special function. It is a name given to the automatic action of the mind or to any of its faculties – to what may not unfitly be called the Hidden Soul.'[132]

Surveying the vast range of existing theories of the unconscious, Dallas notes that while non-mystical theories of hidden thought are nothing new, of the different recent attempts to analyse it (for example, by Hamilton, Mill, Carpenter and Spencer) none are able to get beyond 'the fundamental fact out of which all the fogs of the transcendental philosophy have arisen – the fact that the mind may be engaged in a sphere that transcends consciousness.'[133] The way out of the paradox, he argues, is to embrace its paradoxical aspects. It is not to draw the unconscious into the glare of consciousness, nor to conceive of it in spacial terms, as a box containing forgotten impressions, a hidden place, but to acknowledge that it continually interacts with conscious thought, yet that this interaction itself remains secret:

> I hope to avoid the nonsense and the jargon of those who have discoursed on the sphere of the transcendental – that is, the sphere of our mental existence which transcends or spreads beyond our consciousness; but that consciousness is not our entire world, that the mind stretches in full play far beyond the bourne of consciousness, there will be a little difficulty in proving . . . Comparisons, however, between the two are vain, because each is necessary to the other . . . Between the outer and the inner ring, between our unconscious and our conscious existence, there is a free and a constant but unobserved traffic forever carried on. Trains of thought are continually passing to and fro, from the light into the dark, and back from the dark into the light. When the current of thought flows from within our ken to beyond our ken, it is gone, we forget it, we know not what has become of it. After a time it comes back to us changed and grown as if it was a new thought, and we know not whence it comes.[134]

The qualities of the unconscious mind do not differ essentially from consciousness; they too can be characterized as memory, reason and emotion – reason being 'all that is included in the popular sense of the term – as judgment, invention, comparison, calculation, selection, and the like movements of thought, forethought and afterthought.'[135] Like his contemporaries, Dallas tends to substitute anecdotal description for analysis, but he does this to emphasize that while 'the play of thought' is characterized by this 'constant traffic' in the whole of mental existence, the specific pleasure of art lies in the way that it foregrounds the working of the hidden soul, paradoxically through its *secrecy*. 'Art is poetical in proportion as it has this power of appealing to what I call the absent mind.'[136] It is thus an analogue as much as an extension of all thought – 'As wit is the playful anagram of nature, fantasy is its hieroglyphic alphabet.'[137]

INHERITANCE, ADAPTATION, AND DESTINY

Collins's novels continually conjure with identity. The self is a screen on which others' perceptions are projected and enacted; a collection of physical signs whose meaning is uncertain; a subjectivity struggling to gain coherence, yet bearing secret and forgotten traces. But the self is also formed within a longer history and through the different kinds of legacies it inherits from the past – social, psychic, genealogical – and this sets it within another network of connections (obvious or hidden). The problem of how to both know the past and know how it shapes the future, that sense of 'something obscurely threatening . . . which time was hanging over our heads, is often linked with the mystery of how to place the individual within a family history and thus a fabric of social and organic relations. And it is with these motifs too – lost children, the disclosure of origins, the discovery of immediate or distant kinship – that it is most obvious that Collins is drawing on a familiar stock of fictional conventions in order to exploit the connections that they suggest between the inheritance of property and the formation of identity, and to question the connections between lines of transmission between generations and the reproduction of morbid symptoms. Apparently irrational fears, anxiety about the future, or the burden of an imaginary inheritance are both subjectively real dangers that 'work their own fulfilment' and possible signs of monomania. The sense of an impending fatality contends with the manipulation of coincidence, the notion that the only sure determinant is chance. How do these clashing motifs draw on contemporary notions of inheritance and transmission in order to transform them in new narrative contexts?

The concept of hereditary transmission was certainly not a new one at the beginning of the nineteenth century, but what it meant and exactly how predispositions might emerge was open to different kinds of emphasis. Pritchard identified hereditary factors as among the 'predisposing' causes of insanity that could lie dormant, develop with the growth of the individual, or be excited by environmental causes.[138] Thus changes in the environment might either exacerbate or alleviate a hereditary predisposition, and during the first half of the nineteenth century this was seen as one contributory factor among many. For the notion of hereditary predisposition focused, indeed, on inheritance, often in a way that suggested that it was continuous legacy itself that was morbid. And although nervous disorders might be exacerbated by the frantic pace of modern life, mental malady was just as likely to be the dubious inheritance of the interbred upper classes as the outcome of the excesses of the unruly working classes. It was feudal stagnancy, the weight of an unchanging past, that was felt to breed a decadence that could slide into degeneration. 'It is of little real importance whether it be a predisposition or the malady itself which descends and becomes hereditary', noted George Man Burrows in *Commentaries on Insanity* in 1828. 'But no fact is more incontrovertibly established than that insanity is more susceptible of being propagated; or, in other words, that a specific morbid condition sometimes exists in the human constitution, which, by intermarriage . . . may be perpetuated *ad infinitum.*'[139] The idea is assumed to have gained widespread popular currency by the 1850s. 'Idiots again' in *Household Words* argues that apparent mental defectiveness among paupers is often the result of malnutrition and can be alleviated, but it opens:

> People whose ancestors came in at the Conquest, are apt to have one idea overruling all others – that nobody is worthy of their alliance whose ancestors did not come in at the Conquest. Of course, this has been an idea ever since the Conquest began to be considered an old event; and, of course, there have been fewer and fewer families who had a right to it. Of course, also those families have intermarried, and the intermarriage been more and more restricted. Another 'of course' follows, on which we need not enlarge.[140]

But by the 1860s this notion of the inheritance of morbid traits had been reinterpreted in the context of an evolutionary theory which focused on the relationship of the individual not simply to the family but to the species, and on the interrelationship between the structure of the organism, its function, and its mode of adaptation. Not descent alone but descent with modification was emphasized now. And with this arose questions of whether characteristics which had been acquired by adaptation to the environment could be inherited by succeeding generations; questions which had a significant bearing on the implications of how organic metaphors could be deployed to conceptualize social and sexual forms and divisions, alongside processes of change. The widespread discusion generated by the publication in 1859 of Darwin's *On the Origin of Species by Means of Natural Selection* is the clearest marker of how crucially evolutionary ideas permeated and transformed intellectual culture; but Darwin's work itself emerged out of a complex history of evolutionary theories, and writers made different extrapolations from it, and for different reasons. In Darwin's work the role of chance is a vital factor in the evolutionary process. He stresses the *uneven* and plural nature of change: adaptation and modification draw on and combine disparate and anomalous elements. Thus 'Darwinism' often implicitly challenged many of the overriding assumptions that it could be invoked to demonstrate; it was Darwin's predecessor Lamarck who, with von Baer, had argued that evolution was marked by the increasing drive towards differentiation and complexity (a notion which, we have seen, permeated the analysis of cultural change and the development of fictional forms), and that modification took place as the result of the inheritance of acquired characteristics which thus became structural features.[141] It was this paradigm, primarily, that shaped Herbert Spencer's incorporation of evolutionary concepts into his social and psychological theory – it was he, not Darwin, who coined the term 'the survival of the fittest' in *Social Statics* in 1851.[142]

Like Carpenter (whose work he acknowledges) Spencer's psychological theory had developed initially in phrenological and associationist frameworks, and while he modified these to focus on the nature of the relationship between the internal structures of the organism and the environment, his theory of adaptation retained all the prescriptive attributes of the phrenological tradition that it sought to replace. And although like Darwin and Lewes he refuted teleological explanations of change, his work echoed none of their epistemological challenges – his organic model was essentially extrapolated from a static social one, then deployed to naturalize competitive individualism. While Lewes argued that 'man' had 'a double history', and that organic and social development could never be collapsed into one another, Spencer's use of Lamarckian principles, which seemed to reinforce progressive liberalism, were increasingly to transform it into its own negative image. The first of these principles, that progress is marked by increasing differentiation ('The Law of all progress', he maintained in 'Progress, its law and cause'), underpinned his argument that willed endeavour could become an element of social development; the second, that evolution took the form 'of the continuous adjustment of internal relations to external relations', including the inheritance of acquired characteristics, turned environment into a force of destiny.[143] And psychical transmission, too, followed this path through the inheritance of acquired nervous tendencies. 'Hereditary transmission . . . applies not only to physical, but to psychical peculiarities', Spencer stated in *The Principles of Psychology*:

> It is not simply that a modified form of constitution produced by new habits of life, is bequeathed to future generations; but also that the modified nervous tendencies are also bequeathed: and if

the new habits of life become permanent, the tendencies become permanent.[144]

I have suggested that the worrying links between insanity and the pressures of modernity had been voiced since the eighteenth century and had remained the anxious undercurrent of moral management.[145] In his article on 'Lunatic asylums' in 1857, Andrew Wynter claimed that 'mental ruin springs rather from mental torpidity than from mental stimulation'; but he argued against a growing fear that 'lunacy is on the increase':

Is it true that civilization has called to life a monster such as that which appalled Frankenstein? Is it a necessity of progress that it shall ever be accompanied by that fearful black rider which, like Despair, sits behind it? Does mental development mean increased mental decay?[146]

Over the next twenty years such fears absorbed and helped to shape a discourse of 'degeneration' that was to establish its hegemony by becoming assimilated across biological, psychological, and social theory. John Conolly's son-in-law Henry Maudsley was one of the most vociferous advocates of degenerative explanations of insanity in Britain, replacing the epic story of moral management with an irresistable narrative Nemesis:

that dread, inexorable destiny which has so grand and great a part in Grecian tragedy, and which Grecian heroes manfully contended against, although fore-knowing that they were inevitably doomed to defeat, was in some degree an embodiment of the deep feeling of the inevitable dependence of a man's present being on his antecedents in the past.[147]

His arguments contributed to the legitimation of growing social, economic, and political divisions as the notion of degeneration itself fused distinct biological and social hypotheses, among them Darwin's theory of natural selection. In 1880 E. Ray Lancaster argued in *Degeneration* that some species represented not advanced versions of their earlier selves but atrophied forms of higher species, atrophy being defined as 'a gradual change in the structure, in which the organism becomes adapted to less complex and less varied conditions'.[148] Extrapolations from this modified paradigm adapted it to maintain that the 'unfit' could flourish in a degraded environment in ever-increasing numbers, above all in the 'residuum' expanding at the heart of London's 'nether world'.

Maudsley's theories closely correspond with this new paradigm and contributed to it. Yet by focusing on what he argued were particularly vulnerable points in the process of adaptation and transmission – pauper lunatics and 'nervous women' – he drew on criteria that had already been defined in the mid-nineteenth-century. He was influenced in particular by the French psychopathologists B.A. Morel and Jacques Moreau. Morel's *Treatise on the Physical, Intellectual and Moral Degeneracy of the Human Race* had argued in 1857 that the simultaneously physical and moral taint of degeneration was triggered by environment and accumulated through descent: 'The first generation of a degenerate family might be merely nervous, the second would tend to be neurotic, the third psychotic, while the fourth consisted of idiots and died out.'[149] Maudsley modified this to stress that idiocy was produced by successive breeding in intemperate moral conditions:

> Idiocy is, indeed, a manufactured article. . . . Many cases are distinctly traceable to parental intemperance and excess. . . . Insanity in the parent may issue in idiocy in the offspring, which is, so to speak, the natural form of degeneracy when it goes unchecked through generations.[150]

Morel saw the insane as atavistic throwbacks – 'morbid deviations from a primitive human type'[151] – and while Maudsley cites both Darwin and Esquirol to argue that in madness 'man is seen in all his nakedness . . . he lends not to his passions the chain which seduces, nor to his wiles the appearance which deceives', he follows Morel in stressing the essentially morbid nature of madness by extending Pritchard's concept of moral insanity.[152] For now the boundary between madness and criminality is completely removed, and both are seen as compounded by morbid urban conditions. Thus in *Responsibility in Mental Disease* Maudsley fuses the insane and the casual poor into a single image: 'a distinct criminal class of beings, who herd together in our large cities in a thieves' quarter', a 'degenerate and morbid variety of mankind, marked by peculiar low mental and physical characteristics'.[153] They include, in a reinterpretation of physiognomic conventions,

> an irregular and unsymmetrical conformation of the head, a want of regularity and harmony of the features . . . malformations of the external ear are sometimes observed. . . . There are fits and grimaces, and other spasmodic movements of the muscles of the face. . . . In other cases there are peculiarities of the eyes, which

though they may be full and prominent, have a vacillating movement.[154]

Similarly, debates on the potentially pathological nature of the female body took on more urgent connotations as they became articulated within a degenerative discourse that stressed its reproductive function, though, as with debates on class divisions, the paradigm could be developed in ways that might have opposive political connotations.[155] These debates intensified the contradictions surrounding the image of female insanity within the clear framework of moral management; indeed, here the contradictions within the two discourses often dovetailed. The promotion of women's physical and mental capacities appeared threatening, but in another register their neglect appeared equally so; thus both energy and lassitude now became explicitly morbid. The concept of hysteria as it was cast by the expanding medical profession in the mid-nineteenth century had been linked, paradoxically, with both suppression and energetic self-expression.[156] On the one hand, Robert Carter maintained in *On the Pathology and Treatment of Hysteria* in 1853 that it was attributable to inadequate education and sexual suppression;[157] on the other, F.C. Skey advanced the predominant line in 1867 that while hysteria 'is most prevalent in the young female members of the upper and middle classes of such as live a life of ease and luxury', it will none the less 'often select as its victim a female member of a family exhibiting more than usual force and decision of character, of strong resolution, fearless of danger, bold riders, having plenty of what is termed *nerve*'.[158] Although a few years later Maudsley conceded in *The Pathology of Mind* that 'the range of activity of women is so limited and their available paths of work so few . . . that they have not, like men, vicarious outlets for their feelings',[159] his better-known and controversial article in the *Fortnightly Review*, 'Sex in mind and education', overturns this case, claiming instead that women's bodies contained a fixed amount of energy which would drain away through menstruation or 'unnatural mental exertion'; if through both, debility and thus long-term racial decline would follow.[160] Here the very continuation of the species depended on the enforced segregation of 'male' and 'female' environments and the transposition of resulting characteristics into organic features.

Yet although morbid nervous tendencies were explicitly associated with a growing population of 'other' groups by 1875, the very attempt to establish their physiological and cultural parameters exerted a pressure that took the form of a continual return of the repressed. For the attempts to identify insanity's signs and problematic borderlands meant that now it was the potential strangeness *within* the boundaries of domesticized subjectivity that became apparent rather than the familiarity that dwelt within madness itself. In *The Borderlands of Insanity* (1875) Andrew Wynter suggested that madness now took the form of a vast social unconscious waiting in the wings of history: 'There is an immense amount of latent brain disease in the community, only awaiting a sufficient exciting cause to make itself patent to the world.'[161] And as the inferences of moral insanity came to occupy the territory previously inhabited by intellectual derangement (Maudsley noted 'the effect which a severe attack of insanity sometimes produces on the moral nature of the individual. . . . His intellectual faculties are as acute as ever, but his moral character has changed'), that borderland came to be seen increasingly as a breeding ground rather than a buffer state.[162] Again eccentricity or bohemianism in the male upper class gives rise to anxiety, and the links between madness and genius are stressed, but nervous tendencies now do not even ambivalently signal advance, but are the clear signals that civilization compounds its own atavistic traces, of which the signs are everywhere. 'It is of great importance then to recognise a borderland between sanity and insanity, and of greater importance still . . . to study the doubtful cases with which it is peopled', wrote Maudsley. 'There are a great many people who, without being insane, exhibit peculiarities of thought, feeling and character . . . they bear in their temperament the marks of their peculiar heritage.'[163] In Collins's fiction physiological metaphors combine with competing patterns of inheritance, evolution, and transmission. The weight of various kinds of inheritance spans his work, taking the form of an implied fatality to be resisted or fulfilled in ways that can clash or merge with a moral management that is always its ambivalent concomitant. Collins's first full-length novel, the historical *Antonina, or the Fall of Rome*, was an ambitious attempt to represent imperial decline and to probe the limits of mid-nineteenth-century optimistic expansionism; but in the 1850s inheritance and transmission are above all social and psychic constructs, that shape the tenuous identity of the upper-class male, the sons of redundant ancient families; and this begins with the narrative of *Basil: A Story of Modern Life*.

2

Nervous fancies of
hypochondriacal bachelors
Basil, and the
problems of modern life

> We *hypochondriacks* may console ourselves in the hour
> of gloomy distress by thinking that our sufferings
> mark our superiority.
>
> James Boswell[1]

> In the ravelled skein, the slightest threads are the
> hardest to follow: in analysing the associations and
> sympathies which regulate the play of our passions,
> the simplest and homeliest are the last that we detect.
> It is only when the shock comes and the mind recoils
> before it . . . that we really discern what trifles in the
> outer world our noblest mental pleasures, or our
> severest mental pains, have made a part of ourselves
> – atoms which the whirlpool has drawn into its vortex,
> as greedily and surely as the largest mass!
>
> Wilkie Collins, *Basil, A Story of Modern Life*[2]

Basil, A Story of Modern Life is a modern tale of terror and the
story of a fallen man. It is the confession of an insecure melancholic, a younger son whose family 'dates back beyond the
Conquest', and whose masculinity and class identity are fragile,
attenuated.[3] The confession recalls Basil's chance encounter with
Margaret Sherwin, a linen draper's daughter, on a crowded London
omnibus; his instant obsession with her and his descent into a nether
world of unconsummated probationary marriage in the *petit-
bourgeois* Sherwin family – a nightmare world of anxiety-producing
newness, false clues, and misleading signs. It reveals Basil's
discovery (on the night of the expiry of the false 'long engagement')
of his nominal wife's seduction by the villain Robert Mannion, the
Sherwins' socially ambiguous and undecipherable confidential clerk.
And this revelation discloses a further one: Mannion is fixated,

71

monomaniacally, on persecuting Basil in revenge for his own life-long persecution – the result of his inheritance of the stigma of felony from his father, who had been employed by Basil's father and hanged for forging Basil's father's name. Basil discovers this as the direct outcome of his own simultaneously psychic and social disintegration which is brought on by an attack of 'brain fever' precipitated in turn by disinheritance and social ostracism. It is from this position of namelessness and placelessness that he reconstructs his narrative, a narrative that needs to disintegrate itself before he can be reintegrated as a reformed subject into the family – but a family that seems to have lost the means of renewing itself legitimately.

Collins's first full-length contemporary novel is a remarkable exploration of the formation and breakdown of the codes that shape masculine upper-middle-class identity; it draws on diverse fictional and psychological references which play across a range of ideological registers within the central framework of the confessional narrative. In the first place, it takes up many of the conventions of the self-conscious tale of quasi-supernatural terror by placing the hero in a series of intense and traumatic situations, exploiting his psychological and physiological responses as much as the objective source of terror itself, and thus making the manipulation of subjectivity the primary means of generating shock, indeterminacy, anxiety. It was this quality which prompted *Bentley's Miscellany* to note of the novel: 'In truth the author of that work ought to have been called Mr Salvator Fuseli. There is nothing either of Wilkie or Collins about it'; which caused the *Westminster Review* to consign *Basil* to the ranks of a degenerate supernaturalism: 'It was the fashion then to construct a story out of strange and unnatural *circumstances*, it is the fashion now to elaborate it out of morbid *feelings* and overwrought *sensibilities*.'[4] But 'The progress of fiction as an art' went on to suggest that it was the explicit focus on sexual transgression and the way that the seduction of Margaret Sherwin by Mannion was used as a source of 'terror' that meant that

> Mr Collins has given us nothing which can 'take men from the passions and miserable troubles of life into a higher region'. . . . The incident which forms the foundation of the whole is absolutely disgusting; and is kept so perseveringly before the eyes of the reader in all its hateful details that all interest is destroyed in the loathing it occasions.[5]

It was in this dual sense that *Basil* represented an unacceptable naturalism, and it was thus that the novel pushed the conventions of 'terror' through their earlier limits: not simply by transposing them into a familiar domestic setting, but by transforming anxieties within the family into sources of suspense, and linking this to the threats posed, on the one hand, *to* the upper-class subject by the underworlds of crime and sexual transgression through an encounter with a mysterious and alien class, while on the other implicitly revealing the source of those threats to be the power invested in the figure of Basil's father himself.

Yet *Basil* was the book with which Collins hoped to make his début as a serious contemporary novelist, and despite its obvious risks it was not universally condemned – it certainly won Dickens's admiration.[6] In both the first and revised editions of the novel's Prefaces Collins clearly outlined certain aesthetic principles which, broadly, corresponded with Pre-Raphaelite tenets, stressing a realism founded on the linking of the transcendent and the mundane:

> My idea was, that the more of the Actual I could garner up as a text to speak from, the more certain I might feel of the genuineness and value of the Ideal which was sure to spring out of it. . . . By appealing to genuine sources *within* the reader's own experience, I could certainly gain his attention to begin with; but it would be only by appealing to ther sources (as genuine in their way) *beyond* his own experience, that I could hope to fix his interest and excite his suspense, to occupy his feelings, or to stir his nobler thoughts.[7]

This appeal to, and movement beyond, empirical experience was a way of consciously overturning stale conventions: 'Directing my characters and my story, then, towards the light of Reality wherever I could find it, I have not hesitated to violate some of the sentimental conventionalities of sentimental fiction' – 'conventionalities', above all, of melodrama and romantic fiction.[8]

The novel thus modifies and negotiates two linked but not continuous fictional traditions and with them two modulations of moral sensibility and subjectivity; and these shape the significance of its appropriation of contemporary psychological discourses. For *Basil* also clearly includes many of the elements that are to be found in such late eighteenth- and early-nineteenth-century confessional stories as Godwin's *Caleb Williams*, James Hogg's *The Private Memoirs and Confessions of a Justified Sinner*, Mary Shelley's *Frankenstein*, and, more tacitly and in a different vein, De Quincey's

Confessions of an English Opium-Eater (first published in 1821). It is
an obsessive story of pursuit, revenge, and retribution. It sets up a
pattern of opposition and replication in which pursuer and pursued,
victim and persecutor, become caught in a self-sustaining struggle.
It exploits the sensations of the hero and explores how the outcast
or deviant figure is created as the bad object of the dominant order.
But even as it reproduces them the novel turns these patterns round,
for here it is the privileged son who is duped by a self-created
imposture; the patterns of authority and persecution take on new
combinations as they are internalized by the next generation. The
hero occupies a place, but a place that has been appropriated, and
has a nominal power but a power that has drained away. *Basil*, like
the shorter pieces 'Mad Monkton' and 'A Rogue's Life', focuses on
the problematic position of a son of an ancient family whose real
economic force has waned but whose symbolic power is perpetuated
psychically, internalized into a morbid inheritance as the decline of
the landed patriarchal family is mediated through subjective
disintegration; and it does this by reproducing the unhinging effect
that modern life has on the sensibility of the hero. The figure of Basil
fulfils his dual role as sympathetic yet gullible agent by invoking and
satirizing 'eighteenth-century' sensibility as embodied in the figure
of the man of feeling and acute perception, vulnerable to the
'English malady'. He is constructed as a figure in the narrative by
his assimilation of others' perception as a melancholic hovering on
the brink of monomania – a 'hypochondriac' in both senses of the
term as nervous sensibility merges into the morbid interpretation of
imaginary symptoms.[9]

This gives the discourse of moral management a central yet oddly
absent role in the construction of identity in the narrative. *Basil*
takes the form of a confessional case study which involves both
empathy and estrangement, as the reader follows the reconstruction
of Basil's earlier, gullible self; in order to 'analyse the associations
and sympathies which regulate the play of [his] passions', the
narrative continually draws on psychological patterns which have
close links with the associationist tradition, implying the radical
manipulation of moral and emotional sympathy. Yet this process
becomes fragmented with the fracturing of the narrating voice, for
it is never clear exactly *where* narrative authority resides, nor how the
figure or the text should finally be read. Basil's gullible self is framed
by his later reassessment of it, but this critical distance is framed in
turn within a perspective which extend beyond the parameters of the
first-person narrative and thus takes the form of an authority which

is ubiquitous yet absent, and which directly corresponds to the benign surveillance of a moral management that is both outside and inside the subject. It is this framework that both mediates the declining symbolic power of patrilineal authority within the family and holds that authority up from within, and which is linked with Basil's sensibility, creating an equivocal perspective which is crucial to build up his social self in order to generate the narrative tensions necessary to precipitate his breakdown.

This means, too, that in *Basil* the conditions of writing and the control of it are not only part of the structuring of narrative time itself but are also explicitly bound up with the process of exploration and breakdown of identity as memory, desire, and projection that is at work in the text. Basil's confession constitutes the main body of the story and is written in a remote cottage as he is pursued by the shameful memory of the past which drives him to write. The antagonist Mannion's oppositional narrative is embedded within Basil's reconstruction and three-quarters of the way through the story the process of continual recall breaks down, to be replaced firstly by Basil's disintegrating diary, then by letters. Basil is thus set firstly in the context of his own family and then against Mannion in a way that both counterposes and reproduces the patterns of displacement, transgression, and exclusion that he enacts. He is both caught between class boundaries and is the stage on which the struggle between them is acted out, and his failure to negotiate these boundaries is marked by lack of sexual power. As the younger son, moreover, trapped in a 'feminized' position of perpetual childhood, his dislocated place in the patrilineal line is expressed in his lack of self-possession, and his inability to read or interpret the psychological motivation and social signs that he has to negotiate. He thus represents the weak point in the family history in his very attempt to marry out of the declining family circle; he is the implicit, as Mannion is the explicit, threat, and the two become bound together in an opposition that becomes mutually sustaining.

The opening of the confession is crucial here as the narrator is setting up the terms on which his past may be reconstructed and reinterpreted and placing himself in relation to the authority of the reader, who becomes both analyst and judge, prefiguring and echoing the patterns of controlling observation unfolded in the story. But Basil is also setting up the narrative itself as a piece of moral education. The story begins: 'What am I now about to write? The history of little more than the events of one year, out of the twenty four years of my life. Why do I undertake such employment at this?' In addressing an absent reader while becoming his own interlocutor and thus in a sense substituting himself for the reader, Basil's lack of unity is suggested from the start. This is consolidated:

> Perhaps, because I think that my narrative may do good, because I hope that, one day, it may be put to some warning use. There have been men who, on their death-beds, have left directions that their bodies should be anatomised, as an offering to science. In these pages, written on the death-bed of enjoyment and hope, I give my heart, already anatomised, as an offering to human nature.
>
> Perhaps while desiring to write a confession, I desire to write an apology as well. . . . When these pages are found after my death, they perhaps will be calmly read and gently judged, as relics solemnized by the atoning shadows of the grave. Then, the hard sentence against me may be repented of; the children of the next generation of my house may be taught to speak charitably of my memory, and may often, of their own accord, think of me kindly in the silent watches of the night.[10]

Here, as in most confessions, the act of speaking or writing of past transgressions creates the preconditions of their absolution, and the reader's provisional identification is paradoxically made possible by the critical distance of the remembering voice. The present self is both the wiser product of past culpability and a reformed 'I' who looks at the past self as a renounced identity. Basil thus offers both a cautionary tale, a case history, and an 'already anatomised' heart for scientific investigation. He is on his death-bed, yet has already conducted the post-mortem, just as the readers of the narrative are future members of the family line the continuation of which he himself threatens, and which he has been blanked out of (his father casts him out by tearing his page from the family chronicle). So the position from which he is writing is not only one of imminent death but actual namelessness – blankness.

This opening, where Basil self-consciously and rather ridiculously announces himself and yet has no place to occupy, structurally, in the narrative, produces a qualifying distance in his account which works differently from may other kinds of confession. In William Godwin's *Caleb Williams* and James Hogg's *The Private Memoirs and Confessions of a Justified Sinner*, the central voice is set in a consistent though not necessarily coherent relation to the external authority which vindicates it: for Caleb Williams rational liberalism, for the Justified Sinner divine judgement – though this is implicitly repositioned as insane delusion by the Editor's narrative in the latter.[11] But the opening of *Basil* resists any easy identification with the hero without offering any coherent alternative perspective to it. And this tacitly qualifies the means by which the mystery and sensation of the main body of the story – the hero's frustrated sexual entanglement, his own forced imposture to this family as well as the imposture of the Sherwins, manipulated by Mannion – will be generated and read. This qualification is compounded, too, by Basil's remembrance of his childhood and his description of his family and class history. Here his account of his development as a melancholic, 'sensitive', but imperceptive young man draws on and mingles the concepts of an inherited identity and a constructed one, of inbreeding and moral management. Basil's final recovery and reassimilation into the family with which the story concludes is firmly set 'in the shadowed valley of Repose', and here home becomes a safe place, an asylum, but also a kind of pastoral stasis – a place outside history, outside narrative itself.[12]

But the preconditions of this process are also set up at the beginning in the way in which the figure of the father becomes both the benevolent keeper and the bearer of an exclusive lineage, so that the very shaping of a social identity through a family history becomes the means of its disintegration. Thus the father is the transcendent source of meaning in the first part of the recollection but he is presented initially by Basil as being completely bound up with his own genealogy, and this is described negatively:

> His was not that conventional pride, which the popular notions are fond of characterising by a stiff, stately carriage, by a rigid expression of features. . . . It was that quite, negative, courteous, inbred pride, which only the closest observers could detect; which no ordinary observers ever detected at all.[13]

This displacement of cognitive conventions is compounded by the father's consciousness of his ancestors; they are built up as the only objects of value, taking the place of wealth:

> They were the very breath of his life; the deities of his social worship; the family treasures to be held precious beyond all lands and all wealth, all ambitions and all glories, by his children and his children's children to the end of their race.[14]

Basil, who 'could inherit none of the landed property of the family', is doubly displaced by this himself, and he occupies a 'feminine' position in that he is simultaneously symbol of, and substitute for,

inherited property.[15] He literally lacks self-possession; his upbring-
ing was a series of empty roles: 'The story of my boyhood and youth
has little to interest – nothing that is new. My education was the
education of hundreds of others in my rank of life.'[16] But that position is filled in his early childhood by his father's education of his
moral sense, which is described with almost copy-book explicitness:

> I believe in his own way he loved us all; but we, his descendants
> had to share his heart with his ancestors – we were his household
> property as well as his children. . . . We were taught by his direc-
> tion, that to disgrace our family, either by word or action, was the
> one fatal crime that could never be forgotten and never be
> pardoned. We were formed under his superintendence, in prin-
> ciples of religion, honour, and industry; and the rest was left to
> our own moral sense, to our own gratitude, to our own
> comprehension of the duties and privileges of our station. There
> was no one point in his conduct towards us that we could complain
> of; and yet there was something always incomplete in our
> domestic relations.
>
> It may seem incomprehensible, even, ridiculous, to some
> persons, but it is nonetheless true, that we were none of us ever
> on intimate terms with him. I mean by this that he was a father
> to us but never a companion. There was something in his manner,
> his quiet and unchanging manner, that kept us almost
> unconsciously restrained.[17]

It is not surprising to find that the sense of embarrassment that he
feels in his father's presence as a child is directly transposed at the
moment of his secret, false, wedding to Margaret by his 'morbid
fancy' which he can only, then, interpret as

> wild and monstrous, as if it had been produced by a dream – an
> impression that my father had discovered my secret, and was
> watching me from some hidden place in the church; watching me
> through the service to denounce and abandon me publicly, at the
> end.[18]

The symptoms themselves are recognized as pathological almost on
the condition that here their significance is left unexplained.

Basil's simultaneous subjection to and self-construction through
the perceptions of others (he feels, for instance, that he still exists
while in exile through his sister's remembrance of him though he has
been erased from the official family memory) turn the methods of
moral management into tacit restrictive self-control, and thus

become the means by which the hero is set up as an ineffectual but sympathetic agent. In *The Woman in White* this perceptual structure becomes transformed into the model through which a new, middle-class, resolute masculinity can emerge and disentangle the ravelled skein of the self and the narrative. But here though Basil notes how, just before his illicit marriage,

> bitter thoughts against my father rose in my mind – bitter thoughts against his inexorable family pride, which imposed on me the concealment and secrecy, under the oppression of which I had already suffered so much – bitter thoughts against those social tyrannies . . . which my father now impersonated, as it were, to my ideas

such a quest is always frustrated – even its expression is never taken further than this.[19] Instead, it is the lower-middle class which is pathologized, embodying a predatory modernity, and an unlicensed female sexuality which is turned into a force of terror, by thrusting the protagonist into a liminal, unstable realm. Basil first sees Margaret Sherwin when he impulsively gets on a passing omnibus – a 'perambulatory exhibition-room of the eccentricities of human nature', a place of the disturbing mingling and juxtaposing of classes and types and of unsolicited associations.[20] The lower-middle-class home is essentially an extension of this – the Sherwins' household is in a limbo-like place of unfixed identities: 'a suburb of new houses, intermingled with wretched patches of waste land, half built over. . . . Its newness and desolation of appearance revolted me.'[21] And the means by which Basil traces history back to the traumatic events which precipitated his breakdown are bound up with the means by which the mystery is created and disclosed, a mystery that in another sense is no secret since its outcome is already known. In order for this to happen particular perceptual assumptions and interpretative codes need to be invoked and frustrated, and these manipulate the assumptions of physiognomy, employ different kinds of associations, elicit dreams, and invoke particular methods to decipher their significance.

Basil becomes the upper-middle-class dupe of *petit-bourgeois* sexual intrigue because his sensibility is out of line – he has no control over the codes that govern effective interpretation – and because he is unable to distinguish between distinct kinds of associative mechanisms. But it is through his nervous responses – immediate physiological sensation – that his class and gender identity becomes inexorably attenuated through these skewed associative mechanisms. Here the novel anticipates processes that are to be developed in *The Woman in White*. The hero's wise voice of the present makes retrospective interjections:

> Throughout the whole of that period I walked on surely, step by step, to the verge of the abyss; and never once suspected which course I was taking, never once detected the signs which vainly rose to caution me back, on either side of my path.[22]

Yet this knowledge implies a set of signs that have already been interpreted, clues which conceal another story in their turn, and which the moralized voice of the confession cannot bring itself to utter. He notes of his first meeting with Margaret:

> Remembering what I do, I am ashamed to write, ashamed to think of what I said. . . . Hitherto, I have spoken the stern truth, sacrificing myself to my confessions unhesitatingly . . . but here, at that very part of my story where it might be imagined that I would write minutely and circumstantially with most readiness and most ease – here, for the first and the last time, I must generalise and must hurry on. I can give no good reasons for the sensations that now influence me: I cannot analyse them, and I would not if I could.[23]

The naïve Basil within the narrative is continually misled by his attempt to read his environment in psychological terms, as the world becomes a projection of his own anxiety preciptated in turn by modernity itself. The Sherwins' drawing-room, with its 'fatal newness', exposes their brashness in a way that is turned back on to the perceiving subject; the horror and revulsion experienced in the suburban streets are extended and internalized as Basil becomes the 'nervous man' that he presents as a figure in the scene:

> Everything was oppressively new. The brilliantly-varnished door cracked with a report like a pistol when it was opened; the paper on the walls, with its gaudy pattern of birds, trellis-work, and flowers, in gold, red and green on a white ground, looked hardly dry yet; the showy window-curtains of white and sky-blue, and the still showier carpet of red and yellow, seemed as it they had come out of the shop yesterday; the round rosewood table was in a painfully high state of polish; . . . Never was a richly-furnished room more comfortless than this – the eye ached at looking at it. There was no repose anywhere. The print of the Queen, hanging lonely on the wall . . . glared on you: the paper, the curtains, the

carpet, glared on you: the books, the wax-flowers in glass cases, the chairs in flaring chintz-covers, the china-plates on the door, the pink and blue glass vases and cups ranged on the chimney piece, the over-ornamented chiffoniers with Tonbridge toys and long-necked smelling-bottles on their upper shelves, all glared on you. There was no look of shadow, shelter, secrecy or retirement in one nook or corner of those four gaudy walls. All surrounding objects seemed startingly near to the eye; much nearer than they really were. The room would have given a nervous man a headache, before he had been in it for a quarter of an hour.[24]

The deciphering of faces and figures takes this process of social disorientation further. Mannion baffles him because he can get no interpretative purchase on his face, yet it is presented as a mask concealing an inner nature in a way which uses physiognomic signs to invoke the melodramatic conventions of the smooth-faced villain, with blankness and regularity in themselves presented as significant:

Viewed separately from the head (which was rather large, both in front and behind) his face exhibited, throughout, an almost perfect symmetry of proportion. Such was his countenance in point of form; but . . . in expression – it was, as I beheld it, an utter void. Never had I before seen any human face which baffled all inquiry like his. No mask could have been made expressionless enough to resemble it; and yet it looked like a mask.[25]

It is 'so unexpressive that it did not even look vacant – a mystery for your eyes and your mind to dwell on – hiding something' on to which Basil at first projects his own romantic story:

If there really had been some romance connected with Mr Mannion's early life – if that strange and striking face was indeed a sealed book which contained a secret story, what a triumph and a pleasure, if Margaret and I should succeed in discovering it together![26]

Thus in defusing as much as generating suspense, this method reflects back more emphatically on Basil's obsessional but unsuccessful attempt to follow clues: 'I felt towards him much as a man feels in a labyrinth, where every fresh failure in gaining the centre only produces fresh obstinacy in renewing the effort to arrive at it.[27] It suggests, too, that Mannion represents not so much *his* 'shadow side' as the blanked-out version of his own father, whom 'ordinary observers never detected', and who also silently rules through surveillance.

The aspiring Sherwins' class insecurity, on the other hand, is presented as a double set of expressive nervous tendencies which display and comment on the sources of their conspiracy of social transformation – self-help and moral management. Sherwin's desperate attempt to achieve a proper persona belies as it signals his social mobility, and is written all over his face through a set of unambiguous physiognomic signs:

> All his features were singularly mobile: they were affected by nervous contractions and spasms which were constantly drawing up and down in all directions the brow, the mouth and the muscles of the cheek. . . . His lips were thin and colourless, the lines about them being numerous and strongly marked. Had I seen him under ordinary circumstances, I should have set him down as a little-minded man.[28]

But it is Mrs Sherwin, Margaret's silent, shadowy mother, described by Sherwin himself as nervous, unreliable, and not quite sane, whose body vividly expresses the concealed manipulations most strikingly. She thus reveals the Sherwins' plot to acquire Basil's gentility to be the extension of their legitimate upward mobility and the family drama on which it rests. A ghostly presence within the family, a spectral figure who finally makes a 'death in life' appearance after the revelation of the plot, she appears to Basil less as a set of physiognomic signs, and more as a set of *symptoms*, nervous disorders which, in being written on the body, tell a story that cannot be written, but which can be expressed as an unspoken drama in a secret theatre. Basil's active projection of meaning on to her body again becomes an unmistaken sign which he ignores by seeing it only as the expression of her own private tragedy. And in appearing above all as a silent patient in a county asylum whose meaning is manifested in her nervous symptoms, Mrs Sherwin's body becomes the expressive shadow wide of his own early formation, the enactment of the secret processes that lie within the hidden drama of moral management itself:

> Her pale, sickly, moist-looking skin; her large, mild, watery light-blue eyes; the restless, vigilant timidity of her expression; the mixture of useless hesitation and nervous, involuntary activity in every one of her actions, all furnished the same significant betrayal of a life of fear and restraint; of a disposition full of modest generosities and meek sympathies, which had been crushed down past rousing the self-assertion, past ever seeing the light. There, in

that mild wan face of hers – in those painful startings and hurryings when she moved; in that tremulous faint utterance when she
spoke – *there*, I could see one of those ghastly heart-tragedies laid
open before me, which are not to be written, but which are acted
and re-acted, scene by scene, year by year, in the secret theatre
of home.[29]

This confusion and conflation of physiognomic and interpretative
codes continually produce a double perspective on both the clues
that Basil perceives and on his own liminal identity; but it is through
the representation of femininity and sexuality in the contrast
between his sister Clara and Margaret Sherwin that these social
ambiguities and anxieties are most clearly expressed. Basil's first
view of Margaret is reconstructed as obsession arising from projection; it works through inference and the condensation of meanings,
as he sees her as a collection of parts and fragments of clothing,
bound together by his desire. Clara, on the other hand, is reified
rather than fetishized, and thus becomes a metaphoric expression of
a desire for a perpetual childhood of safety, seclusion, and personal
calm, outside history. For Basil, images of safety and danger,
secluded childhood or terrifying progress, find their allegorical
expression and equivalents in archetypal female figures, figures who
thus become inextricably bound up with his emotional response to
social and cultural meanings and codes. He compares Clara with
'modern women' who 'appear to be ambitious of morally unsexing
themselves before society . . . women of this exclusively modern
order like to use slang expressions in their conversation; assume a
bastard-masculine abruptness in their manners, a bastard-masculine
licence in their opinions.'[30] Clara condenses the softer side of moral
management, as Basil's sensibility, with a retreat into a family past
and a mythic childhood, but what is equally important is the
explicitness with which these emotional associations are made clear:

Few men have not their secret moments of deep feeling –
moments when, amid the wretched flippancies and hypocrisies of
modern society, the image will present itself to their mind of some
woman, fresh, innocent, gentle, sincere; some woman whose
emotions are still warm and impressible, whose affections and
sympathies can still appear in her actions, and give the colour to
her thoughts; some woman in whom we could put perfect faith
and trust as if we were children; whom we despair of finding near
the hardening influences of the world; whom we could scarely
venture to look for, except in solitary places far away in the

country; in little rural shrines shut up from society, among woods
and fields and lonesome boundary-hills.[31]

Yet just as Mrs Sherwin acts as an exaggerated transformation of
Basil's own position within his family, so Clara's symbolic
significance is generated by her concealment of self; the line between
the *petit-bourgeois* 'secret theatre of home' and the gentrified 'rural
shrines shut up from society' has to be continually reasserted and
redrawn in order for both to make sense:

> The strong and deep feelings of my sister's nature lay far below
> the surface – for a woman, too far below it. Suffering was for her
> silent, secret, long-enduring; almost entirely void of any outward
> event or development . . . the very strength of her emotions was
> in their silence and their secrecy.[32]

Thus all three women are 'nervously' susceptible to the influences
around them: Mrs Sherwin's neurotic disorders express the corruption of which she is the innocent victim; Margaret's hysterical
passion, eventually breaking out in typhus fever, indicates her 'own'
moral corruption; Clara's supression both represses emotion and
expresses an imaginary emotional unity. But no single psychological
model can make sense of all of them. The figure of Mrs Sherwin
suggests that suppression itself is morbid, while Margaret's incipient
hysteria imples that unrestrained passion feeds on and breeds itself.
The counterpoint is Clara, whose idealization is founded on self-
restraint.

In conjuring up these projected images so explicitly, the figures of
Margaret and Clara lead into a more self-conscious exploration of the
ways in which archetypes of femininity work through male projection
and fantasy, and this emerges most clearly in the dream Basil has the
night after meeting Margaret, the dream which paradoxically further
undercuts, yet reinforces, an already fragmented moral management. This is the first of a series of different kinds of 'deranged'
states of consciousness that are put to various uses in *Basil*, and they
anticipate many of the processes which are to be developed in *The
Woman in White* and *Armadale*. The use of dreams clearly has a
specific kind of function in the story as an embedded narrative,
which on the one hand suggests that the explicit authority of the
narrator is undermined, opening a space for the emergence of
unsolicited thoughts and emotions; on the other, it is a more
detached premonition or warning interjected into the main body of
the story. The early dream in *Basil* combines these obvious

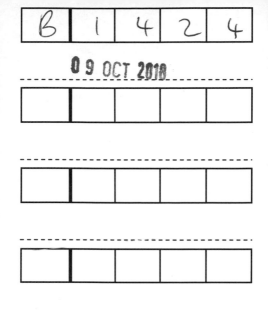

B	1	4	2	4

0 9 OCT 2018

Self service holds

This item is on hold for a Leeds Beckett
student, staff member or guest user.
It must be issued before being
removed from the High Demand Area.

Borrowing

Use the self service issue in the High
Demand Area.
Please note items in high demand may
have a reduced loan period.
Always check and keep your receipt.

Need help?

Please ask a member of Library staff.

0 5 OCT 2016

functions; what qualifies it is the way that Collins uses and develops specific aspects of dream theory in relation to the 'privileged' knowledge offered by the dream text itself, and the relationship between waking and dreaming states that they suggest. The dream itself is both the explicit expression of sexual desire and a moralized comment on it – a text that has already been interpreted. Basil dreams of a landscape that is both a symbolic female body and an iconic moral hierarchy:

> On one side it was bounded by thick woods, whose dark, secret depths looked unfathomable to the eye: on the other by hills, ever rising higher and higher yet, until they were lost in bright, beautifully white clouds, gleaming in refulgent sunlight.[33]

Two women emerge from the woods and hills, predictably one dark and one fair, and 'I was drawn along in the arms of the dark woman with my blood burning and my breath failing me, until we entered the secret recesses that lay amid the unfathomable depths of trees.'[34] The landscape of secret, remote woods that Clara's image had suggested is translated here into sexual engulfment and spiritual defilement.

It is the unreserved quality of the dream that gives it a sophisticated role in the narrative as simultaneously an expression of suppressed desire and an allegorical warning in a way that blurs the boundary between the two kinds of knowledge, and between the two sides of Basil's moral self, as passive subject and ineffectual agent. In the first place, it is clearly presented, following contemporary conceptions of dreams elaborated, for example, by MacNish and Abercrombie, as the temporary suspension or loss of self- control, and as the failure of the dreamer to be able to restrain his own growing sexual obsession, his passion, which was 'deteriorating . . . in its effects on the exercise of my mental powers, and on my candour and sense of duty in my intercourse with home'.[35]

> How could I best crush the desire to see her! . . . Had I resolution enough to wear my heart out by hard, serious, slaving study? . . . I sat by my open window, striving with my burning love thoughts of Margaret; striving to think collectedly and usefully – abandoned to a struggle ever renewing, yet never changing. At last I began to think less and less distinctly. . . . Thoughts and sensations which had been more and more weakly restrained with each succeeding hour of wakefulness, now rioted within me in perfect liberation from all control.[36]

Thus Basil's dream is clearly marked, following Abercrombie, by 'the loss of power over the succession of the thoughts', and combines the associative processes that he outlines as 'recent events and emotions mixed up with past ones though in other respects they were entirely unconnected', and 'trains of images brought up by association with bodily sensations'.[37] But at the same time it is clearly suggested that the dream is conditioned by Basil's self-imposed struggle with himself which later precipitates the breakdown of his tenuous self-control.

And this conditions the way that the dream is interpreted in the double narrative reassessment of it, and how the expression of desire becomes framed as a 'prophetic' text whose meaning is both resisted and confirmed by the way that Basil dismisses it. Immediately on waking, the naïve Basil asks

> Was it warning of coming events, foreshadowed in the wild visions of sleep? But to what purpose could this dream, or indeed any dream, tend? Why had it remained incomplete, failing to show me the visionary consequences of my visionary actions? What superstition to ask![38]

Basil's expectation, then, is that a 'prophetic' dream should take the form of a moral tract (which, indeed, the 'text' of the dream itself, in one sense, does), but within the context of this naïve assessment, it is suggested that Basil's 'divination' or prophetic reading of the dream should take the form of exegesis rather than passive reception. De Quincey had pointed out in *Confessions of an English Opium Eater* that this was the more accurate sense of 'prophetic' readings as elaborated in biblical dream interpretation.

> To unveil or decipher what is hidden – that is, in effect, the meaning of divination . . . in the writings of St Paul the phrase 'gifts of prophecy' never once indicates what the English reader supposes, but exegetic gifts, gifts of interpretation applied to what is dark, of analysis applied to what is logically perplexed, of expansion applied to what is condensed.[39]

J.A. Symonds (who refers to De Quincey in his analysis but to stress simply that dreaming involves a suspension of judgement) developed Abercrombie's point about how dreams can precipitate their own outcome by stressing how 'the mind, vehemently possessed of an idea thus received, almost instinctively acts up to it', and Basil echoes this in his 'wiser' reassessment of the dream, suggesting too that the female images are archetypal projections of the 'real' Margaret and Clara transformed into symbolic polarities which determine his perception of them:[40]

> As I looked out on the reviving, reassuring sunlight, it was easy to dismiss as ridiculous from my mind, or rather from my conscience, the tendency to see in the two shadowy forms of my dream, the types of two real living beings, whose names almost trembled to utterance on my lips; but I could not also dismiss from my heart the love-images which that dream had set up there for the worship of the senses. Those results of the night still remained with me, growing and strengthening every minute.[41]

But this, and Basil's subsequent behaviour after the dream, also overturn the implications of Symonds's argument, in particular his discussion of the relation between waking and dreaming states. Symonds, with others, stressed that the inability to 'wake up' properly from a dream constituted a kind of insanity since the mind becomes completely possessed by the dream, and so the whole world turns into a fantastic projection:

> The healthy waking of the mind is the resumption of the form of consciousness which existed previous to sleep. The objects before the eyes have the same aspect and the same associations; the thoughts return to the same channel; the occupations of the previous day and those projected for the ensuing day, are remembered, and there is no confusion of personal identity. But a man may wake up to that outward world, and that world is all changed to him. . . . Alas! how delicate and fragile a thing is perception! He is awake, and he looks around his chamber in which he has every day hailed the morning sunshine. . . . He looks out on a new world projected from his own inner being. By a melancholy power, a fatal gift, of appropriating and assimilating the real objects perceived by his senses, he takes possession of them, nay, disembodies them, and fuses them into his imaginary creation. . . . They are all shadows; no more the flesh and blood realities of his heart; they are metamorphosed into the unsubstantial figures of a distempered imagination.[42]

In *Basil*, on the other hand, the waking up and the reviving, reassuring sunlight prompt him to resist the possible significance of the dream even as they break down his resistance to Margaret, and this becomes the first stage in a process wherein he is unable to follow clues, distinguish and analyse the logic of different kinds of 'associations and sympathies which regulate the play of [his] passions', except as a process of retrojection.

The first dream is clearly framed as an 'unconscious' revelation through the retrospective narrative analysis, and it is this focus that partially disintegrates in being pushed to its limits in the controlled insanity of brain fever; for here the reference is to an 'outside' infection, generated by 'inner' turmoil, which thus becomes both expression and product of the social crisis of the self.[43] Basil's collapse replays the pattern of the breakdown of self-control of the earlier dream in exaggerated form as he struggles to be his own moral manager after hearing himself described as mad:

> MAD! – that word, as I heard it, rang after me like a voice of judgment . . . I strove hard to separate my thoughts: to distinguish between my recollections; to extricate from the confusion within me any one idea, no matter what – and I could not do it. In that awful struggle for mastery over my own mind, all that had passed, all the horror of that horrible night, became as nothing to me.[44]

Here all past events and impressions are drawn into a vortex of mingled associations which form a replaying of a past and a rewriting of a history in which Basil, now agent as well as passive voyeur, 'toiled and struggled back, over and over again, to seek once more the lost events of the End, through the events of the Beginning'.[45] This is still reinterpreted through a retrospective narrative framework which is to disintegrate as narrative time and story time merge in the increasingly elliptical diary. But the terms of reference of the narrative have been irrecoverably altered by delirium – it is only by looking in at a 'world projected from his own inner being' that Basil is able to disentangle the clues of his waking delusion.

The process of Basil's delirium takes the form of a lifting of a veil and of an analysis applied to what is perplexed, and this qualifies as it licenses the unrestrained visions. It also echoes elements in the process of analysis that John Perceval struggles towards in his *Narrative* of derangement, for here, too, it is only by recognizing the value of the uses of doubt that Basil can disentangle his self-created duplicity by recognizing the plots that surrounded him. This process is rendered ironic, however, for here the truth has been partly determined by delusion, and the most dangerous delusions of all are those which cannot perceive their own irrational traces. And it means, too, that there will always be an element that cannot be recalled, a trace that remains hidden:

It was as if something were imprisoned in my mind, and moving always to and fro in it – moving, but never getting free.

Soon, these thoughts began to take a form that I could recognise. In the clinging heat and fierce seething fever, to which neither waking or sleeping brought a breath of freshness or a dream of change, I began to act my part over again, in the events that had passed – but in a strangely altered character. Now, instead of placing implicit trust in others, as I had done; instead of failing to discover a significance and a warning in each circumstance as it arose, I was suspicious from the first – suspicious of Margaret, of her father, of her mother, of Mannion, of the very servants in the house. In the hideous phantasmagoria of my own calamity into which I now looked, my position was reversed. Every event of the doomed year of by probation was revived. But the doom itself; the night-scene of horror through which I had passed; the brief terrible catastrophe of the weary drama of wickedness and deceit, had utterly vanished from my memory. This lost recollection, it was the unending toil of my wandering mind to recover; and I never got it back. None who have not suffered as I suffered then, can imagine with what a burning rage of determination I followed past events in my delirium, one by one, for days and nights together – followed, to get to the end which I knew was beyond; but which I never could see, not even by glimpses, for a moment at a time.[46]

The endless reconstruction of a past that refuses to reveal its own secrets, where Basil's 'restless memory recoiled before the impenetrable darkness which forbade it to see further', suddenly dissolves into a series of hallucinations which burrow from and comment on their own sources, above all De Quincey's analysis of induced derangement, *Confessions of an English Opium Eater*.[47] In his analysis of 'the pains of opium' De Quincey discussed in detail the way that opium disrupted the workings of the consciousness, and his analysis was often referred to in mid-nineteenth-century psychological theory; it crossed the boundary between a 'literary' exploration of the unpredictable workings of the mind and a medical dissection of an aberrant state of consciousness. Firstly, he noted, 'a sympathy seemed to arise between the waking and dreaming states of the brain' so that 'whatsoever things capable of being visually represented I did but think of in the darkness, immediately shaped themselves into phantoms of the eye.' Secondly, 'a deep-seated anxiety': 'I seemed every night to descend – not metaphorically but literally to descend – into chasms and sunless abysses, depths below depths, from which it seemed hopeless that I could ever reascend.' Thirdly the sense of space and time was distorted: 'Buildings, landscapes, etc, were exhibited in proportions so vast as the bodily eye is not fitted to receive'; and finally, the forgotten events of childhood re-emerge, removing the 'veil between our present consciousness and the secret inscriptions on the mind'.[48] These processes and images are directly and exactly reproduced in Basil's delirium, and here too the allegorical landscape of the earlier dream is transformed into an extraordinary conflation of omniscient vision, eschatological punishment, and metaphorical transformation as he enacts the earlier drama of engulfment and defilement and offers an exegesis of his earlier narrative. This is worth quoting at some length:

Giant phantoms mustered by millions, flashing white as lightning in the ruddy air. They rushed on me with hurricane-speed; their wings fanned me with fiery breezes; and the echo of their thunder-music was like the groaning and rending of an earthquake, as they tore me away with them on their whirlwind course.

Away! to a City of Palaces, to measureless halls, and arches, and domes, soaring one above another, till their flashing ruby summits are lost in the burning void, high overhead. On! through and through these mountain-piles, into countless, limitless corridors, reared on pillars lurid and rosy as molten lava. . . . Still on and on; faster and faster, for years, days, centuries together, till there comes, stealing slowly forward to meet us, a shadow – a vast, stealthy, gliding shadow – the first darkness that has ever been shed over that world of blazing light! . . .

A silence, like no silence ever known on earth; a darkening of the shadow, blacker than the blackest night in the thickest wood – a pause – then, a sound as of the heavy air being cleft asunder; then . . . an apparition of two figures coming on out of the shadow – two monsters stretching forth their gnarled yellow talons to grasp at us; leaving on their track a green decay, oozing and shining with a sickly light. . . . Each laid a talon on my shoulder – each raised a veil that was one hideous network of twining worms. I saw through the ghastly corruption of their faces the look that told me who they were – the monstrous iniquities incarnate in monstrous forms; the fiend souls made visible in fiend shapes – Margaret and Mannion! . . . Anon, the lake of black waters heaved up and overflowed, and noiselessly sucked us away into its centre depths – depths that were endless; depths of rayless darkness, in which we slowly eddied round and round, deeper and deeper at every turn.[49]

This is Collins's most explicit exploitation of the internal configurations of hallucination, which both breaks through its immediate narrative context and the dense set of literary and medical associations within which it is placed, and yet remains caught within them. But the second breakdown, the breakdown of the narrative, though less flamboyant, is inextricably bound up with the story's inability to achieve either a fictional or an ideological resolution of the contradictions that have formed the narrative tensions from the start. Basil's recovery from brain fever leads to further ostracism as his father disinherits him; the figure of Mannion that he encounters in the wildness of Cornwall has become the monstrous vision of the delirium by assuming a mask of disfigurement that Basil himself has imposed. The wildness of Cornwall, too, with its rocks and cliffs, 'beyond the railways' of modern civilization, forms a setting where Basil can engage in the final conflict with Mannion that replicates the landscape of the delirium. It too becomes a projected image of suppressed tumult – a self-conscious evocation of wildness:

> In one of the highest parts of the wall-side of granite thus formed, there opened a black, yawning hole that slanted nearly straight downwards, like a tunnel, to unknown and unfathomable depths below, into which the waves found entrance through some subterranean tunnel. . . . But, high as they leapt up in the rocky walls of the chasm, they never leapt into sight from above.[50]

It is here that Basil finally eliminates Mannion, by flinging him into the abyss. But Mannion then replaces Margaret as the focus for his monomania as he becomes ever less able to obliterate his memory. He notes in the journal:

> The frightful scene that I witnessed yesterday still holds the same disastrous influence over me. I have vainly endeavoured to think, not of Mannion's death, but of the free prospect which that death has opened to my view. Waking or sleeping, it is as if some fatality kept all my faculties imprisoned within the black walls of the chasm.[51]

Increasingly the journal becomes 'the only safeguard that keeps me in my senses', and this use of immediate testimony in the present reveals the earlier retrospection of the confession to be a means not only of self-analysis but of warding off impending disintegration.[52]

The diary breaks off and the story is taken up by letters recounting his rediscovery by his family, his recovery, and assimilation 'in the shadowed valley of Repose' in which the family, in becoming his asylum, is simply an extension of itself. And thus the only conclusion that the story can offer is a statement of suspended animation, which, 'in the interest of Art' as well as of 'Reality', leaves its loose ends hanging open:

> How are the pages which I am about to send you to be concluded? In the novel-reading sense of the word, by story has no real conclusion. The repose that comes to all of us after trouble to *me*, a repose in life: to others, how often a repose only in the grave! – is the end which must close this autobiography: an end calm, natural and uneventful; yet not, perhaps, devoid of all lessons and all value. Is it fit that I should set myself, for the sake of an effect, to *make* a conclusion, and terminate by fiction what has begun, and thus so far proceeded in truth? In the interests of Art as well as the interests of Reality, surely not![53]

I have emphasized the impossibility of locating any source of stable authority in the narrative voice in *Basil*; the novel implicitly poses a set of correspondences between the coherence of the self and the psychological discourses within which it is framed, correspondences which emerge as an explicit source of pleasure and tension in *The Woman in White*. The only means of making sense of shifts in tense and register, or of setting up any implied hierarchy of narrative frames, is by reference to a qualified and ambivalent moral management; yet it is this model, manifested through the controlling gaze of the father, that is suggested as the source of Basil's imposture from the start. And the figure of the villain, Robert Mannion, compounds this ideological incoherence. He emerges as an unambiguous villain, Basil's unsolicited Other, in so far as he can be fitted into the perceptual framework of moral insanity, which enables his own self-possession and control of others to be encoded as a pathological sign. 'Either there has been madness in his family or his brain has suffered from his internal injuries', notes the doctor, offering distinct physiological explanations. 'Legally, he may be quite fit to be at large, for he will be able to maintain the appearance of perfect self-possession in the ordinary affairs of life. But morally, I am convinced that he is a dangerous monomaniac.'[54] Yet Mannion's own confession, his letter written from the public hospital, like the narrative of the monster in *Frankenstein*, sets up an alternative moral and social framework which challenges the one within which it is framed by offering an inverted replication of it. For Mannion's 'moral sense' is also actively constructed by patterns of judgement, surveillance, and inheritance; he too is the product of Basil's father's autocratic power; and these, in becoming new forces of exclusion, turn into a critique of that other legacy of moral management: competitive individualism and self-help; and in this he forms the first stage in the process of the exploration of the construction of deviance and marginality which is to grow progressively more ambitious through the novels of the 1860s:

> The ambition which – whether I was a hack-author, a travelling portrait-painter, or an usher at a school – had once whispered to me: – low down as you are in dark, miry ways, you are on the path which leads upwards to high places in the sunshine afar off; you are not working to scrape together wealth for another man; you are independent, self-reliant, labouring in your own cause – the daring ambition which had once counselled this, sank dead within me at last. The strong, stern spirit was beaten by spirits stronger and sterner yet – Infamy and Want.[55]

In many ways *Basil* is one of Collins's most ambitious novels. The psychic and social processes which it explores are elaborated and transformed in the 1860s in more complex narrative and social contexts, but it is the very obsessive nature of the confessional narrative form, with the elisions and contradictions which I have indicated, that makes this such a bizarre, intense exploitation and exploration of the psychological codes that govern the makeup and breakdown of social identity. *Basil* draws on and merges notions of constructed and inherited identities – discourses of the self which, I have suggested, still had essentially malleable ideological connotations in the 1850s, and which here resonate with older fictional and psychological associations. These 'older' connotations emerge, too, in a reappearance of the figure of the 'hypochondriacal bachelor' in 'Mad Monkton', the story of an obsessed victim of a morbid genealogy, and are debunked in *A Rogue's Life*, the confessions of an unrepentant sinner. Dickens had greatly admired *Basil*, but he rejected 'Mad Monkton' for publication in *Household Words* on the grounds that it offended the journal's view of hereditary insanity, and that it could be read as reinforcing the very myths that it aimed to dispel.[56] But 'Mad Monkton' is above all a reworking of Poe's method of assimilating specific psychological techniques and 'sensations' into the rhetoric of the narrative, and employing this self-consciousness as the means of generating suspense; it is a recasting of his mystery in which the literal and the metaphorical are blurred, and the ancient family line, the material property, and the hypochondriacal sensibility of the hero become morbid extensions of each other: 'The fall of the house of Usher.'

'Mad Monkton', like 'The fall of the house of Usher', is narrated by a sympathetic friend who sees the protagonist's morbid obsessions as a form of hypochondria which he attempts to analyse; but he finally gets caught within the monomaniacal obsessions of the hero, which thus 'work their own fulfilment'. In both, the very self-consciousness of the analysis of the psychological processes by which the delusions are generated serves simply to reinforce them – Usher fears fear of the future as much as the future itself, and the narrator comments at the opening:

> There can be no doubt that the consciousness of the rapid increase of my superstition – for why should I not so term it? – served mainly to accelerate the increase itself. Such, I have long known, is the paradoxical law of all sentiments having terror as a basis.[57]

But in Poe's tale the narrative voice is caught up within the psychic obsession from the beginning: the whole story is 'hypochondriacal' in a way that is subjected to a new kind of scrutiny in 'Mad Monkton'. 'The fall of the house of Usher' takes as its starting point a late-eighteenth-century rhetoric of nervous sensibility to explain Usher himself, the responses of the narrator, and the collapse of the family line with the house at the end. It even echoes Whytt's discussion of how the nerves constitute a weblike structure of sympathy both between parts of the body and between individuals, manifesting itself as a set of vibrations which become morbid through intensification, in his early study of hypochondria and hysteria in 1767.[58] Usher's hypochondria:

> displayed itself in a host of unnatural sensations. . . . He suffered much from a morbid acuteness of the senses; the most insipid food alone was endurable; he could wear only garments of a certain texture . . . his eyes were tortured by even a faint light.[59]

And while the narrator subjects him to phrenological and physiognomic readings, his own perspective from the beginning is saturated by the dreamlike atmosphere of the place in which the physical is inextricably bound up with the moral: 'I wondered to find how unfamiliar were the fancies which ordinary images were stirring up.'[60]

In 'Mad Monkton', too, the decline of the family is expressed by the physical decay, the morbid stagnancy of the environment which thus becomes both projection and cause of the hero's hypochondria. But the terror is generated by being removed a stage further than in Poe's story. The narrator plays the role of analyst, voyeur, and detective, whose relationship with his subject goes through distinct interpretative phases, in which moral management is finally over-powered by internalized inheritance and self-sustaining mythology as the narrator attempts to track the cause of the monomania by investigating the family history. At first the Monkton family is presented as a product of local legend, as manifesting the vaguely defined 'taint' of hereditary insanity. The legend is internalized by the Monktons themselves, who become deviant members of the gentry community, expressing its values in an extreme form by failing to adapt:

> The members [of the Monkton family] shrank from exposing their calamity to others, as they must have exposed it if they had mingled with the busy world about them . . . at intervals almost every form of madness appeared in the family, monomania being the most frequent.[61]

In the second phase, the narrator encounters Monkton directly and contemplates his obsession with the legend that the family will die out if all its members are not buried in the family vault; this lies behind his apparently monomaniacal quest for the lost body of a profligate uncle whose spectral apparition he periodically sees. Here the narrator draws not on the rhetoric of nervous stability so much as on monomania and spectral illusion, separating Monkton's lucid and deluded selves. Monkton's spectral illusions are detached both from the narrator and the protagonist, who does not lack the power to examine them, but cannot rid himself of their emotional power. At the same time the form the monomania takes – that all the members of the family should be included in the vault – compounds its stagnant degeneration. This replaces spectral illusion as a morbid symptom:

> This set me thinking about the extent of his madness, or, to speak more mildly and more correctly, of his delusion. Sane he certainly was on ordinary subjects, nay, in all the narrative parts of what he had said to me on that very evening he had spoken clearly and connectedly. As for the story of the apparition, other men, with intellects as clear as those of their neighbours, had fancied

themselves pursued by a phantom, and had even written about it in a high strain of philosophical speculation. It was plain that the real hallucination in the case now before me, lay in the conviction of the truth of the old prophecy, and on his idea that the fancied apparition was a supernatural warning to him to evade his denunciations. And it was equally clear that both delusions had been produced by the lonely life he had led acting on a naturally excitable temperament, which was rendered further liable to moral disease by the hereditary trait of insanity.[62]

The narrator uses Monkton's ability to 'speak clearly and connectedly' as proof of his sanity, but while never losing his detached, retrospective voice, finds that the distinctions between associations cannot be maintained as they discover the uncle's rotting body, attempt to bring it home, and lose it at sea. Monkton, falling into melancholy, dies, and the narrator concludes by contemplating the involuted framework set up at the beginning. The belief in self-control and moral management of the narrator is progressively broken down as he is drawn into the 'supernatural' framework of the obsession, but it never completely dissolves.

Basil and 'Mad Monkton' both explore the tenacity of the past by intermingling social, psychic, and physical inheritance. In both it is the way in which identities disintegrate through the subject's sensory incorporation of others' projections and expectations that generates not only sensation and suspense, but also a sense of claustrophobia, of the morbidness of inheritance itself. The satirical confession of a gentleman convict, *A Rogue's Life*, breaks free of this stagnancy as the hero facetiously describes his social transformation through crime, and the story parodies the involuted self-analysis of *Basil* by turning case history and moral tale into a pastiche of the exemplary story of self-help and progressive liberalism:

> I am an example of the workings of the social system of this illustrous country of ours on individual nature; and if I may say so without unbecoming vanity, I should like to quote myself for the edification of my countrymen.[63]

Collins's writing in the 1850s often takes a single sensation or situation as its focus, and develops a set of psychological references and narrative strategies to explore these as far as possible within the limits of the specific generic form. *A Rogue's Life* parodies the confessional form of *Basil* and by doing this it also subverts the doubling of hero and villain. Here the hero assumes a self-possessed, healthy criminal identity which even finally becomes respectable in the process of casting off a past. In these novels both inheritance and moral management become vehicles for the taking apart of social self, but in each the central male subject either regresses, dies, or becomes a healthy exile. This is an impasse which is broken in *The Woman in White* as the propertied woman becomes the point of disintegration and the stage for the professional middle-class man's social transformation. But it is an impasse which is negotiated by developing a set of psychological conventions as narrative strategies within the specific context of *Household Words*. And it results not only in Collins's most successful sensation novel, but his most ambitious exploration of the relationship between social perceptions, power, and subjectivity.

3

The Woman in White
Resemblance and difference –
patience and resolution

> What had I done? Assisted the victim of the most horrible of all
> false imprisonments to escape; or cast loose on the wide world of
> London an unfortunate creature whose actions it was my duty,
> and every man's duty, mercifully to control?[1]

Walter Hartright asks himself this question immediately after
encountering the mysterious figure on the road to London, at the
beginning of the second episode of the serialization of *The Woman
in White*. The immediacy of the 'sensation' produced by the sudden
appearance of the spectral woman is both elaborated and qualified
by the double problem that Hartright ponders on discovering that
she is a fugitive from a lunatic asylum; the problem not simply of
whether she is mad, but of whether her derangement is of the kind
to justify confinement in the light of his own observation of her
behaviour. 'I cannot say with truth that the terrible inference which
those words suggested flashed on me like a new revelation', he
remarks. 'But the idea of absolute insanity which we all associate
with the very name of an Asylum, had, I can honestly declare, never
occurred to me in connection with her.'[2]

Thus the shock of first seeing the woman in white becomes a
greater mystery as she is placed in a new light, though this is not a
'new relevation'; the mystery of how to see is linked to the problem
of how to frame and place her. Yet the two contrasting notions of
what she might be, 'victim of false imprisonment' or unfortunate
creature in need of constraint, imply not simply different degrees of
madness, but different conceptions of what it means to be mad. And
yet again 'absolute insanity' itself is a term constructed by the
institution which contains it, while the question that Hartright is
forced to consider makes him distrust the validity of his own senses.

In this way both the sensation of the sudden encounter with, and
the mystery of the identity of, Anne Catherick are compounded out

of a set of suggestions and inferences which in certain respects can never be fully explained or satisfied by the narrative resolutions which are offered. The process anticipates the contradictions and ambiguities set up by the story as a whole, which plays with distinct forms of psychological discourse which are exploited, subverted, and transformed in different ways as they are put to work as narrative strategies in the text. By this process *The Woman in White* becomes a complex investigation of the interaction of psychic and social forces; an exploration of the ways in which social identities are formed by and within particular frameworks of perception, which in turn determine and are determined by social and sexual hierarchies.

On an obvious level as a sensation novel, *The Woman in White* plays with the relationship between ways of seeing, modes of identity, and forms of power. Collins uses the dual device of doubling and substituting Laura Fairlie and Anne Catherick's identities in the asylum not only to question the enigmatic definitions and borderlands of insanity in the 'whited out', drained, figure of Anne, but also to explore how Laura's subjective self is broken down and rebuilt through the controlling interests and perceptions of others. And this in turn breaks down any stable division between the resonances of 'home' and 'asylum' as places of safety and danger. After her rescue from the asylum, stripped of family, property, husband, all social assets, Laura is described by Walter, relating her to Anne:

> The fatal resemblance which I had once seen and shuddered at seeing, in idea only, was now a real and living resemblance which asserted itself before my own eyes. Strangers, acquaintances, friends even who could not look at her as we looked, if she had been shown to them in the first days of her rescue from the Asylum, might have doubled if she were the Laura Fairlie they had once seen, and doubted without blame.[3]

Laura has in a sense 'become' Anne Catherick once the social and psychological contexts that divided them have broken down; she can only regain her place and her identity when she can be shown to others in the revived light of the past.

This takes place, however, in the context of a range of forms of reconstruction at work in the narrative as a whole. Laura, the bearer of wealth, is cast in different lights by others, but never writes herself. The fight over how to possess and repossess her is bound up with the struggle carried on by other figures in the novel: the struggle over how to see, over the control of time and memory, and over the control of writing; a struggle bound up with the battle for self-management and self-definition. This in turn depends on manipulating and soliciting the reader's perception and knowledge. The reader is told at the start that the story will be unravelled through the subjective perspective of the linked testimonies of the different narrators – that their eyewitness accounts are empirically accurate but partial. Suspense and excitement are generated and maintained by the way that the reader's view is limited at any one time to the perspective of each individual narrator whose testimonies are at once reliable and unreliable, and whose means of making sense of the world needs to be continually questioned. Yet actually the narrative forms a more ambiguous embedded chain: each individual utterance gains meaning from the way it has been placed in the chain, which is presented as continual progression but is in reality a continual, contradictory process of reappropriation and redefinition. These narrative paradoxes point to a more general ambiguity; for both the cognitive framework and the process of detection through which the mysteries of Anne Catherick and Percival Glyde's identities are unravelled in order to reconstruct Laura involve a process of realignment within a framework which is essentially and ironically *compatible* with the one through which she is taken apart.

Paradoxically, it was the fictional, cultural, and ideological constraints on the novel which created greater scope for its psychological complexity in the narrative form. *Basil* and 'Mad Monkton' had both used images of madness and the breakdown of identity in pushing a reformulated set of supernatural terror conventions to their limit, set within a reconstructed narrative framework that defused suspense though not intensity of experience. *The Woman in White* was written under particular cultural pressures: it was essential that it should be a compulsively readable story if its serialization was to secure the circulation of the newly launched *All the Year Round*.[4] It needed also, as Margaret Oliphant was later to point out, to be a book 'abounding in sensation', but one in which 'everything is legitimate, natural and possible . . . and there is almost as little that is objectionable in this highly-wrought sensation novel as if it had been a domestic history of the most gentle and unexciting kind'.[5] Collins develops many of the methods and concerns of *Basil* in *The Woman in White*, and in apparently defusing them, actually takes them further. The novel continues to exploit contemporary psychological methods by using them to produce the very anxiety and fears that they were developed to analyse. This puts it on a continuum with the earlier fiction, but in the treatment of insanity the novel is both constrained and presented with a new set of opportunities by the particular discursive framework of insanity which had been set up by *Household Words* – a domesticated, feminized insanity, set within the paternalistic framework of the moral management of the 1850s.

Collins negotiates these constraints firstly by putting the flickering, unstable figure of Anne to different uses in the text as a problematic uncanny figure who hovers on the boundary between madness and sanity, rationality and superstition, literal and figural modes of representation. Joseph Posselthwaite, the pupil at Limmeridge School who functions as the voice of 'popular superstition', is familiar with what Marian sarcastically refers to as the 'manners and customs' of ghosts. He works within a naïve traditional structure of knowledge that determines how he sees 'the ghaist of Miss Fairlie': 'All in white – as a ghaist should be . . . Away yonder, in t'kirkyard – where a ghaist ought to be.'[6] But while this is debunked by Marian and Hartright, the uncertainty of what Anne *does* signify, and how her testimony should be listened to, like their own apparently irrational forebodings, are given a significance, but one they can only decipher as 'unsoundness of mind'. While her contrast with Laura, and the breakdown of the difference between them, mean that the cultural connotations – 'the idea of insanity which we all associate with the name of an asylum' – form a pattern of contrasts which are undermined by the novel while remaining one of the bases of its effects. Anne Catherick, the unpropertied outcast, appears ghostly because, in another way, she *is* Laura's ghost. Simultaneously her other and double, she is the trace, the shadow, and the mirror of the social and subjective transformation which Laura undergoes – undergoes explicitly in the way her identity is taken to pieces, and tacitly in the way it is built up, so that 'the most horrible of all false imprisonments' merges with, while being set against, 'merciful control'.

In order to work in this way *The Woman in White* orchestrates a very precise set of allusions to contemporary debates on confinement, definitions of insanity, and the treatment of the insane within a narrative that enables shifting connotations to be produced by overlapping models of feminine identity through distinct kinds of masculine manipulation. By setting up Laura's obviously wrongful confinement against Anne's, which is also problematic though not in quite the same way, Collins draws on the 'older' resonances of fears about the confinement of the sane in madhouses by relatives aiming to steal their property by bereaving them of social identity (suggested by his use of the late eighteenth-century case of the

Marquise de Douhault); he interweaves this theme with contemporary questions about what justified confinement that were being studied by the Parliamentary Select Committee Inquiry into the Care and Treatment of Lunatics and their Property that reported in 1859–60. But these associations also make up a palimpsest of allusions which go beyond the immediate perimeters of the debates on private asylums as a source of sensation, emphasizing the tensions of these debates, and linking them with the image of domesticated insanity – a reformed madness personified in the inmate of an asylum modelled on a stately home – the model county asylum.

I argued in Chapter 1 that the late 1850s were a contradictory moment in the lunacy reform movement, which in a paradoxical way had helped to shape the very anxieties that it had attempted to institutionalize out of existence. Predominantly, the legacy of progressivist, paternalistic liberalism seemed secured. The practice of moral management and the non-restraint system had domesticated madness itself as it contributed to the reform of the private madhouses and the development of the county asylum system; the study and treatment of insanity had become a respectable, professionalized and rapidly expanding branch of the medical profession – as exemplified above all by Conolly's career. Yet the shaping of insanity within a new kind of institution and a new kind of public professional relation did not dissipate the fears of confinement but merely shifted the focus of the fears, and linked them with the debates on madness itself. 'Wrongful confinement' became more ambiguous now, applying beyond the victims of conscious conspiracy. The problematic borderlands of insanity could be used by the medical profession to argue for increased specialized surveillance and control; but they could equally be used to argue against such surveillance by those who feared the possibility of medical manipulation. Reade's conflation of modern and corrupt asylums, his descriptions of mad-doctors as 'soul murderers who make their lie a truth', depended on collapsing together different images and institutional processes. This might have been disclaimed by Dickens but it echoed a widespread set of fears about the danger of medical expertise legitimizing corrupt motivations that essentially sprang from the tensions within the liberalism of the reform movement itself. Thus *All the Year Round*, discussing the reports of the Commissioners in Lunacy in 1862, two years after the serialization of *The Woman in White* and before *Hard Cash*, modified *Household Words'* almost uncritical admiration of the reform movement on the one hand and Reade's fears of conscious conspiracy on the other.

Like John Perceval and the Conolly of *Indications of Insanity*, it stressed the dangers of total medical control for the liberty of the subject, warning that it 'fixes and renders permanent that which might have passed away'.[7] The difficulties of establishing precisely what constituted 'unsoundness of mind' and whether it justified confinement did not depend on the conscious corruption of the medical profession but on the context in which these judgements inevitably took place:

> Let us at once delare that we do not for an instant, or in the remotest degree, attribute to Dr Winslow, or to any other of these medical gentlemen, a conscious action under mercenary motives. The public danger arising from their influence would be infinitely insignificant if the fact were so. They are highly trained men, who have honestly devoted themselves to a special study of the most difficult questions that can occur to a physician. There is no clear dividing-line between sickness and health of mind; unsoundness of mind is, no doubt, as various and common as unsoundness of body. . . . Every natural defect of temper is unsoundness. . . . But we do not condemn our bodies as unfit for use when there are corns on our toes, or when the sallow tinge on our cheeks supplants the hue of health . . . so it is with the mind. Every man has his weak place, his twist, his hobby. . . .
>
> What opinion are we to form upon the whole case of the facility with which a mad-doctor can insensibly adapt his theories to either side? Even in the less uncertain fields of science, we have seen in great criminal trials eminent chemists as well as eminent mad-doctors retained for the prosecution. The value of the skilled witness has usually its visible measure in questions of material fact that concern the body. In questions that concern the mind, the less heed we pay to the theorist, and the more distinctly we require none but the sort of evidence patent to the natural sense of ordinary men in determining what citizen shall suffer the privations, or what criminal shall enjoy the privileges of unsoundness of mind, the better it will be for us. Let us account no man a lunatic whom it requires a mad-doctor to prove insane.[8]

This echoes the starting-point for Walter Hartright's dilemma on hearing of Anne's alleged insanity in *The Woman in White* just as it picks up on John Perceval's argument to the Parliamentary Select Committee that non-specialists should be involved in the commitment of the supposed insane.[9] 'The natural sense of ordinary men' is dissected in the novel. Yet Collins none the less assumes a tacit identification with Hartright's view of Anne which is, in one register, explicitly confirmed – that of the middle-class, liberal, well-informed observer. This works in the treatment of the confinement and substitution of Anne and Laura, in the effect of confinement on Laura, and in the perception of Anne. Both women are victims of 'wrongful' confinement conspiracies, echoing John Perceval's arguments amongst others that those who have power over the alleged insane 'may be influenced by corrupt motives, such as the desire to possess themselves of a ward or kinsman's estate, or to get a person out of the way who interferes with their selfish gratifications'.[10] They are both confined, however, with the unconscious complicity of not only the medical profession, but the broader institutions of middle-class common sense – the law and the family, all of whom are unable to recognize Laura once she has been pronounced 'socially, morally, legally – dead'.[11] The asylum in which Anne and Laura are confined is a respectable private establishment, an uncontroversial non-restraint institution, that could have been indirectly modelled on one of Fox's establishments, or even one of Conolly's, each patient with her own keeper, in a London suburb rather than a rural retreat.[12] Its proprietor is neither a corrupt profiteer, nor a 'Wycherley' figure, sinisterly collecting mad specimens, but a bland individual who happily opens his doors to Marian, and whose indirectly reported explanation of the changes in Anne/Laura reinforces Hartright's doubts about stable identities and definitions, but within the framework of a medical opinion that bases its authority on physiognomy. It is emphasized that

> such changes, no doubt, were not without precedent in his experience of persons mentally afflicted. Insane people were often, at one time, outwardly as well as inwardly, unlike what they were at another; the change from better to worse, or from worse to better, in the madness, having a necessary tendency to produce alterations of appearance externally.[13]

This echoes Alexander Morison's point that 'the appearance of the face . . . is intimately connected with, and dependent upon the state of the mind.'[14]

The instability of the definition and perception of insanity, and the 'facility with which a mad-doctor can insensibly adapt his theories to either side', are pressed into service to transform Laura in a way that echoes the process by which Conolly himself was able to twist the implications of his own *Indications of Insanity* into their opposite.

But with Anne the asylum works as a crucible in a different way, for, although her confinement is never justified, she is built up through a set of conventions and allusions as a person of 'unsound mind' as an ideal patient of a model county asylum. The article on 'The cure of sick minds' in *Household Words* describes the case of

> a young woman, liable to returns of insanity [who] left her home at four o'clock one wet morning and . . . hurried to the asylum. . . . She said she dreaded being at home, for they treated her badly when mad. She knew the asylum was the best place, and she came as fast as she could, to get help in time.[15]

In one way Anne's escape from the madhouse – 'the most horrible of all false imprisonments' – reverses this, but it also in a curious way reinforces it.

Because from the start Anne's peculiar mental condition is suggested by the way that she is set up as a model patient of moral management. She suffers from monomania, but is able to control herself though not to recognize the extent of her delusions. Like the female patients that Dickens describes in 'A curious dance round a curious tree', she is bizarre in the way that she goes through the motions of passive propriety which in the process become transformed into the mark of hovering on the brink of self-possession. What is weird about Anne is her obedience and docility, her perpetual childlikeness, which is also the sign of her ambiguous class identity, echoing the shadowy class transformation of moral management:

> There was nothing wild, nothing immodest in her manner: it was quiet and self-controlled, a little melancholy and a little touched by suspicion; not exactly the manner of a lady, and, at the same time, not exactly the manner of a woman in the humblest rank of life.[16]

Her obsession with wearing white – instilled into her in the 'asylum' of the substitute home at Limmeridge House – turns Conolly's notion of this 'really proper feeling' as a means of therapy ('many of the women should be indulged in wearing neat articles of dress'[17]) into its opposite and simulacrum. Her weakened intellectual faculties are explained in the First Part of the narrative through the kind of combination of phrenological and associationist criteria that Conolly uses in *Indications of Insanity*; her monomania takes the form of not being able to impose coherent criteria on her own associations, but this can be modified by education. The late Mrs Fairlie cites a doctor's opinion that she will grow out of it. But he says her careful bringing up at school is a matter of great importance just now, because her unusual slowness in acquiring ideas implies an unusual tenacity in keeping them, when they are once received into her mind.[18]

These have become 'fixed and rendered permanent', Hartright notes:

> The old grateful sense of her benefactress's kindness was evidently the ruling idea still in the poor creature's mind – the narrow mind which had but too plainly opened to no other lasting impression since that first impression of her younger and happier days.[19]

Yet they can also be modified and controlled by benign surveillance: 'I appealed to the only anxiety she appeared to feel, in connexion with me and with my opinion of her – the anxiety to convince me of her fitness to be mistress of her own actions.'[20]

What Anne represents, then, is the diffusing and domestication of mania into monomania or partial insanity, able to control itself, and not justifying restraint, or even, necessarily, confinement.[21] But she also suggests the pathologization of feminine passivity. And as Laura's other and double she anticipates a process that the figure of Laura then silently infers as each absorbs the other's connotations. Laura and Anne's doubleness is set on a strictly physiological as well as a figurative level. Hartright notes the similarities as if he were writing a physiognomic report,

> in the general outline of the countenance and in the general proportion of the features; in the colour of the hair and in the little nervous uncertainty about the lips; in the height and size of the figure and the carriage of the head and body.[22]

Anne is primarily differentiated from Laura by 'sorrow and suffering' rather than faculty or constitution and, conversely, it is Laura's delicacy of constitution and faculty that is paradoxically both emphasized and denied as being particularly vulnerable to the changes brought about by confinement: 'Faculties less delicately balanced, constitutions less tenderly organised, must have suffered under such an ordeal as this. No man could have gone through it and come out unchanged.'[23]

This contradictory suggestion that Laura's vulnerability is both constitutional and constituted by social role and social expectation as the bearer of the family wealth becomes further complicated by

Anne and Laura's position in the Fairlie family, which is, tacitly, the 'bleached' version of which the 'white' Anne is the extreme. Anne is finally explained by Hartright in hereditary terms, as the bearer of the biological and moral Nemesis of the father's excesses:

> There rose on my memory the remembrance of the Scripture denunciation . . . 'The sins of the father shall be visited on the children'. . . . With what unerring and terrible directness the long chain of circumstances led down from the thoughtless wrong committed by the father to the heartless injury committed on the child![24]

But in fact the chain of circumstances is far from direct or unerring, for the Fairlie family as a whole, not just its illegitimate strain, is incipiently morbid, in a way that mingles and resists distinct codes of inheritance and transmission. Here Laura is set in different family oppositions: against Anne, her half-sister; her other half-sister, Marian; her uncle Frederick and Eleanor, her formerly wayward aunt, now wife of Fosco.

Each opposition produces a distinct implication, which together resist as well as reinforce a straightforward physiological notion of feminine vulnerability, while linking sensibility and nervous weakness. The inherited weakness of the family, for instance, is all from the father's side – the dark and energetic Marian takes after her mother. It is qualified also by the way in which an implied rhetoric of 'nervous disorder' is juggled with, dislodging it from its sexual referent while still using it as a source of tension. Frederick Fairlie's excessive sensibility echoes Laura's vulnerability in a way that makes his disturbing androgyny generate a sense of unreality: 'His beardless face was thin, worn and transparently pale, but not wrinkled', notes Hartright.

> 'Upon the whole, he had a frail, languidly-fretful, over-refined look – something singularly and unpleasantly delicate in its association with a man, and at the same time, something which could by no possibility have looked natural and appropriate if it had been transferred to the personal appearance of a woman.[25]

This takes the image of the upper-class 'hypochondriacal bachelor' a stage further than *Basil* or 'Mad Monkton', turning artistic sensibility into a caricatured decadence that is the sign of both physiological degeneration and self-indulgent, idle affectation. 'We all say it's the nerves and we none of us know what we mean when we say it', Marian points out, and Fairlie's 'nerves' both parody their earlier reference points and become the means by which Fairlie abdicates his paternal as much as his patriarchal role, leaving his niece the more vulnerable.[26] They also help to turn Limmeridge House into the 'private asylum' of a nervous patient, picture of seclusion and repose where nothing is allowed to irritate, a claustrophobic retreat prefiguring the patterns of confinement and observation that are to be enacted at Blackwater. But to get a coherent view of the way that Collins simultaneously weaves and unpicks this set of psychological and cognitive assumptions it is necessary to look at the way that the narrative itself is controlled and manipulated in more detail.

The tensions of *The Woman in White* hinge on the destruction and re-forming of Laura's identity, but the narrative devices by which it generates and resolves them make it also the story of Walter Hartright's social and psychological transformation – of his progress from marginalized lower-middle-class drawing master to the father of the heir of Limmeridge and revitalizer of the stagnant and incipiently morbid Fairlie family. As his name obviously and emblematically suggests, Hartright operates as the voice of safety, normality, and 'right feeling' in the novel. He is the narrative figure who enables fictional and ideological resolutions to be achieved by presenting them as the outcome of his own resolution. At the same time *The Woman in White* is the more equivocal history of how Hartright's new subjective identity is constructed in order to achieve this closure; how he learns to control the past and thus the present instead of being incapacitated by anxiety about the future, that *ominousness* which is such an important source of suspense in the first part of the novel; how he becomes both his own and Laura's moral manager, and thus successfully opposes the power, also manifested as a form of moral management, of Fosco.

At the beginning of his narrative Hartright is a domesticated artist, a landscape painter dependent on teaching, a male governess figure, drained of social and sexual meaning or effectiveness, who can live almost invisibly at the heart of the patron's family. 'I had trained myself to leave all the sympathies natural to my age in my employer's outer hall', he writes of his arrival at Limmeridge.

> I had long since learnt to understand, composedly, and as a matter of course, that my situation in life was considered a guarantee against any of my female pupils feeling more than the most ordinary interest in me, and that I was admitted among beautiful and captivating women much as a harmless domestic animal is admitted amongst them.[27]

By the opening of the Second Part, when he has rediscovered the 'whited out' Laura and experienced the double shock of recognizing her face above her own gravestone and seeing its transformation 'into' Anne Catherick, it becomes clear that his radical opposition to established privilege merges into his possession of Laura, and that the means and end of his gaining power are founded on *her* social obliteration.

Forlorn and disowned, sorely tired and sadly changed; her beauty faded, her mind clouded; robbed of her station in the world, of her place among living creatures – the devotion I had promised, the devotion of my whole heart and soul and strength might be laid blamelessly, now, at those dear feet. In the right of her calamity, in the right of her friendliness, she was mine at last! Mine to support, to protect, to cherish, to restore. Mine to love and honour as father and brother both. Mine to vindicate through all risks and all sacrifices – through the hopeless struggle against Rank and Power, through the long fight with armed Deceit and fortified Success, through the waste of my reputation, through the loss of my friends, through the hazard of my life.[28]

But the securing of that position of possession and power by rebuilding the social recognition of Laura, by becoming honorary father and brother, and by realigning the cognitive framework through which she is seen, depends in turn on Hartright being able to see differently, partly by appropriating others' perceptions – above all, those of Marian Halcombe who is also, though in a different way and context, struggling for control. 'I answer for my self-control', he states before the final conflict with the villain. 'My nerves were firmly strung, and I felt all the strength of my resolution stirring in me vigorously from head to foot.'[29] But this new-found masculine vigour is the product of a complex process of historical assimilation.

This means that two orders of narrative are at work in the novel – the process by which Hartright discloses the mysteries of the past, and the process by which he covers his traces. 'This is the story of what a Woman's patience can endure and of what a Man's resolution can achieve', the Preamble opens, but the actual pattern of perception and control manifested in the First Part of the novel is Hartright's passive mediation of sensation and Marian's resolution; Marian describes *herself* as 'a woman, condemned to patience, propriety and petticoats, for life.'[30] There is thus no straightforward movement of narrative authority at work in the text, and while the relationship between the control over writing and the consolidation of social identity is more explicit here than in any of the stories I have considered so far, this relationship can be mutually undermining as well as reinforcing, in accordance with the link between the social and psychological frameworks through which they work.

In the Preamble Walter Hartright appears to be the overall narrator and thus the central authority of *The Woman in White*. As General Editor he selects, organizes, and arranges the narratives of others (including his own specific narrative) but in such a way that they seem to tell their own story. He seems to be replacing divine judgement with empirical evidence that emerges as both reliable and relative; absolute morality with contingent experience, wherein the corruption of the Law is replaced by the analysis of the Reader, but within the framework of credibility which the Law confers.

> But the Law is still, in certain inevitable cases, the pre-engaged servant of the long purse; and the story is left to be told, for the first time, in his place. As the Judge might once have heard it, so the reader shall hear it now. No circumstance of importance, from the beginning to the end of this disclosure, shall be related on hearsay evidence. . . .
>
> Thus, the story here presented will be told by more than one pen, as the story of an offence against the law is told in Court by more than one witness – with the same object, in both cases, to present the truth in its most direct and intelligible aspect; and to trace the course of one complete series of events, by making the persons who have been most closely connected with them, at each successive stage, relate their own experience, word for word.[31]

By this use of the passive tense, claiming the neutral authority of the Law even as he reveals its interests, the voice of Hartright the better controls the story as it appears to be its passive medium. He stresses that his authority is based on contingency: 'When his experience fails, he will retire from his position as narrator', yet in the Second Part he continuously uses 'hearsay evidence', and controls the comings and goings of other narrators as well as the story's beginning and end. But the changing relationship between Hartright the General Editor and Hartright the specific narrator, or the voice that frames the story and the narrative utterance itself, becomes increasingly embroiled as the novel progresses.

I have suggested that if one takes the narrative of *The Woman in White* as a whole it seems that two processes are taking place simultaneously: Hartright's editing and reorganizing 'one complete series of events' as a *chain* which forms a narrative totality and is based on a linear set of logically connected associations, and the process of reperception and detection which he goes through himself and which forms a more tangled web. But although the revelation of the former depends partly on making the latter explicit, the two narrative functions are fudged at crucial moments of the story, and this is intimately connected with the contradictory way that the past is reconstructed and Laura restored. It is also crucially bound up with the other narrative relations that are at work in the novel.

So in taking the form of an embedded chain the narrative progresses both along and 'inwards', and this in turn produces a hierarchical order of specific narratives. Firstly, Hartright as General Editor who presents the various narrative testimonies as evidence claiming the legally and empirically verifiable authority of truth; then Hartright the specific narrator, who is on a level, supposedly, with the other specific narrators – Gilmore, Marian, Fairlie, Mrs Michelson, Hester Pinhorn, the Doctor, Jane Gould, 'The Tombstone', Count Fosco. Within this are embedded other narratives, in the form of letters, dreams, or reported speech. But the degree of embedding only partially determines the degree of credibility of each narrating instance, and is itself partly determined by the psychological frame within which the figures themselves are set.

The powerless Anne Catherick and the powerful Fosco are contrasting examples of this. Anne's one autonomous narrative takes the form of a dream related in a letter ('feeble, faint and defaced by blots') to Laura warning her of Glyde's wickedness. This attempts to claim credibility by drawing on biblical authority ('Do you believe in dreams? I hope for your sake, that you do. See what Scripture says about dreams (Genesis XL.8, S.I.24; Daniel IV.18–25); and take the warning I send you before it is too late'), but loses reliability for Hartright and Marian by being triply embedded – in a dream, in a letter, in a deranged person.[32] Here, as I have suggested, this very process of embedding gives it a perverse kind of authority as a means of 'foreshadowing' by making the associations that Marian and Hartright's rationality refuse. It contributes to Anne's general uncanny role in the text, but also prefigures Marian's own dream. with Fosco, on the other hand, the pattern takes a different form. His final narrative has a structurally ambiguous position, being both embedded within Hartright's specific narrative and being a specific one in its own right; but as a figure in Marian's narrative, he has the social and psychological power to burst through the frame through which she sees him, breaking down her sense of the reliability of her own senses and finally snatching the pen from her hand. I will pick up this thread again later, but first it is necessary to investigate the way in which distinct and overlapping methods of perception, control of others, and self-control operate in the specific and implied perspectives of Hartright, Marian, and Fosco in the First Part. I will then consider how they are reappropriated through the control of time and memory in the second half of the novel.

There are two interrelated features of Hartright's early method of perception, which, in creating ominousness, anxiety, and ambiguity, generate and imply the sense of his powerlessness and absence of self-control, in a way that elaborates many of the patterns at work in Basil's consciousness, but from the standpoint of *petit-bourgeois* interloper rather than displaced upper-class younger son. Like Basil, Hartright *projects* meaning into figures and events in the light of his own preconceived expectations, and has his own identity undermined when they are undercut by his sense of the strange and anomalous – this is one of the chief sources of the sense of uncanniness and mystery in the early part of the story. Hartright's perceptual universe – again like Basil's – is dominated by a particular naïve interpretation of associationist and physiognomic methods and assumptions, linked to his problematic social and sexual position, which need to be reconciled and realigned if he is to see to some purpose and act resolutely. Thus the early Hartright's 'commonsense' notion of normality is created paradoxically out of doubt, uncertainty, and insecurity. I have already discussed how this works in his first encounter with, and assessment of, Anne, and in the generalized ways in which the boundaries between 'home' and 'asylum' are undercut in the novel by the anticipating of the asylum at Blackwater Park, and the foreshadowing of Blackwater at Limmeridge, which is a safe, familiar asylum, the place of Anne's early moral treatment, but none the less claustrophobic in its seclusion. These in turn express and contribute to his whole mode of perceiving and operating.

At the opening of the novel Hartright's inability to interpret Anne is the product not only of her own ambiguity, but of the shock to his faculties, and his own inability to control it, that the encounter with Anne had precipitated, but not caused.

> It was like a dream. Was I Walter Hartright? . . . Had I really left, little more than an hour since, the quiet, decent, conventionally-domestic atmosphere of my mother's cottage? I was too

bewildered – too conscious also of a vague sense of something like self reproach, to speak to my strange companion for some minutes.[33]

This anxiety and insecurity, consistently presented as Hartright's inability to interpret any perception that cannot be aligned within established associations as one form or other of partial insanity, are increased by the very retreat-like repose of Limmeridge. Here it becomes clear that the seclusion and isolation do not only compound Frederick Fairlie's hypochondria but also Hartright's own insecure self-control, which also verges on the hypochondriacal. It takes the form, firstly, of loss of memory and control over the perception and marking of time:

> A confused sensation of having suddenly lost by familiarity with the past, without acquiring any additional clearness of idea in reference to the present or the future, took possession of my mind. Circumstances that were but a few days old, faded back in my memory, as if they had happened months and months since.[34]

This is linked to the lack of control over his 'feminized' social situation and over himself. Teaching Laura and Marian to 'represent Nature' in water-colours as part of their feminine formation saps his own self-management: 'I had just enough work to do, in mounting my employer's drawings, to keep my hands and eyes pleasurably employed, while my mind was left free to enjoy the dangerous luxury of unbridled thoughts.'[35]

At this opening stage then, finding himself in an unaccustomed position of privilege and idleness, Hartright both senses that 'unbridled thoughts' are a 'dangerous luxury' and is unable to bridle them. He has the consciousness of the resolute moral superintendent but not the ability to apply it to himself. It is the female asylum qualities of the place that sap his resolution, as it has provided an earlier training ground for Anne. Hartright, in John Barlow's words, does not want 'the power and resolution to examine' his possible delusions; his problem is that he can only explain them as derangement.[36] This applies obviously to his developing response to Anne and her warning dream; it also means that he can only read his own mounting anxiety as monomania. So immediately before discovering Anne's 'Dream' letter, Hartright meditates on the significance of his discovery of Laura's engagement to Percival Glyde, and here his immediate self-control breaks down: 'Thoughts I had hitherto restrained, thoughts that made my position harder than ever to endure, crowded on me now that I was alone.' These thoughts, however, take the form of anxious analysis of his own associations, which enable them to be both suggested and resisted:

> Judging by the ordinary rules of evidence, I had not the shadow of a reason, this far, for connecting Sir Percival Glyde with the suspicious words of inquiry that had been spoken to me by the woman in white. And yet, I did connect him with them. Was it because he had now become associated in my mind with Miss Fairlie; Miss Fairlie being, in her turn, associated with Anne Catherick, since that night when I had discovered the ominous likeness between them? Had the events of the morning so unnerved me already that I was at the mercy of any delusion which common chances and common coincidences might suggest to my imagination?[37]

Like Robert Audley in *Lady Audley's Secret*, Hartright is unable to distinguish between 'monition' and 'monomania'. But while for Robert Audley this is a temporary state of uncertainty, to be replaced by his own sense of the reliability of circumstantial evidence, for Hartright 'the ordinary rules of evidence' cannot help him establish the underlying logic beneath the 'chance' connection, so he sees himself as the victim of a delusion, but in a way that makes him feel the more powerless to predit a dangerous future. The 'sense of something obscurely impending, something invisibly threatening, that Time was holding over our heads' or irrational fears of the future were identified by Pritchard as a sign of monomania.[38] This, together with his reaction to Anne's dream, compounds his own sense of himself as monomaniac and leads him to prescribe his own self-disciplinary moral treatment; to use his 'reason' to 'curb the blind impulse of [his] disordered senses':

> Those words and the doubt which had just escaped me as to the sanity of the writer of the letter, acting together on my mind, suggested an idea, which I was literally afraid to express openly, or even to encourage secretly. I began to doubt whether my own faculties were not in danger of losing their balance. It seemed almost like a monomania to be tracing back everything strange that happened, everything unexpected that was said, always to the same hidden source and the same sinister influence. I resolved, this time, in defence of my own courage and my own sense, to come to no decision which plain fact did not warrant, and to turn my back resolutely on everything that tempted me in the shape of surmise.[39]

What Hartright needs to learn is how to draw 'correct' influences from chance associations and hypothetical surmise, but in the reconstructed framework of his own narrative it never moves beyond the realignment of the process of self-regulation implied by moral management.

Hartright's early perception is not straightforwardly naïve, however. At particular moments of his opening narrative his method of self-scrutiny shifts from contemporary self-consciousness to retrospective assessment, and this undermines its status as immediate evidence, on a par with the other narratives. This emerges particularly clearly in the contrasting way in which he sees Marian and Laura. In both cases the perception of their femininity, or lack of it, is clearly a product of his own projection; but in the case of Marian it works as a satirical subversion of Hartright's preconceptions (as Marian herself satirically subverts femininity); with Laura this process has been assimilated within Hartright's own framework.

Hartright's perception of both Marian and Laura elaborate and manipulate a particular kind of physiognomic idealism, but with Marian this is done at Hartright's expense, in a way that suggests and subverts the idea that natural beauty is a cultural construction. The shock of Marian's 'ugliness' is derived from its disturbing conjunction with the 'rare beauty of her form', and the way that this contradicts 'the old conventional Maxim, that Nature cannot err'. It also immediately echoes and follows his response to Anne. As drawing-master, and professional representer of nature, Hartright's response to Marian's disturbing androgyny, the inverse of Frederick Fairlie's – the ability to recognize, but not to reconcile disparate elements – tacitly questions the implied sexual oppositions that enable his vision, even his sanity, to function, again by the disruption of established trains of association:

The lady's complexion was almost swarthy, and the dark down on her upper lip was almost a moustache. She had a large, firm, masculine mouth and jaw; prominent piercing, resolute brown eyes; and thick, coal-black hair, growing unusually low down on her forehead. Her expression – bright, frank and intelligent – appeared, while she was silent, to be altogether wanting in those feminine attractions of gentleness and pliability, without which the beauty of the handsome woman alive is beauty incomplete. To see such a face as this set on shoulders that a sculptor would have longed to model – to be charmed by the modest graces of action through which the symmetrical limbs betrayed their beauty when they moved, and then to be almost repelled by the masculine form and masculine look of the features in which the perfectly-shaped figure ended – was to feel a sensation oddly akin to the helpless discomfort familiar to us all in sleep, when we recognise yet cannot reconcile the anomalies and contradictions of a dream.[40]

Hartright's physiognomic reading of Marian functions accurately in the novel in that she does manifest all the energy and resourcefulness that he reads in her features. But she realigns them in the context of her own narrative as a desire to be freed from the 'artificial' constraints of femininity. With Laura, the process at first seems to be reversed, though the frame still holds, for it is her very difference from Marian that suggests her femininity and her powerlessness – her 'whiteness'. Hartright begins by acknowledging that his representation of Laura is derived from a memory compounded as a palimpsest of associations and subjective sensations: 'How can I describe her? How can I separate her from my own sensations and all that has happened in the later time?'[41] He then describes his own representation, his portrait, of her, both noting and resisting the signs of inbred weakness and nervous susceptibility:

It is hard to see that the lower part of the face is too delicately refined away towards the chin to be full and fair proportion to the upper part . . . and that the sweet sensitive lips are subject to slight nervous contraction, when she smiles.

He then goes on to contemplate his reading of the significance of the portrait – a self-fulfilling process that manipulates the physiognomic sensation itself by replacing the features with the representation of them and disclosing this and its ideal referent, as a process of neo-platonic self-projection:

Does my poor portrait of her . . . show me these things? Ah, how few of them are in the dull mechanical drawing, and how many in the mind with which I regard it! A fair delicate girl in a pretty light dress, trifling with the leaves of her sketch-book, while she looks up from it with truthful innocent blue eyes – that is all the drawing can say; all, perhaps, that even the deeper reach of thought and pen can say in their language either. The woman who first gives life, light and form to our shadowy conceptions of beauty, fills a void in our spiritual nature that has remained unknown to us till she appeared. Sympathies that lie too deep for words, too deep almost for thoughts, are touched, at such times, by other charms than those which the senses feel and which the sources of expression can realise. The mystery which underlies the beauty of women is never raised above the reach of all expression until it has claimed kindred with the mystery of our own souls.[42]

Hartright's vision of Laura shifts between different implied kinds of projection as he switches between his recall of his first impression of her and his later analysis of it. But it is a shift between forms of absence, both of which mean that 'Laura' can only be perceived as 'the visionary nursling of [his] own fancy'; as neo-platonic ideal, she remains a spirit, a ghost, a spectral illusion. Thus he can only know her through sensations which are but pale reflections of an internal ideal, and which are literally manifested as lack, as 'wanting':

> Mingling with the vivid impression produced by the charm of her fair face and head . . . was another impression, which, in a shadowy way, suggested to me the idea of something wanting. At one time it seemed like something wanting in *her*; at another, like something wanting in myself, which hindered me from understanding her as I ought.[43]

Though this turns out to be, explicitly, a premonition of his recognition of Laura's physical association with Anne, it conceals within it, as its own trace, the construction of meaning through making hidden connections which Hartright's later assessment of his impressions makes clear. This means, too, that while his method of seeing in general needs to undergo a radical transformation between the two halves of the novel, with his vision of Laura there is a fundamental correspondence between his memory of his early impression and his later reconstruction; both simultaneously work through projection, and thus function, in associationist terms, as drawing inferences through comparison.

So Hartright sees others in accordance with their conformity to established conventions, by confusing 'sensations' with 'facts', while attempting a simplistic kind of linear reasoning. This builds up the sense of mystery, of strangeness within familiarity, at the beginning. With Marian's narrative, further into the story, suspense is heightened by the interaction between the greater subtlety and acuteness of her perceptions and the method by which they are narrated. Marian's perspective is not addressed to others as retrospective testimony; it is recorded for herself in her journal, which is crucially important as a means of observation and memory, as a method of self-control, and as a way of marking and controlling time.

It also springs from her contradictory position as a perceptive woman in a world where feminine sensitivity means sinking into vulnerability, and this becomes the source of a new kind of tension. Hartright's 'feminized' place caused him to sink into passivity and lassitude, though aware of the need to impose restraint and discipline on himself. Marian's interstitial position as 'masculine' poor relation, on the other hand, gives her a clear insight into the power relations and social conventions at work within the family, while also bringing the awareness that she can only retain the toe-hold of a limited and circumscribed influence by attempting to control those codes from within, and this means that the concept of 'self-control' for both her and Laura is fundamentally ambiguous – as it was for mid-nineteenth-century feminism. Marian's perception, moreover, goes through various stages during the first part of the story. In her first appearance as a figure in Hartright's narrative her wit and energy take the form chiefly of her resistance to feminine roles – her jokes about female accomplishments, feminine propriety, and so on. Her own narrative falls into two parts, the 'Limmeridge' and 'Blackwater' sections, both of which trace her mounting anxiety, the passage of Laura into an 'other' state, and Marian's own emotional or physical collapse; and it is this that contributes to the sense that Laura's transformation into Anne Catherick and incarceration in the asylum are but a re-enactment of their dress rehearsal – her transformation into Lady Glyde and incarceration in marriage. 'My mind feels almost as dulled and stunned by it, as if writing of her marriage were like writing of her death.'[44] This, however, also involves important shifts in her perception of Laura, herself, and the signs around her, in the 'Limmeridge' and 'Blackwater' sections of Marian's journal.

Initially Marian's analysis is dominated by the need to qualify her own perceptions critically and to control her sensations and reactions, and although she retains her scepticism she comes increasingly to use and analyse unconscious or symptomatic processes. At first she responds to and treats Laura almost as a possessive lover ('she will be *his* Laura instead of mind!') and as a benign keeper: 'There was too much colour in her cheeks, too much energy in her manner, too much firmness in her voice.'[45] But as Laura becomes reconciled to her fate of marriage to Glyde, this gives way to the realization that it is Laura's passivity which is pathological, not her 'hysterical vehemence' against it: 'She used to be pliability itself; but she was now inflexibly passive in her resignation . . . I should have been less pained if she had been violently agitated.'[46] In Marian's journal Limmeridge is a 'safe place', dominated by the wishes of the absent father, and a stage where she begins to be aware of tensions and manipulations. She begins to see expressions and mannerisms symptomatically rather than through a fixed set of physiognomic codes; she notes, for instance, Sir Percival's nervous cough, and his 'suppressed anxiety and agitation' not only 'in every line of his face', but still, after his face had relaxed: 'I saw one of his feet, softly, quietly, incessantly beating on the carpet, and I felt that he was secretly as anxious as ever.'[47] At this early stage, too, Marian uses her journal as a form of self-regulation, as an attempt to force herself to like Sir Percival despite her rising aversion towards and distrust of him: 'I cannot account for the state of my own feelings: the one thing I am certain of is, that it is my duty – doubly my duty, now – not to wrong Sir Percival by unjustly distrusting him', she writes.

> If it has got to be a habit with me always to write of him in an unfavourable manner, I must and will break myself of this unworthy tendency, even though the effort should force me to close the pages of my journal till the marriage is over.[48]

Self-regulation, therefore, means stopping writing; when she attempts to write favourably of Glyde, her comments grow increasingly sarcastic and strained, finally breaking out in the acknowlegement, 'I hate Sir Percival.'[49] This comes to be echoed and elaborated at Blackwater Park: 'It did me good, after all that I had suffered and suppressed in that house – it actually did me good to feel how angry I was.'[50]

The move to Blackwater and the heightening of tension as the gap between narrative time and story time narrows are told through Marian's increasingly acute perception and analysis of empirical processes, combined with a greater willingness to acknowledge the significance of unconscious states. Marian does not always trust her own perceptions, and she uses her distrust as a form of self-analysis, and here the friction between her impressions and her reflexive analysis of them in the journal is crucial. The journal shifts from being a passive receptacle of impressions and a means of self-regulation, to become a vehicle of both confession and analysis. On the one hand, this means fixing and explaining meanings:

> Putting together what I had observed for myself in the library, and what I have just observed for myself from Laura's maid, one

conclusion seems inevitable. The figure we saw at the lake was not the figure of Madam Fosco, or of her husband or any of the servants.[51]

On the other hand though, it means charting her own unconscious mental processes. This emerges most clearly in the premonitory 'supernatural' somnambulant trance that Marian experiences, for which she neither claims divine authority (as Anne does for her dream) nor totally dismisses it as delusion:

> My eyes closed of themselves; and I passed gradually into a strange condition, which was not waking – for I knew nothing of what was going on about me; and not sleeping – for I was conscious of my own repose. In this state my fevered mind broke loose from me, while my weary body was at rest; and, in a trance, or day dream of my fancy – I know not what to call it – I saw Walter Hartright.[52]

And it is immediately after being woken from the trance by Laura's account of a meeting with Anne, that Anne's testimony begins to signify.

Marian's trance is presented as a kind of clairvoyance, as a reverie that blurs the boundaries of consciousness, and as a fantasy through which she transcends the limits of time and space. But she herself is caught in a double bind, since having an acute perception and becoming a 'sensitive subject' to the influences around her do not increase her power but make her more susceptible to the manipulating influences of Fosco. Moral management and self-regulation are the only available means of resisting this, since 'so much depends on my discretion and self-control.'[53] Marian resists Fosco's power by distrusting 'the influence which [he] has exercised over my thoughts and feelings', yet it is through this double process of acknowledgement and resistance that Fosco's force becomes stronger, more flamboyant and pleasurable – he bounces up against Marian's frame and finally cracks it, as he is to do to Hartright's.[54] Distinct psychological codes are inflated and turned into means of manipulation in the figure of Fosco: moral management with his wife and Sir Percival, medical manipulation with Laura and Anne, mesmerism with Marian. He becomes a magical figure, fat and nimble, old and young, through the sheer variety of codes on which he draws as well as simultaneously exploiting and revealing them. Marian notes:

> I think the influence I am now trying to find, is in his eyes. They are the most unfathomable grey eyes I ever saw; and they have at times a cold, clear, beautiful, irresistible glitter in them, which

forces me to look at him and yet causes me sensations, when I do look, which I had rather not feel.[55]

And this is explicitly reinforced by the Count himself, who self-congratulatingly refers to his 'luminous experience of the more subtle resources which medical and magnetic science have placed at the disposal of mankind.'[56]

Thus it is in the paradoxically 'carnivalesque' figure of the upper-class villain that the dominant codes both of the narrative and the social order are displayed and overturned. With his process of moral management, humans and animals become direct equivalents, breaking the very boundaries that the treatment itself depends on. Sir Percival, the neurotic continually teetering on the brink of self-control, responds to the Count's stare 'with the sullen submission of a tamed animal', just as Fosco subdues the violent bloodhound with a withering look.[57] His domestication of the white mice who crawl fondly over his body is a parody and commentary on his management of his wife, the formerly flamboyant and undisciplined Eleanor Fairlee, who is ruled by the combination of fear and a flattery which feeds on what Marian has previously, in relation to Laura, described as 'that despicably-small pride which makes so many women deceitful.'[58] Indeed, Marian's observation of the transformation of her aunt Eleanor Fairlie into Madame Fosco, clothed in her stiff black gowns, is the inversion, the literal negative, of the therapeutic framework of moral managment that is applied 'positively' to Anne, more ambiguously to Laura. She is represented as the subdued, disciplined, previously wayward female patient – the frozen model of propriety of the model asylum:

As Eleanor Fairlie (aged seven-and-thirty), she was always talking pretentious nonsense, and always worrying the unfortunate men with every small exaction which a vain and foolish woman can impose on long-suffering male humanity. As Madame Fosco (aged three-and-forty), she sits for hours together without saying a word, frozen up in the strangest manner in herself. . . . A plain, matronly cap covers her head, and makes her look, for the first time in her life, since I remember her, like a decent woman. . . . Clad in quiet black or grey gowns, made high about the throat – dresses that she would have laughed at, or screamed at, as the whim of the moment inclined her, in her maiden days – she sits speechless in corners; her dry white hands (so dry that the pores of her skin look chalky) incessantly engaged, either in monotonous embroidery-work, or in rolling up endless little cigarettes for the Count's own particular smoking. On the few occasions when her cold blue eyes are off her work, they are generally turned on her husband, with the look of mute submissive enquiry which we are all familiar with in the eyes of a faithful dog.[59]

On contemplating this transformation Marian arrives at an explicit analysis of the process of social and psychic suppression on which it rests:

> For the common purposes of society the extraordinary change thus produced in her, is, beyond all doubt, a change for the better, seeing that it has transformed her into a civil, silent, unobtrusive woman who is never in the way. How far she is really reformed or deteriorated in her secret self, is another question. I have once or twice seen sudden changes of expression on her pinched lips, and heard sudden inflexions of tone in her calm voice, which have led me to suspect that her present state of suppression may have sealed up something dangerous in her nature, which used to evaporate harmlessly in the freedom of her former life. It is quite possible that I may be altogether wrong in this.[60]

The transformed Eleanor Fairlie thus adds another twist to the chain of women, the web of relationships between femininity and insanity, set up by the novel. As a frivolous and ridiculour spinster before her marriage she is Marian's opposite – manifesting all the aspects of unrestrained femininity that Marian resolutely distances herself from; a version of Pritchard's definition of female insanity as breaking the boundaries of propriety in her 'want of self-government, continual excitement, unusual expression of strong feelings, thoughtless and extravagant conduct' and an echo of Conolly's Eliza Nottridge too – confined so that her unseemly exuberance could be regulated.[61] As Madame Fosco, who sees Marian as a rival for the Count's affections, she not only functions as the shadow of Laura and the negative of Anne but, by exaggerating compatible patterns of perception so that they laid bare as a mechanism of control, both inverts and exposes them.

Fosco's power is compounded by his perverse attractiveness, just as Marian acknowledges, 'The man has interested me, has attracted me, has forced me to like him.'[62] And he is such a pleasurable, energetic figure precisely because of the range of ways that he works against the grain of conventions that Hartright's perspective above all depends on. Here there is a direct correspondence between the way the figure operates as a fictional construct that challenges various physiognomic assumptions and queries conventions through his contradictory and anomalous identity, and the way in which he 'pulls the strings' of the narrative itself while remaining a figure within it. 'I had begun to write my story when it struck me that my villain would be commonplace, and I made him fat in opposition to the recognised type of villain', Collins noted in a retrospective assessment of the novel.[63] Fosco resists being a 'recognised type' by the unexpected juxtaposing of different elements, both within himself and in relation to others, and this at once reinforces and overturns his villainy. There is clearly a close relationship between his sexual power and his 'foreignness' for example, but here he eludes any stable stereotypical framework, partly by his opposition to Pesca, the other Italian. While the diminutive Pesca, as presented patronizingly by Hartright, is made ridiculous and childlike by his unsuccessful attempts to imitate English manners and customs and English common sense and propriety, Fosco's power is derived precisely from his command of the language and the codes of 'English common sense' as well as his ability to manipulate', through relativizing, 'English' morality:

> I have met, in my time, with so many different sorts of virtue, that I am puzzled, in my old age, to say which is the right sort and which is the wrong. Here, in England, there is one virtue. And there in China, there is another virtue.[64]

In this way Fosco 'lays bare the device' of dominant social, psychological, and medical conventions even as he makes use of them to manipulate the narrative and conjure with Laura's identity. His diagnosis of Marian's typhus fever is more accurate than the local doctor's and he uses her physical breakdown as the final means of overpowering her.

> I say what other people only think, and when all the world is in a conspiracy to accept the mask for the true face, mine is the rash hand that tears away the plump pasteboard and reveals the bare bones beneath.[65]

Yet it is *because* of the 'conspiracy' of shared recognition that Fosco is able to substitute Laura for Anne; this in turn suggests that Laura's 'true face' is nothing but a constructed mask, laid over 'bare bones'. Hartright's early physiognomic reading of Laura's face – his idealist extrapolations – are here satirically undercut by Fosco's more cynical implied phrenology which lays bare the material base of the mind. It is a materialism that culminates in the physiological determinism of pharmacology, seen here by Fosco as a means of transformation and control, not, as for Ezra Jennings in The *Moonstone*, as a means of psychological investigation, still less of inspiration:

> Mind they say, rules the world. But what rules the mind? The body. The body . . . lies at the mercy of the most powerful of all potentates – the Chemist. Give me – Fosco – chemistry; and when Shakespeare had conceived Hamlet, and sits down to execute the conception – with a few grains of powder dropped into his daily food, I will reduce his mind, by the action of his body, till his pen pours out the most abject drivel that ever degraded paper.[66]

Thus in the First Part of the narrative Hartright, Marian, and Fosco each draw out the contrasting implications of a shared discourse of moral management as an implicit perceptual framework of regulation and control. Hartright is set within it in a way that undermines his self-possession: he is manifested as an ineffectual moral agent, who can only see the future as an obscure and incomprehensible fatality, a transcendent authority which eludes him. Fosco makes this explicit, and in the process inverts the pattern of moral regulation so that indeterminacy is replaced completely by a determined narrative: the hidden tensions of the 'secret theatre' of the family stripped down to the workings of marionettes: 'What are we (I ask) but puppets in a show box? Oh omnipotent Destiny, pull our strings gently! Dance us mercifully off our miserable little stage!'[67]

Fosco's villainy remains ideologically ambiguous in the very way that it is set up to exploit the ambiguity of psychological discourses themselves, to display how social and psychic power works, yet also to wield it by pushing the psychological codes to their grotesque conclusion.[68] But he also expresses what the narrative structure itself makes clear – that history is usually written by the winning side:

> If the police win, you generally hear all about it. If the police lose you generally hear nothing. And on this tottering foundation you build up your comfortable moral maxim that Crime causes its own detection. Yes – all the crime *you* know of. And what of the rest?[69]

This double perspective is achieved by the ambiguous position of Fosco's final narrative – his letter of confession – both embedded within Hartright's specific narrative and a specific narrative in its own right, as I suggested earlier. In order to analyse this, and the process that underlies Hartright's ascendancy and his reconstruction of Laura, it is necessary to pick up the threads I left hanging above, and consider how Hartright's ability to determine the future by reinterpreting the past is bound up with his control over memory and time, and the ideological and fictional dissonance that this endangers.

The control of time is vital in *The Woman in White*. Collins hastily amended his early error in timing, and the central sleight of hand that enables Fosco to substitute Laura for Anne lies in his 'stealing' a day. But the method by which it is controlled undergoes important modifications at different stages of the narrative. In the First Part, it has been seen that ominousness is created by uncertainty about the future, which generates present anxiety; derangement is synonymous with the inability to mark or control time, and this is achieved by the ways in which the two orders of time, progression and reconstruction, narrative time and story time, interrelate. The control of time is crucial for Marian's self-control and opposition to Fosco. It becomes a subtle form of female resistance – the way that patience can be turned into resolution. Marian stresses: 'The question of time, is *our* question, and trust me, Laura, to take a woman's full advantage of it.'[70] Marian's use of her journal as a way of recording and verifying information is crucial, particularly in the way that it is bound up with her control over her own memory:

> It was almost as great a relief to my mind as to Laura's, to find that my memory had served me, on this occasion, as faithfully as usual. In the perilous uncertainty of our present situation, it is hard to say what future interests may not depend upon the regularity of the entries in my journal and upon the reliability of my recollection at the time when I make them.[71]

Thus the tension of the narrative increases as she becomes increasingly obsessed by the control of time. Her breakdown through fever is marked by the gradual convergence of narrative time and story time, finally attained when her own writing peters out and Fosco takes the pen from her hand:

> *June 20th* – Eight o'clock . . . I count the hours that have passed since I escaped to the shelter of this room by my own sensations – and those hours seem like weeks.
> How short a time, and yet how long to *me*. . . . Yes, I heard the

clock strike three . . . I remember my resolution to control myself, I wait patiently for hour after hour. . . . Nine o'clock. Was it nine that struck, or eight?

My head, I am sadly afraid for my head. I can write, but the lines all run together. I see the words. Laura, I can write Laura and I see that I write it. Eight or nine, which was it.[72]

Here too, the merging of the two registers of narrative order is marked by the presence of Fosco.

'I trace these lines, self-distrustfully, with the shadow of after-events darkening the very paper I write on.'[73] Hartright's early ambivalence towards his own testimony, his awareness that all recall involves retrojection, are explicitly overturned in the second half of the novel, where the drive of the narrative becomes increasingly to reach Hartright's and the story's resolution. But the impossible figure that it represents (where, exactly, can the narrating voice be located in this sentence?) is indicative of the narrative paradox that is the fulcrum of *The Woman in White*. The lined chain of evidence that makes up the First Part of the story can only be constructed by an authority that has been produced by it, and in the Second and Third Parts this is made clear in the way in which the two Hartright's, the General Editor and the specific narrator, merge. Closer scrutiny of this process reveals that as a chain, Hartright's method of presenting the evidence involves all kinds of omissions and distortions. Initially he starts out keeping to the rules that he has set up as General Editor, dropping out of the story as he leaves Limmeridge and letting Gilmour take it up. But Gilmour's narrative later turns out to have been written over four years after the events took place. This process of reading is more significant in the case of Marian's journal. This seems to be the most authentic and immediate testimony, yet paradoxically the device which enhances its authenticity – Hartright's note, which makes it clear that the reader is presented with a selection from Marian's absent, fuller journal – creates the illusion that more has been written just beyond the line of vision, in the breaks that interspace the testimony.

By the beginning of the Second Part, with its merging of the two narrative roles, Hartright's increased management of himself, his growing control over the progress of the story, and his gradual reconstruction of Laura are more immediately bound up with the appropriation of absent testimonials. 'No circumstance of importance, from the beginning to the end of this disclosure, shall be related on hearsay evidence.' The statement in the Preamble is tacitly reversed here. The crucial section of the story – Hartright's analysis of Laura's experience leading to her confinement in the asylum, and his construction of the chain of circumstantial evidence that leads to his discovery of the *absent* names in the marriage register, testifying to Sir Percival's illegitimacy ('That space told the whole story') and to the true identity of Anne – is dependent on his own interpretation of testimonials that cannot be presented directly to the reader.[74] Indeed, in opposing 'the eye of reason and of law' and 'every received formality of civilised society'; and in perpetuating a false deception in order to unmask the true one by appearing 'in the estimation of others [as] at once the dupes and the agents of a daring imposture', Hartright becomes the *reader's* moral manager, and upturns both narrative construct and psychological framework.[75] And this in turn also involves the suppression of memory in order for Hartright to emerge as a resolution agent. The Second Part opens:

> I open a new page, I advance my narrative by one week.
> The history of the interval which I thus pass over must remain unrecorded. My heart turns faint, my mind sinks in darkness and confusion when I think of it. This must not be, if I, who write, am to guide, as I ought, you who read. This must not be if the clue that leads through the windings of the Story is to remain, from end to end, untangled in my hand.[76]

Thus the clue, or thread, which leads through the labyrinth of the story itself can only be woven by the deliberate forgetting of part of Hartright's own narrative of 'how he came to be there . . . poring over it'. And he can only transform the ravelled skein of the story into a coherent web by assimilating the separate memories of the witnesses, and turning them into a chain of associations which regulate it, as he switches from directly presenting the separate narratives as evidence to the reader, to analysing the different testimonials, the accounts of Marian, Mrs Clements, Mrs Catherick, Laura, and pieces together Anne's confused associations. 'I shall relate both narratives, not in the words (often interrupted, often inevitably confused) of the speakers themselves', he notes of Marian and Laura's rememberance of the confinement, 'but in the words of the brief, plain, studiously-simple abstract which I committed to writing for my guidance of my legal advisor. So the tangled web will be most speedily and most intelligibly unrolled.[77] In the case of Mrs Clements this involves replacing open testimony with interrogation:

Knowing by experience that the plainest narrative attainable from persons who are not accustomed to arrange their ideas is the narrative which goes far enough back at the beginning to avoid all impediments of retrospection in its course, I asked Mrs Clements to tell me, first, what had happened after she left Limmeridge; and so, by watchful questioning, carried her on from point to point till we recalled the period of Anne's disappearance.[78]

This in turn leads to the decoding of Anne's knowledge of Sir Percival's secret, the realization that the secret contained another, but that Anne's threateningness was itself unconscious – that she knew a secret existed without knowing what it contained. Thus the truth is built up by cross-currents of delusion. Sir Percival confines Anne because he believes the delusion which is 'perfectly in character with [her] mental affliction', which in turn 'afterwards fixed in his mind the equally false suspicion that his wife knew all from Anne.'[79] Hartright discloses that Laura has been confined for another's fear of a knowledge she never possessed as well as for her property. But the process by which her identity is restored can never take the form of the complete exploration of her memory, since this itself would upset the moral treatment of her cure, through which distressing associations are laid to rest. 'The fair companion of your retreat shall not be pursued. She has found a new asylum, in your heart', Fosco writes to Marian.[80] It is in the anonymous safety of the London streets that the sinister connotations of the asylum now become transformed back into friendly ones, as Laura's cure takes the form, in the first place, of the imaginary reconstruction of the past at Limmeridge that could almost be based on combining Conolly's *The Treatment of the Insane Without Mechanical Restraints* with Samuel Tuke's *A Description of the Retreat* – 'nursing the faculties' by recreating the 'first home' that Hartright had earlier found so enervating:

> The only events of former days which we ventured on encouraging her to recall were the little trivial domestic events of that happy time at Limmeridge when I first went there, and taught her to draw. Tenderly and gradually, the memory of the old walks and drives dawned upon her; and the poor weary pining eyes, looked at Marian and me with a new interest, with a faltering thoughtfulness in them, which, from that moment, we cherished, and kept alive. I bought her a little box of colours, and a sketch-book like the old sketch book which I had seen in her hands on the morning when we first met. . . .

We helped her mind slowly by this simple means; we took her out between us to walk, on fine days, in a quiet old City square, near at hand, where there was nothing to confuse or alarm her; we spared a few pounds from the fund at the bankers to get her wine, and the delicate strengthening food that she required; we amused her in the evenings with children's games at cards, with scrapbooks full of prints . . . by these, and other trifling attentions like them, we composed and steadied her, and hoped all things, as cheerfully as we could, from time and care, and love that never neglected and never despaired of her. But to take her mercilessly from seclusion and repose; to confront her with strangers, or with acquaintances who were little better than strangers; to rouse the painful impressions of her past life which we had so carefully hushed to rest – this, even in her own interests, we dared not do. Whatever sacrifices it cost, whatever long, weary, heart-breaking delays it involved, the wrong that had been inflicted on her, if mortal means could grapple with it, must be redressed without her knowledge and without her help.[81]

Laura can only finally have her social identity restored and regain her property through the recognition of the family and the law, a recognition which takes place by Hartright's struggles on her behalf, in control of himself and finally in control of the story. But just as Hartright's own resolution springs from social obliteration and displacement with Marian as 'help meet', so Laura's reconstitution also depends on her class transformation:

We are numbered no longer with the people whose lives are open and known. I am an obscure, unnoticed man, without patron or friend to help me. Marian Halcombe is nothing now, but my elder sister, who toils for our household wants by the toil of her own hands.[82]

Laura's growing self-possession is marked by her realization that she is economically and sexually powerless and treated like a child: 'You work and get money, Walter . . . why is there nothing I can do? You will end up in liking Marian better than you like me.' This realization is marked by Hartright's 'innocent deception' whereby he pays her phantom wages for her drawings.[83] So just as Anne learnt, as a child, to be a proper lady at Limmeridge House, so it is only through poverty and imaginary work that Laura can retake her place as member of the landed gentry and as Hartright's property; a proper 'self-made' woman who has really been made by others in the theatre of a simulated family.

Finally *The Woman in White* depends on transforming particular patterns of suspense into the means of closure. There is nothing particularly unusual about this, and if if were not the case, the story would not be able to end at all. Nor is it strange that the mystery should open up questions and contradictions that exceed the perspective of the 'resolute' consciousness that is finally able to control both the self and the narrative. But the novel is extraordinary in the way in which the narrative discourse itself displays the impossibility of drawing a precise boundary between fictional and psychological codes. And this is a reciprocal process: psychological references and allusions produce narrative tensions, yet at the same time the narrative manipulation of these methods subverts them in one register and highlights their contradictions in another. Thus the discourse of moral management remains the ascendant framework in the story, yet its meaning is continually transformed both as it combines with other psychic mechanisms, and as these mechanisms come to correspond more and more closely to different forms of social definitions through the manipulation of psychological power.

4

Skins to jump into
Femininity as masquerade in
No Name

It might be worthwhile, sometimes, to inquire what
Nature is, and how men work to change her, and
whether, in the enforced distortions so produced, it is
not natural to be unnatural.

Charles Dickens, *Dombey and Son*[1]

Nothing in this world is hidden for ever. The gold
which has lain for centuries unsuspected in the
ground, reveals itself one day on the surface. Sand
turns traitor, and betrays the footsteps that have
passed over it; water gives back to the tell-tale surface
the body which has been drowned. Look where we
will, the inevitable law of revelation is one of the laws
of nature: the lasting presentation of a secret is a
miracle that the world has not yet seen.

Wilkie Collins, *No Name*[2]

If you're all rakes, Miss Garth, the sexes are turned
topsy-turvy with a vengeance; and the men will have
nothing left for it, but to sit at home and darn the
stockings.

Wilkie Collins, *No Name*[3]

'It will be seen that the narrative related in these pages has been
constructed on a plan, which differs from the plan followed by my
last novel', Collins' emphasized in the Preface to *No Name*.

The only secret contained in this book is revealed halfway through
the first volume. From that point, all the main events in the story
are purposefully foreshadowed, before they take place – my present
design being to rouse the reader's interest in following the train of
circumstances by which these foreseen events are brought about.[4]

131

No Name takes the form of an obsessive pursuit of a lost social self – a transgressive quest that culminates in a breakdown that leads finally to the restitution of identity and a legitimate social role. The secret revealed half-way through the first volume is the disclosure of illegitimate origins. But while in *The Woman in White* this was the final exposure and explanation of the villain's pathological behaviour – and of the meaning of the shadowy Anne – here it is the initial absence, a revelation that creates the precondition for a new kind of mystery, as the reader is drawn into contemplating the relationship between the outcome and the precipitating causes of events, and psychological responses. The strategy works precisely because of the uncertainty of the 'how' rather than the 'what' of the story, and by the tension that is generated between the means by which events are 'purposefully foreshadowed' and the processes through which they remain indeterminate in order to retain suspense. In *The Woman in White* a cloud of ominous 'foreshadowing' hung over the multiple narrative voices. In *No Name* a range of rhetorics play with the discursive resources of the omniscient narrative voice, parodying it even as they carry it forward. It is a story of 'perversity', Collins's most explicit treatment of the formation of social identity and of the cultural construction of femininity outside and inside the family. It is also a perverse story – not simply one in which the narrative rhetoric is the direct analogue of identity and subjectivity, but one in which self and narrative become equivocal through working against the grain of the dominant voice, following instead the story's elements of plotting, play and diversity.

No Name is the story of what happens to two young middle-class women, Magdalen and Norah Vanstone, when they discover that they literally have no name: that they are illegitimate and have no claim to their dead parents' property or class position. The novel opens with a leisurely account of a domestic idyll which is made to seem the more nostalgically safe and natural when contrasted with the loss which is hinted at from the start. It is quickly followed by the parents' untimely death and the revelation that the property is to revert to the father's enemy, their uncle, and on *his* death, to Noel Vanstone, his sickly son. The story traces how the sisters' 'natures' respond to this sudden withdrawal of a given social self as they are projected into a hostile and indifferent world. Norah patiently submits to her fate and takes on the ready-made identity for genteel femininity fallen on hard times, predictably becoming a governess; but Magdalen casts herself out into the world to speculate on the open market – initially by acknowledging her lack of a given self by taking to the stage. From here she moves from one disguise to another and, in collaboration with her mother's stepbrother (or false uncle) the unashamed confidence trickster Captain Wragge, succeeds in marrying her cousin under an assumed name, a performance that fails in turn with *his* untimely death. She then takes on the role of servant in the *next* heir's family, her obsessive desire to retrieve her lost name finally breaking down into hysteria and nervous collapse from which she is improbably rescued by a substitute strong father – the merchant seaman, Captain Kirke. Meanwhile, the good sister, Norah, regains the name and position 'legitimately' by marrying the inheriting cousin, subjectively filling the role that Magdalen had taken on as a masquerade, and again, as in *The Woman in White*, transforming the initial sources of ambiguity and tensions into the means of narrative closure.

Like *The Woman in White*, *No Name* was written for publication both as a weekly serial and as a three-volume novel; it was serialized in *All the Year Round*, and nearly all the 4,000 copies of the first edition were sold on the day of publication, the majority bought by Mudie's for library circulation. In spite of Dickens's intervention in its planning, *No Name* was crucial in consolidating Collins's career as an independent professional novelist; he received £3,000 for the copyright of the novel from its publishers Sampson Low, but he was only able to command this price as a result of the massive success of *The Woman in White*.[5] And in generating suspense by focusing on the process of plotting *within* the narrative, rather than a secret revealed at the end, *No Name* illustrates particularly clearly the constraints as well as the possibilities open to sensation fiction – that the excitement lies in the strategies pursued by a deviant heroine yet this transgression has finally to be morally and fictionally assimilated. Magdalen is no fallen woman, despite the unmistakable connotations of her name, yet her machinations were bound up with the novel's 'morbid' obsession with plot in many critics' minds.

> The Magdalen of *No Name* does not go astray after the usual fashion of erring maidens in romance. The pollution is decorous, and justified by law; and after all her endless deceptions and horrible marriage, it seems quite right to the author that she should be restored to society, and have a good husband and a happy home

commented Margaret Oliphant in *Blackwood's*, after insisting,

> Mr. Wilkie Collins . . . has chosen, by way of making his heroine piquant and interesting . . . to throw her into a career of vulgar

and aimless trickery and wickedness, with which it is impossible to have a shadow of sympathy, but from all the pollutions of which he intends us to believe she emerges, at the cheap cost of a fever, as pure, as high-minded and as spotless as the most dazzling white of heroines.[6]

'Everything is tense, strained and unnatural', noted the *North British Review*, anticipating the response to *Armadale*. 'The characters are preternaturally acute . . . every incident is charged with oppressive importance.'[7]

Yet the complexities of *No Name* cannot simply be explained by suggesting that Collins was attempting to 'evade the censor' of the assumptions of his readers, for of all the novels of the 1860s this has the most apparently tendentious as well as the most 'playful' tone; it is the book in which he most clearly counterposes a 'false' and meretricious social morality with a superior one that exposes its limitations, even as this is mediated through a narrative voice that continually undercuts the sources of its own ideological coherence. For like *Basil*, *No Name* is set up as a psychological case study; its tensions emerge from the inconsistencies within the central figure. But that central figure is now a woman, without a given social identity, and the internal contradictions that she poses are mediated not through the convolutions of the confessional form, but through the external 'anatomising' voice of the narrator. 'Here is one more book', Collins wrote in the Preface:

> that depicts the struggle of a human creature, under those opposing influences of Good and Evil which we have all felt. . . . It has been my aim to make the character of 'Magdalen', which personifies this struggle a pathetic character even in its perversity and its error: and I have tried hard to retain this result by the least obtrusive and least artificial of all means – a resolute adherence, throughout, to the truth as it is in Nature.[8]

As in *Basil*, the loss of name and exile from the family reveal the patterns of power through which identity is built up within it; and these forms of power are consolidated through bringing together discourses of moral management and inheritance. But the terms of that combination have shifted with the means of constructing identity in the narrative itself; for what *No Name* reveals above all is the impossibility of representing a coherent female subjectivity, a 'true nature'. Within the overarching narrative rhetoric it inverts the conventions of moral management to take apart the social codes that make up femininity, and this turns into a satirical exploration of the relationship between progress and decadence, of what constitutes fitness and what is meant by survival, by invoking an ambiguous rhetoric not simply of inheritance, but of evolution and natural selection.

In the first chapter I argued that there was no one interpretation or inflection of evolutionary discourse in the mid-nineteenth-century. Indeed the early 1860s can be seen as a moment of extraordinary diversity within contrasting and overlapping discourses of inheritance, transmission, and genealogy. Notions of progress begin to transmute into degeneration; the concept of continuous transmission is transformed by adaptation; a unilinear narrative of change combines and clashes with plurality, diversity, and chance, even as organic metaphors and models are overwhelmingly deployed to fix social and sexual identity and to naturalize difference. Identity is both shaped and objectified through these dissonant codes in *No Name*, and it is thus that the natural itself is revealed to be socially shaped – reinforcing class and gender boundaries, yet at the same time providing the terms that undermine them. In this way 'truth as it is in Nature' is a continually shifting term in the narrative, and it can be used for distinct purposes in contexts that play with different kinds of oppositions. It implies inexorable processes, organic laws beyond human intervention, while suggesting that the parameters of the natural and the social are impossible to pin down. The sisters turn out to be 'natural' children, illegitimate and outside the law, but there is no 'natural order' to which they can return. It implies an inner core of being, but that subjectivity is shaped in ways that provide contradictory models of development.

Initially, however, the tensions and pleasures of *No Name* depend on making the ideological concerns of *The Woman in White* more explicit. And here the very intrusiveness of the moral voice of the narrator opens up a space in which the conventions and presuppositions of moral management that were the sources of contradiction and coherence in the previous book can be pushed to their limits. Both novels hinge on probing the boundaries of the social self, and explore how a 'legitimate' identity is in many ways a trick of the light created by the manipulation of self-possession and propriety, underpinned by economic interests. 'Shall I tell you what a lady is?' Magdalen asks her maid whom she is training to be her substitute, so that she can pose as a servant. 'A lady is a woman who wears a silk gown, and has a sense of her own importance.'[9] Both novels explore the position of women stripped of property and inheritance, but while

in *The Woman in White* the literal extension and analogue of this position were found in the non-restraint asylum, Magdalen and Norah
Vanstone have inheritance and identity stolen, not through a dubious
conspiracy but by the legitimate workings of the law. Structurally,
Magdalen's plot to reclaim her name puts her in a position
corresponding to that of Percival Glyde, but the patterns of sympathy
and identification are reversed, not least because she comes from a
position of powerlessness. The sisters' *literal* illegitimacy is now the
dramatic analogue of their economic powerlessness as women, as well
as being an anomaly in itself. The narrator might explicitly question
Magdalen's assertion that 'any conspiracy, any deception, is justified
to my conscience by the vile law which has left us helpless', but not
the fact that the law *is* vile.[10]

The use of these different devices as fulcrums for the transformation of identity also amends the way in which *No Name*, like *The
Woman in White*, undercuts any stable division between 'same' and
'other', wildness and domesticity, putting moral management as the
means of that subversion to distinctive kinds of use. In both,
apparently aberrant or perverse forces are threatening because they
display the workings of the social conventions that create them by
setting up boundaries founded on their exclusion; at the same time,
too, both depend on reinforcing these boundaries by the contrast
between passive and resolute women. Anne Catherick, the
illegitimate outcast of unsound mind, echoed passive domesticity
rather than unassimilable wildness, just as her asylum was modelled
on 'home'; Laura's powerlessness was compounded therefore by
moving 'inwards' into an exclusion that was an extreme version of
that from which it was excluded, a contrast reinforced by Marian,
whose strength resided in her marginality. In *No Name* both sisters
are cast out of the middle-class family into a competitive and indifferent world, but their struggle for survival both brings them back
into it and in different ways reveals its concealed underside. At first
there seems to be a clear contrast between the passive Norah, who
takes on the protective colouring of a governess, and Magdalen, who
is described as 'resolute and impetuous, clever and domineering . . .
not one of those model women who want a man to look up to, and
to protect them.'[11] But this contrast is broken down in an
ambivalent way that on the one hand reinforces the 'moral fable'
aspect of the story, emphasizing Norah's patient moral force, but on
the other explicitly demonstrates the very propriety from which the
sisters are exiled to be a masquerade.

For in moving 'out' the heroine is again, in effect, moving

'inwards', and the use of the theatre rather than the asylum as the crucible for the shaping and transformation of identity is a crucial focus for this involuted process. Magdalen transgresses not because the roles she plays are themselves unseemly but because they are obviously a series of seemings, pursued shamelessly to autonomously advance her own ends. And while this behaviour is seen as a sign that she is 'not sufficiently mistress of herself to exert her natural judgment', it is none the less essentially an aping of the process by which female self-possession and propriety are built up by enacting a domestic tableau in the 'theatre of home' within the moral management framework.[12] Magdalen's self-consciously assumed roles are exaggerated re-enactments of the world that she has lost: her first public entertainment is 'A young lady at home', a performance of private feminine domesticity. Her dramatic skills are first developed in the prelapsarian days of the family in an amateur production of *The Rivals*. Here Magdalen plays two parts, representing two roles of femininity: Julia, which she bases on a 'cool appropriation of Norah's identity', and Lucy, the coquettish maid, which prefigures her own later role.[13] She disguises herself as her governess to gain entrance to Noel Vanstone's household; and in collaboration with Wragge she takes on the character of what he calls one of his many 'Skins to Jump Into',[14] a ready-made identity to be assumed at a moment's notice, acting the role of innocent middle-class girl to lure Noel into marriage. This in turn displays the economic underpinnings of female legitimacy: 'Thousands of women marry for money, why shouldn't I?' Magdalen asks herself.[15] And thus the conscious assumption of a role becomes a more 'honest' dissimulation than the reality on which it is based. 'You may depend on my never making the general Sense of Propriety my enemy again: I am getting enough knowledge of the world to make it my accomplice this time', she writes to her governess: 'My life as a public performer is at an end. It was innocent enough, God knows.'[16] And again, having married Noel:

> I don't wish to tell you I was the reformed and repenting creature whom *you* might have approved . . . I am no longer the poor outcast girl, the vagabond public performer . . . I have made the general sense of propriety my accomplice. . . . Do you know who I am? I am a respectable married woman, accountable for my actions to nobody under heaven but my husband. I have got a place in the world, and a name in the world at last. . . . You forget what wonders my wickedness has done for me. It has made Nobody's Child, Somebody's Wife.[17]

Thus Magdalen's transgression is transformed into adaptation by pushing the codes of moral management through their own limits. The 'skin' into which she jumps has been formed by the 'general Sense of Propriety' and is already shaped by social use, but the satirical use of the evolutionary analogy equally imples that the 'self' that jumps into the skin is nothing more than a previously discarded role. The cynical philosopher asks Magdalen 'What is this mask of yours hiding?' and in a sense all that can be revealed is another mask.[18] This highlights the paradox that I mentioned earlier, that narrative tension, and therefore the survival of the story itself, is generated by perversity taking the form of multiplicity, while needing to be continually realigned within a linear narrative of moral growth and improvement. The contrast between Magdalen and Norah explicates this in a completely straightforward way. Norah is continually referred to as the touchstone of worthiness by the narrator, but her dilemmas and struggles can never be made interesting. She can only hover, boringly, on the periphery of the story to be wheeled on as a means of narrative closure, along with that even more improbable *deux ex machina* figure, the paragon of colonial fitness, Robert Kirke. The dominant narrative voice undergoes a pattern of development that corresponds to Lamarck's model of willed transformation, setting itself against the perverse resolution of the heroine.[19] But this is qualified by other figures, most notably Captain Wragge; and there is always a countervailing element within the the narrative which is foregrounded in the open pattern generated by the serial instalment rather than the final three-volume form. This tacit process resorts to chance and hidden associations to reach its premonitored conclusion, so that the rhetoric which shapes the terms which shapes the figures does so by juxtaposing contrasting definitions of 'fitness' itself, and it is through the dissonance of these notions of fitness that it questions the 'natural' of natural selection.

This question of the 'natural' is posed, above all, around the quest and metamorphosis of Magdalen, the central problematic identity. But the heroine is also an anomalous figure in that collective entity, the family, and the novel explores the family's organic identity as well as illusionary social coherence. Both sisters regain their place by marrying cousins – Magdalen the morbid one, Norah the healthy one – so that the conventional means of refitting the heroine into a right place here also transforms organic diversity back into unity. Yet there is a shift in the significance of inheritance here, in contrast with *Basil* and *The Woman in White*; genealogy is not transmuted into social and psychic transmission in quite the same way. The withdrawal of the original family as a social mould leaves the sisters in a liminal state and disrupts the natural order as they are catapulted into a hostile environment. Yet the original family itself is presented as the inversion of Collins's earlier symbolic roles – the father is a benign and ineffectual figure, and Magdalen treats him 'as if he was a kind of younger brother of hers'.[20] Instead, vestiges of parental positions are perpetuated in the shape of honorary elder relatives who have no biological link with the central figures: Miss Garth, the governess; Francis Clare, Senior, father of Magdalen's unworthy lover; Wragge, who claims the place of honorary uncle; Mme Lecount, Noel's housekeeper and manipulative substitute mother.

Miss Garth, the governess, with her 'air of habitual authority', is not simply a substitute for the absent parents but takes their place as the focus of 'friendly authority' even before their death. The psychological questions that are explicitly set up as the sisters respond to their calamity are focused through the indirectly reported thoughts of the governess who has 'studied the natures of her two pupils in the daily intimacy of twelve years', thoughts which have a correspondingly copy-book quality about them, and could be taken as extracts from a popular treatise on the incubation of inherited latent traits, revealing at the same time their allegorical moral quality through physiognomic signs.[21]

Does there exist in every human being, beneath that outward and visible character which is shaped into form by the social influences surrounding us, an inward, invisible disposition, which is part of ourselves, which education may directly modify, but can never hope to change? Is the philosophy which denies this, and asserts that we are born with dispositions like blank sheets of paper, a philosophy which has failed to remark that we are not born with blank faces – a philosophy which has never compared together two infants of a few days old and has never observed that those infants are not born with blank tempers for mothers and nurses to fill up at will? Are there, infinitely varying with each individual, inbred forces of Good and Evil in all of us, deep down beneath the reach of mortal encouragement and moral repression – hidden Good and hidden Evil, both alike at the mercy of the liberating opportunity and the sufficient temptation? Within these earthly limits is earthly circumstance ever the key; and can no human vigilance warn us before hand of those forces imprisoned in ourselves which that key *may* unlock?[22]

The governess, like Norah, operates as the tacit and marginal voice of common sense in the novel, but her perspective – moral management modified by predetermined inheritance – is qualified in the first place by Francis Clare, honorary absent father and alternative voice from the prelapsarian world. The member of the 'younger branch of a family of great antiquity' whose 'views of human nature were the views of Diogenes, tempered by Rochefoucault', and who is set up as a personification of 'eighteenth-century' scepticism ('his favourite poets were Horace and Pope; his chosen philosophers Hobbes and Voltaire'),[23] Clare's analysis of the likely future of his vapid son is also set up as an explicit hypothesis. His voice becomes an alternative peripheral form of 'traditional good sense', a modified Hobbes as Miss Garth's is a modified Locke, and in his view established privilege favours the incompetent, as against 'native' wit:

> I have always maintained that the one important phenomenon presented by modern society is – the enormous prosperity of Fools. Show me an individual fool, and I will show you an aggregate society which gives that highly favoured personage nine chances out of ten – and grudges the tenth to the wisest man in existence. Look where you will, in every high place there sits an Ass, settled beyond the reach of all the greatest intellects in this world to pull him down. Over our whole social system, complacent Imbecility rules supreme, snuffs out the searching light of Intelligence, with total impunity – and hoots, owl-like, in answer to every form of protest, See how well we all do in the dark! One of these days that audacious assertion will be practically contradicted; and the whole rotten system of modern society will come down with a crash.[24]

These contrasted established positions, typified by archetypal figures as representing alternative discourses of development, each pessimistic, each emphasizing a 'truth of nature' to be modified by circumstance either as unlocking hidden dispositions or as selecting them, are set up as ideologically dissonant hypotheses that foreshadow the unfolding of the central drive of the narrative. But another process is also taking place here in which the narrative itself questions its own teleological implications, elaborating Spencer's use of von Baer's principle that development takes the form of 'the continuous adjustment of internal relations to external relations', suggesting different hypotheses of development as the story shifts its conceptual emphasis and moves beyond its early presuppositions.[25]

The narrative progress of *No Name* goes through three stages – stages which are further fragmented by the tension between the serialized and three-volume form. The first sets up the socially constructed natural order, the domestic catastrophe, and the hypothetical speculations on possible outcomes. The second is the 'Wragge'-dominated part of the story which hinges on trickery, manipulation, and disguise, and is the stage in which identities become provisional and attenuated. The third stage follows Magdalen's decline, breakdown, and final penitential reassimilation; here the third-person narrative literally comes to occupy her consciousness. Each stage both develops out of the previous one and overturns its presuppositions. Within this overall process, each expresses different degrees of cognitive ambivalence about how to interpret the significance of physical signs of identity – linking them to a conception of male and female 'proper natures' manifested as adjustment or otherwise to roles that are, as I have already argued, in the process of being revealed as masquerades. Thus 'the continuous adjustment of internal relations to external relations' is itself an ambiguous process – it can take the form of either conformity or perversity.

In the first stage Magdalen is set in the context not only of established 'development hypotheses', but in a network of family characteristics that suggest that continuous lines of transmission lead to morbidness, weakness, and degeneration in a way that suggests that physiological features can only acquire meaning in the light of the established cultural references of masculinity and femininity. This method of perception qualifies the dichotomy that was central to Hartright's method of perception and interpretation in *The Woman in White*, and is built up in the contrasted figures of Norah, Frank Clare, and Noel Vanstone; figures in which directly contrasted physical signifiers carry different social and moral referents. Norah and Frank both apparently manifest the same process of wearing out through genealogical transmission.

Inheriting the dark majestic quality of her mother's beauty, [Norah] had yet hardly inherited all of its charms. Though the shape of her face was the same the features were scarely so delicate, their proportion was scarely so true. She was not so tall. She had the dark-brown eyes of her mother . . . and yet there was less interest, less refinement and depth of feeling in her expression: it was gentle and feminine, but clouded by a certain quiet reserve, from which her mother's face was free. If we look closely enough, may we not observe, that the moral force of character and the higher intellectual capacities in parents seem often to wear out mysteriously in the course of transmission to children? In these days of insidious nervous exhaustion and subtly-spreading nervous malady, is it not possible that the same rule may apply, less rarely than we are willing to admit, to the bodily gifts as well?[26]

This passage moves rapidly through a range of speculations about Norah's incipient 'nervous exhaustion' and possible moral weakness and sets up an image of vulnerability that is to be explicitly refuted by the very unsettled status of the narrative gaze itself. At first she seems to be a cruder version of her mother; transmission here breeds 'less refinement and depth of feeling', but not femininity. But the location of this bluntness or vagueness suddenly shifts from the structure of the features to their expression, signalled by its blankness, its quiet reserve. The narrator then stands back, making the general speculative statement that Norah's actual development is to overturn, as adverse circumstances become the key that unlocks the forces of hidden strength; but this means that her extreme reserve and self-control – the symptoms hinted here of her 'degeneration' – have to become the primary sources of her resolution. This inverts the pattern of references that made sense of Laura's passivity and Marian's resolution in *The Woman in White*, for here resolution can only be expressed as patience, a passivity that is also in itself morbid.

Frank Clare's organizational weakness on the other hand is expressed in a way that develops Frederick Fairlie's disturbing androgyny in *The Woman in White* into femininity:

The small regular features, which he was supposed to have inherited from his mother, were rounded and filled out, without having lost their remarkable delicacy of form. . . . His gentle wandering brown eyes would have looked to better advantage in a woman's face – they wanted spirit and firmness to fit them for the face of a man. He was undeniably handsome, graceful, well bred – but no close observer could look at him without suspecting that the stout old family stock had begun to wear out in the later generations, and that Mr Francis Clare had more in him of the shadow of his ancestors than of the substance.[27]

This is pushed even further in the figure of Noel Vanstone:

His complexion was as delicate as a young girl's, his eyes were of the lightest blue, his upper lip was adorned by a weak little white moustache, waxed and twisted at either end into a thin spiral curl. When any object specially attracted his attention, he half closed his eye-lids to look at it. When he smiled, the skin at the temples curled up into a nest of wicked little wrinkles.[28]

Here decadent sensibility withers into atrophy – 'feminine' is the initial association, replaced by 'wizen', finally compounding his 'reptile temperament'.[29]

These figures all depend on a set of references which link organic and moral decline by compounding a connection between femininity and 'subtly spreading nervous malady'. But the figure of Noel also realigns this network of associations, since his nervous debility and intellectual decline stem from an atrophied circulation that is presented by conflating organic and directly economic process: 'He had inherited his father's love of money, without inheriting his father's capacity for seeing the uses to which money can be put. His one idea in connection with his wealth, was the idea of keeping it.'[30] And Noel himself is first introduced in his father's house in Lambeth, at the centre of what is presented by a suddenly detached and polemical narrator to be the inevitable concomitant of modern progress – urban degeneration; the 'street-labyrinth of a remote London', of which the inhabitants are both products and victims:

> In this district, as in other districts remote from the wealthy quarters of the metropolis, the hideous London vagabond lounges, lowering and brutal . . . the public disgrace of his country, the unheeded warning of social troubles that are yet to come. Here, the loud self-assertion of Modern Progress – which has reformed so much in manners, and altered so little in men – meets the flat contradiction that scatters its pretensions to the winds. Here, while the national prosperity feasts, like another Belshazzar, on the spectacle of its own magnificance, is the Writing on the Wall which warns the monarch, Money, that his glory is weighed in the balance, and his power found wanting.[31]

Thus the nervous weakness of the hypochondriacal bachelor and the late-nineteenth-century threat of the degenerate casual poor meet in the figure of Noel, and become the double product of his father's commercial enterprise, and his waning patriarchal line.

Magdalen is set within this matrix of family resemblances as a 'wild type', the healthy strain in the family, who can only be defined by difference, the absence of any fixed characteristics, transparency. The first presentation of her implies what turns out to be true, though in an unexpected way: that she is a bastard. But it is done by emphasizing her flexibility and strength, so that initially anomalousness implies healthiness. So while Magdalen is introduced as a 'caprice of Nature' that seems to be scientifically inexplicable, she draws on a set of references that correspond most closely of all to the Darwinian model of natural selection that makes anomalousness itself the central element of development:

> By one of those caprices of Nature, which science still leaves unexplained, the youngest of Mr Vanstone's children presented no recognisable resemblance to either of her parents. How had she come by her hair? How had she come by her eyes? . . . It was here exactly that the promise of her face failed of performance in the most startling manner. The eyes, which should have been dark, were incomprehensibly and discordantly light: they were of that nearly colourless grey which, though little attractive in itself, possesses the rare compensating merit of interpreting the finest gradations of thought, the gentlest changes of feeling, the deepest trouble of passion, with a subtle transparency of expression which no darker eyes can rival. Thus quaintly self-contradictory in the upper part of her face, she was hardly less at variance with established ideas of harmony in the lower. . . . The whole countenance – so remarkable in its strongly-opposed characteristics – was rendered additionally striking by its extraordinary mobility. . . . She bloomed in the full physical maturity of twenty years or more – bloomed naturally and irresistibly, in right of her matchless health and strength. Here, in truth, lay the mainspring of this strangely-constituted organisation.[32]

Magdalen's 'fitness' therefore is manifested as a refusal to fit into any perceptual category, while her 'unexplainable' identity disrupts the cognitive perspective that makes sense of Norah. But it also suggests that there are no stable signs or clues that can manifest feminine strength and this is reinforced by the fact that the roles she plays are exaggerated versions of established feminine ones. This paradox takes on a new set of connotations in the second stage of the story where Magdalen, in collaboration with Wragge, adapts herself to an assumed role in plotting to marry Noel – an act of individual survival that threatens to compound the family's degeneration.

Wragge's anomalous and perverse attraction lies more openly in the way that he manipulates and exposes dominant social, psychological, and narrative codes. He reproduces Collins's recurrent technique of subverting the dominant discourse of the narrative by replicating it in an unexpectedly familiar form rather than in a directly grotesque or uncanny way – but in another key. Like Fosco in *The Woman in White*, his attraction lies in his total shamelessness, but here it is as a 'rogue' or trickster, a figure that has different kinds of class connotations from 'villain', and which replicates and over-turns a moral management now pressed into the service of self-made competitive individualism rather than the 'fortified Success' of the Count's counter-republicanism. While it is structurally necessary that Frank Clare should fail to fulfil his father's expectations by *not* surviving – 'he drifted away into the misty commercial future – as aimless, as helpless, as gentlemanlike as ever' – so Wragge's pastiche of free enterprise (imposture masquerading as respectability) depends on his particular status as a bastardized form, a trickster who is composed from a montage of overlapping rhetorics, pushing their terminology to a ridiculous conclusion while also managing finally to flourish in defiance of the conditions he exploits.[33] He appears for the second time as the victim of a more widespread economic catastrophe, the same catastrophe from which Michael Vanstone profited, the overreaching of the commercial speculation of 1846 which is described as collective insanity: 'The railway mania of that famous year had attacked even the wary Wragge; had withdrawn him from his customary pursuits; and had left him prostrate at the end, like many a better man.' But this reinforces the sense of his capacity for survival while turning respectable poverty into a caricature of respectability: 'From top to toe every square inch of the captain's clothing was altered for the worse; but the man himself remained unchanged – superior to all forms of moral mildew, impervious to the action of social rust.'[34]

Wragge's own rhetoric deflates horticultural metaphors of individual self-culture by inflating them to their absurd conclusion, so that he becomes a pastiche of a moral management that bolsters competitive individualism – human intervention shaping a mean-ingless 'Nature'. He describes himself as

> a moral agriculturalist; a man who cultivates the field of human sympathy. . . . Consult my brother agriculturalists in the horticultural line – do they get their crops for the asking? No! they must circumvent arid Nature, exactly as I circumvent sordid man. They must plough, and sow, and top dress, and bottom dress, and deep drain, and surface drain and all the rest of it. Why am I to be checked in the vast operation of deep draining mankind?[35]

His wife is a parodied patient of a non-restraint asylum, a

145

grotesque image of wifely propriety, whose 'personal appearance' he fails to 'mould' into 'harmony with the eternal laws of symmetry and order' although she desperately attempts to present a domestic tableau.[36] Wragge's speculation eventually leads to commercial success, based on his widespread use of advertising and his shift 'from moral agriculture to medical agriculture. Formerly I preyed on the public sympathy, now I prey on the public stomach. . . . Don't think me mercenary – I merely understand the age I live in.'[37] It is balanced by the intrigues of his antagonist and counterpart, Mrs Lecount. Like Count Fosco, Mrs Lecount wields a magnetic power through her simultaneous foreignness and familiarity. Combined with this is her ability to turn moral management into medical control, but this power is now brought about more decisively by her feminine manipulation of her own appearance, which as 'little less than a triumph of physical resistance to the deteriorating influence of time', and an artificial counteraction to degeneration.[38] Mrs Lecount's favourite pet, moreover, is no white mouse, an echo of Laura, but a more atavistic equivalent of Noel – a tame toad.

So it is through the parodying of the rhetorics of self-help and moral management, within the contexts of an overlapping set of evolutionary discourses, that the focus of tension in *No Name* becomes the battle of plot and counterplot between Magdalen and Lecount: the *Saturday Review* went as far as to maintain that 'the whole point of the story, the one source of interest it possesses, is the contest between these two wicked, deceitful, obstinate women'.[39] This 'vying with each other in politeness and propriety' has the effect of suspending the 'purposeful' line of the narrative precisely because masquerading now takes on a life of its own in its very satirical correspondence with the codes of propriety on which it is based. Conversely, the reassertion of narrative authority needs to be based on pushing those plots to a morbid conclusion, so that the final stage of the story both enacts the already established premonition of Magdalen's decline, and reverses the implications of the way that her early healthy self was built up by transmuting them into the symptoms of *hysteria*. The figure of Magdalen here corresponds to the medical perception of the hysterical patient put forward, for example, by F.C. Skey – 'the hysterical passion swelling at her heart' is the excess of resolution, of 'nerve'.[40] The quest that drove the narrative forward is now turned into the obsessive sign of monomania, as Magdalen's resolution now takes the form of a force dominating her *as* the product of her own will: 'Time . . . had made her purpose part of herself; once she governed it, now it governed her'.[41] Nervous collapse now becomes the outcome of the heroine's 'perversity' through the reassertion of a linear narrative, of which it now becomes a morbid deviation: and in this the nervous collapse itself is both the product of Magdalen's fall and the magical means of effecting her social reconstitution through intellectual rather than moral disintegration: 'her whole nervous system has given way: all the ordinary functions of her brain are in a state of collapse', notes the doctor.[42]

The resolution of *No Name* now depends on the heroine's identity being reframed within a newly assertive narrative that has gained its authority by charting the heroine's decline, and this means that 'moral management' takes on a completely different position as a means of effective narrative closure from its place in *The Woman in White*. For while Magdalen's resolution pushed the story forward, now, in becoming necessarily morbid, it has to be replaced by a kind of narrative surveillance that both mediates, diffuses, and interprets it, and the narrative voice negotiates this ambivalence between identification and distance by shifting between different registers. Magdalen becomes a 'patient' by this process but she can never gain a coherent subjectivity; she is positioned as an opaque collection of physical signs at one moment, through directly reported internal monologue at another, now through letters, now through explicit interjection. At times the narrative voice becomes overtly judgemental: 'Let this be said of her; let the truth which has been told of her fault be told of her expiation as well. Let it be recorded of her that she enjoyed no secret triumph on the day of her marriage.'[43] At times it 'homes in' on the consciousness, by merging with her 'inner voice':

> Faintly and more faintly the inner voices now pleaded with her to pause on her downward way. . . . But one refuge now. She turned to the relentless Purpose which was now hurrying her to her ruin, and cried to it with the daring of her despair – Drive me on![44]

This modifies her 'organic' identity, too, for as she 'declines' her features freeze, and 'fix and render permanent what might have passed away': 'There was a settled composure on her face which . . . made it look still and cold as marble'; or just before her marriage to Noel: 'In one mysterious instant, all her beauty left her; her face stiffened awfully, like the face of a corpse.'[45]

In *No Name* the inherent ideological tensions within conceptions of development and fitness are absorbed within the figure of the heroine who can never be incorporated within a single organic model, yet who is refracted through the discursive contexts which I have outlined. The novel sets up a continually unstable relationship between gender and organic identity and change: a comparable set of codes that signify survival and decline work differently for men and women, and this can break down the organic basis of sexual difference itself. And although the novel has none of the structural complexity of *The Woman in White* it continually qualifies the sources of its own apparent coherence in the face of the obtrusiveness of the narrative voice itself. *No Name* does not explore an internalized subjectivity; even Magdalen's breakdown occurs off-stage; the narrative does not focus on social ambiguity by playing with cognitive codes, and its 'underside' is comic rather than uncanny. 'Unconscious' or secret processes manifest themselves automatically, through the workings of an 'inevitable law of revela-tion' – a return of the repressed that is one of the 'laws of nature', even as that natural law is itself denaturalized.

But while this explicitly reinforces the dominant performative structure of the story, the narrative itself tacitly draws on a more ambiguous process of 'revelation' in order to focus its sources of tension and keep the story moving forward, while postponing its end. The third-person narrative is broken up by letters – the 'Progress of the Story through the Post' – and by Wragge's chronicle that works on a different time-scale from the dominant narrative as well as disrupting its omniscience and qualifying its authority over Magdalen. The story continually resorts to chance and coincidence to reach its predestined end. It is only when that end has been revealed that this is reinterpreted as providential intervention. Magdalen, on the brink of despair, counts the ships passing her window to decide whether she should commit suicide; she is accidentally discovered in the last stages of nervous exhaustion by Kirke, the paragon of colonial fitness, as her quest takes an ever more obsessive form after the death of Noel. Preternatural and 'uncanny' devices are increas-ingly used when, disguised as a servant rather than a wife, she penetrates the house of the new heir and attempts to find the 'Secret Trust' outlining the future of the inheritance. Hidden links of association, lost keys, dark and winding passages abound in this section, and Magdalen is 'unconsciously' put on the trail of the document by the somnambulant heir, so that the means by which she pursues her social self become more weird as her own subjective coherence disintegrates. Mesmerism also makes an appearance, but fleetingly and in a deflated way through the indirectly reported speech of Noel, as Magdalen has a momentary collapse, explained as a 'neuralgic attack', under the strain of dissembling in the 'Bygrave' plot: 'Mesmerism was frequently useful in these cases. Mr Noel Vanstone's father had been the most powerful mesmerist in Europe; and Mr Noel Vanstone was his father's son. Might he mesmerise?'[46] It becomes the sign here of Noel's gullibility and lack of power.

There is, however, one moment where Collins does directly exploit internalized psychological processes, drawing on specific developments in associationist psychology to make possible the necessary conceptual leap in order to be able to recognize masquerade. This is where Mrs Lecount first meets Magdalen disguised as Miss Bygraves after meeting her masquerading as Miss Garth. Before falling asleep, Lecount's mind drifts along its own uncontrolled chain of associations:

> She had got no further with this during the day; she could get no further now: the chain of thought broke. Her mind took up the fragments and formed another chain which attached itself to the lady who was kept in seclusion – to the aunt who looked well and yet was nervous; who was nervous, and yet able to ply her needle and thread. . . . Were the members of this small family of three, what they seemed on the surface of them?
>
> With that question in mind, she went to bed.
>
> As soon as the candle was out, the darkness seemed to communicate some inexplicable perversity to her thoughts. They wandered back from present things to past, in spite of her. They brought her old master back to life again: they revived forgotten sayings and doings in the English circles at Zurich; they veered away to the old man's death-bed at Brighton; they moved from Brighton to London; they entered the bare comfortless room at Vauxhall Walk. . . . At this point her thoughts broke off once more, and there was a momentary blank. The next instant she started up in bed; her heart beating violently, her head whirling as if she had lost her senses. With electric suddenness, her mind pieced together its scattered multitude of thoughts, and put them before her plainly under one intelligible form. In the all-mastering agitation of the moment, she clapped her hands together and cried out suddenly in the darkness: 'Miss Vanstone again!'[47]

'She was quite incapable of tracing the mental processes which had led her to discovery', notes the narrator, switching from tracing these processes to analysing them.

She could not get sufficiently far from herself to see that her half-formed conclusions on the subject of the Bygraves, had ended in making that family objects of suspicion to her; that the association of ideas had thereupon carried her mind back to that other object of suspicion which was represented by the conspiracy against her master; and that the two ideas of those two subjects of mistrust, coming suddenly into contact, had struck the light.[48]

This self-consciously echoes a process that Abercrombie's discusses in the analysis of 'automatic' memory in *Intellectual Powers and the Investigation of Truth*, manifested in that borderland state of reverie that is neither dreaming, nor trance, nor logical association, but an intermediate state in which apparently disconnected ideas directly recall each other:

Besides this tendency, by which thoughts formerly associated are brought into the mind in a particular order, there is another species of association, into which the mind passes spontaneously, by a suggestion from any subject which happens to be present to it. The thought or fact, which is thus present, suggests another which has some kind of affinity to it; this suggests a third, and so on, to the formation of a train of series which may be continued at great length. A remarkable circumstance likewise is, that such a train may go on with very little consciousness of, or attention to it.[49]

Here, as elsewhere in the novel, a process of 'inexplicable perversity' simultaneously disrupts and reaffirms the central 'train of circumstances'. *No Name* is an extraordinary exploration of a process that *A Rogue's Life* satirically suggested: it is a study of 'the workings of the social system . . . on individual nature'. But in his next novel, *Armadale*, Collins takes the figure of the transgressive heroine one step further, this time in the context of an enquiry into the interaction of subjective identity, social power, and 'psychic' forces, and here elaborates a set of narrative conventions that does more than demonstrate the provisional nature of the natural – it completely takes it to pieces.

5

Armadale
The sensitive subject as palimpsest

> The Mind is not a passive recipient of external
> impulses but an active co-operant . . . it is a variable
> mechanism which has a *history*. What the senses
> inscribe on it are not merely changes in the external
> world, but these characters are co-mingled with
> characters of preceding inscriptions. The sensitive
> subject is no *tabula rasa* but a *palimpsest*.
>
> G.H. Lewes, *Foundations of a Creed*[1]

In the Prologue of *Armadale*, Allan Armadale II (Senior), father of
Allan Armadale II (Junior), alias Ozias Midwinter, warns his son in
his deathbed confession of the possible consequences of his
namesake's murder:

> Guiltless minds may see nothing thus far but the result of a series
> of events which could lead no other way. I . . . with my crime
> unpunished and unatoned, see what no guiltless minds can
> discern. I see danger in the future, begotten of the danger in the
> past . . . I look into the Book which all Christendom venerates;
> and the Book tells me that the sins of the father shall be visited
> on the child. I look out into the world; and I see the living
> witnesses round me to that terrible truth. I see the vices that have
> contaminated the father, descending and contaminating the child;
> I see the shame which has disgraced the father's name descending
> and disgracing the child. I look in on myself – and I see My
> Crime, ripening again for the future in the self-same circumstance
> which first sowed the seeds of it in the past; and descending in
> inherited contamination of Evil, from me to my son. . . .
>
> My son! The only hope I have left for you, hangs on a Great
> Doubt – the doubt whether we are, or are not, the masters of our
> own destinies.[2]

Armadale opens with a confession, a complicated narrative of a guilty past involving doubling, pursuit, and retribution. But the confession does not form a reconstruction and reassessment of that past which will lead to atonement and reassimilation. It turns it into a force that will determine the future progress of the story, but not in a straightforward way. The confession is the novel's opening assertion, setting up a framework of expectation wherein the language of scriptual judgement merges with moral transmission. Armadale's son, the receiver of the confession, is placed in a similar position to Robert Mannion in *Basil* as the threefold 'look' of the father – into the 'Book', into the world, into himself – becomes his own social and psychic inheritance. That destiny is thus simultaneously resisted and fulfilled by the progress of the narrative. It is internalized by the hypochondriacal obsessions of the son, the sensitive subject who indirectly transmits the tensions and mysteries of the story, and the subject of a psychological investigation of the way that a monomania can work its own fulfilment. He is the victim, too, of a plot to steal the name and identity that are the subject of so much complication and confusion, a plot that depends for its sensation on fulfilling the very expectations that have been rendered problematic.

Armadale is a fascinating and elusive novel which combines, in a bizarrely kaleidoscopic way, many of the narrative elements and psychological methods that have already been identified in Collins's fiction. The narratives of *The Woman in White* and *No Name* hinged on one of the basic conventions of sensation fiction: gaining a name and an identity by assuming another false one. In *Armadale* there are plots, and plots within plots, which in turn become the breeding ground for further plots, all proliferating around the name 'Allan Armadale' – a name without an identity, not, as in *No Name*, an identity that has been rendered problematic by the loss of name. It is a blank space standing for a property that has no real owner, a stage on which various psychological propensities and dispositions are acted out, though the replications and inversions take on different meanings in different contexts. The confessional narrative of the Prologue – the letter addressed to the son – sets up the basic conflict around the inheritance of name, property, and morbid traits that works in two directions, between self and other, and father and son, and it shapes the presuppositions that both determine and undermine the story. The fathers, the two Allan Armadales of the Prologue, are set in opposition by directly replicating the other's transgression in a way that presents the excess of power itself as morbid, as a form of moral insanity. The conflict is given the apparently exotic setting of Barbados, but the colony primarily gains its 'wild' connotations from its position as the site of unlicensed *domestic* feudal power, an imaginary reversion to an earlier historical epoch. The confessing Armadale, née Wrentmore, inherited the Armadale name and estates in both England and Barbados in the place of the Armadale who had 'disgraced himself beyond redemption', though Wrentmore's own youth had echoed this absence of restraint:

> My mother was blindly fond of me . . . she let me live as I pleased. My boyhood and youth were passed in idleness and self-indulgence, among people – slaves and half-castes mostly – to whom my will was law . . . I doubt if there was ever a young man in this world whose passions were left so entirely without control of any kind.[3]

Both echo Pritchard's case of

> an only son of a weak and indulgent mother [who] gave himself up habitually to the gratification of every caprice and passion of which an untamed and violent temper was susceptible. . . . The money with which he was lavishly supplied removed every obstacle to the indulgence of his wild desires.[4]

But Wrentmore is then displaced himself by the original Armadale, who takes on another assumed name to steal back his inheritance and to marry an English heiress and gain an English estate; in revenge Wrentmore drowns him by locking him in a sinking ship; when dying himself of a degenerative (implicitly venereal) disease, he confesses this to his son.

There are no stable oppositions between self and other, reality and imposture here, and this process of displacement of significance is taken further in that there is nothing but displacement; even the desire to (re)claim a name becomes another form of imposture. The story itself re-enacts the 'gaining a name and identity through dissemblance' plot through two counterveiling registers, which follow the way in which the projected narrative that is the father's legacy is resisted and fulfilled. The first revolves round the relationship between the two Armadales, focusing on the morbid self-consciousness of Wrentmore's son, discovered as an outcast under the bizarre name of 'Ozias Midwinter', a name now assumed to avoid inheriting the property and the prophecy. The junior Armadales deconstruct the discourses through which their fathers are set up while at the same time upsetting the very expectations generated by their own opposition. They are respectively dark and fair, burdened with anxiety and harmlessly irresponsible, yet this involves a complex notion of the splitting, shadowing, or doubling of the self, which emerges most clearly in the premonitory dream which foreshadows the future and which 'belongs' to both of them. The second focuses on the one surviving figure from the Prologue, the extraordinary villainess, the red-haired Lydia Gwilt, who conspires to acquire the English inheritance by assuming the Armadale name through marriage, not to Armadale, but to his replica Midwinter, under his 'real' name. The 'fatal' force of the father's prophecy and projected threat now turns out to be the power of manipulative female sexuality.

So *Armadale* juggles with the concept of transmission, scrutinizing the way in which a legacy of the past is reproduced by the next generation, becomes internalized within the consciousness, and then is again transmitted through various 'psychic' phenomena – most notably the dream in which one morbid state is transposed into the subjectivity of another. It uses the devices of doubling and substitution of names and identity and exploits the links between names and inherited property to question the stable boundaries of the self, as well as to explore its social construction. It draws on contradictory psychological conventions and assumptions in building up and breaking down outcast and deviant figures, figures who are either shown to be threatening and anomalous because of others' fears and preconceptions, or who make use of those projections and fears to build up Collins's most ambitious villainess in a way that can never be assimilated, as it is in *The Woman in White*, within the overall framework of moral management. *The Woman in White* explored how identity could be built up and broken down by manipulating a consistent rhetoric that simultaneously covered and disclosed its interests, with the asylum as the pivot. A secluded asylum for nervous patients also makes an appearance in *Armadale*, but as an 'overwrought' melodramatic device at the climax of the story.

This replicates the contrast in the way the novels operate, for *Armadale* draws on a set of psychological processes that suggest opposing interpretations. By continually replaying a plot with modifications the novel elicits distinct interpretations which succeed and overlap with one another, and which form a set of interlocking but dissonant frameworks. In this respect, *Armadale* generates a sense of mystery by continually undermining the terms on which its own cognitive assumptions are founded while allowing them, on another register, to remain intact. Towards the beginning of the novel the naïve and boorish Allan Armadale I (Junior) tells his surrogate father, Decimus Brock, a joke about 'three Bedouin brothers at a show':

Ali will take a lighted torch, and jump down the throat of his brother Muli – Muli will take a lighted torch, and jump down the throat of his brother Hassan – and Hassan, taking a third lighted torch, will jump down his own throat, and leaving the spectators in total darkness.[5]

Armadale is a story which 'jumps down its own throat', and unlike *The Moonstone* and *The Woman in White*, there are no sympathetic detectives, only victims and conspirators. There is no reconstruction which proceeds through distinct narrative frameworks as part of a process of detection, yet neither is there an overall omniscient narrative authority as there is in *No Name*.

Armadale works as a sensation novel as the conventions of the mode are pushed to their limits, and Collins took as many explicit aesthetic and moral risks with this novel as he had done with *Basil*. But he wrote *Armadale* when his economic security and position as a popular writer seemed most assured. Smith, Elder had lured him from *All the Year Round*, following the serialization of *No Name* as the result of the phenomenal success of *The Woman in White*. He serialized *Armadale* in the well-established middle-class, middle-brow *Cornhill Magazine*, paying Collins no less than £5,000 for the publishing rights.[6] Again the Preface offers defence and justification:

Readers in particular will, I have some reason to suppose, be here and there disturbed – perhaps even offended – by finding that *Armadale* oversteps, in more than one direction, the narrow limits within which they are disposed to limit the development of modern fiction – if they can.[7]

Armadale certainly was condemned by critics as an exaggerated sensation novel, Miss Gwilt – 'a portrait drawn with masterly art, but one from which every rightly constituted mind turns with loathing' – being singled out for their special detestation.[8] But although the novel was attacked for both aesthetic and moral distortion, on the one hand winding up the narrative to such a pitch as to render the characters 'puppets', on the other producing dangerously attractive and realistic criminals, it was also accorded a grudging admiration. The *Athenaeum* complained:

Those who make plot their first consideration and humanity the second – those, again, who represent the decencies of life as so often too many hypocrisies – have placed themselves in a groove which goes, and must go, in a downward direction, whether as regards fiction or morals. We are in a period of diseased invention, and the coming phase of it may be palsy.[9]

But the *Saturday Review* was more ambivalent, acknowledging Collins's

> strange capacity for weaving extraordinary plots; *Armadale*, from first to last, is a lurid labyrinth of improbabilities. It produces upon the reader the effect of a literary nightmare. . . . If it were the object of art to make one's audience feel uncomfortable without letting them know why, Mr Wilkie Collins would be beyond doubt a consummate artist. . . . As a whole the effect is clever, powerful, and striking, though grotesque, monotonous, and to use a French word, *bizarre*.[10]

Though the review is finally dismissive it points to the real complexities of the way the novel works – that it produces the same effect that Marian had on Hartright, 'a sensation oddly akin to the helpless discomfort familiar to us all in sleep, when we recognise yet cannot recognise the anomalies and contradictions of a dream'.[11] And here the dream itself and the way that it is offered up to distinct kinds of interpretation are both the fulcrum of the plot and a direct analogue of a more generalized process whereby meaning is rendered problematic in the novel. Collins wrote an Appendix to *Armadale* where he made it clear that he left the meaning of the dream deliberately opaque:

> My readers will perceive that I have purposely left them, with reference to the Dream in this story, in the position that they would occupy in the case of a dream in real life – they are free to interpret it by the natural or the supernatural theory as the bent of their own minds may incline them.[12]

This means that overlapping forms of 'double consciousness' are at work in the novel: firstly, the 'double consciousness' of contemporary dream theory that is put to work in the text; secondly, the ambiguous possible interpretations of the dream focused through the consciousness of individuals; and thirdly, the way in which the text works as a dream through mingling its own past and present. *Armadale* works in a way that is analogous to Elliotson's analysis of dreams in *Human Physiology*: he reiterates that dreams are marked by loss of control over the thoughts, but goes on to argue that the mind can, in fact, 'perceive the grossest incongruities and impossibilities . . . thoughts riot on in confusion . . . more like the cross reading of a newspaper. . . . A dream sometimes continues rational or consistent till near the end, when suddenly it becomes absurd.'[13] The novel 'jumps down its own throat' through its juxtaposition of these different modes, without signalling that anything peculiar is happening. The effect is to collapse the natural into the supernatural, but in ways which never move beyond the devices of the manipulation of sensation and perception. It thus extends the dream theory of physiological psychology, even as it points to its limitation of explaining psychical realities as morbid phenomena by investigating the social construction of a morbid consciousness in the figure of the 'sensitive subject' of Ozias Midwinter. To analyse how this works it is necessary to look at the dream, its own immediate relationship to contemporary dream theory, and the way both are manipulated by the workings of the narrative and the shaping of identities that this involves.

Armadale's dream, which takes the form of a series of static tableaux which then 'work their own fulfilment' in the later narrative through strategies that are open to contrasting interpretation, is itself subjected to two contrasting analyses immediately the dreamer wakes, which straightaway puts it on a different footing from the dreams that have emerged so far in Collins's novels.[14] In *Basil* and *The Woman in White* (with the exception of Marian's trance) unexplainable forebodings were discussed by the partial view of sceptical but naïve narrators who were sensitive to the 'influences' around them, but unable to perceive the hidden connections that the dream or 'other' state represented. They therefore interpreted monition as a monomania but in a way that could then be reworked (by Basil in delirium, by Hartright by gaining self- and narrative control) as part of a process of transformation or reassimilation. In *Armadale* there is also a split between superstition and rationality, but it is given a different emphasis and serves a different narrative function. The dream is given a superstitious 'supernatural' reading by Midwinter, reworked in the framework of expectation that he is set within as 'sensitive subject'; yet also given a materialist interpretation by the local doctor, Hawbury, who serves no other function than as the voice of medical authority. This sets up a direct correlation between the dream's narrative function, enabling the bizarre juxtaposing of anomalous elements, and the use of dream theory to explain it. This means that Hawbury's theory should be credible in external terms in order for it to be effectively qualified and developed in the narrative itself.

Hawbury's explanation of Armadale's dream corresponds closely to the dream analysis of MacNish, Abercrombie, Symonds, and other contemporaries, but it does so selectively. Like his non-fictional counterparts, Hawbury is more concerned to offer a causal explanation of the dream's different elements than a reading of its meaning, and like them, too, he offers a purely physiological explanation with an account of how the dream selects and combines past traces, working 'as the shuffling of a deranged kaleidoscope'.[15] Hawbury opines:

> We don't believe that a reasonable man is justified in attaching a supernatural explanation to any phenomenon which comes within the range of his senses, until he has certainly ascertained that there is no such thing as a natural explanation of it to be found in the first instance. . . .
> There is nothing at all extraordinary in my theory of dreams: it is the theory accepted by the great mass of my profession. A Dream is the reproduction, in the sleeping state of the brain, of images and impressions produced on it in the waking state; and this reproduction is more or less involved, imperfect or contradictory, as the action of certain faculties of the dreamer is controlled more or less completely, by the influence of sleep.[16]

Hawbury, Armadale, and Midwinter then attempt to 'trace [their] way back to these impressions', speculating on how they will be transformed in the dream, which is 'like guessing a riddle'.[17] This process directly corresponds with Abercrombie's outline of the different processes at work in dreaming, where he notes that 'one of the most curious objects of investigation is to trace the manner, in which the particular visions or series of images arise'.[18] The process of tracing back in the dream analysis of *Armadale* correlates with Abercrombie's identification of 'Recent events and recent mental emotions, mingled up into one continuous series';[19] Allan combines the image of the landscape of a recent trip with a scene he has been reading about, and condenses this with other memories and suggestions: 'And behold the dream, Mr Midwinter, mixing up separate waking impressions just as usual!'[20]

But Hawbury's analysis only gives a partial account of the theory outlined by Abercrombie. It focuses on the recent past, while Abercrombie stressed 'Recent events . . . mingled up . . . with old events', and 'Dreams consisting in the revival of past associations, respecting things which had entirely passed out of mind, and which seem to have been forgotten', as well as those in which 'a strong mental emotion is embodied in a dream and is fulfilled'.[21] The text suggests a more complex understanding of the dreaming process, corresponding to the concept of 'double consciousness' current in contemporary theory which was developed by associationist analysis and mesmerism, and was a starting-point for Dallas's *The Gay Science*.

'In dreams each man's character is disintegrated, so that he may see the elements of which it is composed.'[22] Frank Seafield's summary of methods of dream interpretation is taken literally in *Armadale*. On hearing that a bad dream has been had, the doctor immediately assumes that Midwinter has had it: 'with your constitution, you ought to be well used to dreaming by this time'.[23] By giving Allan the dream which reproduces Midwinter's anxieties, the novel directly makes use of one the tenets of mesmerism – that impressions can be directly transmitted – as well as the claim that clairvoyance offers a method of prediction which is not 'contrary to nature': 'Say, now, what can be concealed from us, present and future?' Elliotson asks, 'the soul of magnetiser and the magnetised can be mingled, and afterwards separated again.'[24] This further blurs the boundary between natural and supernatural explanation as well as between Midwinter's and Armadale's identities. But the novel mixes this with less obviously transcendental processes in both the text of the dream itself and its narrative setting.

Allan's dream is presented as an embedded narrative carefully itemized and noted by Midwinter:

1. The first event of which I was conscious, was the appearance of my father. He took me silently by the hand, and we found ourselves in the cabin of a ship.

2. Water slowly rose over us in the cabin; and I and my father sank through the water together.

3. An interval of oblivion followed; and then the sense came to me of being left alone in the darkness.

4. I waited.

5. The darkness opened and showed me the vision – as in a picture – of a broad, lonely pool, surrounded by open ground . . .

6. On the near margin of the pool, there stood the Shadow of a Woman.[25]

Like Basil's early dream (in *Basil*) it takes the form of a set of static tableaux, which have an allegorical, already interpreted quality about them, but which are themselves embedded in the narrative as the dreamer sinks into the other world of double consciousness, and he and the father sink beneath the water in a state which is neither past nor future. This use of the language of sinking and drowning is closer to Basil's delirium and Hartright's fear (in *The Woman in White*): 'my mind sinks in darkness and confusion when I think of it', making literal use of the metaphors of unconscious activity to describe the process within the dream itself.[26] The use of metaphors or currents or tides to conceptualize unconscious processes within the self, either as a force linking the individual to the surrounding world or as a set of currents forming channels within the mind that could be developed, blocked, or controlled, was developed in different contexts within physiological psychology.[27] But Dallas in particular conceptualized the unconscious as a sea or expanse of water containing a range of different currents or tides that both frame the perimeters of the self and exist within or beneath it.

> When one is most struck with the grandeur of the tides and currents of thought that belong to each of us, and yet all beyond our consciousness, one is apt to conceive of it as a vast outer sea or space that belts our conscious existence. . . .
> In the dark recesses of memory, in unbidden suggestions, in trains of thought unwittingly pursued, in multiplied waves and currents all at once flashing and rushing, in dreams that cannot be laid . . . we have glimpses of a great tide of life ebbing and flowing, rippling and rolling and beating about where we cannot see it. . . . Our conscious existence is a little spot of light, rounded or begirt with a haze of slumber.'[28]

Thus the device of sinking beneath the waters with the father to produce the 'visions' of the preternatural state of consciousness simultaneously moderates and disrupts the distinction between alternative states of consciousness within the dream. And this corresponds with Dallas's sense that

> this unconscious part of the mind is so dark and yet so full of activity; so like the conscious intelligence and yet so divided from it by a veil of mystery, that it is not much of a hyperbole to speak of the human soul as double, or at least leading a double life.

But a double life in which there is a secret 'constant traffic' between conscious and unconscious existence, and where each is necessary to the other.[29]

It also directly echoes the patterns at work in creating the immediate conditions of dreaming and disrupts the linear sequence of time. The 'sinking beneath the waters with the father' sequence mixes Allan's 'unconscious past' (the drowning of the father in the ship) with the immediate one (the two Armadales finding themselves stranded on the wreck of the same ship) here coincidence perversely reproduces the patterns of the intractable past. But it also seeps into the language describing the waking present, and suffuses the terms of reference of the novel as a whole. Allan Armadale's lack of discipline in early life evaporates harmlessly but it means that he becomes a principle of free association in the novel, flitting from one idea to the other, but never being anchored to any meaning. His passion for sailing and the sea both underpins this and is made explicit when the narrator comments on his confusion about the dreams: 'In both senses of the word his mind was at sea already'; a disruption of the distinction between the metaphorical and the literal reinforced by the way that Midwinter, the more obvious outcast, is continually described as being 'cast adrift'.[30] And this comes to permeate the language of the narrative itself. As the story moves into the sequence of the fulfilment of the dream with the trip to the Norfolk Broads and the first encounter with the fatal Lydia the landscape becomes increasingly dreamlike – not, as in *Basil*, through the dramatic Fuseli-like imagery of cliffs and chasms, but in the way that the flat monotony of the Norfolk Broads is built up by the juxtaposing of unexpected elements, presented by a dissociated narrative consciousness that does not know how to make sense of it.

All the strange and startling anomalies presented by an island agricultural district, isolated from other districts by its intricate surrounding network of pools and streams – holding its communication and carrying its produce by water instead of land – began to present themselves in closer and closer succession. Nets appeared on cottage palings; little flat-bottomed boats lay strangely at rest among the flowers in cottage gardens; farmer's men passed to and fro clad in the composite costume of the coast and the field, in sailor's hats and fisherman's boots and ploughman's smocks, – and even yet the low-lying labyrinth of waters, embosomed in its mystery and its solitude, was a hidden labyrinth still.[31]

Armadale also turns into a bizarre or dreamlike text as processes of psychical transmission are explored through a narrative which continually displaces any stable authority. Yet this displacement is still aligned in a social framework where the meaning of identity is overdetermined by the expectations and perceptions of others, which can compound or undermine the legacy of the past. There is neither a clear shift between narrators nor an identifiable moralized narrative rhetoric in *Armadale*. It modulates between different kinds of narrative moods which can correspond to different modes of remembering the past. For example, the most clearly identifiable benign authority is Armadale's substitute father, the rector Decimus Brock. The Epilogue of the novel closes with the posthumous re-reading of his letter, which states his belief in rational religion, autonomy, and moral management, and which finally cancels out the opening of the scriptual denunciation of the absent father in the Prologue. The opening of the Story is focused through Brock's memory and presents his immediate response to Midwinter. It takes place *after* the two Armadales have met and after some of Midwinter's past is known, but *before* Brock has read the confessional letter of the Prologue.

The reader thus has a latent knowledge of the past which qualifies the way that the opening events of the story are transmitted through the retrospective analysis of the rector. Brock recalls Armadale's early life, his mother's self-imposed exile, and the mysterious appearance of Midwinter as a vagabond through a process of 'natural or philosophical association', which, following Abercrombie, takes place 'when a fact or statement, on which the attention is fixed, is, by a mental process, associated with some subject which it is calculated to illustrate'.[32]

> One by one the events of those years – all connected with the same little group of characters, and all more or less answerable for the anxiety which was now intruding itself between the clergyman and his night's rest rose, in progressive series, on Mr Brock's memory.[33]

So narrative mood and the modes of focus and recall are bound up with the control of narrative time, which is itself built up as a palimpsest of distinct kinds of memory. As the novel progresses suspense is heightened as knowledge of the past turns into anticipation of the future via the dream, and this involves a shift from 'natural' to 'fictional' forms of association in Abercrombie's term. This process coincides with a shift in the use of narrative voice as well as focus. The main body of the story takes the form of continuous narration into which other texts – the dream, letters – are embedded. But as the plot thickens the significance of the embedding shifts; as Lydia Gwilt gains power over Midwinter her

diary substitutes itself for continuous narration. She becomes in
both senses the author of the plot, while remaining a shadow within
it – in both capacities the fatal force of the past.

The dream disrupts the coherent order of the narrative and is the
means by which the past, in another register, exerts a pressure on
the future, and is also the means by which the 'double
consciousness' of Armadale and Midwinter becomes a means of
resisting and replaying the drama of the past. The junior Armadales,
I have suggested, overturn the expectations by their fathers' and
their own opposition, and they add a twist to Collins's methods of
doubling and replicating identity and exploring patterns of exclusion
through the means by which the unitary self is disintegrated in the
dream. Midwinter at first seems to represent Allan's 'unconscious',
as repository of the guilty knowledge of the past, describing himself
as 'an ill-conditioned brat, with my mother's negro blood in my face
and my murdering father's passions in my heart, inheritor of their
secret, in spite of them', and is the source of the dream.[34] But it is
as Allan's conscience as much as his submerged consciousness that
Midwinter compounds as well as resists his 'destiny' – turning an
over-anxious gaze back on himself. The figure of Midwinter
represents Collins's most sophisticated treatment of the ways in
which 'sensitive' subjectivity is perceived as pathological and
becomes morbid without being constructed by the narrative as
pathological itself. He represents a complex overlapping of
psychological codes, not only in the mingling of contrasting sets of
expectations through which he makes sense, but in the way that
these implied terms themselves are rendered problematic and provisional, and resist any coherent set of correspondences between identity and physical sign.

Midwinter is burdened by a social and a psychic inheritance, but
he is developed in a way that goes against the grain of Spencer's
development of the organic paradigm to discuss psychical
inheritance: 'Hereditary transmission . . . applies not only to
physical but psychical peculiarities . . . modified nervous tendencies
. . . are also bequeathed.'[35] He is built up as a palimpsest in a way
that corresponds more closely with the way Lewes developed the
metaphor to emphasize the 'double root, the double history' of
development, which 'passes quite out of the range of animal life, and
no explanation of mental phenomena can be valid which does not
allow for this extension of range', an extension which here includes
the traces of others' projections and the force of memory.[36] The
narrative voice shifts between indirect narration focused through

others' views of Midwinter, his own consciousness, and his own
embedded confessional accounts of his past. In the first place this
takes the form of an interrogation of even the more liberal assumptions of moral management. Midwinter is introduced through
Brock's perspective as a mixed-race outcast and the precise method
of narrative focus used emphasizes Brock's pathologizing response
as much as its object:

> Ozias Midwinter, on recovering from brain-fever, was a startling
> object to contemplate on first view of him. His shaven head, tied
> up in an old yellow silk handkerchief; his tawny, haggard cheeks;
> his bright brown eyes, preternaturally large and wild; his rough
> black beard, his long supple, sinewy fingers, wasted by suffering
> till they looked like claws – all tended to discompose the rector at
> the outset of the interview. When the first feeling of surprise had
> worn off, the impression that followed it was not an agreeable one.
> Mr Brock could not conceal from himself that the stranger's
> manner was against him. The general opinion has settled that if
> a man is honest, he is bound to assert it by looking straight at his
> fellow-creatures when he speaks to them. If this man was honest,
> his eyes showed a singular perversity in looking away and denying
> it. Possibly they were affected in some degree by a nervous
> restlessness in his organisation which appeared to pervade every
> fibre of his lean, lithe body. The rector's healthy Anglo-Saxon
> skin crept responsively at every casual movement of the usher's
> supple brown fingers, and every passing distortion of the usher's
> haggard yellow face. 'God forgive me!' thought Mr Brock, with
> his mind musing on Allan and Allan's mother, 'I wish I could see
> my way to turning Ozias Midwinter adrift in the world again.'[37]

This manifestation of the figure through the shifting response to
it moves through a succession of interpretative modes and calls each
of them into question. The first two sentences, concentrating on him
as a 'startling object' who surprised the rector's habitual perception,
present him simply as a collection of disembodied objects. Here
there are no clear boundaries of the body: head, handkerchief,
cheeks, eyes, beard, claw-like fingers, both discompose the rector
and are presented as the product of a process of suffering which itself
only makes sense within a particular analytical framework. This is
taken further in the rector's response to Midwinter's 'shiftiness',
which in turn distances Brock's unquestioning appropriation of 'the
general opinion's' use of a set of vaguely defined physiognomic
codes. Midwinter's shiftiness and twitchiness are both cultural – the

particular interpretation of a set of physical responses – and physiological, but it is a physiology that has no meaning beyond its cultural reception. Thus the initial impression is gradually qualified as his history of social isolation and rejection is revealed, Brock's perception being replaced by a distanced and anonymous stranger:

> The fatal reserve which he had been in a fair way of conquering some minutes since possessed itself of him once more. Again his eyes wandered, again his voice sunk in tone. A stranger who had heard his story, and who saw him now, would have said: 'his look is lurking, his manner is bad, he is, every inch of him, his father's son'.[38]

'Nerves' are a key term in defining Midwinter. But the particular class and gender connotations that the rhetoric of 'nervous sensibility' had absorbed through Basil's hypochondriacal fancies or Laura's vulnerability, are here transformed by being applied to a physically resilient, racially ambiguous, male vagabond even as the rhetoric itself is developed to suggest Midwinter's sensitive subjectivity. It is a sensitivity, however, that is put forward in gender terms rather than class ones: his 'sensitive feminine organisation' coexists with resilience while remaining the sign of vulnerability; anxiety continually hovers on the brink of *hysteria* – not hypochondria – as he struggles for control over his own nervous fancies and associative processes. This not only gives his sensations feminine connotations, but also shifts the emphasis from the delusion itself to the subject's immediate response to it in a way that expose the limitations of a moral management that simply takes the form of an exhortation to pull oneself together. For Midwinter's hysteria arises from his struggles to suppress his nervous fancies, not from giving in to them; from his attempts to enact an exaggerated cheerful sociability, not from his customary melancholy. Thus 'the hysterical passion rose, and conquered him' as he describes his history to Brock, but the passion is the strength of his gratitude to Armadale.[39] The chapter in which he attempts to build an acceptable persona is headed 'Midwinter in disguise' and here he presents a face which takes the form of throwing off reserve, which was 'no new side of Midwinter's character . . . it was only a new aspect of the ever-recurring struggle of Midwinter's life'. This leads to his most morbid and bizarre behaviour, loss of control and hysterical breakdown.

> His artificial spirits, lasted continuously into higher and higher effervescence since the morning, were now mounting hysterically

beyond his own control. He looked and spoke with that terrible freedom of licence which is the necessary consequence, when a diffident man has thrown off his reserve, of the very effort by which he has broken loose from his own restraints. . . . He looked backwards and forwards from Miss Milroy to Allan and declared jocosely that he understood now why his friend's morning walks were always taken in the same direction. He asked her questions about her mother, and cut short the answers she gave by remarks on the weather. . . .

There are limits even to the licence of laughter; and these limits were ere long so outrageously overstepped by one of the party as to have the effect of almost instantly silencing the other two. The fever of Midwinter's false spirits flamed out into sheer delirium as the performance of puppets came to an end. His paroxysms of laughter followed one another with such convulsive violence, that Miss Milroy started back in alarm.[40]

The dream is the most explicit example of how the narrative both analyses the basis of Midwinter's morbid delusions and makes his superstitious reading of it work while scrutinizing the effects of his ability to resist its implications. Hawbury's explanation of the dream, and his subsequent interpretation of its elements as having a limited significance, provide a framework for Midwinter's 'prophetic' response to it. This interpretation continues to operate even as Midwinter's interpretation itself qualifies it. This in turn reinforces the sense of fatality in the text itself, as he is caught in the spell of the dream. In sinking under it, he hastens the very end that he is seeking to evade while struggling to control the delusion and reassert the claims of moral management. Yet in attempting to control his associations Midwinter enacts the prescriptions set up by Abercrombie and Conolly in their outline of 'the qualities and acquirements which constitute a well-regulated mind'. He does so by reworking the associations and impressions of the dream into different contexts, and this becomes a process of self-analysis.[41] For example, he is able to dispel the superstitious connotations of Armadale's mother's old room, not by shutting it away and turning it into a site of repressed associations but by opening it up and transforming those past accretions:

Here, more strangely still, he looked on a change in the household arrangements, due in the first instance entirely to himself. His own lips had revealed the discovery that he had made on the first morning in the new home; his own voluntary act had induced the son to establish himself in his mother's room.

This turns into a more sustained analysis:

It was only after he had unreservedly acknowledged the impulse under which he had left Allan at the Mere, that he had taken credit to himself for the new point of view from which he would now look at the Dream. Then, and not till then, he had spoken of the fulfilment of the first vision, as the doctor on the Isle of Man might have spoken of it – he had asked, as the doctor might have asked, where was the wonder of their seeing a pool at sunset, when they had a whole network of pools within a few hours drive of them? And what was there extraordinary in discovering a woman at the Mere, when there were roads that led to it, and villages in its neighbourhood, and boats employed on it, and pleasure parties visiting it? So again, he had waited to vindicate the firmer resolution with which he looked to the future, until he had first revealed all that he now saw himself of the errors of the past. . . . The glaring self-contradictions betrayed in accepting the Dream as the revelation of a fatality, and in attempting to escape that fatality by an exertion of free will – in toiling to store up knowledge of the steward's duties for the future, and in shrinking from letting the future find him in Allan's home – were, in their turn, unsparingly exposed.[42]

Yet here, too, the very effort that Midwinter makes to shake off the past reinforces the sense of the strength of its hold; the weighty, convoluted sentences themselves all build up the sense of its intractability while working through the processes by which it has gained its power.

But the legacy of the past is most decisively enacted in the future by the plots of the *femme fatale*, Lydia Gwilt. She is the figure of all-embracing, disarming, and suffocating female power – in whom fear of the father and his legacy of male violence becomes transformed into the threat of the castrating women. She is everything that men desire in the feminine and everything they fear, a villainess who comes to control the narrative and who is never overpowered by successful detection, though her past is revealed by it; she only finally overpowers herself through the retribution of suicide. As most critics realized, Miss Gwilt's villainy make her the most forceful character in *Armadale*, and one aspect of her dangerous attraction is the initial absence of shame with which, like Fosco in *The Woman in White*, she perpetuates her conspiracies. But this takes on a completely different set of meanings: firstly, her villainy is mediated through her femininity and secondly, her diary plays an important role in compounding and undermining this villainy as she experiences contrition and attempts to reform herself.

'Gwilt' is emblematically set up as a study of 'guilt' in the dual sense of both wickedness and conscience; but she also operates as a study of the limitations of conventions of feminine transgression and remorse – the repentant fallen woman – and she enacts the narrator's remark that

> a man entering on a course of reformation ought, if virtue is its own reward, to be a man engaged in an essentially inspiring pursuit. But virtue is not always its own reward, and the way to reformation is remarkably ill-lighted for so respectable a thoroughfare.[43]

She is first seen as the embodiment of the shadow in the dream, as a shadow, and is built up through the juxtaposing of her appearance manifested as shadow with the self that manipulates that appearance as a means of gaining power. But while with Midwinter the delusions are dispelled through his gaining self-control, Lydia's lack of shame and ability to control her appearance can only be interpreted as moral insanity. Pedgift, the lawyer, compares her to other female criminals: 'All had a secret self-possession which nothing could shake.'[44]

This means that Lydia gains power when she is not what she appears to be, and loses it when she becomes subjected to her own desire for Midwinter, when she wants to fill the role that she had been able to manipulate as a masquerade. She first puts herself in the position of being able to seduce both Armadale and Midwinter by becoming the neighbour's governess. She acts the role of governess the more successfully by seeming to be too attractive and too self-possessed to be one: 'The sudden revelation of her beauty, as she smiled and looked at him inquiringly, suspended the movements of his limbs and the words on his lips. A vague doubt beset him whether it was the governess after all.'[45] She seduces through simulating the apparent passivity of the *femme fatale*, while in reality actively conspiring:

> Perfectly modest in her manner, possessed to perfection of the graceful refinements of a lady, she had all the allurements that feast the eye, all the Siren-invitations that seduce the sense – a subtle suggestiveness in her silence and a sexual sorcery in her smile.[46]

She plays the role of repentant fallen woman as a means of concealing her real history (which remains concealed from the reader for most of the story) and uses the conventions of melodrama to persuade Midwinter of the 'truth' of her past: 'There was nothing new in what I told him: it was the commonplace rubbish of the circulating libraries. A dead father, a lost fortune, vagabond brothers whom I dread ever seeing again.'[47] And the 'repentant fallen woman' story is further dismantled when Armadale thinks he has discovered Lydia's past. Here an intrusive narrator switches from sensation-novel conventions to a pastiche of melodrama:

> One conclusion, and one only . . . forced itself into his mind. A miserable, fallen woman, who had abandoned herself in her extremity to the help of wretches skilled in criminal concealment – who had stolen her way back into decent society and a reputable employment, by means of a false character – and whose position now imposed on her the dreadful necessity of perpetual secrecy and perpetual deceit in relation to her past life –such as the aspect in which the beautiful governess at Thorpe-Ambrose now stood revealed to Allan's eyes!
>
> Falsely revealed or truly revealed? Had she stolen her way back into decent society and a reputable employment by means of a false character? She had. Did her position impose upon her the dreadful necessity of perpetual deceit in relation to her past life? It did. Was she some such pitiable victim to the treachery of a man unknown as Allan had supposed? *She was no such pitiable victim.* The true story of the house in Pimlico – a house rightly described as filled with wicked secrets, and people rightly represented as perpetually in danger of feeling the grasp of the law – was a story which coming events were yet to disclose: a story infinitely less revolting, yet infinitely more terrible, than Allan or Allan's companion had either of them supposed.[48]

Lydia Gwilt's attempted reform, as she falls for Midwinter and attempts to fill subjectively the role that was previously an imposture, is negotiated and shown to be impossible in the terms of her own self-defining identity, in the shifting confessional function of her diary. The diary is the means by which Miss Gwilt both mediates the tensions of the plot – where she meditates on the significance of coincidence – and is 'haunted' by the resemblance of names and by herself:

> My nerves must be a little shaken, I think, I was startled just now by a shadow on the wall. It was only after a moment or two that I mustered sense enough to notice where the candle was, and to

see that the shadow was my own. . . . Here is my own hand-writing startling me now! . . . The similarity of names never struck me in this light before.[49]

It is also the place where her 'wicked' self speaks and where she incubates the plot against the Armadale property, and a means of self-control (as it was for Marian in *The Woman in White*):

> Would it help me to shake off these impressions, I wonder, if I made the effort of writing them down? There would be no danger, in that case, of my forgetting anything important, and perhaps, after all, it may be the fear of something I ought to remember, this story of Midwinter weighing as it does on my mind.[50]

But while with Marian the gradual loss of this self-control is the sign of defeat by forces beyond it, with Lydia a split gradually arises in the function of the diary between the conspiring and controlling self, and the 'guilty' self as she becomes 'reformed'. Thus the movement of penitence is marked by the merging of narrative time and story time as Lydia renounces her diary and herself, and loses self-possession: 'Six o'clock. . . How is it that he alters me so that I hardly know myself again? . . . I felt a dreadful hysterical choking in the throat when he entreated me not to reveal my troubles.[51] '*Sunday August 10th* The eve of my wedding-day! I close and lock this book, never to write in it, never to open it again. I have won the great victory; I have trampled my own wickedness underfoot. I am innocent.'[52] But as she finds the sheer boredom of domesticity and wifely dependence to be the falsest role of all, she comes to depend on her diary as much as her 'drops' of laudanum: 'My misery is a woman's misery and it *will* speak here rather than nowhere; to my second self, in this book, if I have no-one else to hear me.'[53] The diary is the only place where she achieves a sympathetic subjectivity, but self-imposed moral management and reform involve that loss of self-possession, a contradiction which in the end can only be expressed by suicide.

The climax of *Armadale* and of the Gwilt conspiracy is when Lydia, with the accomplice Dr Downward, now transformed into the sinister Dr le Doux, lures Armadale and Midwinter into le Doux's newly built model 'Sanitorium' for nervous patients; Gwilt uses one of the asylum's boasted non-restraint methods as a means to attempt to poison Armadale by 'drowning' or suffocating him in poisoned air – a method she finally applies to herself. While the non-restraint asylum was the means of Laura's transformation in its very acceptability in *The Woman in White*, here the image of the sanitorium winds up the elements that are disturbing for their realism in the earlier novel, and draws on the 'older' image of the asylum as a melodramatic force of evil, a means of sensational conspiracy and horror. But it does this, as in Reade's *Hard Cash*, by blowing up moral management itself as a sinister force and transforming seclusion and repose into literal sources of suffocation – firstly of the hero, finally of the repentent villainess – and thus creates a sensational framework to achieve the 'fatal' end that is a pastiche of the very means by which it is resisted.

The sanatorium is an explicit parody of a private asylum for nervous patients directly based on those aspects of Conolly's *The Treatment of the Insane Without Mechanical Restraints* that stress suppression and seclusion rather than self-control, and it turns the image of the theatre round to parody those presuppositions. It is a theatre of its own techniques, open to public inspection and offering a welcome relief to the visitors from the propriety of their private lives while replicating its essential forms:

> In the miserable monotony of the lives led by a large section of the middle classes of England, anything is welcome to the women which offers them any sort of harmless refuge from the established tyranny of the principle that all human happiness begins and ends at home.[54]

Doctor le Doux has graduated to the proprietorship of the sanatorium from an earlier position as 'ladies' medical man': 'One of those carefully constructed physicians . . . he had the necessary bald head, the necessary double eyeglass, the necessary black clothes and the necessary blandness of manner, all complete.'[55] His description of the asylum is a direct echo of Conolly's argument. Conolly wrote in *The Treatment of the Insane*:

> Many English superintendents speak of seclusion as something worse than mechanical restraint; seeming to forget that it is as much adapted to secure an irritable brain from causes of increased irritability as a quiet chamber and the exclusion of glare . . . is adapted to the same state of brain in a fever. The patient needs repose, and every object, or every person seen, irritates him. . . . It is often seen that the mere moving of the cover of the inspection-plate in the door of a patient's room if not cautiously done, rouses the patient from tranquility and causes him to start up and rush violently to the door. Seclusion gives him the benefit of continued tranquility, by removing at once every cause of excitement.[56]

Le Doux extends this to cover all forms of nervous disorders of modern life:

> Literally a word, on nervous derangement first . . . I throw up impregnable moral entrenchments between Worry and You . . . I assert the medical treatment of nervous suffering to be entirely subsidiary to the moral treatment of it. That moral treatment of it, you find here. . . . [The patient's mind] is one mass of nervous fancies and caprices, which his friend (with the best possible intentions) have been ignorantly irritating at home . . . I pull a handle when he is snug in his bed, and the window noiselessly closes in a moment. Nothing to irritate him, ladies and gentlement, nothing to irritate him![57]

The two doctors, Hawbury and le Doux, thus form two poles in the use of psychological discourse – dream theory and moral management – around which the plot revolves; but they do so by having contradictory fictional functions; the function of le Doux (to transform perception through transforming moral management into a bizarre and uncanny device) undermines Hawbury's role as realigning the trains of association.

Armadale has two endings as well as two beginnings: the end of the Story with Lydia's suicide and the Conclusion, 'Midwinter', where Midwinter himself finally reaches a satisfactory interpretation of the dream, and a means of explaining coincidence, and reversing the terms of his father's letter: 'I have learnt to view the purpose of the Dream with a new mind. . . . In that faith I can look back without murmuring at the years that are past, and can look on without doubting to the years that are to come.[58] Brock's rational Christianity is the final means of closing the novel. But it is in seeking out the resolution and generating the mystery that the cognitive complexity of *Armadale* is created; and it is never finally able to emerge from its involuted heuristic structure and either reach a final interpretation of the dream, or offer a stable interpretation of itself to the reader. *Armadale* seems to be set up as a struggle between fate and chance, destiny and autonomy, but it quickly turns into a novel about the different ways the present and present identity are over-determined by the forces of the past, emerging in coincidence as much as conspiracy. Finally the great doubt – 'the doubt whether we are, or are not, masters of our own destiny' – of the father remains unresolved, but in the process the meaning of destiny has splintered through the process of working out what that process of working out might mean. And as a palimpsest of traces of the past, *Armadale* – both the name and the title – anticipates Collins's most ambitious attempt to investigate that process of investigation, set within a psychological context that incorporates an analysis of the unconscious – *The Moonstone*.

6

Lost parcel or hidden soul?
Detecting the unconscious in
The Moonstone

Is there a form of hysterics that bursts into words
instead of tears?
Wilkie Collins, *The Moonstone*[1]

What have I lost? Nothing but Nervous Force – which
the law doesn't recognise as property.
Wilkie Collins, *The Moonstone*[2]

Here was our quiet English house suddenly invaded by a devilish
Indian Diamond – bringing after it a conspiracy of living rogues,
set loose on us by the vengeance of a dead man. Who ever heard
the like of it – in the nineteenth century, mind; in an age of
progress, and in a country that rejoices in the blessings of the
British constitution?[3]

Thus Gabriel Betteredge, who has the edge on all the narrators in
The Moonstone, describes his reaction to the news of the advent of
the oriental jewel, seized by imperialist plunder, into the apparently
calm, stable world of the English upper-middle-class country house.
The Moonstone has become dangerous because it has been stolen,
displaced; it is stolen and misplaced a second time, precipitating
wispread anxiety and a disruption of social and sexual relationships
within the family, manifested above all in the apparently hysterical
behaviour of the heroine: 'The cursed Moonstone had turned us all
upside down.'[4] The drive of the narrative, then, is to track down
the lost object not simply for itself, but to restore what its lack
signifies, socially and sexually, within the family. Suspicion falls
predictably on the alien, marginal figures: on the Indians hovering
about the grounds, relying on the occult device of clairvoyance to
ascertain the diamond's whereabouts; on the deformed penitent
thief turned housemaid, Rosanna Spearman; even on Rachel. But it
is the hero, Franklin Blake, possessed of what Ezra Jennings

describes as 'youth, health, riches, a place in the world, a prospect before you. You and such as you, show me the sunny side of human life',[5] who is revealed, three-quarters of the way through the story, to have stolen the diamond without realizing it himself. The quest now becomes to find the lost object through the reinterpretation of the meaning of the past. And this means learning not only to see differently, but to redefine what constitutes knowledge and experience in a way that involves a new kind of remembering, one which leads to a historical and psychological reconstruction. But the traces of the past are ambiguous and shifting, there is no focal point from which they can be surveyed, and the physiological experiment that is interpreted as proof is essentially a piece of theatre projected out of a fictional hypothesis which claims the authority of science – an opium-induced re-enactment of an opium-induced action, set up by an opium-dependent doctor.[6] They never get the diamond back either. It is revealed to have been stolen from Blake by the heroine's false suitor and representative of English hypocritical philanthropy, Godfrey Ablewhite; but then taken from *him* by the Indian brahmins and finally restored to its proper place in the Hindu temple.

The Moonstone is Collins's most compulsively readable and pleasurable novel. Again it was written within specific constraints, partly shaped by the risks that Collins had taken with *Armadale*; again it was phenomenally popular, doing more to boost the circulation of *All the Year Round* than *Great Expectations* had done.[7] It is also his most conceptually complex work; in it Collins most clearly appropriates theories through telling stories in a way which suggests that theories themselves are interpretative narratives. As a prototypical detective novel, which offers multiple means of exploring those forms of symbolic transformation focused above all on the heroine's tacit sexuality, *The Moonstone* has attracted a host of psychoanalytic readings. The most sophisticated of these is Albert D. Hutter's essay, 'Dreams, transformations and literature: the implications of detective fiction'.[8] It argues for extending the dream as the paradigm for the text by moving beyond a reductive reading of dreaming itself purely as a form of infantile wish-fulfilment while interpreting the novel itself as a detailed allegory of sexual repression. These readings have stressed the novel's fundamental cognitive ambiguity – the way that it continually asserts and undermines the sources of its own coherence, most notably by breaking down the boundary between 'objective' and 'subjective' reality, so that it becomes a palimpsest of overt and covert meanings. On the one hand, it has been seen in the light of the interpretative framework shaped by the later development of the 'whodunit' school: a cosy 'three pipe problem' which deals with the disruption of order in an isolated community, through the subjective impressions of individual narrators, presented from the safe standpoint of retrospection and empirical proof. Here the pleasure of reading is bound up with the construction of a rational solution out of the fragmented testimony of the different narratives – putting the reader in a comparable position to the one s/he occupied for *The Woman in White*. On the other, it has been read as tacitly overturning all these procedures.[9] Without discounting the importance of those readings, this chapter investigates how the novel becomes Collins's most ambitious exploration of social and psychic identity, as a study in ambiguity itself. I want to raise questions here both about how mid-nineteenth-century discourses on the unconscious are appropriated in *The Moonstone* (discourses which do not straightforwardly prefigure later Freudian or Jungian psychoanalytic models, though they might contribute to their formation) and about the interpretative challenges that they pose. *The Moonstone*'s simultaneously cosy and disturbing quality was noted by Dickens, who wrote in a letter to Wills: 'It is a very curious story, wild yet domestic . . . nothing belonging to disguised women or the like'.[10] The concerns of the earlier fiction are pushed beyond their own limits here, but they are paradoxically also reassimilated. They are taken up on a register that is at once more 'homely' and more abstract and conceptual, and it is this which gives the novel its uncanny yet canny, 'wild yet domestic', quality – cosy and reassuring even as it overturns the discursive boundaries on which that security rests.

The Woman in White derived its means of narrative tension and closure from using a dominant psychological ambivalently, as a means of both creating mystery and resolving it. The benign asylum was the crucible for both the destruction and the reconstitution of Laura's identity, displaying the contradictions of the overall framework of moral management even as it reaffirmed it. A more complicated piece of cognitive juggling is at work in *The Moonstone*; the novel does not so much twist one model round as conjure with countervailing yet collusive paradigms, paradigms which, more decisively even than in *Armadale*, cannot be brought into interpretative alignment. The 'discovery of the truth' hinges on Blake 'bringing into the light' the secret contained in the murky and entangled past – the secret that he had taken the diamond but while 'unconscious' and for benign motivations – only to have it stolen from him. This discovery could only take place when the psychic conditions of the year before were exactly reproduced through a physiological experiment initiated by the doctor's assistant, the bizarre and cross-grained Ezra Jennings, who is basing his hypotheses on principles derived from combining the writings of William Carpenter and John Elliotson. The model of the unconscious that this implies can, I shall argue, be assimilated within a dominant physiological mould – the domesticated, 'Carpenter' one – but it also fuses into a 'wilder' model, the one suggested by 'Elliotson', and this has the effect of reinforcing and undercutting a moral management that has no coherent focus. In an immediate sense this paradox discloses and conceals an unresolved question: what is Blake's 'self'? Can all its secret places be finally brought into the light, moral ambiguity displaced on to Ablewhite, the whited sepulchre, the leader of a double life? And this again suggests that the underlying tensions of the text concern not only the tacit definition of feminine sexuality but the problematic nature of masculinity.

These tacit questions about Blake's identity and, by metaphor and analogy, the meaning of the Moonstone are both the absent centre and analogue of the process of detection and the narrative relations at work in the story as a whole: the process by which identity is created through generating both resemblance and difference – a process that can never be located in a stable set of oppositions. The two countervailing models of the unconscious are the pivot of the plot; they transform the meaning of the narrative contexts in which they are placed, yet they are also transformed by it, and in this way *The Moonstone* itself works as a complex model of the mind. And that narrative process, the means of generating pleasurable suspense, also, I want to argue, tacitly draws on another conception of the unconscious – one that hovers, as it were, just out of the field of vision of the text itself: that analysis of aesthetic pleasure, the 'hidden soul', and the 'play of thought' – *The Gay Science*.

But it is not enough to set up psychological paradigms as interpretative hypotheses and then try to fit the novel into them or see it reflecting them in order to demonstrate how this process works: this would too easily imply a given set of prior meanings, which the novel somehow approximates to. I argued in Chapter 1 that mid-nineteenth-century debates about consciousness signalled the tenuousness of a knowable subjectivity fixed through clear discursive boundaries in the very drive to establish that subjectivity. *The Moonstone* continually exploits the tenuousness of these boundaries by juggling with these distinct hypotheses, and again it is this that shapes its possible subversive ideological meanings. Its relation to these theories moves between correspondence, analogy, and homology, and thus the narrative relations of the novel slide between transforming the significance of their sources, and remaining finally bounded by them. This is a process which needs to be analysed, starting with the narrative itself, for metaphors of levels, depth, and surface are inadequate to conceptualize what happens in the novel – and here it takes the implied scrutiny of interpretative paradigms discussed in *Armadale* a stage further. I have suggested that all the novels of the 1860s unpick their own discursive assumptions as they go along. This culminates in *The Moonstone* in the particular way in which the pleasure of the search is a direct analogue of the mental processes that are investigated as part of it. For it is through this narrative method that the novel becomes 'wild yet domestic' – creating direct parallels between the subverting of oppositions in scrutinizing the terms which construct social, psychic, and cognitive resemblance and difference. The undermining of the boundaries between homely and uncanny, inside and outside, normal and deviant, are homologous with the function of the boundaries between the 'rational' and 'occult' on the one hand, between 'Englishness' and 'foreignness' on the other, a process which culminates, through metaphoric transference and analogy, in a direct correspondence between the social construction of psychic marginality, and the process whereby colonial 'otherness' works as the projection of 'English' fascinations and fears. So this chapter starts with the narrative, and works through its patterns to reach the psychological discourses that both frame it and are set within it.

The Moonstone is a novel about remembering; about how, and under what conditions, the unconscious past might be reclaimed, about how its traces might be interpreted and understood, about how this might be transmitted to posterity. It shows the inadequacy of the lawyer, Bruff's, commonsense suggestion:

> I tell you, we shall be wasting our time . . . if we attempt to try back, and unravel this frightful complication from the beginning. Let us close our minds resolutely to all that happened last year at Lady Verinder's country house; and let us look to what we *can* discover in the future, instead of what we can *not* discover in the past.

It is shown to be inadequate in the light of Blake's stricture: 'Surely you forget . . . that the whole thing is essentially a matter of the past.'[11] But in order to show this it equally needs to be a novel about forgetting, about what is intractable, about silence, suppression, and concealment. On a straightforward level, of course, this is a basic precondition of the story; there would *be* no mystery if Rachel had not suppressed her knowledge of the theft (this also makes it impossible for her to be a narrator) or if Rosanna's letter had not been sunk in the quicksand, to be dragged back, much later, on a chain. The pleasure of the 'discovery of the truth' thus depends on the interplay between conscious and unconscious forms of resistance involved in the 'loss of the diamond' in the first place; but it is an equivocal pleasure, that is enhanced by disclosing marginal and half-hidden texts that not only exist on the perimeters of the central narrative, but are written by those who labour under the yoke of various kinds of social and psychic inheritance, and who finally sink without trace. The narrative thus needs to overturn its own apparent order in order for meaning to emerge, but the order that takes its place never takes the form of a fixed set of relations. Rather, it works as a set of interlocking frameworks: on the one hand, the overall structure of the story, within which the viewpoints of the specific narrators are set: on the other the linear ordering of narrative time through which the past in repossessed within the overall reconstruction.

Thus, structurally, *The Moonstone* seems to develop and combine many of the narrative features of *The Woman in White* and *Armadale*: it is narrated by different characters through different interpretative and psychological perspectives; it is divided into Prologue, Story, and Epilogue, and these together take the form of an 'English' chain embedded within an 'Indian' frame. The 'Indian' Prologue is 'extracted from a family paper' of 1799 – the story is set in 1848 – and it supplies both the long-term history of the Moonstone as a religious object and source of passion and violence, and the more recent story of the Verinder family's guilty past of colonial expropriation – a past shared by Rachel, Blake, and Ablewhite in that they are all cousins, but not directly known by them. As in *Armadale* the Prologue forms the central narrative's history by presenting *English* passion and violence let loose in a colonial setting. But it is more thoroughly separated from the Story here – the autonomous family is referred to indirectly; the history of the diamond remains 'unconscious' and it is this which compounds its occult and invasive connotations, and means that Prologue and Story hold a different relation to each other from their opposite numbers in *Armadale*. The Story is itself subdivided between the history of the loss and the restoration. 'The loss of the diamond' has one narrator, Gabriel Betteredge, the old family retainer, and covers the appearance of the diamond, the budding courtship of Rachel and Franklin, the loss on the birthday night, the inadequacy of the police search, and the suicide of Rosanna. 'The discovery of the truth' has multiple narrators: Miss Clack, the fanatic evangelical; Bruff, the solicitor; Blake; Jennings; Cuff, the detective; Dr Candy and Betteredge again. It covers Rachel's confusion over Ablewhite and hostility to Blake; Blake's discovery that she witnessed his stealing the diamond; the disclosure of Rosanna's confession and the stained nightshirt; the experimental reconstruction of the birthday night; the re-emergence of the police search and the move to London, and the tracking down of the disguised Ablewhite in the city streets. The Epilogue is principally narrated by Murthwaite the anthropologist, who describes the 'Finding of the diamond' in the Hindu temple. The resolution of the double mystery is thus structurally separated from the return of the colonial plunder – the original crime – which takes place beyond the perimeters of the Story itself.

But this embedded chain structure has an alternative meaning. Just as the frame is marginal in both senses of the word – defining the story even as it remains at its edges, so those other kinds of marginal texts – the brahmins' clairvoyance, Rosanna's letter, Jennings's incomplete book on the brain and nervous system – become central by *remaining* peripheral. So the more embedded and qualified a testimony, the stronger its significance becomes, and this completes the reversal of narrative authority that was the tacit undertone of *The Woman in White*. Moreover, there is no Walter Hartright figure to double as general editor and specific narrator in *The Moonstone*. Structurally, Blake fills the role: Betteredge reveals at the beginning that he is writing at the behest of Blake who is himself following Bruff's suggestion: 'Mr Bruff thinks, as I think, that the whole thing ought, in the interests of truth, to be placed on record in writing and the sooner the better', and it then emerges that it was Blake who had extracted the 'family paper' of the Prologue.[12] But whereas in *The Woman in White* the 'loss' of Laura was told through multiple viewpoints and the reconstruction through Hartright's reappropriation of the past, this pattern is reversed here, and although the discovery depends on appropriating information buried in the loss, the relationship between the narrative focus and the control of narrative time is more uncertain; Blake is collecting retrospective evidence *after* the resolution of the mystery. Although he makes editorial interventions in the form of notes, or disputes with participating narrators, the whole is constructed retrospectively. Indeed it is the voice of Betteredge which closes the Story:

'I am the person (as you remember no doubt), who led the way in these pages and opened the story. I am also the person who is left behind, as it were, to close the story up'; he thus frames the frame he is set within.[13] Within this frame, the obviously subjective perceptions of the different narrators work principally to get the reader to search for truth by having it continually frustrated by offering evidence 'unconsciously', through lapses, or symptomatic mannerisms rather than having it operate as a chain of linked associations.

There are several interwined implications to this narrative structure. Firstly, there is a remarkable set of correspondences between the way that the process of pleasurable detection works in the narrative patterns of the *The Moonstone* as a whole and Dallas's outline of the working of aesthetic pleasure in the 'play of thought' itself given in *The Gay Science*. Dallas, as I suggested in Chapter 1, argued that pleasure in art was derived from its direct correspondence with the workings of the unconscious, or the 'hidden soul'; that this kind of mental activity took place automatically and that its power lay above all in its secrecy. He argued that no experience was ever entirely lost though it might pass out of the range of the beam of light of consciousness, and it was the process of 'unconscious seeking' that compounded the apparently magical effects of imagination; the process of transformation whereby a thought resurfaces 'changed and grown as if it were a new thought, and we know not whence it comes'.[14] He maintained that in order to appreciate this process it was necessary to recognize the simultaneous marginality and centrality of the unconscious: 'trains of thought are continually passing to and fro, from the light to the dark and back again from the dark into the light' and yet this unconscious mental activity is most evident

> when memory halts a little. Then we are aware that we are seeking for something that we know not, and there arises a strange contradiction of a faculty knowing what it searches for, and yet making the search because it does not know.[15]

Similarly in *The Moonstone* the 'outer and the inner ring' of consciousness are paradoxically both absent and present in the text, and part of the pleasurableness of searching is in reading through the inconsistencies, the 'gaps and lapses of memory, the trains of thought unwittingly pursued', that are central not only to the overall process of narrative reconstruction, but to the detective process in the story itself.

But this is only one possible reading (one which I shall come back to), and to apply Dallas's analysis of the 'play of thought' as an external narrative paradigm that the text reproduces through direct correspondence leaves out a crucial process of internal scrutiny implied within the story itself, and through this *The Moonstone*'s ideological ambivalence. For in a literal sense the novel is precisely concerned with 'the slow and toilsome journey from the darkness to the light', with exposing what is 'hidden in the obscure recesses of the mind'.[16] And this affects the cognitive status of psychic marginality, Blake's identity as analogue of the workings of the mind in the novel as a whole, and his relation to the figures that surround him, the tacit correspondence between dominant and marginal forms of knowledge, and the way that the past determines the present. *The Moonstone* is not just a reconstruction: it is the reconstruction of a reconstruction of a reconstruction, which means that suspense and indeterminacy also need to arise from *within* the process of memory itself and the way it in turn is remembered. Thus, although narrative time and story time remain structurally separate in the novel (with the important exception of Jennings's journal), both enact the circuitous process of drawing on and exposing, while covering, their own traces.

And here the explicit reference to external psychological authority, as well as the means by which it is mediated, is crucial. Ezra Jennings repeatedly claims the credibility of scientific validity in explaining the psychological experiment with the opium to Blake:

> I think myself bound to prove, in justice to both of us, that I am not asking you to try this experiment in deference to any theory of my own devising. Admitted principles, and recognised authorities, justify me in the view that I take. . . . Science sanctions my proposal, fanciful as it may seem. Here, in the first place, is the physiological principle on which I am acting, stated by no less a person than Dr Carpenter. . . . Observe, Mr Blake, that I am now referring to one of the greatest of British physiologists. The book in your hand is Dr Elliotson's *Human Physiology*; and the case which the doctor cites rests on the well-known authority of Mr Combe. . . . Are you satisfied that I have not spoken without good authority to support me?[17]

In this way Jennings repeatedly claims the authority of externally verifiable texts, and Collins, too, emphasizes the validity of the physiological experiment in the Preface:

Having first ascertained, not only from books, but from living authorities as well, what the result of the experiment would really have been, I have declined to avail myself of the novelist's privilege of supposing something which might have happened, and have so shaped the story as to make it grow out of what actually would have happened – which, I beg to inform my readers, is also what actually does happen, in these pages.[18]

But of course the credibility here depends on hypothetical speculation, and it is this that gives scientific credibility its particular role in producing a fictional *frisson*; the reader, like the sceptical observers, Bruff and Betteredge, is drawn, as voyeur and spectator, into the 'secret theatre' of the action. The experiment and what it reveals are thus the pivot of the story while being set within its own internal framework of coherence by the citing of the 'external' Carpenter and Elliotson texts. But Collins uses Carpenter and Elliotson in this particular context in a very precise way as a means of highlighting the dramatic elements of the story and of bringing together the homely and the exotic, the scientific and the occult – the particular use of opium and the double conception of the unconscious that is excavated is crucial here.

In what way does Jennings's experiment draw on and transform specific aspects of the unconscious? In conflating Carpenter and Elliotson in this way Collins is condensing two figures whose names, as we have seen, would have had very different resonances in the 1860s: Carpenter, the respected voice of mainstream physiological psychology; Elliotson, the marginalized advocate of mesmerism. Jennings tests the hypothesis that Blake had stolen the diamond in an artificially induced state of aberrance by juxtaposing the two figures in a way that, mimetically fits completely within the bottom line of physiological psychology that Carpenter and Elliotson share: the basic assertion that there *is* an unconscious, that nothing that has been assimilated by the mind is ever entirely lost though the lines of transmission may be broken. The familiar image of the unconscious mind as a 'lumber room' filled with misplaced articles, is evoked by the passage from Carpenter's *Principles of Human Physiology* that Jennings cites:

There seems much ground for the belief that *every* sensory impression which has once been recognised by the perceptive consciousness, is registered (so to speak) in the brain, and may be reproduced at some subsequent time, although there may be no consciousness of its existence in the mind during the whole intermediate period.[19]

This spatial metaphor is vividly encapsulated in Jennings's verbatim quotation from Elliotson, reinforcing the well-worn notion of double consciousness which he explicitly extrapolates from the phrenological tradition:

'Dr Abel informed me', says Mr Combe, 'of an Irish porter to a warehouse, who forgot, when sober, what he had done when drunk; but, being drunk, again recollected the transactions of his former state of intoxication. On one occasion, being drunk, he had lost a parcel of some value, and in his sober moments could give no account of it. Next time he was intoxicated, he recollected that he had left the parcel at a certain house, and there being no address to it it had remained there safely, and was got on his calling for it.[20]

This 'lost parcel' model of the unconscious provides the means of re-enacting the night of the theft 'as it happened', while enabling Blake's identity to remain not simply innocent of conscious complicity, but as safe, if obscure, as the lost parcel itself. But a dissonance between 'Carpenter' and 'Elliotson' is also at work. It has been seen that Carpenter recognized that memory operated selectively, but that 'consciousness of agreement', or recognition of the traces of the past, 'constitutes the basis of our feeling of personal identity', by stressing the importance of continuous lines of transmission between past and present.[21] He reiterated that

the *unconscious* prejudices that we thus form are often stronger than the *conscious*, and they are more dangerous because we cannot knowingly guard against them . . . the conceptions of childhood will appear latent in the mind, to reappear in every hour of weakness . . . when the tension of the reason is relaxed, and the power of old associations is supreme.[22]

But his precise interpretation of the implications of this premise underwent important modifications during the late 1840s and this resulted in a realignment of the claims of moral management through his reassessment of the significance of the distinction between reflex and volitional action.

Carpenter had claimed, following Pritchard and anticipating Maudsley, that individuals could not be held responsible for actions that they had performed reflexively, or automatically:

Nor can we say a human action is morally wrong . . . when it directly results from a powerful impulse which he has no power to restrain. . . . According to this view, what is termed conscience is nothing less than the idea of right or wrong character which becomes attached to an action, when we place in comparison the motives that prompted it.[23]

The implications of this argument, however, underwent important modifications, and during the 1840s moved towards extending the range of the controlling powers of the mind, and thus individual responsibility, bringing reflexive and automatic actions themselves into moral management's sphere of influence. His study of the effects of artificially induced derangement was crucial here, since these provided examples of mental states in which volitional activity was suspended but not entirely abolished; his analysis of Jacques Moreau's *Psychological Studies on Hachisch and on Mental Derangement* of 1847 maintained that even under the influence of cannabis the mind was capable of self-direction:

> One of the first effects of the hachisch . . . is the gradual weakening of that power of voluntarily controlling and directing the thoughts, which is so characteristic of the vigorous mind. The individual feels himself incapable of fixing his attention on any subject; his thoughts being continually drawn off by a succession of the ideas that force themselves (as it were), into his mind without his being able in the least to trace their origin. . . . By a strong effort of will, however, the original thread of the ideas may still be recovered, and the interlopers may be driven away, their remembrance, however, being preserved, like that of a dream recalling events long past.[24]

Thus with the right training the unconscious would itself become fully recuperated, and the mind would be 'not only concerned with carrying into the effect the suggestions of the desires. In the well-regulated mind it ought to have a controlling effect over the desires themselves, so as to prevent them from exercising themselves with undue force.'[25]

This becomes one of a palimpsest of hidden scripts that make up *The Moonstone*, enabling the detective process to follow clues and drive interlopers away even as it legitimizes Blake as interloper himself. It is well known that Collins was himself thoroughly dependent on laudanum by the time he wrote the novel, although his account of having dictated sections of the story while directly under its influence may well be exaggerated. Opium provides the explicit means of inducing a trance-like state in which 'volitional activity' is suspended in Blake, but it does so primarily as a medicine rather than as a hallucinatory drug, and this is underlined by Jennings's reference not only to Carpenter, but to his other authoritative source: De Quincey's *Confessions of an English Opium-Eater*.[26] For the reference to De Quincey simultaneously gives 'opium' exotic and romantic connotations and diffuses them along Carpenter-like lines. Jennings cites the *Confessions* as a self-conscious analysis of the drug to stress the distinction between its stimulant and narcotic effects. The section on 'The pleasures of opium' in the *Confessions* itself reinforces this: 'Whereas wine disorders the mental faculties, opium on the contrary (if taken in the proper manner), introduces among them the most exquisite order, legislation and harmony.'[27] Here, then, it is used to produce a kind of unconscious that is tacitly still regulated, a state of passive derangement that does not necessarily involve or imply the disintegration of Blake's social identity, and which offers him a past to be visited, not a history to be narrated. Moreover, Blake's original 'morbid' condition, which led to Candy secretly spiking his nightcap with laudanum on the night of the original theft, is, in a literal sense, another ostensibly innocent form of artificially induced nervous disorder. And this, together with the anxieties that explicitly rise to consciousness in the deranged state in both its original and replayed versions, indeed suggest that his is a 'Carpenter' unconscious – a set of indirectly willed reflexive gestures beyond volitional control, yet which take the form of a relatively 'moral' impulse in response to immediate impressions. Jennings describes the process thus:

Under the stimulating influence, the latest and most vivid impressions left on your mind – namely, the impressions relating to the Diamond – would be likely, in your morbidly sensitive nervous condition, to become intensified in your brain, and would subordinate to themselves your judgement and your will – exactly as an ordinary dream subordinates to itself your judgement and your will. Little by little, under this action, any apprehensions about the safety of the Diamond which you had felt during the day would be liable to develop themselves from the state of doubt to the state of certainty – would impel you into practical action to preserve the jewel – would direct your steps, with that motive in view, into the room which you had entered – and would guide your hand to the drawers of the cabinet until you had found the drawer which held the stone. In the spiritualised intoxication of opium, you would do all that.[28]

So in the means of disclosure Collins combines aspects of Carpenter with the less contentious side of Elliotson, and this is reinforced by the management of the experiment itself. Jennings's aim is to reproduce exactly the conditions of the night of the crime in the belief that Blake will provide an action replay by taking up an identical subject position:

> We shall have to put you back into something assimilating to your nervous condition on the birthday night. If we can next revive, or nearly revive, the domestic circumstances which surrounded you; and if we can occupy your mind again with questions concerning the Diamond which formerly agitated it, we shall have replaced you, as nearly as possible, in the same position physically and morally, in which the opium found you last year.[29]

But the device itself – Blake's trance watched by hidden observers – immediately recalls one of the 'Magnetic evenings at home': the controlled experiment of the private mesmeric display. Blake's re-enactment can be seen both as a reflexive response and as a somnambulist's trance, artifically induced; for it is the voyeuristic process of observation of the revelation of the past that is the source of tension and fascination as much as what is actually revealed. And this means that the 'Elliotson' of the fifth edition of *Human Physiology* – outcast of the scientific establishment, advocate of magnetism as a means of disclosing the sources of nervous disorders and thus precipitating their cure, who notes, citing Gall, 'how often in intoxication . . . under violent emotions . . . through the effect of such poisons as opium . . . are we not transformed in some measure into totally different beings?'[30] – becomes the ambiguous subtext of the official physiological experiment. Bruff's initial distrust of the scheme ('It was quite unintelligible to *his* mind, except that it looked like a piece of trickery, akin to the trickery of mesmerism, clairvoyance, and the like'[31]) is principally a means of displaying his naïve empiricism, for mesmerism as an implied mode of influence and power that has both occult and scientific connotations is put to complicated use in *The Moonstone*.

The explicit and mimetic use of mesmerism is the role its most extreme and 'occult' form – clairvoyance – has in compounding the 'wild', or romantic implications of the Indian brahmins. This 'orientalism' is made clear by Murthwaite the anthropologist, who offers an account that immediately replicates the dominant English explanation of the phenomenon:

The clairvoyance in this case is simply a development of the romantic side of the Indian character. It would have been a refreshment and an encouragement to these men – quite inconceivable, I grant you, to the English mind – to surround their wearisome and perilous journey with a certain halo of the marvellous and the supernatural. Their boy is certainly a sensitive subject to the mesmeric influence – and under that influence, he has no doubt reflected what was in the mind of the person mesmerising him. I have tested the theory of clairvoyance – and I have never found that the manifestations get beyond that point. . . . We have nothing whatever to do with clairvoyance; or with mesmerism, or with anything that is hard of belief to a practical man, in the inquiry that we are now pursuing. My object of following the Indian plot, step by step, is to trace results back, by rational means, to natural causes.[32]

I will come back to this description, but it needs first to be specifically placed within the context of the multiple manifestations of 'mesmerism' in the novel, which together form key pieces in the pattern of interwoven hypotheses in the text as a whole. 'Mesmerism' is a means of signalling wildness, difference, 'otherness', but it is also much more than this – it is a method of generating a sense of cognitive confusion, disrupting stable means of signification, and this transforms the significance of wildness as much as domesticity. And in suggesting not simple irrationality so much as the logic underlying the workings of the unconcious, 'magnetic' imagery – above all in the signifier of the Moonstone itself – again works in a way that is analogous to Dallas's 'play of thought'; displacing the 'lost parcel' notion of the unconscious with the 'hidden soul'. Like Combe, Elliotson, and Jennings, Dallas refers to the 'lost parcel' anecdote in *The Gay Science*; but he does so to criticize the most simplistic aspects of the physiological tradition:

We laugh to hear of the drunken Irish porter who forgot when sober what he'd done when drunk . . . so that having once in a state of intoxication lost a valuable parcel, he could give no account for it, but readily found it again in his next drinking bout. . . . The physiologists attempt to account for this by regarding the brain as a double organ.[33]

He went on to argue that

these physical explanations are not satisfactory. . . . If memory has its hiding place in the mind, and if there too is to be found a hidden reason; so also, nearly all that we understand by passion, feeling, sympathy . . . is an energy of the hidden soul.[34]

As I suggested in the discussion of *Armadale*, Dallas includes mesmerism and the 'nightly rising of the somnambulist' as symptoms of the 'hidden soul'; *The Moonstone* extends this exploration of the secret interaction within the mind through the language of animal magnetism, but again in a way that implicitly questions any straightforward pattern of projection and transference: marginality is actively constructed, and is more than simply an analogue of the unconscious mind – and conversely, *as* an analogue, it is rooted in explicit social hierarchies.

The linchpin of the social and psychic significance of mesmerism is Jennings himself: a figure of ambiguity who uses psychological discourse ambiguously and who plays a double role as agent and subject, doctor and patient, in the progress of the story. As narrator, Jennings obviously provides the crucial pivot: his journal recounting the course of the experiment offers the tensest moment of the detective process by being the point at which narrative time and story time merge, and retrospection turns into prospective chronicle in which 'subjective' and 'objective' impressions merge. Furthermore, Jennings collapses different kinds of knowledge and authority together in his own transgressive identity. As Collins's most explicitly cross-category figure, he operates as the point at which all the systems of difference in the novel – and the means of interpreting and explaining them – break down; pushing the disruptive patterns of projection and inverted expectation involved in the perception of Marian Halcombe (in *The Woman in White*) and Ozias Midwinter (in *Armadale*) through their own limits by turning them into a force of 'magnetic' attraction as he reciprocates Blake's look:

Judging him by his figure and his movements, he was still young. Judging by his face, and comparing him to Betteredge, he looked the elder of the two. His complexion was of a gypsy darkness; his fleshless cheeks had fallen into deep hollows, over which the bone projected like a pent-house. His nose presented the fine shape and modelling so often found among the ancient people of the East, so seldom visible among the newer races of the West. His forehead rose straight and high from the brow. His marks and wrinkles were innumerable. From this strange face, eyes, stranger still, of the softest brown – eyes dreamy and mournful and deeply sunk in their orbits – looked out at you, and (in my case at least) took your attention captive at their will. Add to this a quality of thick closely-curling hair, which, by some freak of Nature, had lost its colour in the most startling and capricious manner. Over the top of his head it was still the deep black which was its natural colour. Round the sides of his head – without the slightest gradation of grey to break the force of the extraordinary contrast – it had turned completely white. The line between the two colours preserved no sort of regularity. At one place, the white hair ran up into the black; at another, the black hair ran down into the white. I looked at the man with a curiosity which, I am ashamed to say, I found it quite impossible to control.[35]

Jennings and Blake are drawn to each other through mutual attraction and sympathy. 'It is not to be denied that Ezra Jennings made some inscrutable appeal to my sympathies, which I found impossible to resist', Blake muses, while Jennings asks himself, 'What is the secret of the attraction that there is for me in this man? . . . Is there something in him that answers the yearning I have for a little human sympathy?'[36] Like the Armadale/Midwinter doubling, Jennings operates as Blake's 'unconscious', the site of the painful and intractable memories of which Blake is blissfully ignorant, as well as being the possessor of scientific knowledge of how the unconscious works. The language of mesmerism is vital here not simply in blurring the boundaries between self and other, but in connecting this process to the blurring of the boundaries between 'the body and the surrounding world' – a process of projection and displacement that is simultaneously material and figurative. Jennings notes before the experiment, 'Without professing to believe in omens, it was at least encouraging to find no direct nervous influence – no stormy or electric perturbations – in the atmosphere', and this process of correspondence and transference becomes progressively more widely diffused as 'nervous' energy and disorders are presented in magnetic terms.[37]

There is thus at once a correspondence and a contrast between Blake's artificially induced nervous derangement and Jennings's. This paradoxical relationship surfaces in the way that Jennings's medical methods operate as extension and inversion of the conceptual authority that he draws on in explaining the physiological experiment to Blake, even as he remains the unwritten object of psychological enquiry himself. It also means that he functions as the inversion of the flamboyant manipulation of 'medical and magnetic science' as manifested by Fosco (*The Woman in White*) and uses pharmacological transformation in the opposite way. The techniques that Jennings uses as a doctor are all designed to stimulate rather than soothe, suppress, or sedate. He rallies the strength of the fever-struck Dr Candy with the use of 'champagne, or brandy, ammonia and quinine', following the practice of the late-eighteenth-century Edinburgh doctor John Brown, rather than sticking to the orthodox method of administering 'gruel, lemonade, barley water and so forth'.[38] He uses opium to stir up Blake's past, in contrast with Candy, who intended it as a narcotic. And this is based on the testing of an even more speculative hypothesis that he is elaborating in his unfinished book on 'the intricate and delicate subject of the brain and nervous system', a hypothesis that develops those assumptions of associationist psychology that correspond with those elements of both Carpenter and Elliotson that come closest to Dallas. For Carpenter and Abercrombie, like Hamilton, did acknowledge that the chains of association at work in the memory include hidden links 'which might be reproduced, as by the touching of a spring, through a nexus of suggestions'.[39] As a doctor, Jennings, too, concentrates on the logic underlying the associative processes at work in delirium in the first stage of disentangling the clues which will lead to the replaying of the past – his decoding of Dr Candy's feverish ramblings which reveal that he had secretly drugged Blake as a practical joke the year before.

Jennings doubts 'whether we can justifiably infer – in cases of delirium – that the loss of the faculty of speaking connectedly, implies of necessity the loss of the faculty of thinking connectedly as well',[40] a theory he tests by rewriting Candy's ramblings, projecting meaning into the gaps in his speech. But although this process of 'thinking connectedly' involves ironing out inconsistencies and creating 'a smooth and finished texture out of the ravelled skein',[41] it does this through the symptomatic decoding of fragmented testimony that is the direct analogue of the Janus-faced process of reading the novel itself. But this can only happen on the condition that Jennings's own text be allowed to remain disconnected and his past to comprise an unconfessed and unvindicated taint. His own medicinal use of opium imples none of the reassuring reflexes of Blake's trance; for him the past becomes a 'hideous phantasmagoria' that refuses to be laid to rest, rising up like an exhalation in a way that directly recalls Basil's delirium and De Quincey's account of opium's *pains*; this is immediately chronicled with no reassuring retrospection:

June 16th. – Rose late, after a dreadful night, the vengeance of yesterday's opium pursuing me through a series of frightful dreams. At one time I was whirling through empty space with the phantoms of the dead, friends and enemies together. At another, the one beloved face which I shall never see again, rose at by bedside, hideously phosphorescent in the black darkness, and grinned at me.[42]

For Jennings, as for Mannion (*Basil*) and Midwinter (*Armadale*), memory takes the form of the continual pursuit of unsolicited testimonials from the past that turn him into an outcast and whose social and psychic burdens cannot remain concealed. But while for Mannion and Midwinter the confessional disclosing of the past can either reinforce difference or realign the perception through which it is made aberrant, with Jennings it *remains* unspoken, concealed as the undisclosed, intractable element within the novel itself. For Jennings, 'obscurity is the only hope'; the one trace that remains is the fragmented extracts of the diary that he himself selects: 'He opened the volume for this year, and tore out, one by one, the pages relating to the time that you and he were together', recalls Candy, and he consigns the rest, his book on the brain and himself, to a nameless grave. 'His story is a blank.'[43]

So the figure of Jennings embodies the double process whereby the two kinds of reason at work in the text are brought together yet remain unassimilable, always containing an intractable element, in his dual position as subject and agent. Like Dallas's model of the secrecy of hidden thought, he searches the 'dark recesses of memory, unbidden suggestions, trains of thought unwittingly pursued'.[44] Yet in producing a 'smooth texture' on the one hand, consigning his own history to a nameless grave on the other, he emphasizes what is painful and difficult about this process far more than what is pleasurable, even in Dallas's extended sense of the term. Jennings operates as the point at which the different kinds of oppositions at work in the novel break down (east/west, dark/light, rational/occult, masculine/feminine) – 'Physiology says, and says truly, that some men are born with female constitutions – and I am one of them!'[45], but again (like Marian Halcombe in *The Woman in White*) he represents bizarre juxtaposition rather than reconciliation or compromise. And this suggests that there needs to be another concept of the unconscious that remains tacit in the text, one which in Dallas's terms corresponds with the most fictive or 'magical' element within the 'play of thought' and which emerges primarily through metaphoric transference, a transference again brought about by extending and transforming the language of mesmerism. Collins thus extends the implication of the figure of Jennings by using mesmerism as a means of invoking the mysterious, the occult, hidden sources of energy and power; yet at the same time he reframes the convoluted patterns of the social mechanism by which that psychic power is produced.

It has been seen that the Indian brahmins are the most explicit representation of the way in which 'occult' processes are invoked as the strange and indecipherable product of dominant fears and anxieties. Clairvoyance is projected on to them as a form of romantic fascination, which they then internalize and represent. And here Murthwaite's rational explanation of the phenomenon itself overturns its ostensible meaning: clairvoyance is described as 'simply a development of the romantic side of the Indian character'; but if the 'sensitive subject to the mesmeric influence' does nothing but 'reflect what is in the mind of the person mesmerising him', then logically the Indians function primarily as reflections of what is in the English mind. The Indians, like the diamond itself, are present in the text through being absent, seen out of the corner of the eye; through their very absence another process of transformation is at work which shifts both their cognitive and ideological status. They link the framing Prologue with the Story, but they also move across the parameters of the narrative itself through a set of indirectly focalized perspectives which imperceptibly shift the centre of gravity so that they finally emerge as the real owners of the Moonstone; the Hindu temple is seen to be its right place, and its right function to be purely a symbolic image of transcendence. Clairvoyance works as a kind of familiar exoticism here; but though *The Moonstone* exploits the 'occult/oriental' association (an association shaped in part by De Quincey's 'oriental' opium dreams in the *Confessions*), it is also a precise elaboration of the more critical and resistive ways that Collins uses 'colonies' as sites of fantastic otherness in his fiction – places whose position is structured by their simultaneous marginality and annexation to England, transmitters of a nervous disorder that remains an English malady, one of the more dubious 'blessings of the British constitution'. And this too can be connected with the implied investigation of the meaning of the 'occult' in the novel.

In *The Woman in White*, for example, South America is essentially given the function of a purely marvellous device, a magical place to which Hartright can disappear and learn both tracking skills and masculine, 'self-made' resolution. In *No Name* this function is already qualified: Canada is the licensed space of Andrew Vanstone's youthful excesses, colonial trading the testing ground of constitutional weakness which enhances Kirke's strength and Frank Clare's atrophy. In *Armadale* the setting of Barbados is the analogue of the father's passion and violence in the Prologue, creating the expectation of doubling and transgression which are undermined in the Armadale/Midwinter opposition itself. 'Colonies', therefore, are not an undifferentiated 'other place'; they are associated with distinct kinds of psychic projection; and although Collins remains ultimately caught within the cultural framework that constructs them as incubators of violence and sexuality, this is never naturalized into a pathological difference, but always turned into a scrutiny of its homely source.[46] The story of the Moonstone is, after all, indirectly an inversion of the story of the Koh-i-Noor diamond – literally the jewel in the imperial crown. As John Reed has suggested, Collins decisively goes against the grain of the prevailing representation of 'India' as extreme signifier of savage violence, a representation that had been fuelled by media reaction to the Indian mutiny of 1857. He instead portrays a rapacious imperialism as the barbaric invader and destroyer of an established culture.[47] And while this initially reinforces a pathologized image of 'oriental despotism' in the form of the Muslim moguls in the history of the diamond in the Prologue, the account of the Siege of Seringapatam is unambiguous in its presentation of the English army as the unrestrained invading force, generating 'riot and confusion'. It is Herncastle, the transgressive cousin, who is 'exasperated to a kind of frenzy by the slaughter through which we had passed'.[48] It is he who transforms the diamond into a morbid inheritance by suppressing the crime, and who returns to England to dwell in an underworld of moral insanity that none the less anticipates the fascination with experimental chemistry and artificially induced mental states that is to be unfolded later:

> Sometimes they said he was given up to opium smoking and collecting old books; sometimes he was reported to be trying strange things in chemistry; sometimes he was seen carousing and amusing himself among the lowest slums in London. Anyhow a solitary, vicious, underground life was the life the Colonel led.[49]

This split between transcendent and 'horrid' otherness is thus given a particular historical framework in the history of the Moonstone in the Prologue, one that relativizes its position in the Story, and this contributes to the way that 'magnetic' codes are given a social significance. The direct continuum between the Indians and Jennings is significant here – they are both seen by Bruff and Betteredge as disturbingly indecipherable and conjuring tricksters;

both only make sense through an absent story that cannot be incorporated into the central narrative. But the discontinuities are also important, for it is only with the off-stage conclusion of the Indians' story (mediated by Murthwaite, who also crosses the two worlds, and of whom Bruff notes, 'Lawyer as I was, I began to trust Mr Murthwaite to lead me blindfold through the last windings of the labyrinth, along which he had guided me thus far'[50]) that *The Moonstone* can end. Mesmerism, therefore, does not provide a coherent alternative model of the unconscious as a 'place' so much as a set of allusions that enables different processes of transference to take place and various forms of psychic power to be connoted; forms of power which can be 'traced back, by rational means, to natural causes', but which also frustrate any consistent cognitive framework.

Of course the Moonstone itself is the apotheosis of the means by which meaning, desire, and value are created out of projection, displacement, and transference. It represents 'wild' nervous energy that operates both metaphorically and metonymically. It is the signifier and the object of desire; it disrupts the distinction between literal and figural, depth and surface, manifest and latent, through its very absence in the narrative. 'What have I lost? Nothing but Nervous Force – which the law doesn't recognise as property', jokes Ablewhite, describing his attack by the Indians, but the Moonstone gains its dangerous and threatening power when treated as a piece of property dislodged from its purely symbolic role.[51] As 'Nervous Force', it is again the language of animal magnetism that conveys the diamond's influence and attraction, turns it into the conductor of the disruptive forces of the past, suggests links between psychic power and sexual energy. The meaning of the Moonstone is continually merging with the objects and people that surround it, even as it emanates from its own self-reflected light. 'When you looked down into the stone you looked down into a yellow deep that drew your eyes into it so that they saw nothing else', Betteredge notes. 'No wonder Miss Rachel was fascinated; no wonder her cousins screamed. The Diamond laid such a hold of *me* that I burst out with as large an "O" as the Bouncers themselves.' Like the mesmeric 'fluid', or ether, it resists either material or 'spiritual' status. Betteredge goes on, 'It seemed unfathomable . . . we set it in the sun, then shut the light out of the room, and it shone awfully out of the depths of its own brightness.'[52] This draws on C.W. King's point in *The Natural History of Precious Stones* (one of Collins's sources of information on the diamond) that 'the diamond is highly electric, attracting light objects when heated by friction, and alone among many gems has the peculiarity of becoming phosphorescent in the dark, after prolonged exposure to the sun's rays';[53] the Moonstone's 'occult' qualities are thus given a physical base, while its assimilation of its psychological environment – the 'nervous influences' that surround it – is expressed metaphorically.

The Moonstone, like the language of mesmerism itself, upsets the distinction between the physical and the transcendental in connoting hidden sources of energy and power, linked to multiple possible identities. This does not detract from its purely romantic and exotic connotations, but it does suggest that these have a psychological as well as a symbolic base, and that the novel thus extends into an investigation into the psychic roots of imagination itself. For even at its apparently most transcendental, the significance of the diamond itself can again be recast within that aspect of Dallas's analysis that forms part of his own extended critique of 'transcendental' interpretations of the way that unconscious mental processes operate through metaphoric transformation.

> To lay bare the automatic or unconscious action of the mind is indeed to unfold a tale which outvies the romances of giants and ginns, wizards in their palaces and captives in the Domdaniel roots of the sea. As I am about to show how the mind and all its powers work for us in secret and lead us unawares to results so much above our wont and so strange that we attribute them to the inspiration of heaven or to the whispers of inborn genius, I seem to tread enchanted ground. The hidden efficacy of our thoughts, their prodigious power of working in the dark and helping us underhand, can be compared only to the stories of our folk-lore and chiefly to that of the lubber-fiend who toils for us when we are asleep or when we are not looking. . . . We have such a fairy in our thoughts, a willing and tricksy worker which commonly bears the name of Imagination, and which may be named – as I think more clearly – the Hidden Soul.[54]

Dallas's ambitious aim in *The Gay Science* was to demonstrate that existing theories of the imagination inevitably either dismissed it as irrational or resorted to a mystical vagueness by characterizing it as a separate *faculty* rather than a process, or function. To do this he attempted to pin down the underlying processes of mental transformation that are essential not simply to poetry but to meaning itself – the power to construct comparisons, correspondences, symbolic types, the power to generalize. And this led him to the conclusion that this assimilating capacity stretched far beyond what was conventionally characterized as imagination, though in 'imaginative' productions it has its most obvious forms, since 'imagination means no more than the automatic action of any and every faculty.'[55] For example, it undercuts the conventional distinction between 'sympathy' (in which the subject identifies with person or object – 'I am that or like that'); 'egotism' (in which the subject sees himself reflected back in the object of perception – 'That is I or like me), and 'imagination' in itself (which focuses on the actual process of metaphoric transformation – 'That is that or like that'). The function of the diamond in *The Moonstone* directly corresponds to this slipperness of definition in the way that it resists any clear distinction between its metaphoric and its metonymic meanings. It is that vague force itself which operates primarily as the analogue and signifier of the meanings that are projected onto it. This process is most explicitly conveyed in 'magnetic' terms; and it is thus that the diamond itself represents 'the assimilating power of the mind' and the working of the 'hidden soul' in the 'play of thought'. It operates simultaneously as a principle of sympathy – by which 'we are transformed . . . into the image of what we look on. We personate each other, nay, we personate things . . .'; and as egoism – the loss of the jewel in a fundamental way means loss of identity and sanity.[56]

The 'devilish' or disruptive side of the Moonstone as displaced or dangerous energy mediated through the language of mesmerim also has its echo in *The Gay Science*: it corresponds to that disturbing element in all aesthetic pleasure that Dallas terms the *weird*, and which he argues is an indispensable complement to the 'dramatic' and the 'beautiful'. He is vague about the term – preferring simply to invoke it through poetic example: Southey's 'In full-orbed glory yonder moon divine/Rolls through the dark blue depths', is quoted as an example of the flatly beautiful; Coleridge's 'Yea slimy things did crawl with legs/Upon a slimy sea', as a case of the undiluted weird.[57] *The Moonstone*, too, picks up these connotations, for as signifier of free-floating nervous energy, the diamond is set against that other image of magnetic yellow deeps – the Shivering Sand. The physical connections and contrasts between the two 'forces' suggest that the Sand represents the purely 'horrid' elements of a psychic process of which the Moonstone is the more ambiguous, sublime, and awful sign; yet the Sand paradoxically suggests a process of unconscious activity that again works at the limits of Dallas's notion of pleasure. The diamond is hard, transparent, self-contained – but with a flaw. It is a source of unconscious energy which, when lost, produces hysteria – inherited by Rachel yet arriving into the Story bearing a history that lies just beyond its field of vision. The Shivering Sand is *viscous*; unlike the stone, it is a totally meaningless natural phenomenon with no human or social use. It represents a 'wild' Nature that can never be assimilated as a romantic object of pastoral contemplation; it exists in a space beyond the poetic realm in its obdurate secrecy. 'We have got beautiful walks all round us, in every direction but one', reports Betteredge. 'That one I acknowledge to be a horrid walk.'[58] The unassimilable force of the Sand lies in its hidden tides and currents; a double consciousness that repels rather than attracts.

> At the turn of the tide, something goes on in the unknown deeps below, which sets the whole face of the quicksand shivering and trembling in a manner most remarkable to see. . . . A great bank, half a mile out, nigh the mouth of the bay, breaks the force of the main ocean coming in from the offing. Winter and summer, when the tide flows over the quicksand, the sea seems to leave the waves behind it on the bank, and rolls its waves in smoothly with a heave, and covers the sands in silence. A lonesome and horrid retreat, I can tell you! No boat ever ventures into this bay. No children from our fishing village . . . ever come here to play. The very birds of the air, as it seems to me, seem to give the Shivering Sand a wide berth.[59]

Unlike the sand in *No Name*, which inevitably 'turns traitor and betrays the footsteps that have passed over it', the Shivering Sand is expressive because it *absorbs* its secrets, and thus sucks energy into itself rather than transforming it through continual interaction. It conceals its own past and the pasts of others, which have to be dragged back, painfully, on a chain of submerged associations. This is bound up with its disturbing weirdness: neither liquid nor solid, exerts pressure on the waking subject by remaining intractable. Rosanna 'reads' the Sand, telling Betteredge, 'Something draws me to it . . . I try to keep away from it, but I can't. Sometimes . . . I think my grave is waiting for me here.'[60] Her deliberate concealment of the secret of her concealed knowledge in the Sand reproduces her own self-obliteration, which reproduces in turn her interpretation of the Sands themselves as signifying enforced social obscurity: 'Do you know what it looks like to *me*? . . . It looks as if it had hundreds of suffocating people under it – all struggling to get to the surface, and all sinking lower and lower in the dreadful deeps!'[61] There is no free and constant traffic between outer and inner ring here.

And just as Jennings is buried in an unmarked grave having rendered up his knowledge, so Rosanna Spearman leaves her confessional letter (which is itself initially forgotton by Blake) to be dragged back while being absorbed into the Sand without leaving a trace herself. This 'hidden parcel' image thus moves through the language of magnetism to a further implicit critique of Carpenter's 'lost parcel' analogy, and the framework of mid-century moral management which it reinforces; this time around the representation of feminine sexuality. In *The Moonstone* there is an obvious attack on evangelical piety and hypocritical philanthropy in the figure of Godfrey Ablewhite, which transmutes into an explicit parody of the evangelical end of the spectrum of moral management in the narrative of the fanatical Miss Clark. Her sexual obsession for Ablewhite is clearly displaced on to religion, and she presents herself as a paragon of early training and of 'energetically exercising the will': 'I am indebted to my parents . . . for having had habits of order and regularity instilled into me at a very early age'.[62] But the figure is so grotesque, the parody of 'frustrated spinster' as well as religious fanatic laid on so heavily, that its effectiveness is diffused into an uncontroversial stereotype. With Rosanna and her counterpart, Rachel, a far more subtle process is at work, and as a linked opposition they also qualify and reframe the critique of the relationship between femininity and pathology through the codes of moral management posed by Laura Fairlie and Anne Catherick (*The Woman in White*).

Rosanna Spearman (whose so obviously emblematic name needs no comment), the negative reflection of Rachel as Jennings is of Blake, is never compared to Rachel (as Anne is to Laura in *The Woman in White*); the elimination of the difference between them is eroded by the elimination of Rosanna, not of the difference itself. But Rosanna clearly connects the articulation of an implied critique of self-determination in the face of a psychic inheritance that *refuses* to be laid to rest with the negotiation of illicit sexual desire. For what is primarily transgressive about Rosanna is that as an ugly working-class woman she *has* a subjectivity and a sexuality that she has the audacity to express openly. 'It's quite monstrous that she should forget herself and her station in that way. But she seems to have lost pride, and proper feeling, and everything', notes the good servant, Penelope, who keeps to her place.[63] It is a desire that cannot be suppressed but can only be articulated posthumously, and it reveals the cracks in the ideological foundations on which her 'proper feeling' – her reformed subjectivity – is built, and the submission which is its precondition. Rosanna points out the banality of Betteredge's paternalistically benevolent comment, 'Your past life is all sponged out. Why can't you forget it?', extending the metaphor to highlight its copybook complacency: 'The stain is taken off . . . but the place shows, Mr Betteredge – the place shows!'[64] Her confessional letter is buried with the nightshirt that bears Blake's stain; like Rachel, she is the bearer of Blake's unconscious guilt. But the submerged letter itself links her hopeless desire to her class history, as the Prologue provides the history of the diamond. This makes it clear that it was moral treatment itself that compounded a self-consciousness that made self-hatred rather than self-esteem a concomitant of reform – which built up the expectation of a 'proper' subjectivity that is, structurally, inevitably denied:

> My life was not a very hard life to bear when I was a thief. It was only when they taught me at the reformatory to feel my own degradation that the days grew long and weary . . . I don't regret, far from it, having been roused to make the effort to be a reformed woman – but indeed it was a weary life. You had come across it like a beam of sunshine at first – and then you too had failed me. I was mad enough to love you – but I could not even attract your notice.[65]

'Suppose you put Miss Rachel in a servant's dress and took her ornaments off?'[66] Rosanna's question is never tested in the novel; Rachel Verinder sidesteps the problems posed by the overtly transgressive identities of Magdalen Vanstone (*No Name*) or Lydia Gwilt (*Armadale*) – she remains an heiress though she loses the diamond, she does not step beyond the limits of propriety to regain a name or regain a property. But although Dickens noted that there is 'nothing of disguised women' in *The Moonstone*, the codes and methods by which Rachel *keeps* to her place both expresses and suppresses a 'nervous force' that is interpreted as hysteria: she becomes transformed, as Blake makes clear in his 'Objective/Subjective' explanation, into 'Somebody Else' by concealing his secret, by remaining caught within her own limits.[67] And thus, just as there is a correspondence between Rachel and the diamond, in the same way as there is a symbolic interaction betwen Rosanna and the Sand, so Rachel is set in opposition to Rosanna as an ambiguous figure, not as the positive to which Rosanna is the negative. Rachel thus tacitly upsets the conventions of feminine propriety, while both inverting and breaking down the Laura/Marian contrast (*The Woman in White*): she is dark, positive, purposeful, independent – yet silent.

And like Magdalen, in this she displays all the characteristics that F.C. Skey identified as the symptoms of hysteria in young, middle-class women, an exaggerated rendering of the self-controlling elements of moral management: 'She judged for herself, as few women twice her age judge in general', Betteredge notes, ambivalently in presenting Rachel; 'never asked your advice; never told you beforehand what she was going to do; never came with secrets and confidences to anybody, from her mother downward'.[68] Rachel's silence is the essential secret that generates the Story; but in its very structural indispensability this suppression turns the conventions of moral management into hysterical repression on the one hand, and on the other suggests that the ascription of hysteria is the uncomprehending response to female autonomy. 'I have never seen her so strange and reserved as she is now', Lady Verinder remarks, 'the loss of her jewel seems almost to have turned her brain.'[69] Thus, in demanding 'Is there a form of hysterics that bursts into words instead of tears?' and in providing an unwritten testimony that the narrative can only rewrite, the figure of Rachel suggests that the 'form of hysterics' is, literally, the text as a whole.

I have argued that in *The Moonstone* occult, deviant, and marginal traces become significant in their very secrecy, and that this implicitly overturns the pattern of narrative authority that is set up by the novel's overall structure. But the implications of this depend on how one interprets the psychological paradigms as well as the narrative frameworks of the novel, and in concluding I want to suggest that in a curious way *The Moonstone* becomes the victim of its own cognitive relativism. At an early stage in the Story, Blake and Betteredge speculate on the possible interpretations of the significance of the Colonel's legacy. 'Oh, that's your interpretation of his motive, is it? The Subjective interpretation again! Have you ever been in Germany, Mr Betteredge?' remarks Blake. 'There is a totally different interpretation from yours, Betteredge, taking its rise in a Subjective-Objective point of view. From all I can see, one inter-pretation is just as likely to be right as the other.' To which Betteredge remarks, 'Having brought matters to this pleasant and comforting issue, Mr Franklin appeared to think that he had completed all that was required of him.'[70] The novel suggests and undermines competing hypotheses, framed by different narrative voices placed in an elusive narrative hierarchy; but all revolving round the problematic and slippery identity of Franklin Blake, the absentee landlord, object of desire and implied general editor as well as subject of psychological investigation. And to assess the significance of placing Blake as the absent centre of the competing models of the unconscious in the text initially means returning again to its narrative structure.

There are at least five distinct cognitive frameworks that are set up within their own terms in the novel, although they are not on a par with each other, either in terms of credibility or in terms of space. There is Betteredge, voice of English common sense, who assures Blake, 'you'll soon get over the weakness of believing in facts'; Bruff, 'immersed in Law, impenetrable to Medicine'; Cuff, working by logical inference, based on the speculative interpretation of empirical evidence; Murthwaite and Jennings, both cognitively liminal figures; and Blake, a palimpsest of clashing methodologies.[71] These overlap with the specific function of the actual narrators in the novel, who, like the specific narrators of *The Woman in White*, are asked to keep within the perimeters of their own experience, but whose equally important function, I have argued, is to highlight the shifting and provisional nature of evidence, the arbitrary and unreliable nature of memory, so that the reader reads simultaneously through and against their testimony. But at the same time their lack of reliability does not simply operate as a retarding device – it works as a direct analogue of the problematic nature of memory in the text as a whole, and thus has a specific cognitive function. These perspectives in turn overlap with the overall method of structuring time, which at first seems to echo the implied inversion of narrative authority in that, inevitably, the narratives that have the greatest immediate impact on the story, and which are in a sense the 'closest' to it in temporal terms, can only do so by disrupting the pattern of retrospective progression supplied by the linked testimonies. It been seen that Jennings's journal is the main example of this; Rosanna's letter and Candy's lost recollection are others, and both these are, as it were, on a time fuse, since their function in creating suspense depends on their action being delayed. Thus the very means that Collins uses to produce indeterminacy in a retrospective narrative reinforces the relative inaccessability of the past.

But suppose one reads these countervailing tendencies the other way, as mutually collusive, so that in collapsing wildness and domesticity into each other the disruption itself becomes domesticated? Betteredge, that crucial analogue of the lapses and ramblings of memory, is a crucial figure here. Old retainer, trace of an era of feudal loyalty and bearer of the family's unofficial memory, he is the safely cross-category figure who moves between the upper and lower worlds of the family. In doing so, unlike Rosanna, he stays in his place; he finally achieves a reconciliation between his different roles as unreliable witness. Betteredge stands as the primary model introducing the reader to the provisional way that truth operates, providing the necessary digressions that delay the main line of the story. He represents the process of narrative itself, in which all memory becomes significant, and immediately establishes the correspondence between 'Persons' and 'Things':

> Still, this doesn't look much like starting the story of the Diamond
> – does it? I seem to be wandering off in search of the Lord knows
> what, the Lord knows where . . . I am asked to tell the story of the
> Diamond and instead of which I have been telling the story of my
> own self. Curious and quite beyond me to account for. I wonder
> whether the gentlemen who make a business and a living out of
> writing books, ever find their own selves getting in the way of their
> subjects, like me.[72]

Betteredge, too, lives his life through explicit and continual reference to an overall paradigm: *Robinson Crusoe*, that colonial manual of self-help, sandwiched in popularity in the first third of the nineteenth century between the Bible, *Pilgrim's Progress*, and Combe's *Constitution of Man*. This book provides an explanatory framework for all unaccountable phenomena through his active projection of meaning into it, at one stage becoming a text that explains the nature of supernatural terror itself: 'Fear of Danger is ten times more frightening than danger itself when apparent to the eyes.'[73] He thus works as a kind of friendly unconscious, one constructed after the event, a ravelled skein of friendly associations and sympathies which simultaneously conveys and defuses the anxieties surrounding the Moonstone.

Betteredge frames the frame that he is set within, and thus is, in a sense, turned inside out by the story; but his status as the pivot of the narrative also shapes the meaning of the elusive General Editor, Franklin Blake – that other analogue of the model of consciousness of the Moonstone and *The Moonstone* as the central yet absent figure around which the narrative inversions turn. And here it is significant that Blake's final establishment of control does in a sense take place through his own efforts and his own process of detection; but that he does not, like Hartright, have to struggle for self- and narrative control, because of his social and psychic position as the centre of the narrative. His power and 'magnetic' attraction are reasserted, and his marriage to Rachel finally assured, as he moves along 'the slow and toilsome journey from the darkness to the light', by researching the recesses of others' memories, which thus replace his own.[74] He even has to ask Betteredge about his own possible childhood somnambulism: 'I knew I could trust his memory, in a matter of a kind.'[75] And this process of erasure itself suggests that Blake, indeed, remains healthy because he continually becomes dissociated from the past or any fixed identity. He is caught up in the family's morbid legacy, but he is no 'hypochondriacal bachelor' subjectively embroiled in the mesh; he appropriates others' memories, but this does not involve any social or psychic transformation – the most intense moment of 'superstitious terror' that has clear sexual undertones is when he feels Rosanna's submerged chain beneath the Shivering Sand. And in this respect *The Moonstone* can be read not only as a novel of disruption and transformation, but also as a novel of how things stay the same, how hierarchies are established apparently outside history. Blake becomes Jennings's healthy counterpart through also being the point at which the cognitive boundaries of the novel break down, as he evades any national identity or discursive framework. And this means that he is really, as Betteredge describes, a palimpsest of national identities; yet this is not ultimately incompatible with his Englishness:

> At an age when we are all of us most apt to take our colouring, in the form of a reflection from the colouring of other people, he had been sent abroad, and had been passed on from one nation to another, before there was time for any one colouring more than another, to settle on him firmly. As a consequence of this he had come back with so many sides to his character, all more or less jarring with one another, that he seemed to pass his life in a state of continual contradiction with himself. . . . He had his French side, his German side, and his Italian side – the original English foundation showing through, every now and then, as much as to say, 'Here I am, sorely transmogrified as you can see, but there's still something of me at the bottom of him still.'[76]

Blake is the figure in whom fragmented elements of identity become entangled theoretical hypotheses; who, in becoming satirically enmeshed in a labyrinth of speculation on the night before the experiment, makes it both the echo and the 'sunny side' of Jennings's psychic legacy and cognitive ambiguity:

> To speak seriously, it is perhaps possible that my German training was in some degree responsible for the labyrinth of useless

speculations in which I involved myself. For the greater part of the night I sat smoking, and building up theories, one more profoundly improbable than the other. When I did get to sleep, my waking fancies pursued me in dreams. I woke the next morning, with Objective-Subjective and Subjective-Objective inextricably entangled in my mind; and I began the day which was to witness my real effort at practical action of some kind, by doubting whether I had any sort of right (on purely philosophical grounds) to consider any sort of thing (the Diamond included) as existing at all.[77]

Of all Collins's novels, *The Moonstone* is the clearest case of a story 'in a state of continual contradiction with itself', and that contradiction is crucially shaped by the process of interplay and transformation between the models of the unconscious in the text and those which implicitly frame it, models which in turn shape how to interpret both its internal transmogrifications and the links between its outer and its inner rings. 'Carpenter' and 'Elliotson' blend and clash as the unconscious and the Moonstone shift between 'lost parcel' and 'hidden soul'. To detect this dynamic sense of unconscious transformation means incorporating a contemporary hypothesis that hovers outside the margin of the text – Dallas's *The Gay Science*. *The Moonstone*'s pleasurableness lies in its ambiguity, but this ambiguity is itself ambiguous, for in concealing and revealing its own problematic and intractable traces it simultaneously demonstrates their power and domesticates the very generation of secrecy itself. And this, too, is commensurate with Dallas's 'play of thought', and suggests that his 'hidden soul', too, can be recuperated into the dominant framework. For while Dallas's notion of the unconscious strikingly seems to anticipate elements of the model that would be applied in a psychoanalytic reading of the novel, a reading that would interpret it as an 'uncanny' exploration of the transformative processes at work in repression, his 'hidden soul' finally manifests its Utopian connotations even in its very resistance to transcendentalism. And in his discussion of the social meaning of art, Dallas clearly put the discussion of the role of the unconscious in a moral and evolutionary context, though he challenges the 'high/popular' dichotomy. Pleasure, he argued, should not be 'connected in our minds with forbidden gratifications'; and 'if art, in the pleasure which it yields, does not satisfy the moral sense of a people, it is doomed'; though the appeal to this sense should never take the form of a self-conscious didacticism.[78] But perhaps this, too, is framing the challenges that *The Moonstone* poses too simply, and not only pinning the novel's meaning to the narrative's final resolution and Dallas's concluding argument, but the significance of the 'unconscious' itself to a set of unified meanings in the correspondences between the discourses within which it is framed.

7

Resistless influences
Degeneration and its negation
in the later fiction

> The resistless influences which are one day to reign
> supreme over our hearts and to shape the sad short
> course of our lives, are sometimes of mysteriously
> remote origin, and find their devious ways to us
> through the hearts and lives of strangers.
>
> Wilkie Collins, *The Fallen Leaves*[1]

> So do we shape our own destinies, blindfold. So do we
> hold our poor little tenure of happiness at the
> capricious mercy of Chance. It is surely a blessed delu-
> sion which persuades us that we are the highest
> products of the great scheme of creation, and sets us
> doubting whether other planets are inhabited, because
> other planets are not surrounded by an atmosphere
> which *we* can breathe!
>
> Wilkie Collins, *Man and Wife*[2]

A central figure in *Jezebel's Daughter* is a lunatic, Jack Straw. Like
the 'meagre man' in *The Lazy Tour of Two Idle Apprentices*, he is
undersized, and at once childlike and prematurely aged. Like the
'meagre man', he is obsessed by matting and plaiting, and spends
a large proportion of his time weaving straw hats and baskets. But
the emphasis has shifted, and with it the fictional and discursive role
of madness. *Jezebel's Daughter*, a reconstruction of events in 1828
narrated in 1878, is Collins's most explicit discussion of moral
management: the widow of a lunacy reformer discovers a copy of
Tuke's *A Description of the Retreat* among her husband's books,
rescues Jack Straw from an old-fashioned 'whips and chains'
asylum, and reforms him in complete accordance with non-restraint
ideals. Yet while this directly echoes Dickens's earlier philanthropic
humanitarianism, the more radical connotations of the 'meagre man'
passage have drained away. The plaited straw no longer offers a

conceptual metaphor that merges with the interwoven clues of the narrative of how he came to be there, or of how we might interpret it; it has become externalized into a handicraft, a suitably feminine piece of occupational therapy.

Jack Straw remarks,

> Once there was a time when my hands were the maddest things about me. They used to turn against me and tear my hair and flesh. An angel in a dream told me how to keep them quiet. An angel said, 'Let them work at your straw.' All day long I plaited my straw. I would have gone on all night, too, if they would only have given me a light.[3]

Even Jack's dreams provide their own paternalistic keeper; but the image has already become a historical curiosity. The non-restraint system is explicitly and favourably contrasted with the 'old' corrupt asylum in *Jezebel's Daughter*, but the function of Jack Straw himself is to be a kind of domesticated court jester, to provide the light relief that offsets the horror of the central villainy of the story – the plots of Madame Fountaine, the 'Jezebel' of the title, who is a case of qualified moral insanity. In using the contrasting images of madness so explicitly in this way, Collins seems to be resorting to desperate, worn-our remedies. Yet they are images which, in harking back to earlier models, both depend on and resist the shift in discourses on insanity itself in 1880. The suspense of *Jezebel's Daughter* hinges on uncertainty over how Jack's well-intensioned actions will turn out – whether he will cure the heroine of an earlier attempt to poison her, or inadvertently administer the fatal dose himself.

Collins's later fiction poses its own particular interpretative problems. To treat a selection of his novels written during the 1870s and 1880s in a single chapter and inevitably schematically, tracing developments between novels rather than exploring the complexity of individual narratives, seems to make assumptions about the second half of his career that concur with the overwhelming consensus on his later work – that it represents a process of steady and irreversible decline. Many discussions of Collins's work present this in an extremely simplistic and often a somewhat prurient way, collapsing biographic circumstances, literary influences, explicit ideological shifts, cultural context, and the use of particular fictional conventions into one another. Both author and works tend to be discussed in a degenerative framework: Collins's poor health, his accelerating gout, and increasing dependence on laudanum, the disappearance of the benign influence of Dickens who died in 1870, and the ascendancy of the supposedly detrimental effects of his growing friendship with Reade, can be pressed into service to make Collins seem like a figure in one of his own narratives, gradually growing weaker, his writing becoming more and more 'feeble, faint and defaced by blots'.[4] Collins's fiction does decline – the late work does not have either the narrative complexity or the cognitive sophistication of the 1860s. But the process is much less relentless than is often assumed, and many of the novels deserve a fuller investigation than I have space to develop here. Moreover, the factors that contribute to the shifts in the later writing need to be disentangled.

To analyse Collins's 'decline', it is necessary to ask a slightly different question: why was he able to sustain his writing for so long? The novels of the 1860s were written when a particularly productive range of constraints and possibilities converged. These included the beginning of the enormous expansion of middle-range publishing that was signalled by the sensation novel, a factor which combined with the limitations and opportunities offered by the Dickens-dominated *Household Words* and *All the Year Round*. This, together with the competing claims of Collins's publishers, George Bentley and George Smith, who offered him £5,000 for *Armdale*, meant that by the late 1860s Collins was in a strong position to set his terms as an independent writer wishing to expand his audience while avoiding the more extreme pressures of serial production. In 1875 he signed a contract with Andrew Chatto transferring the copyright of all his published and future works to Chatto and Windus; his works were to be published first in three-volume form, but to be made quickly available in two-shilling and ultimately sixpenny editions. This was an experiment in cheap popular publishing that Richard Bentley had unsuccessfully attempted to initiate with *Basil* in 1852, but which was only now economically and culturally feasible.[5] By the mid 1870s, therefore, Collins was in a relatively secure position, though he still needed to maintain a steady output of fiction: he was potentially able to reach a more broadly based lower-middle-class mass audience than ever before, yet he remained structurally constrained by the three-volume form which dragged out its weary life until the early 1890s.

Thus while Collins, like Hardy, Moore, and Gissing, was affected by the economic and ideological crisis of novel production at the end of the nineteenth century, he was also in a position to take advantage of the revolution in middle-range publishing that was one offshoot of it: the production of cheap editions which undermined, while remaining under the shadow of, the three-decker form.[6] However, this also meant that his conception of both his actual and potential audience became oddly skewed. Collins always felt constricted by a narrowly moralistic element in the critical establishment and by Mudie's evangelicalism: 'This ignorant fanatic holds my circulation in his pious hands. What remedy have we? What remedy have his subscribers?' he stressed angrily to Bentley in 1873 when Mudie refused to accept *The New Magdalen* unless the title was modified.[7] Yet his continuing popularity, as witnessed by the Chatto sales, gave him the sense of a radical, popular public just beyond his grasp, that was, in a real sense, not simply an unknown but a mythical one.

Late-nineteenth-century literary culture was marked not so much by the disintegration of a previously coherent readership (the fears of that sort of disintegration had surrounded the rise of the sensation novel itself as a mass middle-class form in the 1860s and before that the Minerva Press had appealed to a predominantly female audience in the late-eighteenth-century) as by the development of specific forms of publishing aimed at increasingly specific readerships.[8] While the sensation novel had emphasized that culture was a commodity, it helped to create the conditions that enabled publishing to expand *as* a commodity and in a way that further consolidated the already established split between 'serious' and 'popular' literature. Collins became more explicitly radical, more openly socially committed, in the second half of his career, and also like E.S. Dallas, came increasingly to pin his cultural hopes on a mass popular audience rather than a Bohemian avant-garde or liberal coterie, as his critique of social institutions became more open and outspoken.[9] But it was a public that remained elusive. For example, he had originally intended that his most explicitly political novel, *The Fallen Leaves*, should be in two series, the second series following the hero and heroine's adventures in America. The second series was indefinitely postponed, ostensibly because of the negative critical reaction to the first, and Collins justified this in the Letter of Dedication to the following novel, *Jezebel's Daughter*:

> The first part of that story has, through circumstances connected with the various forms of publication adopted thus far, addressed itself to a comparatively limited class of readers in England. When the book is finally reprinted in its cheapest form – then, and then only, it will appeal to the great audience of the English people. I am waiting for that time, to complete my design by writing the second part of *The Fallen Leaves*.[10]

But the time never arrived.

So there are connections between the permutations of Collins's cultural and economic circumstances, his political position, his discursive context, and his adaptation of particular fictional conventions, but they are indirect and entangled ones. The later work, for example, continually shifts between genres though on the whole the novels are clearly recognizable within definite categories, as purpose novels, high melodrama, domestic realism. They adapt a shared stock of conventions from the earlier sensation fiction, yet it is impossible to draw precise generic boundaries around them. In much of the later work too Collins clearly encounters a problem that had not emerged as a problem before: how to revitalize the pleasurable potential of 'sensation' conventions by making them 'work harder' while at the same time intensifying the fictional and psychological codes they draw on, by giving them a more clearly tendentious purpose? Collins's late novels have a strangely disturbing, dissonant, bizzare quality. Yet though they often employ similar devices to the earlier stories, the effect, on the whole (*The Law and the Lady* is an important exception here), is not so much to blur cognitive boundaries as to return to them in an unexpected way, developing an alternative method of producing a critical distance by turning particular assumptions against themselves. Many of the later novels seem to be concerned not with creating a range of possible meanings, but with narrowing meanings down, although this still often involves parody and play. In the 1870s and 1880s Collins develops particular conventions to overturn the assumptions of what had become a dominant discursive model – the narrative of degeneration. In the 1860s he could draw on a range of psychological and experimental scientific methods, speculatively and hypothetically. Now science itself comes increasingly to be used as a monolithic form of power and manipulation – an externalized source of melodrama and horror.

Here Collins's dissension from dominant contemporary psychological, biological, and social theory becomes in a curious way an appropriation of and adaptation to it. In Chapter 1, I argued that conceptions of degeneration were not a new feature of social and psychological theory of the 1870s. The general notion of the inheritance and transmission of morbid symptoms and propensities within families was a well-established one throughout nineteenth-century psychological theory, and the more concrete notion of madness accumulating within families through the inexorable stages of eccentricity, insanity, idiocy, and extinction, which was to be developed in the late 1870s and 1880s by Maudsley, was a direct appropriation of Morel's writings from the 1850s. But by the mid-1870s, the emphasis had changed: 'degeneration' was no longer one explanatory model interwoven with others. It became the dominant paradigm, in a way that also involved a shift in the cognitive status of the paradigm itself, and in the nature of the relationship between biological, psychological, and social theory that it posed. Thus degenerative explanations of insanity and pathology directly contributed to post-Darwinian biological theory, and were themselves reinforced by it. This took place in an ideological context that increasingly drew on biological and organicist ideas less as a conceptual metaphor or analogue, more as a direct model wherein the social became collapsed into the biological. The 'tyranny of organization' implied not only that the physiological explained and defined individual psychology. It suggested also that this could only make sense in a framework which placed the individual, on the one hand, in a long-term history of degenerative genealogy; on the other, in the context of a theory that conceptualized all social, racial, and sexual divisions as manifestations of the biological determinism that it relied on to legitimize them.

The concept of degeneration as an implied concomitant of the process of inheritance and transmission is a strand that runs throughout Collins's fiction, and is set against moral management in a variety of ways, which take on different connotations as their narrative context and their social focus shift. The novels of the 1850s and 1860s that I have analysed all depend for their sensations on tensions generated within the family – echoed or articulated by the excluded or marginal figures outside it. The upper-middle-clas family, left to itself, needed to be roused from atrophy in order to renew itself, but moral management was also a source of manipulation, its presuppositions overturned by the tenacity of a psychic legacy. Collins uses similar narrative motifs in the 1870s and 1880s but the elements within the stories as well as their context have changed. The later novels often attempt to locate the tensions in a wider structural network than the immediate one of the family, to trace the determinants, the 'resistless influences', that shape identity. They seek remote origins in a social fabric woven out of economic divisions as well as a meretricious morality. The meliorist beliefs of moral management are set within this wider implied analytical framework, and emerge most explicitly in *The New Magdalen* and *The Fallen Leaves* through the rhetoric of Christian Socialism. It is a rhetoric that clashes and combines with organic metaphors in exploring structural processes, expressed through physiological signs, and stresses that destinies are shaped 'blind-fold', by chance as much as a predetermined origin. But now, the devices through which the novels explore the position of powerless groups within this structure transform the way that physiological and psychological codes can be transformed themselves by being put to work as fictional conventions. It also transforms the meanings of the sensation conventions themselves.

MAN AND WIFE AND THE NEW MAGDALEN

Man and Wife (1870) and *The New Magdalen* (1873), for example, take up certain of the central concerns and conventions of *The Woman in White* and *No Name* to focus on the way that feminine identity is constituted through marriage as a property relationship, and Collins pushes the conventions of *No Name* further to explore the structural position of more obvious outcasts: the fallen woman, the servant, and the penitent prostitute (the latter the subject of much ambivalent fascination). But because Collins deals with these questions of class and sexuality so openly here, he is forced into covering his tracks as he goes along. He implies that the anomalousness of the powerless is completely the product of the codes of a dominant social structure whose morbidity lies in its very power, but he ends up by reinforcing the split between purity and danger that earlier is made so ambiguous.

Man and Wife in particular is an extraordinary exploration of male violence and the position of women in marriage. It uses the familiar ingredients of forced marriage, masculine villainy, and feminine vulnerability, but, in contrast with *The Woman in White*, uses these conventions to focus not on the vulnerability of the heiress but on the plight of the unpropertied middle-class woman and the self-reliant and productive working-class woman able to earn her own living. In a modified return to the older melodramatic conventions of the seduction of the working-class girl by the upper-class villain, the victims are vulnerable either because of their lack of property or their lack of ability to earn money, not because of their inheritance – though that vulnerability is itself passed on from mother to daughter. The narrative revolves around three problematic, inter-related marriages, and it draws explicit connections, at the beginning, between the two Anne Silvesters – middle-class, unpropertied mother and daughter, both seduced and betrayed – and towards the end, between the positions of Anne Silvester the younger and the mysteriously dumb cook Hester Dethridge. The latter's written confession, describing her oppression by, and final murder of, her drunken and brutal husband, is revealed as part of the process by which Anne's wicked husband Geoffrey Delamayne attempts literally to smother Anne herself.[11]

Hester Dethridge's ambiguously pathological identity absorbs and expresses the unspoken connotations of the middle-class marriage; but it is the figure of Geoffrey Delamayne who both echoes and is contrasted with her feckless, drunken, and dead working-class husband, in a way that suggests that it is the latter's gender which is morbid rather than his class. This turns *Man and Wife* into a polemical attack on the 'inbred' violence that lies at the heart of the dominant culture. Published in 1870, the year after the appearance of Arnold's *Culture and Anarchy*, it takes up the increasing middle-class fear of the violence of a degraded urban working class and turns this round into an attack on the 'savagery' of English upper-middle-class customs and ideals of masculinity in a way that extends Arnold's discussion of 'Barbarians' while pushing it to a pathological conclusion. In doing this Collins detaches the physiognomic sign from its superficial moral referant in a way that makes 'fitness' itself the corollary of cultural atrophy and decay; yet this also finally leads to a transformed but reasserted realignment of the moral and the physiological. The Preface claims medical authority in exposing the rigours of the 'national eccentricity', the 'mania for muscular cultivation', and goes on:

> As to the moral results, I may be right or I may be wrong in seeing as I do a connection between the recent unbridled development of physical cultivation in England, and the recent spread of grossness and brutality among certain classes of the English population. But, is it to be denied that the grossness and brutality exist? and more, that they have assumed formidable proportions among us of late years? We have become so shamelessly familiar with violence and outrage that we recognise them as a necessary ingredient in our social system, and class our savages as a representative part of our population under the name of 'Roughs'. Public attention has been directed by hundreds of other writers to the dirty Rough in fustian. If the present writer had confined himself within these limits, he would have carried all his readers with him. But he is bold enough to direct attention to the washed Rough in broadcloth – and he must stand on his defence with readers who have not noticed this variety, or who, having noticed it, prefer to ignore it.[12]

Thus the very terms that he uses to question the framework through which 'Roughs' are seen as expressions of working-class degeneration can only do so by reinforcing the assumptions that contribute to its formation.

Geoffrey Delamayne is the figure who marks and reinforces the point of shift in the interpretations and modifications of the notion of 'fitness' itself – the point where evolution slides into degeneration. His excessive physical strength is both cause and symptom of moral atrophy which in turn is finally explained physiologically. It is stressed that he is representative of modernity, but as a result of upper-class 'barbarism' rather than over-refinement. And in modifying the degenerative model that produced the attenuated 'inbred' nervous disorder of Noel Vanstone (*No Name*) and Frederick Fairlie (*The Woman in White*), Delamayne can only be presented as a 'savage' throwback to a primitive state that is fostered and required by modern social conditions rather than as a product of a worn-out but tenacious heritage:

> The savage element in humanity . . . began to show itself furtively in his eyes, to utter itself furtively in his voice. Was he to blame for the manner in which he spoke to her? Not he! What had there been in the training of his life (at school or at college) to soften and subdue the savage element in him? About as much as there had been in the training of his ancestors (without the school or the college) five hundred years since.[13]

Moral insanity is now incubated at the heart of English progress, but Geoffrey none the less needs to be presented as a primitive throwback for this to stick.

In *Man and Wife*, moreover, power and strength become degenerate through turning out not really to be power and strength after all – Vanbrough, Anne Silvester Senior's husband, turns to suicide when his own relentless ambition and success turn to dust in his hands; Delamayne's muscularity is finally revealed to be a deceptive mask concealing a vital weakness. But the manipulation of these conventions is made dependent here on a narrative rhetoric that actively projects interpretations into physiological signs, and this paradoxically reinforces the patterns of control that fix Delamayne as pathological, and, by contrast, Anne as unconsciously attractive through physiognomic irregularity. Here nervous symptoms, as with Laura Fairlie (*The Woman in White*), become the sign of desirability itself; but this now extends to actual physical defect – in Maudsley's terms 'a want of regularity and harmony in the features . . . there are tics, grimaces, other spasmodic movements . . . of eyelids, or lips':[14]

> Worse even than this, there were positive defects in her face, which it was impossible to deny. A nervous contraction at one corner of her mouth, drew up the lips out of the symmetrically right line, when they moved. A nervous uncertainty in the eye on the same side narrowly escaped presenting the deformity of a 'cast'. And yet, with these indisputable drawbacks, here was one of those women – the formidable few – who have the hearts of men and the peace of families at their mercy.[15]

Anne's innocent vulnerability is the outcome of her attractiveness being at once perverse and beyond her control. And her counterpart, Hester Dethridge, becomes an uncanny figure by both functioning as the extended analogue of Anne's position, and as the literal manifestation of a psychic response to violence and repression.

Hester, like Anne Catherick (*The Woman in White*), is a spectral manifestation of a psychic response who is herself 'psychic'; she sees visions but refuses to speak. While her written confession disrupts both narrative voice and narrative time in the story – it emerges from underneath the dominant narrative as a trace of the past – it also enacts a parodied return to the model of moral management now transformed into opposing but related forms of spectral delusion. For the confession is not only addressed to a vengeful God, replaying the history behind her murder of her husband, but also recounts the punishment itself: 'I was commanded in a vision to open the Bible, and vow on it to set my guilty self apart from my innocent fellow-creatures from that day forward: to live among them a separate and silent life.'[16] Thus her hysterical dumbness turns out to be restraint imposed by the controlling gaze of a punitive Deity. And this vision of a controlling God turns into another kind of revelation, this time a vision of her guilty self, unambiguously presented as her pathological other:

> The Thing stole out, dark and shadowy in the pleasant sunlight. At first I saw only the dim figure of a woman. After a little, it began to get plainer, brightening from within outwards – brightening, brightening, brightening, till it set before me the vision of MY OWN SELF – repeated as if I was standing before a glass: a double of myself looking at me with my own eyes. . . . It pointed to the boy, with my own hand. And it said to me, in my own voice: kill him.[17]

216

Thus Hester Dethridge functions as an uncanny, ghostly figure within the overall naturalistic narrative by remaining embedded within its implied terms of reference as pathological – though it is a pathology that has become more self-conscious. And while Anne Catherick and Laura (*The Woman in White*) directly echoed each other through their shared ghostly whiteness, Hester's absence, her silence and 'deathliness', finally breaks out into mania as she attacks Delamayne; but it is a violence that has to take the form of doubling within the self, if Anne Silvester is to remain sympathetically vulnerable.

In *The New Magdalen* these patterns of guilty and innocent identities are more complex, but they still finally reinforce the fixed purity of the victim. While *Man and Wife* took up the unspoken questions of *The Woman in White* in the interrelated figures of unpropertied women, *The New Magdalen* reruns its familiar sensation conventions – the substitution of identity to gain a new one – to elaborate what by the 1870s was also a familiar convention, the figure of the chaste 'Magdalen'. This explicitness imposes another layer of necessity for subterfuge, which is enacted as much by the novel's narrator as its heroine. *The New Magdalen* is about the need to evade the stigma of an intractable past and an intolerant morality, but the deception and disguise that this involves both produce the remorse that can only be experienced by the penitent and reveal the true self that is expressed by the role. The novel contrasts respectable pathology and penitent transgression. Two women meet by chance in the neutral ground of a war zone. The orphaned middle-class Grace Roseberry is returning from Canada to a well-established position as paid companion to an aristocratic dowager; the Red Cross nurse, Mercy Merrick, reveals herself both as an angel of mercy, and as *at* the mercy of her past. Her account of her past and present position is not so much a reformed sinner's confession as a philanthropist's case history. It is a study of ostracism told by an assimilated voice that conjures up a familiar image of the penitent fallen woman:

> I am accustomed to stand in the pillory of my past life. I sometimes ask myself if it was all my fault. I sometimes wonder if society had no duties towards me when I was a child selling matches in the street – when I was a hard working girl fainting at my needle for want of food. . . . What I *am* can never alter what I *was*. . . . Everybody is sorry for me. . . . Everybody is kind to me. The lost place is not to be regained.[18]

A literal bolt from the blue – a bomb – leaves Grace for dead; Mercy takes her place as the companion but is then persecuted by her own remorse and by Grace herself, who returns to claim her place and name, claims initially dismissed as insane delusion.

A process of double displacement is thus developed throughout the novel. It is only through imposture that Mercy can find her right place, while the respectability that has been stolen from Grace turns out to be an empty shell; it is only through another emigration with the radical preacher Julian Gray that the heroine can finally be assimilated. Echoing *The Woman in White* and *No Name*, the social self is seen to be the product of others' interpretations and projections – which, in disintegrating, lead to madness. At first Grace's response to the stealing of her identity seems to enact Laura's plight (in *The Woman in White*) – she is shown Mercy's clothes to prove that that is who she is; she is stripped of all the reference points that link her to the past. With Mercy, as with Magdalen Vanstone (*No Name*) the greatest form of imposture is duping respectability, and both heroines break down under the strain of dissembling, even as Mercy comments, 'Remorse is the luxury of an honest woman'.[19] But it is a remorse that has been internalized, none the less. Collins often protested in his Prefaces that he drew a distinction between 'true' and 'false' morality, and exposed the latter as a way of reassessing the former, but this was qualified by narrative complexity in the 1860s. In *The New Magdalen* it is more clearly affirmed, but this in turn depends on images of unequivocal guilt and innocence as well as remorse and reform that are reinforced by the contrasting psychological reference points that make sense of Mercy and Grace.

I have suggested that Collins needed to resort to an unambiguous notion of purity in order to represent an actual prostitute. Here a rhetoric of radical philanthropy is pushed through moral management into a state of 'grace' – as Mercy finally acknowledges she is not really Grace. The moral centre of the story is the Christian Socialist priest, Julian Gray, a figure who clearly states his own position as he is introduced: 'Pitiless Political Economy shall spend a few extra shillings on the poor as certainly as I am that Radical, Communist and Incendiary – Julian Gray.'[20] He reinforces Mercy's self-analysis by presenting the plight of the ex-prostitute to the midde-class household:

She may long to make atonement, and may not know how to begin. All her energies may be crushed under the despair and horror of herself, out of which the truest repentance grows. Is such a woman as this all wicked, all vile? I deny it! She may have a noble nature, she may show it nobly yet.[21]

And he later refers to this symbolic figure as Mercy struggles under the strain of dissembling: 'Be the woman whom I once spoke of – the woman I still have in my mind – who can nobly reveal the noble nature that is in her.'[22] Thus he transforms Mercy into absolute virtue by holding up an idealized image of her for her to emulate. The disguise is literally a mask rather than a metaphor for identity shaped by perception; her final confession reveals that even her apparent former life a a prostitute was forcibly imposed.

Mercy Merrick represents a modification of the self-regulating perspective of moral management projected on to an idealized image that functions almost as an allegorical figure. Her counterpart, Grace Roseberry, on the other hand, depends on the expectations generated by the conventions of moral insanity, wherein self-possession becomes the sign of perversion, which is in turn manifested through unambiguous physiognomic signs: 'The forehead was unusually low and broad; the eyes unusually far apart; the mouth and chin remarkably small.'[23] Just as Mercy's purity defies as it manifests 'society's' exclusion of its outcasts, so Grace's 'perversion' is the extension of the very propriety that consolidated that exclusion. Collins often suggested that the very attempt to enact the social codes that are the sign of self-possession through propriety can easily slip over the edge into weird behaviour: Midwinter's collapse into hysteria in *Armadale* as he attempts to enact a parody of good-humoured politeness is one clear example. But this depends on a pattern of self-sustaining contradictions within the self that are reversed in the figure of Grace Roseberry in *The New Magdalen*. Again, her moral insanity resides in the strength of her self-control, though not in the skill with which she can manipulate others sexually, but this coherence must again depend on the simple realignment of the physiological and the moral: the connotations of Grace's low forehead and receding chin – her arrested moral development – are borne out by her subsequent behaviour.

But although the transformation and disguise of identity in *The New Magdalen* paradoxically end up by reinforcing the very physiological assumptions that the earlier novels questioned, Mercy and Grace are none the less placed in the context of a set of marginal or contingent figures who represent different gradations of the inter-pretative realignment as they shift down the social scale. Horace

Holmcroft, the false hero from an ancient upper-middle-class family, combines the decadence of Fairlie (*The Woman in White*) with the degeneration of Delamayne (*Man and Wife*), but again it is healthy conformity that breeds a morally deficient type signalled by the stock conventions of physiognomy:

> Men – especially men skilled in observing physiognomy – might have noticed in the shape of his forehead and in the line of his upper lip the signs indicative of a moral nature deficient in largeness and breadth – of a mind easily accessible to strong prejudices, and obstinate in maintaining those prejudices in the face of conviction itself.[24]

The plain-clothes policeman – a hybrid voyeur who crosses the boundaries between classes, between public and private zones, between crime and respectability – is presented more comically, as a sinister creature whose degradation is the product of adaptation: 'He had odiously watchful eyes – eyes that looked skilled at peeping through keyholes. His large ears, set forward like the ears of a monkey, pleaded guilty to meanly listening behind other people's doors.'[25] But the East End pauper child, whom Mercy wants to save in order to save herself, has become a polluted and polluting victim, adapted to the conditions which have formed her in a way that suggests that Mercy's own story is formed by the very 'halo of romance' that her 'sister' negates:

> There was no beauty in *this* child; no halo of romance brightened the commonplace horror of *her* story. She came cringing into the room, staring stupidly at the magnificence all around her – the daughter of the London streets! the pet creation of the laws of political economy! the scourge and terrible product of a worn out system of government and of a civilization rotten to its core! Cleaned for the first time in her life, dressed in clothes instead of rags for the first time in her life, Mercy's sister in adversity crept fearfully over the beautiful carpet and stopped wonder-struck before the marble of an inlaid table – a blot of mud on the splendour of the room.
>
> Mercy turned from Julian to meet the child. The woman's heart, longing in its horrible isolation for something it might harmlessly love, welcomed the rescued waif as a consolation sent from God. She caught the stupefied little creature up in her arms. 'Kiss me', she whispered in the reckless agony of the moment. 'Call me sister!' The child stared vacantly. Sister meant nothing to her mind but an older girl who was strong enough to beat her.[26]

The narrative rhetoric here is forced to overturn the very structure of liberal philanthropic sympathy that is activated by and manifested in the figure of Mercy in order to emphasize the social and political laws that form the pauper child. And it can only do this, it can only set her as a figure in a political rhetoric, by reinforcing her alien identity through the physiological signs of urban degeneration.

THE LAW AND THE LADY, JEZEBEL'S DAUGHTER, HEART AND SCIENCE

Man and Wife and *The New Magdalen* each take the questions that sensation conventions raise about the perception of social identity beyond their earlier limits, yet need to strip away much of their psychological and cognitive equivocation in order to elicit their reader's sympathy. But in *The Law and the Lady* (1875) Collins approaches the cognitive complexity of *The Moonstone*, and develops his most bizarre and contradictory image of insanity in the figure of Miserrimus Dexter. Here, and in *Jezebel's Daughter* (1880) and *Heart and Science* (1883), there is a return to distinct methods of psychological investigation, which are self-consciously used as sources of narrative tension in ways that turns the stories themselves into more detailed enquiries into the methods that are exploited. Collins's brief note to the reader in *The Law and the Lady*, 'Be pleased then to remember (first) that the actions of human beings are not invariably governed by the laws of pure reason', is enacted by the narrative itself, in which the process of disclosing the past involves the exploration of psychic mechanisms which have to be hidden again if the social and sexual balance that their disclosure achieved is to be maintained.[27]

The Law and the Lady is neither as structurally nor as conceptually complex as *The Moonstone*, nor does it draw explicitly on contemporary theories of the unconscious. But in consequence it merges legal and psychological definitions and psychic and social identities the more effectively, and gives Dexter as madman a range of competing roles to play as agent in the narrative. The heroine Valeria Macallen's story opens with her marriage, but then goes on to reveal her husband's hidden secret as she discovers that he had been tried for the murder of his former wife, the verdict pronounced 'not proven'. Her own resolution to reopen the case and vindicate her husband's innocence in order to gain full possession of him and consolidate her own subjective identity as his wife, makes her in some respects a female equivalent of Walter Hartright (*The Woman in White*). But the truth that is disclosed, the ghostly trace of the first marriage and the final discovery of the first wife's confession embedded in Valeria's narrative and in fragments in a dust-heap, leaves the husband's guilt ambiguous: the wife's confession describes how she was gradually driven to suicide, not by her husband's violence, but by his contemptuous indifference and sexual aversion – evidence that Valeria suppresses herself.

Thus 'the discovery of the truth' confirms the husband's legal innocence though in a manner that allows it to remain morally opaque. And although the reconstruction of the dead wife's diary is finally confirmed through the excavation of the past's traces, the disclosure of the existence of the trial and the courtroom drama itself, merges cognitive opacity with the unreliability of legal perceptions. Valeria first discovers that all is not well with her husband when she accidentally meets his mother (whom she recognizes from a photograph). The mother fails to show any sign of recognition when Valeria tells her her name, and then fails to acknowledge her son. Her husband's friend, an ageing roué, refuses to reveal his secret, but leaves her in a room which contains the clue to it; this means that every object becomes overburdened with significance, as she notes and analyses in detail her own sensations and associations: 'the longer I searched the farther I seemed to remove myself from the one object I had it in my heart to attain'.[28]

The secret, when she does discover it, is presented as a piece of sensation drama in a volume of 'celebrated trials', which is then replayed at length as an embedded narrative within the story. And the transcript of the trial reinforces the device that produces the unresolved tension in the story; the verdict *does* seem 'not proven' as the evidence itself is open to contradictory implications. The post-mortem proves 'beyond the possibility of doubt' that the wife died poisoned. But it is more difficult to interpret the significance of the husband's diary in which he acknowledges his distaste for his wife; Dexter denies that it should be read as a 'true confession' despite the way it is paraded as such:

A Diary (when it extends beyond a true record of facts and dates) is, in general, nothing but an expression of the weakest side in the character of the person who keeps it. It is, in nine cases out of ten, the more or less contemptible outpouring of vanity and conceit which the writer dares not exhibit to any mortal but himself.[29]

Equivocation hinges firstly on the controversial identity of the wife – presented alternately as ugly, aggressive, pathologically jealous, and demanding and as intelligent, charming, compassionate, and witty; and secondly on the status of the evidence of Dexter himself.

Dexter has a range of contrasting functions in the narrative. He plays a crucial role in achieving its final resolution by possessing a knowledge of the truth that he refuses to reveal, so that it has to emerge through the disintegration of his consciousness and the piecing together of the fragments of his memory (as Jennings does with Candy in *The Moonstone*). Here the business of disentangling and realigning the elements of his unconscious associations directly prefigures the means by which the wife's confessional letter is recovered from the forgotten detritus of the household's past. And his 'craziness' is a crucial means for compounding the mystification of the trial itself. But the excesses of Dexter go far beyond this. They take the form of a fantastic magnification of competing psychological codes; above all, of competing definitions of the perception and significance of the borderlands of insanity.

In the first place Dexter is presented not simply as a fantastic image, but as a figure who works, on different registers, in a way that is directly analogous to the dreaming process. He is initially introduced in the transcript of the trial, wheeled on the courtroom stage as exhibit as well as witness. He literally appears as the unexpected justaposing of fragments that can be recognized but no reconciled: 'a strange and startling creature – literally the half of a man' but 'to make the deformity all the more terrible, the victim of it was – as to his face and his body – an unusually handsome and well-made man'. And further, although 'Never had Nature committed a more careless or a more cruel mistake than in the making of this man', he is presented as both natural and mechanical, half man, half chair: 'My Chair is Me', thus pushing physiological psychology to an absurd conclusion.[30] As in a dream, Dexter's physical manifestations are metaphoric expressions of mental processes which are in turn dreamlike. Mrs Macallen describes how he 'mixed up sense and nonsense in the strangest confusion' after a lucid opening in the trial.

> In short, he was just like himself – a mixture of the strangest and opposite qualities; at one time perfectly clear and reasonable, as you said just now; at another breaking out into rhapsodies of the most outrageous kind, like a man in a state of delirium.[31]

This openly acknowledges that physical identity has become a deconstructed analogue of a mental process.

Moreover, just as Dexter is presented in the language of dreams, and inhabits the uncanny borderlands at the edge of logical associations, so the overlapping narrative views of him progressively both deconstruct and reinforce competing perceptions and definitions of insanity. 'Miserrimus Dexter – First View' presents him in a state of high mania, complete with the classic symptoms of delusions of grandeur, in his sombre house in the indeterminate suburbs which is found by driving 'through a dingy brick labyrinth' of streets. Here the *frission* of what he signifies depends on magnifying his grotesqueness:

> A high chair on wheels moved by, through the field of red light, carrying a shadowy figure with floating hair and arms furiously raised and lowered, working the machinery that raised the chair at its utmost rate of speed. 'I am Napoleon, at the sunrise of Austerlitz!' shouted the man in the chair as he swept past me, on his rumbling and whistling wheels, in the red glow of the firelight. 'I give the word; and thrones rock, and kings fall, and nations tremble, and men by tens of thousands fight and bleed and die!' The chair rushed out of sight and the man in it became another hero – 'I am Nelson!' the ringing voice cried now. 'I am leading the fleet at Trafalgar. . . .' The frightful and fantastic apparition, man and machinery blended in one – the new Centaur, half man, half chair – flew at me again by the dying light. 'I am Shakespeare!' cried the frantic creature now. 'I am writing "Lear", the tragedy of tragedies. Ancient and modern, I am the poet who towers over them all.'[32]

This passage, however, qualifies, as it sets up, the terms of its own interpretation. Dexter is seen fleetingly, in a lurid half-light in a way that 'works the machinery' of his dramatic performance as he works the machinery of his chair. He is thus giving a performance of a performance, a display of contrasting personas, presented as a 'fantastic and frightful apparition' and concluding with the performance of a playwright.

This 'apparition' is extended and modified in the 'Second View' where again 'the whole man appeared to have undergone a complete transformation', but this time a transformation across an earlier boundary between madness and eccentricity:

> I saw plainly now the bright intelligent face, and the large clear blue eyes . . . the deformity which degraded and destroyed the manly beauty of his head and breast was hidden by an Oriental robe of many colours. . . . He wore lace ruffles at the ends of his sleeves, in the fashion of the last century.[33]

Here he analyses his own behaviour, in a way that turns it into the excess of hypochondriacal nervous sensibility: 'I have an immense imagination; it runs riot at times. It makes an actor of me. I play the parts of all the heroes that ever lived . . . I merge myself in their individualities.'[34] Thus Romanticism is pushed beyond its own limits, beyond any conception either of orginality of self or truth to nature. 'Persons who look for mere Nature in works of Art are persons to whom Mr Dexter does not address himself with the brush', he writes of his grotesque paintings; 'Nature puts him out.'[35] And while Dexter is unmistakably morbid, Valeria's response to him is inconclusive. She acknowledges in the 'Second View': 'It may well have been due to want of perception on my part – but I could see nothing mad in him, nothing in any way repelling, as I now looked at him.'[36] And this leads into a more detailed analysis of the way he expresses latent or suppressed impulses. She tells Mrs Macallen:

> I never felt more surprised, more confounded in my life. But now that I have recovered from my amazement, and can think it over quietly, I must continue to doubt whether this strange man is really mad, in the true meaning of the word. It seems to me that he openly expresses – I admit in a very reckless and boisterous way – thoughts and feelings which most of us are ashamed of as weaknesses, and keep to ourselves accordingly. I confess I have often fancied myself transformed into another person, and have felt a certain pleasure in seeing myself in my new character. One of our first achievements as children . . . is to get out of our characters, and to try the characters of other personages for a change – to be fairies, to be queens, to be anything, in short, but what we really are. Mr Dexter lets out the secret, just as the children do – and if that is madness he really is mad . . . I am not learned enough to trace the influence of that life in making him what he is. But I think I can see the result in an over-excited imagination.[37]

As with the figure of Hester Dethridge (*Man and Wife*), Collins here self-consciously includes the psychological explanation of uncanny figures as part of the process of representing them.

Miserrimus Dexter's ability to play with identity and undermine the concept of stable character thus mirrors and extends the ambiguous nature of reality, the danger in trusting the evidence of the senses, and the instability of self explored in the first part of the novel. Valeria herself needs to be disguised as a 'pretty girl' in order to be able to search for the clue leading to the disclosure of her husband's past: 'From the moment when I had resigned myself to the hands of the chambermaid, I seemed in some strange way to have lost my ordinary identity – to have stepped out of my own character.'[38]

But the resolution of the mystery depends not only on evacuating Dexter's unconscious but reducing him to one meaning as a specimen framed within contemporary medical discourse; here the language of moral management merges into that of degeneration, in a way that involves the interpretation of the borderlands of eccentricity, insanity, and idiocy. Valeria's modified view of Dexter claims a kind of kinship and common sympathy with him which, in stressing his childlikeness, is compatible with the perspective of moral management, even as it goes beyond it. This is realigned by the doctor's initial report on his mental condition, which presents his very self-control as another mode of performance. 'He may say and do all sorts of odd things; but he has his mind under the control of his will, and you can trust his self-esteem to exhibit him in the character of a substantially intelligent witness.' But this analysis is immediately modified in a way that links the breakdown of the conditions of self-control with disintegration into total insanity:

That he will end in madness (if he lives), I entertain little or no doubt. The question of *when* the madness will show itself, depends entirely on the state of his health. His nervous system is highly sensitive; and there are signs that his way of life has already damaged it. If he conquers the bad habits to which I have alluded in an earlier part of my report, and if he passes many hours of every day quietly and in the open air, he may last as a sane man for years to come. If he persists in his present way of life – or, in other words, if further mischief occurs to that sensitive nervous system – his lapse into insanity must inevitably take place when the mischief has reached its culminating point. Without warning to himself or to others, the whole mental structure will give way; and at a moment's notice, while he his acting as quietly, or speaking intelligently as at his best time, the man may drop (if I may use the expression) into madness or idiocy . . . The balance once lost, will be lost for life.[39]

The doctor's report hovers, as the figure of Dexter does, on the boundary between self-control and degeneration, finally collapsing into the latter, which is seen as a latent feature of the former, intertwining physical organization and mental responsibility. As with both Henry Maudsley and Andrew Wynter's analyses of mental degeneration, Dexter's latent insanity is an inevitable destiny, a Nemesis which he might struggle against by virtuous living, but not one that he can evade. Moreover, Dexter simultaneously corresponds with and parodies Maudsley's description of eccentric individuals who 'exhibit peculiarities of thought, feeling and character which render them unlike ordinary beings', and in whom 'a vein of madness in the constitution sometimes displays itself . . . in a morbid vein of poetical delusion.'[40] Wynter's argument that 'it is the sustained departure from the normal condition of life which should suggest a grave suspicion of impending insanity' is taken to an absurd extreme in his lifestyle.[41] But this focus then becomes another view, another assumed persona, for Dexter's disintegration telescopes the degenerative process that both Maudsley and Wynter, for example, considered to stretch over generations. His figure, moreover, collapses the shift from late-eighteenth-century nervous sensibility into late-nineteenth-century degenerate eccentricity, but in an overtly improbable way. He finally comes to resemble his idiot cousin Ariel, who is presented as an evolutionary freak, a throwback – 'I could now see the girl's round, fleshy, inexpressive face, her rayless and colourless eyes, her coarse nose and heavy chin. A creature half alive; an imperfectly-developed animal in shapeless form', Valeria notes.[42] Dexter 'showed an animal interest in his meals, and a greedy animal enjoyment in eating and drinking as much as he could get – and that was all.'[43] So in resolving the narrative and ideological contradictions that Dexter poses in this way, the figure can be read as playing with and qualifying degenerative discourse as much as finally emphasizing it.

Collins's use of specific notions of degeneration in these novels highlights some of their interpretative problems by analysing how psychological codes take on different meanings in shifting contexts. The different combinations of emphasis in the interrelated social, physiological, and psychological influences suggested in the figures of Delamayne in *Man and Wife*, the East End child in *The New Magdalen*, and in Dexter himself, for example, suggest that 'degeneration' itself can take on different connotations; it can be used to satirize the conception of 'fitness' to qualify the complacencies of philanthropy – no matter how radical – and to parody its own presuppositions. It is twisted further with Jack Straw in *Jezebel's Daughter*, a figure who seems to be compounded out of the opposite elements from those that made up Miserrimus Dexter, and who serves a completely different narrative function in a novel that represents a modified reconsideration of the moral polarities of high melodrama, rather than the interpretative subtleties of the detective story. 'You will . . . find two interesting studies of humanity in these pages', Collins claimed in the Letter of Dedication.

> In the character called 'Jack Straw' you have the exhibition of an enfeebled intellect, tenderly shown under its lightest and happiest aspects, and used as a means of relief in some of the darkest scenes of terror and suspense in the story. Again, in 'Madame Fountaine', I have endeavoured to work out the interesting moral problem, which takes for its ground work the strongest of all instincts in a woman, the instinct of maternal love, and traces to its solution the restraining and purifying influence of this one virtue over an otherwise cruel, false, and degraded nature.[44]

In hinging the 'terror and suspense' around an act of conscious villainy, Collins again consolidates the split between moral insanity and responsibility, medical and moral definitions, while pressing them into service in a narrative process that draws on and reinterprets early-nineteenth-century perceptions.

Jezebel's Daughter is a reconstruction, by a detached narrator, of events in 1828 written in 1878; it is further distanced by being set in Germany, although the madhouse, Bethlehem, has very specifically 'English' connotations. The story contrasts the effects of the intellectual legacies of two men on their widows. Wagner was a successful merchant involved as a philanthropist in the lunacy reform movement – his widow carries on his work by rescuing Jack Straw from the madhouse. Fountaine was an experimental chemist who had been working on an antidote to poisons; his work is twisted by the villainess, who uses all the machinery of experimental medicine as a means of consolidating her power. Jack is a crucial figure in the narrative because he turns out to have been an earlier accidental victim of Fountaine's experiments, and this gives him the knowledge necessary to reverse the effects of Madame Fountaine's attempts to poison Mrs Wagner. He is thus primarily an agent of narrative resolution, although the crucial focus of suspense hinges on whether he has correctly understood the medical instructions.

It also means that he has to be absolutely and unequivocally innocent (just as Mercy Merrick has to be (*The New Magdalen*)), and this partially explains why he is, like Anne Catherick (*The Woman in White*), so firmly and explicitly set within the discursive framework of moral management. It is, moreover, the moral management of Tuke, rather than Conolly; moral treatment here again involves removal to a home, a curative asylum where Jack takes up permanent residence as a cross between a household pet and an adoring servant. But the novel sidesteps the interacting resonances of 'home' and 'asylum' that provide so much of the tension of *The Woman in White*, by splitting the home into two polarized places of safety and danger – the site of moral treatment on the one hand, of medical manipulation on the other. The thrill of horror conveyed by the image of the 'old' corrupt asylum is created from the same stand-point of half-purient self-congratulation that produced the early descriptions of moral treatment and the articles in *Household Words*:

> The man put his hand into the big pocket of his coat, and produced a horrible whip, of many lashes. He exhibited this instrument of torture with every appearance of pride and pleasure. 'This is what keeps him in order, my lady', said the brute cheer-fully. 'Just take it in your hand.'[45]

Jack Straw, himself, moreover, is drawn from Tuke's *A Description of the Retreat* but never in a way that confirms the reciprocity of its moral treatment. He is first presented as being prone to fits of mania, but already has his own internal keeper – the 'angel' of his dreams who instructs him in basketwork. Just as the maniac in Tuke's account 'promised to restrain himself', so Jack struggles with his 'morbid propensities'.[46] Like Tuke's patients, he is exag-geratedly grateful for his kind treatment: 'On the one occasion when he did lose self-control, you saw how he recovered himself when he was calmly and kindly reasoned with', Mrs Wagner argues.[47] Jack is caught in a perpetual childhood and thus becomes a magical agent; a figure who can be assimilated into the Wagner family as quasi-servant and child, but who has no family, no history, of his own: 'the memoirs of Jack remain unwritten'.[48] The focus on inbred or inherited traits is all on the 'moral insanity' side of the narrative and the figure of Madame Fountaine. Like Lydia Gwilt in *Armadale*, Collins attempts to set up a self-divided character here, but is unable to do so by exposing the limitations of the resources of moral management as Gwilt does. As a result Madame Fountaine becomes completely the product of a 'perverted' nature: even her 'better nature', her desire to protect her daughter, becomes the expression of an amoral instinct of biological destiny. The narrative never completely overturns the cynical Frau Meyer's comment: 'It's as much part of woman's nature to take to her child when she has got one, as it is to take to her dinner when she is hungry. A fond mother? What stuff! A cat is a fond mother.'[49]

Jack Straw and Madame Fountaine become self-sustaining opposi-tions, and this is bound up with the equally decisive polarization of medical and moral means of tranformation. In *Armadale* the parodied curative asylum merged into medical control and became the means for melodramatic manipulation; in *Jezebel's Daughter*, the terror of the well-established convention of malignancy manifested through poisoning becomes more potent as a fantastic form of alchemy through being a perversion of 'legitimate' science. In the 'Story of the Present Time', *Heart and Science*, the split between morality and medicine is amplified and finally modified as physiological investigation into the brain and nervous system becomes a source of both horror and reconciliation. Again, as in *The Moonstone*, Collins invokes the authority of physiological psychology, but this time it is the externalized phrenological authority of David Ferrier. 'A supposed discovery in connection with brain disease, which occupies a place of importance, is not (as you may suspect) the fantastic product of the author's imagination', he stresses in the Preface. 'Finding his materials everywhere he has even continued to make use of Professor Ferrier – writing on "The Localisation of Brain Disease".'[50] Indeed Ferrer's *The Localisation of Brain Disease* (1878) was one of the most important developments of experimental physiology derived from the earlier tenets of phrenology in the late nineteenth century. His findings established that the brain's different hemispheres produced distinct sensory-motor functions. A report to the British Association for the Advancement of Science stated of Ferrier's observations:

> A new, but this time a true, system of phrenology will probably be founded upon them: by this, however, I do not mean that it will be possible to tell a man's faculties from the configuration of his skull; but merely this, that the various mental faculties will be assigned to definite territories of the brain.[51]

But although Collins concludes 'plenty of elbow-room here for the spirit of discovery', it is not the curiosity that motivates the narrative and cognitive complexity of *The Moonstone* and the shift in emphasis is important.

The critical reception of *Jezebel's Daughter* had highlighted how much Collins's well-established reputation as 'master of plots' had undermined his claim to seriousness. The *Spectator* reiterated:

> Is Mr Collins in fact, as he declares himself to be in purpose, a moral reformer, or is he merely an ingenious story-teller? Are his ends greater than his means, or are his means so cunningly devised as to make his ends comparatively insignificant or invisible? Do

his puppets exist purely for the sake of the dance, or is the dance contrived to elucidate the mechanism of the puppets? Is a noble warmth at the heart, or a creepy sensation down the spine, the commoner consequence of reading one of Mr Collins's novels?[52]

In the Preface to *Heart and Science* Collins takes up a position where he simultaneously claims to his 'Readers in General' that he is 'still refusing to get up in a pulpit and preach, or to invade the platform and lecture', yet makes his didactic intention clear to his 'Readers in Particular'. Here, too, in contrast with his earlier balancing of plot and character in the Preface to *The Woman in White*, he concedes that he has 'never succeeded in keeping an equal balance' between the two elements:

> In the present story you will find the scales inclining, on the whole in favour of character and humour. . . . It has been my chief effort to draw the characters with a vigour and breadth of treatment derived from the nearest and truest view that I could get of one model, Nature.[53]

This claim to naturalism takes on a new meaning here, for in a curious way the fictional techniques of the novel are caught up in the contradictions of the very belief in naturalistic empirical observation that it simultaneously exploits and criticizes. Conversely, Collins concedes an incompatibility between emotional and sensational response by stressing that he deliberately plays down the macabre potential of the vivisection laboratory, as this would outrage the very sympathies to which he was appealing: 'From first to last you are purposely left in ignorance of the hideous secrets of vivisection. The outside of the laboratory is a necessary object in my landscape – but I never once open the door and invite you to look in.'[54]

Heart and Science depends on the dichotomy implied by its title even as it attempts to redraw its boundaries within science by invoking a moralized physiology. Again the plot hinges on a vulnerable heroine who breaks down under the strain of malicious family intrigue, but now it is experimental physiology rather than moral management that becomes the crucible of breakdown and restoration. Moreover, this is a science which is wheeled on as a magical solution rather than producing a sense of cognitive opacity, for the story also revolves around the opposition between the good and bad physiologist. The hero discovers the significance of Ferrier's theory of brain disease in order to rescue the heroine from a vaguely defined nervous prostration, while the villain resorts to the necessarily obscure horrors of vivisection to advance his researches on the nervous system. Thus there are two kinds of experimental subjects. The polemic against vivisection, advanced by stressing the 'common sympathies' between humans and animals (the most sympathetic figure is 'Zo', a wayward child), serves, however, only to reinforce a paternalism based on experimental observation that finally becomes its humane equivalent. There are, moreover, distinct modes of naturalistic scrutiny in the narrative method itself. The novel set the hero up as sympathetic agent by tracing his associative processes as he wanders round London; the villain is 'vivisected' by a narrative gaze that also penetrates his mental processes.

THE FALLEN LEAVES AND THE LEGACY OF CAIN

Collins aimed to transform the well-worn conventions of mistaken or substituted identity in *Man and Wife* and *The New Magdalen*, and self-consciously turned the manipulation of the physiological experiment back into a qualified critique of science itself in *Heart and Science*. *The Fallen Leaves* (1879) and *The Legacy of Cain* (1889) are sharply contrasting adaptations of the conventions of mysterious coincidences, misplaced children, the discovery of origins, and contrasting projections of inheritance and destiny. These now link the connections within the family into wider social and organic networks whose strands and origins are shaped by a structure in which chance is a crucial determining element. *The Fallen Leaves* is Collins's most politically explicit novel. Commercial capitalism, social divisions, and the ideology that both exploits and attempts to explain them are critically scrutinized through the framework of Christian Socialism, and this in turn is qualified and shown to be inadequate by being placed in different contexts by a narrative rhetoric which alternatively identifies with and distances itself from it. The novel attempts to resist the influence of two organic models of social structure: Spencer's notion of competitive individualism, with its naturalization and validation of 'fitness', and clearly degenerative explanations of growing class divisions produced by adaptation to the environment. Yet this resistance also modifies radical liberalism itself and focuses on the determining influence of social structure as well as the effects of economic contradictions. The outcasts and cast-offs, the 'fallen leaves' of the title, 'the people who have drawn blanks in the lottery of life'[55] are the victims of an arbitrary process and the product of specific circumstances. So the novel grapples with the problem of how to develop a narrative perspective which resists the naturalizing connotations of the metaphor, that the 'fallen leaves' are the necessary detritus of an organic process of change, while constantly attempting to relate this to the establishment and analysis of dominant forms of power.

Collins often attempted to develop a method that allowed various means of tension, dissonance, and coincidence to work quasi-legitimately in the story, while scrutinizing the various causes that lay behind and affected their outcome, but they are linked most clearly to the rhetorical purpose of the novel in *The Fallen Leaves*. Moreover, the novel does more than question a new kind of natural order by incorporating the legitimated improbability of sensational conventions. It attempts to combine this with more openly allegorical, Utopian, and social investigative methods and the development of a narrative voice that oscillates between exploratory, explanatory, and distancing modes. The central narrative and ideological focus is the figure of Amelius Goldenheart – like Hartright (*The Woman in White*), obviously the perspective of 'good feeling'. He is an innocent who arrives from the 'other world' of an American Utopian Christian Socialist community, and is a figure whose optimism is modified but whose identity is never fundamentally contaminated by his encounter with the divided London of the drawing-room and the East End. His focusing perception is set within the narrative of the social evolution of the Farnaby family. The Prologue, set fifteen years before the beginning of the story, describes how Farnaby, epitome of self-made, competitive individualism, builds his own success on jettisoning his future wife's illegitimate child to a shady fate in an unknown London; fifteen years later the wife is still obsessed by the loss. Here the fairy-tale device of the 'stolen child' is used to mock its own complacent expectations even as it fulfils them. Similarly, Mrs Farnaby depends on the sustaining illusions of her dreams of reunion even as she derides them as delusions:

> O, you needn't remind me that there is a rational explanation to my dream. I have read it all up, in the Encyclopaedia in the Library. One of the ideas of wise men is that we think of something, consciously or unconsciously, in the daytime, and then reproduce it in a dream.[56]

Amelius is both the innocent agent who is able to discover the child – now a prostitute – by traversing the zones of London, and the means of her reformation, but he never becomes the eye through which contradictions can be resolved or a figure that can be assimilated. He remains almost a dream figure himself.

This means that the dominant narrative voice is distanced from the hero even as it identifies with him, and this in turn shapes the way that his Christian Socialism (outlined early on through the familiar device of 'explanation to a stranger') functions as the qualified ideological centre of the book. This is a curious blend of earlier nineteenth-century co-operative socialism, and contemporary models. Collins himself clearly knew something about American Utopian socialist communities, but in *The Fallen Leaves* the Tadmor community is always presented as a memory or a future possibility.[57] It becomes a pastoral myth that combines co-operation and the abolition of private property with an idealized belief in education and self-management, echoing Owenism. But the political ideas that the hero puts forward in London – most obviously in the 'fatal lecture' – correspond with many of the tensions that marked late-nineteenth-century English Christian Socialism.

Christian Socialism was always fundamentally a middle-class attempt to defuse the threat of violent social revolution, rather than aiming to radically transform the social structure, but there was an important shift in emphasis between its founding movement in the 1840s and its revival initiated by Stuart Headlam in the late 1870s. Maurice had made it clear that the movement was a response to the twin threats of Chartism and the revolutionary upheavals in France. He wrote to Ludlow in 1848:

> The sovereignty of the people, in any sense or form, I not only repudiate as one of the silliest and most blasphemous of all contradictions, but I look on it as the *same* contradiction, in its fullest expansion, of which kings have been guilty.[58]

Headlam, in reviving the movement, redirected its concerns away from the fears of class conflict and focused instead more on the structural divisions that might bring the threat of social disintegration. The 'Socialism' of the equation here was clearly of the Fabian kind; Headlam considered the Guild of St George to be the religious wing of the Fabian Society, and published a pamphlet with them on Christian Socialism. The fear of organized revolution was now replaced by equally profound anxieties about the demoralization leading to contagion and degeneration of the casual poor.[59]

The figure of Amelius Goldenheart enables these contrasting political resonances – the Utopian ideals of the willed transformation of self and society through education and progressive social reorganization, as against the need for planned intervention to defuse the disintegrating forces of a degeneration accelerating under capitalism – to be telescoped together. In the 'fatal lecture' he uses the Bible as a moral reference point and as a means of distancing his audience from their habitual assumptions, revealing the 'bare bones' under the 'plump pasteboard' of international capitalism:

> Look at our commerce. What is its social aspect, judged by the morality which is in this book in my hand? Let those organised systems of imposture masquerading under the disguise of banks and companies, answer the question. . . . You know how our poor Indian customer finds his cotton-print dress a sham that falls to pieces . . . how the half-starved needlewoman who buys her reel of thread finds printed on the lable a false statement of the numbers of yards she buys. . . . Do you believe in the honourable accumulation of wealth by men who hold such opinions and perpetuate such impostures as these?[60]

The rhetoric of contagion and corruption – 'demoralisation and disgrace' – is deflected here from its morbid symptoms and linked to its structural causes. But in the next stage of the analysis, Amelius claims scriptual authority as a means of resolving the conflict as well as providing the perspective from which to view it:

> Do I unjustly ignore the capacity for peaceable reformation which has preserved modern England from revolutions, thus far? . . . And I do personally fear (and older and wiser men than I agree with me), that the corruptions at which I have only been able to hint are fast extending themselves – in England as well as in Europe generally – beyond the reach of that lawful and bloodless reform which has served us so well in past years. . . . The one sure foundation on which a permanent, complete and worthy reformation can be built – whether it prevents a convulsion or whether it follows a convulsion – is only to be found within the covers of this book.[61]

Amelius's speech is embedded in the narrative as his solution is embedded in the 'book', while always remaining alien and distanced. But the lecture also serves a more immediate narrative purpose. It loosens the fixed separateness of the different classes of London, leading to the recognition of Farnaby from the nether world to which he had jettisoned his daughter Sally, and it projects Amelius into his random wanderings round London and his chance encounter with the 'lost child'. But it is also an extreme expression of the problem of social perception that is played out tacitly in the text as a whole: the problem of how to transform dominant perceptions rather than simply inverting them. *The Fallen Leaves* in this respect takes the specific ideological tensions of *Man and Wife* and *The New Magdalen* into another dimension, and grapples with the problem of how to resist the 'resistless influences' of the degenerative connotations of evolutionary language, but in a framework which depends on interlocking social, psychological, and organic, as well as more narrowly physiological, metaphors. In *The New Magdalen* Collins encountered the problem of how to elicit sympathy for the 'contagious' figure of the prostitute in a way that presented her as shaped by social influences while remaining morally uncontaminated. Here this process has become more complex; the prostitutes are the ultimate 'fallen leaves' of society, and this both changes the meaning of the metaphor itself and the transgressive connotations of 'fallen'. But again this also implies that the contrasted 'pet creations of the laws of political economy' are also the creations of organic laws.

The boundaries between the different zones of London are both reinforced and blurred by describing the city itself as a ubiquitous virus: 'with its monstrous extremes of wealth and poverty, and its all-permeating malady of life at a fever heat'.[62] This means that the corruption of commercial capitalism exposed in the lecture is reproduced in and contaminates the nether world; the costermongers have become a parody of the 'organised system of imposture' of legitimate commerce, but poverty itself is alternately a state of grace and contamination. Amelius's response to 'the sight of utter misery around him, and the sense of his utter inability to remedy it' makes him doubt whether 'his happy brethren of the community and these miserable people [were] creatures of the same all-merciful God'.[63] But the prostitutes themselves are again idealized as asexual madonnas: 'All that is most unselfish, all that is most divinely compassionate and self-sacrificing in a woman's nature, was as beautiful and undefiled as ever in these women – the outcasts of the hard highway!'[64] And this contradiction is even more exaggerated in the childish figure of Sally:

She was little and thin; her worn and scanty clothing showed her frail youthful figure was still waiting for its full perfection and growth. . . . But for the words with which she had accosted him, it would have been impossible to associate her with the lamentable life that she led. The appearance of the girl was artlessly virginal and innocent; she looked as though she had passed through the contamination of the streets without being touched by it, without fearing it or feeling it or understanding it.[65]

Her apparent 'simple mindedness' is both a sign of her innocence and proof against environmental contamination; her rescue involves re-education but not a fundamental transformation.

The hereditary link between mother and daughter, which becomes the clue that Amelius attempts to trace as he threads his way through the streets of London, is their webbed toes – an unmistakable stigma in degenerative terms.[66] Here the ideological connotations of those terms are overturned but not the language of degeneration itself; it becomes a sign of those 'mysteriously remote origins' whose negative significance is displaced as Sally is able to adapt into a middle-class girl, by being presented, like Amelius, as a 'child of Nature'. But when the poor actually adapt to their surroundings they absorb all the degenerate connotations that the figure of Sally resists. Sally's stepfather extends the fear of the demoralized vagabond that hovered on the periphery of *No Name*: 'a half-drunken ruffian; one of the swarming beasts of low London, dirtied from head to foot the colour of street mud – the living danger and disgrace of English civilization'.[67] *The Fallen Leaves* slides between different rhetorics and employs different models of social and individual identities and forms of change, but it clearly works within and against a culture steeped in degenerative assumptions. There can be no final assimilation within the terms of the known world here; the vigorous colonial can no longer vitalize the culture, but must return to colonial exile in order to survive.

These degenerative assumptions have become paramount in *The Legacy of Cain*, a story of inheritance and psychic transmission which overturns the methods of *Armadale* and *No Name* even as it seems to be developing them. *The Legacy of Cain* is set up as a parable that both debates and extrapolates from contemporary theories of inheritance, exploring hypotheses tested through the parallel development of questionable identities. But the framework of the story now determines both the progress of the narrative and the terms within which it is read. This framework is set up in the Prologue, set in a prison, where three representative types – the Doctor, the Minister, and the Prison Governor – debate criminal responsibility, moral insanity, and the inheritance of morbid propensities, focusing their remarks on the case of a condemned murderess. The Doctor's position clearly corresponds to contemporary degenerative theory concerning the accumulation of morbid traits through transmission; he echoes Maudsley in stressing 'I have found vices and diseases descending more frequently to children than virtue and health.'[68] His fatalism is countered by the moral management of the Minister, who agrees to adopt the murderess's child and to bring her up with his own daughter, keeping her identity concealed. The Story traces the girls' parallel development, adding the complication that the Minister's own daughter, too, might have inherited morbid propensities from *her* dead mother.

So the terms of the narrative are set up speculatively, yet they constitute a framework which can never be fundamentally reformulated by the Story. The narrative as a whole is a reconstruction by the Prison Governor, who mediates the opposing positions and who tells the Story from the position of knowledge which is its outcome. Thus the Story itself teases the reader's expectations by keeping him or her in ignorance of the girl's true identity, but the reader still knows more than the girls do about themselves. Their development is charted by the parallel presentation of their diaries, and their propensities emerge through these narratives, which gradually disclose that the Minister's daughter, Helena, has incubated and compounded the latent pathological propensities of her mother. The murderess's daughter, Eunice, on the other hand, has a fundamentally good nature, but contains the trace of her mother's 'evil genius', which is excited by extreme provocation, yet which she is finally able to control. Thus the Prison Governor's conclusion takes the form of an equivocal reconciliation of the claims of determinism and self-control. He doubts, in relation to Eunice, 'the conclusion which sees, in the inheritance of moral qualities, a positive influence over moral destiny', but follows this by asserting that 'there are inherent emotional forces in humanity to which the inherited influences must submit; they are inherently influences under control.'[69] But this once more means that the contrasting figure, Helena, must embody a melodramatic wickedness and become absolutely guilty: 'It was weak, indeed, to compare the mean vices of Mrs Grace Dieu with the fundamental depravity of the daughter. . . . There are virtues which exalt us and vices which degrade us which are not in our parents but in ourselves.'[70]

The story thus closes with a moral management that now leaves no space for ambiguity of identity, and in this respect the novel is, as J.A. Noble pointed out, a 'protest against the fatalism that is more or less bound up with any full acceptance of the modern doctrine of heredity'. But Noble is also right to note that 'our interpretation may be mistaken, and . . . the doctrine in question is not really discredited by the story'.[71] The doctrine of inheritance needs to be set up as a foil for the Story, providing a set of terms that produce the necessary tension over whether they will be resisted or fulfilled in order for it to work as a story at all. It also forms a new kind of unconscious in the text that invokes a completely different kind of tension between determinism and indeterminacy from that which generates the narrative of *Armadale*.

For in *The Legacy of Cain* psychic legacies have narrowed down to a single strand of biological inheritance rather than operating as a metaphor which gains its meanings from breaking down the boundaries between social and psychological transmission. So while the Prison Governor asserts that we are 'masters of our own destinies' the actual interest of the narrative focuses on unconscious influences, conveyed through the device of the girls' contrasting diaries which present their impressions and secret thoughts but reveal propensities of which they are unconscious. Thus Eunice, in an artifically induced state of somnambulism brought about by a 'composing draught', hears the 'voice' of her mother urging her to violence, and asks 'where does this horrid transformation of me out of myself come from?'[72] But the reader knows where it comes from, and the unconscious force of the trace does not permeate the narrative itself, as it does in *Armadale*. The dream does not work its own fulfilment through the sensitive subject's self-conscious morbid fancies; Eunice is no palimpsest but a moralized self whose pathological unconscious must be suppressed rather than buried as the pivot of narrative tension. Herditary theory becomes a doctrine exerting a fatal pressure that the story now perversely confirms by resisting, for that resistance means resorting to the revelation of a true self pressing against the grain of dominant assumptions.

CONCLUSION

In the Preface to *Armadale* Collins maintained that his writing 'overstepped, in more than one direction, the narrow limits within which [critics] have been disposed to restrict the development of modern fiction'. What has emerged from this investigation is that his fiction does not simply overturn a given set of meanings so much as work at the edges of a range of discourses that are themselves shifting and contradictory; it oversteps their limits by pushing their implicit incongruities through and beyond their own recognizable forms. Psychological perceptions and heuristic models can be manipulated to produce radically different kinds of meanings as literary strategies, and Collins's novels appropriate an extraordinary range of possible models within an overarching paradigm of moral management, and transform them into the means of generating ambiguity, but in a way that is itself ambiguous. For they build up the sense of a real world and a knowable self, even as they make it strange and blur the distinction between literal and figural; and while this doubleness of signification continually renders meaning and identity unstable and provisional, it is through its historical position in its culture, grounded in these psychological devices, that Collins's work, in its very indecidability, has a precise social significance that makes sense now.

In *Basil, The Woman in White*, and *No Name* the relationship between patterns of narrative authority and the construction and breakdown of the self make the *family* the centre of social and psychic tension, not as a fixed object or institution, but as a collection of imaginary constructs and projections – a genealogical story, a set of transmitted property relationships, a set of 'skins to jump into', which only take on subjective reality when reinforced by the recognitions of others – that none the less have real power. It is also, in a far more elementary sense, the 'asylum' in which subjectivity is fundamentally shaped. 'The emotions are the nurses of the faculties', Collins wrote in his biography of his own father, 'and the first home is the sanctuary in which they are created and reared'; but this sanctuary is also the asylum in which emotions and faculties begin to vibrate, become uncertain, lead to breakdown.[73] This manipulation of emotions and faculties through both internalized and objectified projection contributes to the subtle interaction between class and gender identity in these novels that is crucially mediated through an equivocal evocation of the codes of moral management and a rhetoric of nervous sensibility. Identities become fragile, attenuated, vulnerable, and thus 'feminized'. This is given primarily a class association as the languid male vestiges of inherited 'rank and power', as much as 'whited out' heroines, sink into lassitude, hypochondria, and thus a disturbing androgyny. This dissociates the signs of feminity from their biological referents, and while it means that female fortitude is also perceived as the opposite kind of androgyny (as with Marian Halcombe in *The Woman in White*), this alternative female identity can only become strong through being anomalous, and in being anomalous both displays the oppositional potential of resolution and self-control, and (as with

Magdalen Vanstone in *No Name*) becomes a kind of deviance that is ultimately interpreted as hysterical in order to be recuperated or assimilated within the dominant narrative framework.

The equivocal implications of this breaking down of difference in order to display the elements of which it is composed emerges still more strikingly in the representation of split and double selves, deviance, and marginality in Collins's fiction. For Collins's rhetoric of difference and overstepping limits modifies and challenges the very model of subversion that it seems so clearly to embody, undergoing a continual transformation which can never be explained by a unified figure either of repression or of 'carnivalesque' inversion. Fosco (*The Woman in White*) and Wragge (*No Name*), the magnetic villain and the engaging trickster, most clearly embody a world turned upside-down, playfully conjuring with dominant codes and thus 'saying what other people only think', becoming the hand that 'tears away the plump pasteboard and shows the bare bones beneath', in a way that challenges a dominant authority by reinforcing it. But elsewhere transgressive figures carry other meanings. In the first place, oppositions are often split themselves rather than being placed simply in a binary polarity. Basil and Mannion (*Basil*), Armadale and Midwinter (*Armadale*), are placed not simply against each other but also against their fathers, and this gives their meaning in relation to each other an internal historical dimension that challenges the terms on which they are opposed. It is the despotic feudal power of the earlier generations that becomes internalized into a fatal and morbid force, and in both cases this challenges the simple bourgeois alternative to feudal 'rank and power' – self-help and competitive individualism, that 'place in the sunshine afar off'. Mannion remains Basil's sinister other to be eliminated in a final combat, but Midwinter, the other Armadale, challenges the implication of the fathers' mutual destructiveness, becoming Armadale's over-anxious 'moral sense' even as he compounds his own psychic inheritance by morbidly dwelling on it.

And this, too, is part of the complex way that Collins's fiction implicitly challenges the cultural construction of racial difference as a form of pathological primitivism, exoticism, or barbarism. Psychic forces *are* projected on to 'colonies', and there is a continual process of correspondence between marginal psychic states and colonial difference, but even as Collins's fiction draws on these cultural associations he turns them against their prevailing meaning, firstly by self-consciously representing them as projections, annexations of, and reflections on, Englishness itself, secondly by denaturalizing the perceptions through which these representations emerge as pathological, or even different – thus exploring the social shaping of subjective perception as much as the subjective construction of the apparent world. This culminates in the figure of Ezra Jennings, that equivocal manipulator of notions of 'unconscious cerebration'.

Observing the 'meagre man' in *The Lazy Tour of Two Idle Apprentices*, the narrator noted that as he projected meaning on the madman's weaving of clues through the matting, he constructed an explanatory narrative that threw his own cognitive framework into question even as it enabled him to empathize with the figure. Finally, only our own interpretative hypotheses can make sense of Collins. One of the starting-points for this book was a desire to develop feminist analysis of the construction of subjectivity springing from debates on the relationship between psychoanalysis and history; but to develop it experimentally outside an immediate psychoanalytic framework. Collins's fiction, however, is also fascinating in the way that it challenges our own cognitive assumptions, our own consciousness of how consciousness is mediated in fictional texts, and it does this in the interrelationship between the patterns of authority within the narratives themselves, and between the story and its discursive parameters. *The Moonstone* is the clearest example of how a set of hypotheses about the unconscious transform and are themselves transmuted into something else by the secret position that they held within the structure of the story and the way the narrative manoeuvres between dominant and marginal forms of knowledge, between what emerges as a story and what sinks without trace, but this process of negotiation is at work in all the texts explored here. Collins's fiction might 'appal the imagination' but it also 'satisfies the intellect', and, although the mystery and the trace often offer more than the final resolution, both depend on the tension, which emerges from the interplay of resemblance and difference, between the stories' cognitive framework and our own.

NOTES AND REFERENCES

INTRODUCTION: COLLINS AS A SENSATION NOVELIST

1 Henry James (1865) 'Miss Braddon', *The Nation*, 9 November 1865, p. 594.
2 Wilkie Collins (1908) Preface to *Armadale*, 3 vols, London, p. i (1st edn 1866).
3 The main studies of the development of the sensation novel are Walter C. Phillips (1919) *Dickens, Reade and Collins – Sensation Novelists: A Study of the Conditions and Theories of Novel Writing in Victorian England*, New York; Kathleen Tillotson (1969) 'The lighter reading of the 1860s', Introduction to *The Woman in White*, Boston; Winifred Hughes (1980) *The Maniac in the Cellar: The Sensation Novel of the 1860s*, Princeton; Patrick Brantlinger (1982) 'What is "sensational" about the sensation novel?', *Nineteenth-century Fiction* 37 (June 1982), pp. 1–28. The critical response to sensation fiction is analysed in Elizabeth K. Helsinger, Robin Lauterbach Sheets, and William Veeder (1983) *The Woman Question: Society and Literature in Britain and American, 1837–1883*, 3 vols, New York, 3, pp. 122–44, and Keith Brown Reierstad includes a brief discussion of the form in 'The demon in the house, or the domestication of gothic in the novels of Wilkie Collins (unpublished Ph.D. dissertation, University of Pennsylvania, 1976).
4 Margaret Oliphant (1862) 'Sensation novels', *Blackwood's Edinburgh Magazine* 91 (May 1862), pp. 564–5.
5 (1863) 'Not a new sensation', *All the Year Round*, 22 July 1863, p. 517. The point that 'sensationalism' is mainly symptomatic of critics' anxieties is developed in Charles Dickens (unsigned, 1864) 'The sensational Williams', *All the Year Round*, 13 February 1864, pp. 14–15: 'Life itself is similarly sensational in many of its aspects, and nature is similarly sensational in many of her forms, and art is always sensational when it is tragic.' The piece considers Shakespeare's likely reception as a sensation dramatist.
6 (1863) 'Sensation novels', *Medical Critic and Psychological Journal* 3, p. 514.
7 The connections between fears about the 'drug-like' qualities of sensation fiction and dominant definitions of femine sexuality are discussed in greater detail in Kate Flint (1986) 'The woman reader and the "opiate" of fiction 1855–1870', in Jeremy Hawthorn (ed.) (1986) *The Nineteenth-Century British Novel*, London. In the same book D.A. Miller's essay, '*Cage aux folles*: sensation and gender in Wilkie Collins's *The Woman in White*', also draws out the complex ways that physiology mediates and undermines gender difference in sensation fiction in general and *The Woman in White* in particular, in a way that overlaps at

times with my own analysis. As is so often the case, these essays appeared as work on this book was nearing completion.

8 Henry Mansel (unsigned, 1863) 'Sensation novels', *Quarterly Review* 113 (April 1863), pp. 482–3. Henry Mansel, author of *Metaphysics, or the Philosophy of Consciousness Phenomenal and Real* (Edinburgh 1860), was a professor of Moral and Metaphysical Philosophy at Oxford and in 1868 appointed Dean of St Paul's. A high Church Tory, he was an admirer of William Hamilton and the editor of his *Lectures on Metaphysics*.

9 Oliphant, 'Sensation novels', p. 568.

10 (1866) 'Belles lettres', *Westminster Review* 20 (October 1866), p. 270.

11 (1865) 'Sensation novelists: Miss Braddon', *North British Review* 4, p. 204. For a discussion of the Minerva Press, see J.M.S. Tomkins (1932) *The Popular Novel in England 1770–1800*, London, pp. 243–95.

12 (1860) 'Novels of the day: their writers and readers', *Fraser's Magazine* 62 (August 1860), p. 210.

13 (1853) 'The progress of fiction as an art', *Westminster Review* 60 (October 1853), p. 358.

14 For a full analysis of the development of this mode, and the argument that it should be clearly distinguished from Gothic romance as it uses different techniques and has distinct epistemological origins, see Peter Denman (1981) 'The supernatural referent: the presence and effect of supernatural terror in English fiction in the mid nineteenth century' (unpublished Ph.D. dissertation, University of Keele), especially pp. 142–60 on the *Blackwood*'s stories. In contrast, in 'The demon in the house, or the domestication of gothic in the novels of Wilkie Collins' Reierstad develops the argument that Collins's fiction transforms and adapts gothic conventions to explore sexual and modal ambiguity; his study includes an interesting discussion of Collins's early novella, *Mr Wray's Cash Box, or The Mask and the Mystery* (1852). On the formal links between different forms of 'Gothic' writing, see Eve Kosofsky Sedgwick (1986) *The Coherence of Gothic Conventions*, 2nd edn, London.

15 George Eliot (unsigned, 1856) 'Arts and belles lettres', *Westminster Review* 9 (April 1856), p. 640.

16 (1861) 'The enigma novel', *Spectator*, 28 December 1861, p. 1428.

17 (1866) 'Belles lettres', p. 270.

18 Alexander Bain (1877) *English Composition and Rhetoric*, 4th edn, London, p. 224 (1st edn 1866).

19 E.S. Dallas (1866) *The Gay Science*, 2 vols, London, II, pp. 293–4. He goes on:

> In the novel of character man appears to be moulding circumstance to his will, directing the action for himself, supreme over incident and plot. In the opposite class of novels man is represented as made and ruled by circumstance, he is the victim of change and the puppet of intrigue. Is either of these views of life wholly true or wholly false? We may like the one better than the other. We may like to see men generally represented as possessed of decided character, masters of their destiny and superior to circumstance; but is this view of life

a wit more true than art that pictures the mass of men as . . . tossed hither and thither by the accidents of life which we sometimes call fate and sometimes fortune?

For a more detailed discussion of the sensation novels' position in debates on the theory of fiction, see 'The sensation novel and Victorian theories of fiction' in Hughes, *The Maniac in the Cellar*, pp. 38–73; also relevant here is Richard Stang (1959) *The Theory of the Novel in England 1850–1870*, London, and A.H. Warren (1963) *English Poetic Theory 1825–1865*, London.

20 E.S. Dallas, *The Gay Science*, II, p. 295.
21 E.S. Dallas, (1862) '*Lady Audley's Secret*', *The Times*, 18 November 1862 p. 8.
22 (1866) 'Madness in novels', *Spectator*, 3 February 1866, p. 135.
23 Mary Elizabeth Braddon (1862) *Lady Audley's Secret*, 3 vols, London, I, p. 141.
24 ibid., II, pp. 202–3. The narrator reinforces this point at the end of the novel, where Robert's hypochondria is linked to his own analysis of reading sensation fiction.

'I haven't read Alexandre Dumas and Wilkie Collins for nothing', he muttered, 'I'm up to their tricks, sneaking in at doors behind a fellow's back, and flattening their white faces against window panes, and making themselves all eyes in the twilight.' (III, p. 190)

Do not laugh at poor Robert because he grew hypochondriacal after hearing the horrible story of his friend's death. There is nothing so delicate, so fragile, as that invisible balance on which the mind is always trembling. Mad today and sane tomorrow. (III, p. 193)

25 ibid., I, p. 104.
26 Mrs Henry Wood (1885) *St Martin's Eve*, 3 vols, London, p. 158 (1st edn 1866).
27 Charles Reade (1885) *Hard Cash*, 3 vols, London (1st edn 1863), Note p. 158. Reade wrote a lengthy reply to the *Daily News*, and this, with Bushman's letter and other related correspondence, is added to the Note in later editions of the novel.
28 Note to the first edition, reprinted with additions, p. 626. It opens: 'I request all, – who, by letter or by *viva voce* have during the last five years, told me of persons incarcerated or detained in private asylums, and other abuses, to communicate to me by letter' (p. 626).
29 Tzvetan Todorov (1973) *The Fantastic: a Structural Approach to a Literary Genre*, trans. Richard Howard, London. Todorov breaks the fantastic category down into four basic divisions: at one end the 'marvellous', in which there is a complete break from the real; the 'fantastic marvellous' in which inexplicable occurrences are given a supernatural cause; the 'fantastic uncanny', in which they are given a subjective origin, and the pure 'uncanny', rooted in unconscious projection.
30 Sigmund Freud (1919) 'The uncanny', *Standard Edition of the Complete Works*, XVII, pp. 224–5. Freud draws in detail on Otto Rank (1914) *The Double*, London, in his analysis.
31 Rosemary Jackson (1981) *Fantasy, The Literature of Subversion*, London.

Jackson's work is the clearest and best exposition of the 'subversiveness' of fantasy and the problems of defining it as a mode. She combines psychoanalytic discussion of theoretical approaches to fantasy with Bakhtin's discussion of the generic features of the 'menippea' in *Problems of Dostoevsky's Poetics* translated by R. W. Rotsel (Ardis, 1973) and Foucault's account of the changing meanings of madness. Other relevant studies in this area include: Glen St John Barclay (1978) *Anatomy of Horror: the Masters of Occult Fiction*, London; Julia Briggs (1977) *Night Visitors: the Rise and Fall of the English Ghost Story*, London; William R. Irwin (1976) *The Game of the Impossible: a Rhetoric of Fantasy*, Illinois; Howard Lovecraft (1973) *Supernatural Horror in Literature*, New York; Irving Massey (1976) *The Gaping Pig: Literature and Metamorphosis*, California; David Punter (1980) *The Literature of Terror*, London; David Rabkin (1976) *The Fantastic in Literature*, Princeton; Otto Rank (1971) *The Double: a Psychoanalytic Study* trans. and ed H. Tucker, N. Carolina; Karl Miller (1985) *Doubles: Studies in Literary History*. The 'transgressive' interpretation of the significance of madness is also a central feature of such radical feminist criticism as Sandra Gilbert and Susan Gubar (1980) *The Madwoman in the Attic*, London. For an explanatory critique of their position, see Toril Moi (1985) *Textual/Sexual Politics: Feminist Literary Criticism*, London.

32 Oliphant, 'Sensation novels', p. 566.

33 T.S. Eliot (1932) 'Wilkie Collins and Dickens', *Selected Essays 1917–1932*, London, pp. 460–70. See also Robert Ashley (1951) 'Wilkie Collins and the detective story', *Nineteenth-Century Fiction* 6 (June 1951), pp. 47–60; Gavin Lambert (1975) *The Dangerous Edge*, London; Ian Ousby (1976) *Bloodhounds of Heaven: English Detective Fiction from Godwin to Doyle*, Cambridge, Mass.; Julian Symons (1972) *Bloody Murder: from the Detective Story to the Crime Novel*, London. An important counterbalance to the dominant approach is D.A. Miller (1980) 'From *roman-policier* to *roman-police*: Wilkie Collins's *The Moonstone*', *Novel* 13 (Winter 1980), pp. 153–70.

34 See, for example, Ernst Bloch (1980) 'A philosophical view of the detective novel', trans. R. Morella and S. Thaman, *Discourse* 2 (summer 1980), pp. 32–51; John G. Cawelti (1977) *Adventure, Mystery and Romance*, Chicago; Carlo Ginsburg (1980) 'Morelli, Freud and Sherlock Holmes: clues and scientific evidence', trans. Anna Davin, *History Workshop Journal* 9 (spring 1980), pp. 5–37; Stephen Knight (1980) *Form and Ideology in Detective Fiction*, London; Franco Moretti (1983) 'Clues' in *Signs Taken for Wonders*, London; Dennis Porter (1981) *The Pursuit of Crime: Art and Ideology in Detective Fiction*, Yale; T. Todorov (1977) 'The typology of detective fiction', *The Poetics of Prose*, trans. Richard Howard, Oxford.

35 Geraldine Pederson-Krag (1957) 'Detective stories and the primal scene', *Psychoanalytic Quarterly* 26, pp. 229–45; Charles Rycroft (1957) 'The analysis of a detective story', *Psychoanalytic Quarterly* 26, pp. 229–45; Lewis A. Lawson (1963) 'Wilkie Collins and the detective story', *American Imago*, 20, pp. 61–79; Albert D. Hutter (1975) 'Dreams, transformations and literature: the implications of detective fiction', *Victorian Studies* 19 (December 1975), pp. 181–209.

36 In the development of the great series of animal organisms the Nervous System assumes more and more of an imperial character. . . . In like manner, in the development of the social organism, as the life of nations becomes more complex, thought assumes a more imperial character; and literature in its widest sense, becomes a delicate index of social evolution. . . .

Literature is at once the cause and effect of social progress. It deepens our natural sensibilities and strengthens by exercise our intellectual capacities. It stores up the accumulated experience of the race, connecting Past and Present into a conscious unity; and with this store it feeds successive generations, to be fed in turn by them. As its importance emerges into more general recognition, it necessarily draws after it a large crowd of servitors, filling noble minds with noble ambitions. ('The principles of success in literature', Part I, *Fortnightly Review* 1 (May 1865), p. 85)

On the relation between the 'real' and the 'ideal' in realism, see G.H. Lewes (1858) 'Realism in art: recent German fiction', *Westminster Review*, 70 (October 1858), pp. 488–504.

37 G.H. Lewes (1865) 'Criticism in relation to novels', *Fortnightly Review*, 3 (December 1865), pp. 353–4. He goes on to note:

It is quite fair to praise Miss Braddon for the skill she undoubtedly displays in plot interest of a certain kind. But I have no hesitation in concluding that her grasp of character, her vision of realities, her regard for probability, and her theoretical view on human life, are very far from being on a level with her power over plot-interest. (p. 354)

38 E.S. Dallas, *The Gay Science*, I, p. 5. For some biographical details see *The Dictionary of National Biography* edited by Lesley Stephen and Sidney Lee, 22 volumes (Oxford 1917), Vol. V, pp. 394–5. For a brief discussion of Dallas's work, see J.H. Buckley (1951) *The Victorian Temper: A Study in Literary Culture*, Harvard, pp. 145–8, and John Drinkwater (1932) 'Eneas Sweetland Dallas' in John Drinkwater (ed.) *The Eighteen-Sixties*, London; Jenny Taylor (1984) '*The Gay Science*: the "hidden soul" of Victorian criticism', *Literature and History* 10 (autumn 1984), pp. 189–203. Dallas was probably the critic who pointed out the error in timing in *The Times* review of *The Woman in White* on 30 October 1860 (p. 6).

39 ibid., I, p. 19.

40 ibid., I, pp. 127–9.

41 ibid., I, pp. 42–4.

42 ibid., I, p. 199.

43 'Recent novels', *Spectator*, 26 January 1889, p. 120.

44 Full-length studies of Collins are the two biographies, Kenneth Robinson (1951) *Wilkie Collins, A Biography*, London, still a useful though limited source, and Nuel Pharr Davis (1956) *The Life of Wilkie Collins*, Urbana, Ill., a highly speculative and unreliable one, that contributes to the 'underworld' image. Also Robert P. Ashley (1952) *Wilkie Collins*, London; R.V. Andrew (1959) *Wilkie Collins: a Critical Survey of his Prose Fiction*, New York; Dorothy Sayers (1977) *Wilkie Collins*,

a *Biographical and Critical Survey* (uncompleted), Toledo. William
Marshall (1970) *Wilkie Collins*, New York, is still a useful study, and the
fullest recent account of Collins's methods and relation to his readership
is Sue Lonoff (1982) *Wilkie Collins and His Victorian Readers: a Study in
the Rhetoric of Authorship*, New York, which brings together a wide range
of hitherto unpublished manuscript material. Interesting essays, in addition to those cited, include: David Blair (1979) 'Wilkie Collins and the
crisis in suspense', in Ian Gregor (ed.) *Reading the Victorian Novel:
Detail into Form*, New York; Mark Hunelly (1980) 'Reading detection
in *The Woman in White*', *Texas Studies in Language and Literature* 22
(winter 1980), pp. 449–67; Walter M. Kendrick (1977) 'The sensationalism of *The Woman in White*, *Nineteenth-Century Fiction* 32 (June
1977), pp. 18–35; John Reed (1973) 'English imperialism and the
unacknowledged crime of *The Moonstone*', *Clio* 2 (June 1973). Two
essays that do discuss the question of Collins's representation of insanity
in *The Woman in White*, but from radically different positions are
Barbara Fass Leavy (1982) 'Wilkie Collins's Cinderella: the history of
psychology and *The Woman in White*', *Dickens Studies Annual*, 10, pp.
90–141, and D.A. Miller, '*Cage aux folles*: sensation and gender in
Wilkie Collins's *The Woman in White*' (see Note 7).

45   Wilkie Collins (1875) Preface to *My Miscellanies*, 2nd edn, London, p.
vi.

46   On Collins's complex position in relation to mid-nineteenth-century
patterns of novel-publishing and reception, see Lonoff, *Wilkie Collins
and his Victorian Readers*; Norman Page's Introduction to Norman Page
(ed.) (1974) *Wilkie Collins, the Critical Heritage*, London; John
Sutherland (1976) *Victorian Novelists and Publishers*, London;
Guinevere Griest (1970) *Mudie's Circulating Library and the Victorian
Novel*, Bloomington, Ind.

47   These biographical details are taken from Lonoff, *Wilkie Collins and His
Victorian Readers* and Robinson, *Wilkie Collins, A Biography*, pp. 25–
60. Collins was asked to write a popular article explaining the Pre-
Raphaelite Brotherhood's aims and principles for *The Germ* (Robinson,
Wilkie Collins, p. 60). Collins himself gives an account of his grand-
father's affiliations and his father's connections with Wordsworth,
Coleridge, and Fuseli (1848) *Memoirs of the Life of William Collins,
E'qu., R.A., with Selections from his Journals and Correspondence*, 2 vols.
In addition, Nigel Cross (1986) *The Common Writer*, Cambridge, pp. 95-
-103, describes the loosely defined radical and republican group of
writers that surrounded Dickens and were involved in amateur
dramatics, including George Augustus Sala, Blanchard Jerrold, and
Collins's good friend and admirer Edmund Yates.

48   See Kirk H. Beetz (1982) 'Wilkie Collins and *The Leader*', *Victorian
Periodicals Review* 15, pp. 20–9. As Beetz points out, articles signed
'W.W.C.' can only speculatively be ascribed to Collins, who prefixed
'William' to Wilkie in the early 1850s, but on this basis, his main
contributions were reviews of plays, books, and art exhibitions,
together with a short series on mesmerism, 'Magnetic evenings at
home', and a piece arguing for the lifting of Sunday leisure restrictions,
'A plea for Sunday reform', expressing paternalistic liberal views:

I want . . . a system of Sunday observance that is both religious and rational. . . . You establish a code of religious exercises and restraints which suits *your* condition of life; and no matter what the difference in your station that code must be his code too. ('A plea for Sunday reform', *The Leader*, 27 September 1851, p. 925)

49 (1852) *'Esmond* and *Basil'*, *Bentley's Miscellany* 32 (November 1852), p. 586.

50 Dickens invited Collins to become a member of the salaried staff of *Household Words* towards the end of 1856, writing to Wills, the journal's sub-editor:

It strikes me that the best thing we can do for *H. W.* is to add [Collins] on to Morley and offer him five guineas a week. . . . Being industrious and reliable besides, I don't think we shall be at an additional expense of £20 a year by the transaction. (Letter to Wills, 16 September 1856, from R.C. Lehmann (ed.) (1912) *Charles Dickens as Editor*, London, p. 221)

Collins engaged in a short dispute with Dickens over the question of signed authorship, and it was agreed that *The Dead Secret* should be serialized under his name (Dickens, letter to Wills, 18 September 1856, in Lehmann, *Charles Dickens as Editor*, p. 222). The serial sales of *The Woman in White*, Dickens's position as a publisher, and his relationship to Collins in this respect are given in Sutherland (1976) *Victorian Novelists and Publishers*, pp. 165–70; see also John Sutherland (1977) 'Two emergencies in the writing of *The Woman in White'*, *Yearbook of English Studies* 7, pp. 148–56. Collins's collaboration with Dickens during the 1850s and 1860s included fiction and plays, but it is impossible to establish its precise nature. In his *Wilkie Collins: An Annotated Bibliography (1889–1976)* Kirk Beetz (1978) lists 'The seven poor travellers' (1854); *The Lazy Tour of Two Idle Apprentices* (1857; published in book form, 1980); 'The perils of certain English prisoners' (1857); 'No thoroughfare' (1859). For further accounts of Dickens/Collins collaborations, see R.L. Brannan (1966) *Under the Management of Mr Charles Dickens: His Production of 'The Frozen Deep'*, New York, and Anne Lohrli (ed.) (1973) *Household Words*, Toronto, pp. 233–5.

51 Charles Dickens (unsigned, 1850) 'A preliminary word', *Household Words*, 30 March 1850, p. 1.

52 The main accounts of the development of reading patterns and literacy which contributed to the establishment of these journals are Richard Altick (1957) *The English Common Reader, a Social History of the Mass Reading Public*, Chicago; R.K. Webb (1955) *The British Working Class Reader 1789–1948*, London; Margaret Dalziel (1957) *Popular Fiction 100 Years Ago: an Unexplored Tract of Literary History*, London; Louis James (1962) *Fiction for the Working Man 1830–1850*, Oxford; Sally Mitchell (1981) *The Fallen Angel: Chastity, Class and Women's Reading 1835–1880*, Bowling Green, Ohio. Collins's own fascination with the lower-middle- and working-class readership of the penny journals that were just outside *Household Words'* circle is expressed in the essay 'The unknown public', which appeared in the journal in 1858: 'A public of three millions . . . right out of the pale of literary civilisation . . . a

phenomenon worth examining'. In examining the journals themselves, however, he detects 'the same dead level of the smoothest and flattest conventionality . . . an intense in-dwelling respectability in their dulness', and argues that 'the Unknown Public is, in a literary sense, hardly beginning, as yet, to learn to read' ('The unknown public', *My Miscellanies*, second edition (1875) London, pp. 260–3).

53 Dickens, 'A preliminary word', p. 1.
54 Oliphant, 'Sensation novels', p. 584.
55 If I predominantly apply any one model of narrative analysis, it is that of Gerard Genette (1980) *Narrative Discourse*, trans. Jane Lewin, Oxford, though I do not use his precise terminology.

1 THE PSYCHIC AND THE SOCIAL: BOUNDARIES OF IDENTITY IN NINETEENTH-CENTURY PSYCHOLOGY

1 Quoted in V. Skultans (1975) *Madness and Morals: Ideas on Insanity in the Nineteenth Century*, London, p. 172.
2 *The Lazy Tour of Two Idle Apprentices*, Household Words, 24 October 1857, p. 385. Compare this with 'A walk in a workhouse':

> Groves of babies in arms; groves of mothers and other sick women in bed; groves of lunatics; jungles of men in stone-paved down-stairs dayrooms. . . . In all these Long Walks of aged and infirm, some old people were bedridden and had been for some time. (*Household Words*, 25 May 1850, p. 206)

3 *The Lazy Tour of Two Idle Apprentices*, p. 386. For a brief summary of Collins's and Dickens's collaborations, see Introduction, Note 50.
4 'A walk in a workhouse', p. 205.
5 The main articles on insanity in Household Words (HW) are: 'The treatment of the insane', 6 September 1851, pp. 572–6 (probably by Richard Oliver); 'A curious dance round a curious tree', 17 January 1852, pp. 385–9 (Charles Dickens); 'Idiots again', 15 April 1854, pp. 197–200 (Harriet Martineau); 'Grand jury powers', 16 May 1857, pp. 457–63 (Henry Morley); 'The star of Bethlehem', 15 August 1857, pp. 144–50 (Henry Morley); 'Things within Dr Conolly's rememberance', 28 November 1857, pp. 518–23 (Henry Morley); 'The cure of sick minds', 2 April 1859, pp. 415–19 (Henry Morley).
6 'The cure of sick minds', HW, 2 April 1859, p. 415. The articles goes on to paraphrase pieces from *The Journal of Mental Science*.
7 For example, *The Journal of Psychological Medicine and Mental Pathology*, *The Asylum Journal*, and *The Journal of Mental Science* were all established during the 1840s.
8 On Collins's use of Mejan's *Recueil des causes célèbres*, see Clyde K. Hyder (1939) 'Wilkie Collins and *The Woman in White*', PMLA 54, pp. 297–303. Collins described in *The World*, 26 December 1877, how he received a letter in the late 1850s 'asking him to take up some case of real or wrongful confinement in a lunatic asylum'. (Reprinted as 'Wilkie Collins in Gloucester Place', in Edmund Yates (1879) *Celebrities at Home*, third series, London, pp. 145–56, and Hall Caine (1908) *My Story*, London, p. 336.) The relationship of *The Woman in White* to the

lunacy reform movement is also discussed in Barbara Fass Leavy (1982) 'Wilkie Collins's Cinderella: the history of psychology and *The Woman in White*', *Dickens Studies Annual* 10, pp. 91–141. Our historical perspective overlaps at times, but Leavy concentrates on the character of Anne Catherick as case study in *The Woman in White*.

9 Michael Foucault (1973) *Madness and Civilization: a History of Insanity in an Age of Reason*, trans. Richard Howard, New York, and (1975) *The Birth of the Clinic: an Archaeology of Medical Perception*, trans. A.M. Sheridan Smith, New York. Foucault's work traces the discursive shifts in the history of insanity in the west between the Middle Ages and the nineteenth-century: from the Middle Ages, where it was seen as a kind of sanctity, an expression of an essentially human wisdom, through the sixteenth century, where the figure of the fool was identified with and transcended an essentially human wisdom, through the seventeenth and eighteenth centuries which led to the 'Great Confinement' in which madness was progressively excluded and hidden, becoming the repository of unreason by representing everything that reason denied. He argues that by the end of the eighteenth century this image became a threat that was reinforced by the means deployed to defuse it. This meant that the eighteenth-century madhouse gave the mad a perverse kind of reciprocity and subjectivity, a threat which in turn needed to be assimilated by internalizing the patterns of control through the reformed asylum and the rise of moral management in the early nineteenth-century. Histories of psychiatry directly or indirectly influenced by this approach include: K. Koerner (1981) *Madmen and the Bourgeoisie: a Social History of Insanity and Psychiatry*, Oxford; Michael Donnelly (1983) *Managing the Mind: a Study of Medical Psychology in Early Nineteenth-Century Britain*, London; Andrew T. Scull (1982) *Museums of Madness: The Social Organization of Insanity in Nineteenth-Century England*, Harmondsworth. An important recent feminist study that develops this work and corrects its implicit gener bias is Elaine Showalter (1985) *The Female Malady: Women, Madness and English Culture*, New York.

10 The overlapping connotations of 'moral' for the concept of moral management are briefly discussed by Vieda Skultans in the Introduction to *Madness and Morals*, but she tends to argue that the connotations of its two uses were consistently conflated. For the development of the concept within associationism and late eighteenth-century utilitarianism, see Elie Halevy (1928) *The Growth of Philosophic Radicalism*, trans. Mary Morris, London, and Leslie Stephen (1876) *English Thought in the Eighteenth Century*, 2 vols, London.

11 Cited in Foucault, *Madness and Civilization*, p. 242. On the setting up of the Retreat, see R. Hunter and I. MacAlpine (1964) Introduction to Samuel Tuke, *A Description of the Retreat*, London, and Anne Digby (1986) *Madness, Morality and Medicine: a Study of the York Retreat, 1786–1982*, London.

12 However, although Pinel's and Tuke's methods were broadly similar, they were not absolutely compatible. 'Moral' had different connotations in English and French, and Pinel's methods concentrated more on behaviour modification, Tuke stressing self-control and judgement. See

Kathleen Jones (1971) 'Moral management and the therapeutic community', *Society for the Social History of Medicine* 5 (October 1971), pp. 6–10; William Bynum (1974) 'Rationales for therapy in British psychiatry', *Medical History* 18, pp. 310–25.

13 W.A.F. Browne (1837) *What Asylums Were, Are, and Ought to Be*, Edinburgh, p. 135.

14 'A curious dance round a curious tree', *HW*, 17 January 1852, p. 385.

15 'The star of Bethlehem', *HW*, 15 August 1857, p. 146. The case of Norris, who was kept for years chained to his bed in a steel harness and became the emblem of the cruelty of the private madhouse treatment, is vividly described in John Conolly (1856) *The Treatment of the Insane Without Mechanical Restraints*, and is directly quoted in this article. For a discussion on the significance of this case, and Bethlehem Hospital, see Patricia Allderidge, 'Bedlam: fact or fantasy?', in W.F. Bynum, Roy Porter, and Michael Shepherd (eds) (1985) *The Anatomy of Madness: Essays in the History of Psychiatry*, vol. II, *Institutions and Society*, London, pp. 17–34.

16 'Things within Dr Conolly's rememberance', *HW*, 28 November 1857, pp. 518–23.

17 Andrew Wynter (unsigned, 1857) 'Lunatic asylums', *Quarterly Review* 101 (April 1857), p. 353.

18 See Roy Porter (1983) 'The range of party: a glorious revolution in English psychiatry?', *Medical History* 73, pp. 35–50. Porter's work is concerned with exploring the complexities of eighteenth-century treatment and perception of madness, which have tended to be obscured by the rather monolithic histories of insanity that have been directly or indirectly inspired by Foucault's *Madness and Civilization*. For a critique of Foucault's method, as manifesting many of the problems of 1960s anti-psychiatry, see Peter Sedgwick (1982) *Psycho-Politics*, London.

19 George Cheyne (1733) *The English Malady*, p. 44, cited in Porter, 'The rage of party', who points out that similar characterizations of English madness continue throughout the eighteenth century. See also Vieda Skultans (1978) *English Madness: Ideas on Insanity, 1580–1890*, London, and Michael V. De Porte (1974) *Nightmares and Hobbyhorses, Swift, Sterne and Augustan Ideas of Madness*, San Marine, California.

20 Tuke, *A Description of the Retreat*, p. 132.

21 See Anne Digby, 'Moral treatment at the retreat, 1796–1846', in Bynum, Porter, and Shepherd (eds) *Anatomy of Madness*, II, pp. 52–73.

22 Tuke, *A Description of the Retreat*, p. 141.

23 ibid.

24 ibid., p. 178. See also Fiona Godlee, 'Aspects of non-conformity: Quakers and the lunatic fringe', in Bynum, Porter, and Shepherd (eds) *Anatomy of Madness*, II, pp. 73–98. On the shift between early moral treatment and the mid-nineteenth-century development of the psychiatric profession, see Scull, *Museums of Madness*, especially pp. 125–58.

25 'A curious dance round a curious tree', p. 387.

26 Kathleen Jones (1972) *A History of the Mental Health Services*, London, pp. 64–70, and W. Parry-Jones (1972) *The Trade in Lunacy: A Study*

of Private Madhouses in England in the Eighteenth and Nineteenth Centuries, London, pp. 29–74.

27 See Scull, *Museums of Madness*, pp. 50–70.

28 John Conolly (1968) *The Construction and Government of Lunatic Asylums and Hospitals for the Insane*, London, facsimile of the 1847 edn, pp. 8–9.

29 John Conolly (1973) *The Treatment of the Insane Without Mechanical Restraints*, London, facsimile of the 1856 edn, pp. 58–9. Other important mid-nineteenth-century descriptions of the non-restraint system include W.A.F. Browne, *What Asylums Were, Are and Ought to Be*, and (1864) 'The moral treatment of the insane', *Journal of Mental Science* 101, pp. 309–37; John Haslam (1817) *Considerations on the Moral Management of the Insane*, London; Robert Gardiner Hill (1838) *The Total Abolition of Restraint in the Treatment of the Insane*, London.

30 For an analysis of the development of the ideology of domesticity, as the linchpin of the reform of manners and morals, which was developed by early-nineteenth-century evangelical reformism (particularly in the work of William Wilberforce and Hannah More), but which had become assimilated as a cultural norm by the mid-nineteenth-century, see Catherine Hall (1979) 'The early formation of Victorian domestic ideology', in Sandra Burman (ed.) *Fit Work for Women*, London, pp. 15–33; Leonora Davidoff, Jean l'Esperance, and Howard Newby (1976) 'Landscape with figures: home and community in English society', in Juliet Mitchell and Ann Oakley (eds) *The Rights and Wrongs of Women*, Harmondsworth, pp. 139–76; Barbara Taylor (1983) *Eve and the New Jerusalem*, London, especially pp. 238–88; Jeffrey Weeks (1981) *Sex, Politics and Society*, London; and Sara Delamont and Lorna Duffin (eds) (1978) *The Nineteenth-Century Woman: Her Cultural and Physical World*, London. For further discussion of the 'domestication' of madness, see Andrew Scull (1983) 'The domestication of madness', *Medical History* 27, pp. 233–48, and Donnelly, *Managing the Mind*.

31 Again, there is a danger in simplifying processes in the late eighteenth century for the sake of contrast; for discussion of the earlier links between sensibility, femininity, and propriety, see Janet Todd (1986) *Sensibility*, London; Mary Poovey (1984) *The Proper Lady and the Woman Writer*, Chicago; and J.M.S. Tomkins (1984) *The Popular Novel in England 1770–1800*, Chicago.

32 See Elaine Showalter (1981) 'Victorian women and insanity' in Andrew Scull (ed.) *Madhouses, Mad-Doctors and Madmen*, London, pp. 313–39; and Showalter, *The Female Malady*, discusses this process in far greater detail than can be given here. On the position of women in nineteenth-century medicine, see also Ludmilla Jordanova (1980) 'Natural traits: a historical perspective on science and sexuality', in Carolyn MacCormack and Marilyn Stratham (eds) *Nature, Culture and Gender*, Cambridge; Ludmilla Jordanova (1981) 'Mental illness, mental health: changing norms and expectations', in Cambridge Women's Study Group, *Women in Society, Interdisciplinary Essays*, London, pp. 95–114; Sally Shuttleworth, 'The surveillance of the sleepless eye, the constitution of neurosis in *Villette*' in her forthcoming book on Charlotte Bronte and nineteenth-century psychology.

33 'A curious dance round a curious tree', p. 386.
34 Andrew Wynter, 'Lunatic asylums', pp. 358–9.
35 *The Construction and Government of Lunatic Asylums*, pp. 59–60. Conolly remarks, too: 'Among the most constant indications of insanity are to be observed negligence or peculiarity as to dress; and many patients seem to lack the power of regulating it according to the seasons, or the weather, or the customs of society' (p. 59).
36 'Insanity: its cause and cure', *The English Woman's Journal* 4 (September 1859), 1–14 (pp. 12–13). The series also includes 'Insanity, past and present, part 1, 6 (January 1861), pp. 305–32, part 2, 7 (February 1861), pp. 383–97; 'A lunatic village' (an account of the famous moral managing community at Gheel), part 1, 7 (March 1861), pp. 19–33, part 2, 7 (April 1861), pp. 94–102; Daniel Hack Tuke, 'Insanity among women', 7 (May 1861), pp. 145–7.
37 Report of the Select Committee of the House of Commons on Lunatics, 1851, p. 45. Cited in Andrew Scull, 'A Victorian alienist: John Conolly, FRCP, DLC (1794–1866)', in Bynum, Porter, and Shepherd (eds), *The Anatomy of Madness*, vol. I; *People and Ideas*, p. 103. This essay, together with R. Hunter and I. MacAlpine's Introductions to the reprinted editions of *Indications of Insanity, the Treatment of the Insane Without Mechanical Restraints*, and *The Construction and Government of Lunatic Asylums*, are the most useful sources on Conolly. See also Showalter, *The Female Malady*, pp. 23–51.
38 See Scull, 'A Victorian alienist', pp. 115–23.
39 John Conolly (1964) *An Enquiry Concerning the Indications of Insanity*, London, p. 17 (1st edn 1830).
40 ibid., p. 35.
41 Conolly set up Lawn House 'for the reception of ladies', in 1845, and Hayes Park in 1850. See Hunter and MacAlpine, Introduction to *Indications*, p. xc.
42 John Conolly (1849) *A Remonstrance with the Lord Chief Baron Touching the Case Nottridge Versus Ripley*, 3rd edn, London, p. 3. Cited in Scull, 'A Victorian alienist', p. 129, and p. 146, note 217. Scull also mentions that Bulwer-Lytton sought advice from Conolly and Forbes Winslow regarding the confinement of his wife Lady Rosina Bulwer-Lytton (p. 145, note 209).
43 Hunter and MacAlpine, Introduction to *Indications*, p. xl.
44 Dickens's disclaimer reads:

> The statements and opinions of this journal generally are, of course, to be received as the statement and opinions of its conductor. But this is not so, in the case of a work of fiction first published in these pages as a serial story, with the name of an eminent writer attached to it. When one of my literary brothers does me the honour to undertake such a task, I hold that he executes it on his own personal responsibility, and for the sustainment of his own reputation; and I do not consider myself at liberty to exercise that control over his text which I claim as to other contributions. (*All the Year Round*, 26 December 1863, p. 419)

For a discussion of this incident, and Dickens's relationship with

Conolly, see R. Hunter and I. MacAlpine, 'Dickens and Conolly: an embarrassed editor's disclaimer', *The Times Literary Supplement*, 11 August 1961, pp. 534–5.

45   Pascal, according to Wycherley, was a madman with an illusion about a precipice . . . Napoleon an ambitious maniac, in whom the sense of impossibility gradually became extinguished by visceral and cerebral derangement. . . . But without intending any disrespect from these gentlemen, he assigned the golden crown of insanity to Hamlet. (*Hard Cash*, p. 438)

Cf. Conolly's *Indications of Insanity*: 'The celebrated Pascal was the subject of a false sensation, representing to him the edge of an immediate and fearful precipice . . . the hallucination is mistaken for reality, then the man is mad' (p. 315).

46   Three of the most well-known of these exposures were John Mitford's pamphlets, *The Crimes and Horrors of Warburton's Private Madhouses*, and *The Crimes and Horrors of Kelly House* (both probably 1825), together with Richard Paternoster's more sober *The Madhouse System* (1841). See W. Parry Jones, *The Trade in Lunacy*, pp. 36, 227. Kathleen Jones, *History of the Mental Health Services*, pp. 160–6, argues that Reade directly adapted Paternoster's case in *Hard Cash*.

47   *Hard Cash*, p. 427.

48   Charles Reade (1883) 'Our dark places', *Readiana*, London. See also Wayne Burns (1961) *Charles Reade, a Study in Victorian Authorship*, New York, pp. 203–8. Burns argues, not altogether convincingly, that Reade's interest was in part motivated by fears for his own sanity.

49   *Hard Cash*, p. 428.

50   On the specific role of the Lunacy Commission, see N. Harvey, 'A slavish bowing down: the Lunacy Commission and the psychiatric profession 1845–60', in Bynum, Porter, and Shepherd (eds) *Anatomy of Madness*, II, pp. 98–131.

51   Cited in K. Jones, *A History of the Mental Health Services*, p. 29.

52   Mary Wollstonecraft (1980) *The Wrongs of Woman* (unfinished in 1797, when she died), ed. James Kingsley and Gary Kelly, Oxford, p. 85.

53   Both Scull, *Museums of Madness*, and W. Parry-Jones, *The Trade in Lunacy*, develop excellent analyses of this process.

54   W. Parry-Jones, *The Trade in Lunacy* pp. 234–40. Also Peter McCandless, 'Liberty and lunacy: the Victorians and wrongful confinement', in Scull (ed.) *Madhouses, Mad-Doctors and Madmen*, pp. 339–63. One of the most widely publicized cases was that of Miss Turner, a patient at Acomb House, York, who was believed to be 'of sound mind' following the 1858 Enquiry (W. Parry-Jones, *The Trade in Lunacy*, p. 237). Reade mentions the case in *Hard Cash* (p. 360).

55   Report of the Parliamentary Select Committee on the Care and Treatment of Lunatics and Their Property (1859), pp. 15–17. In addition to his evidence to the Select Committee, Perceval had published a pamphlet aiming to expose the inadequacy of the 1845 Act to deal with improper detention: 'Letters to the Right Honourable Sir James Graham, Bart, and to other noblemen and gentlemen, upon the reform of the law affecting the treatment of persons alleged to be of unsound mind (1846). See

also R. Hunter and I. MacAlpine (1962) 'John Thomas Perceval (1803–1876), patient and reformer', *Medical History* 6, pp. 393–4.
56 C.J. Fox, who founded both Brislington House and Ticehurst Asylum was one of the early pioneers of the non-restraint system in private asylums. See W. Parry-Jones, *The Trade in Lunacy*, pp. 112–27.
57 John Perceval, *A Narrative of the Treatment Experienced by a Gentleman in a State of Mental Derangement, Designed to Explain the Causes and the Nature of Insanity, and to Expose the Injudicious Conduct Pursued Towards Many Unfortunate Sufferers under that Calamity*, two vols (1838 and 1840), edited, as *Perceval's Narrative*, by Gregory Bateson (1962), London, p. 4.
58 ibid., p. 3.
59 ibid., pp. 99–100.
60 ibid., p. 37.
61 ibid., p. 25.
62 ibid., pp. 270–1.
63 But this may with truth be said, that the study of man's understanding requires to be pursued to a certain extent, to enable medical practitioners to perform an important part of their practical duties with credit. . . . Without such principles, the cure of lunatics may indeed be professed as a trade and a profitable trade . . . those who would really be master of the whole subject of mental impairment and error, must make a wider survey of the functions of the mind, must study both its peculiar philosophy and the philosophy of morals. (Conolly, *Indications of Insanity*, pp. 37–9)
64 'In the year 1830, I was unfortunately deprived of the use of reason. . . . The Almighty allowed my mind to become a ruin under sickness – delusions of a religious nature, and treatment contrary to nature. My soul survived that ruin' (*Perceval's Narrative*, p. 3).
65 The use of the term 'unconscious' investigated here should not be confused with the later development of the concept by Freud. Although there are some correspondences between some aspects of the earlier theories and its psychoanalytic development, the mid-nineteenth-century 'unconscious', if anything, comes nearer to Freud's notion of the 'preconscious' than to his idea of the unconscious proper; the crucial difference being that for Freud the unconscious itself was constructed by the transformation of sexual drives through a process of repression that was itself unconscious. Thanks to Ann Scott for helping to clarify this point.
66 See Gillian Beer (1983) *Darwin's Plots: Evolutionary Narrative in Darwin, George Eliot and Nineteenth-Century Fiction*, London, and Sally Shuttleworth (1984) *George Eliot and Nineteenth-Century Science: The Make-Believe of a Beginning*, Cambridge.
67 These methodological questions are raised and discussed in detail in Roy Wallis (ed.) (1979) *On the Margins of Science: the Social Construction of Rejected Knowledge*, Keele; Michel Foucault (1970) *The Order of Things: An Archaeology of the Human Sciences*, London.
68 Mary Braddon (1862) *Lady Audley's Secret*, 3 vols, London, II, p. 202.
69 For a detailed analysis of the interrelationship between the legal and medical professions, their establishment of criteria for defining insanity

and criminal responsibility, and in particular the emergence of the administrative category of 'criminal lunacy' during the 1840s, see Roger Smith (1981) *Trial by Medicine: Insanity and Responsibility in Victorian Trials*, Edinburgh.

70 James Cowles Pritchard (1835) *A Treatise on Insanity and Other Disorders Affecting the Mind*, London, p. 3.
71 ibid., p. 6.
72 See Smith, *Trial by Medicine*, pp. 37–40.
73 John Barlow (1843) *On Man's Power Over Himself to Prevent and Control Insanity*, London. Barlow's is a popular manual of moral management, part of a series 'Small Books on Great Subjects'. Monomania, and the different subdivisions thereof, are also discussed in detail in J.C. Bucknill and D.H. Tuke (1858) *A Manual of Psychological Medicine*, London; Alexander Morison (1847) *The Physiognomy of Mental Diseases*, London; and Browne (1837) *What Asylums Were, Are and Ought to Be*.
74 Pritchard, *Treatise on Insanity*, p. 12. 'Moral Insanity – Dr Mayo's Croonian Lectures', *Fraser's Magazine*, March 1855, 245–59 (p. 246). This article gives a detailed account of Thomas Mayo's *Medical Testimony and Evidence in Cases of Lunacy: being the Croonian Lectures delivered before the Royal College of Physicians in 1853. With an Essay on the Conditions of Mental Unsoundness*. It quotes Benjamin Brodie's *Psychological Inquiries*: '[Mayo] has shown that other [cases], in which the plea of "moral insanity" was set up as an excuse for a crime, deserved no better appellation than that of "brutal recklessness"' (p. 247).
75 Review of Benjamin Brodie's 'Psychological Inquiries: In a series of Essays, intended to illustrate the mutual relations of the Physical Organisation and the Mental Faculties (1854)', *Quarterly Review* 96 (December 1854), p. 115. The article precedes the discussion of moral insanity with a detailed discussion of recent research on the brain and nervous system, discussed by Brodie. Pritchard, p. 24.
76 ibid., pp. 14–15.
77 ibid., p. 21.
78 ibid., pp. 156–80.
79 See Sander Gilman (1982) *Seeing the Insane*, New York, especially p. 58.
80 J.C. Lavater (n.d.) *Essays on Physiognomy*, trans. Thomas Holcroft, London, pp. 31–2. Lavater's original nine-volume study was published in English in the late eighteenth century. See also John Graham (1961) 'Lavater's *Physiognomy* in England', *Journal of the History of Ideas* 22, pp. 561–72. Graham notes how Lavater's *Physiognomy* was described in the *Gentleman's Magazine* as 'popular as the Bible itself' in 1801, and that there were over fifty-five editions in under forty years. His work had a strong influence, he argues, on Mary Wollstonecraft, Fuseli, Godwin, and Mary Shelley.
81 Gilman, *Seeing the Insane*, pp. 72–102, 164–79.
82 Let us imagine to ourselves the overwhelming influence of grief on woman, the object in the mind has absorbed all the power of the frame. . . . What causes the swelling and quivering of the lips, and the deathly paleness of the face? (Charles Bell, *The Anatomy and*

Philosophy of Expression as Connected with the Fine Arts, cited in Julie F. Codell (1986) 'Expression over beauty: facial expression, body language and circumstantiality in the paintings of the Pre-Raphaelite Brotherhood', *Victorian Studies* 29, p. 271)

E.S. Dallas's unsigned article 'On Physiognomy' in the *Cornhill* in 1861, compared the method favourably with phrenology precisely because it did not have phrenology's scientific pretensions: 'The absurdities of Lavater are as laughable as those of the phrenologists, and they are only less pernicious, because the good man had no scientific pretentions' ('On Physiognomy', *Cornhill Magazine* 4 (July-December 1861), p. 481).

83 For a very interesting discussion of Darwin's adaptation of physiognomic conventions in *The Expression of the Emotions in Man and Animals* (1872), see Janet Browne, 'Darwin and the face of madness', in Bynum, Porter, and Shepherd (eds) *The Anatomy of Madness*, I, pp. 151–66.

84 The role of Bell's physiognomy and its contribution to Pre-Raphaelite naturalism is discussed in Codell, 'Expression over beauty'. Other contemporary discussions of physiognomy include: 'Physiognomy', *Quarterly Review* 90 (December 1851), pp. 62–91; 'The physiognomy of the human form', *Quarterly Review* 99 (September 1856), pp. 452–91.

85 Wilkie Collins (1886) *The Evil Genius*, 3 vols, London, I, p. 34.

86 Roger Cooter (1984) *The Cultural Meaning of Popular Science: Phrenology and the Organisation of Consent in Nineteenth-Century Britain*, Cambridge, p. 3. This is a superb exploration of the social and cultural constitution of scientific knowledge in the nineteenth century. For an outline of Gall's theory of cerebral localization, see also Robert M. Young (1970) *Mind, Brain and Adaptation in the Nineteenth Century: Cerebral Localisation and its Biological Context from Gall to Ferrier*, Oxford, pp. 9–54.

87 Cooter, *The Cultural Meaning of Popular Science*, p. 20.

88 George Combe (1827) *The Constitution of Man in Relation to External Objects*, Edinburgh, pp. 46–8.

89 Dallas, 'On physiognomy', p. 476. Cooter offers a detailed account of how phrenologists initially stressed the 'inventive' aspect of the method and were pushed into stressing empirical accuracy by establishment scepticism in *The Cultural Meaning of Popular Science*, pp. 19–35.

90 Andrew Combe (1831) *Observations on Mental Derangement*, Edinburgh, p. 62.

91 Johann Spurzheim (1825) *A View of the Philosophic Principles of Phrenology*, pp. 133–4. Cited in Angus McClaren (1974) 'Phrenology, medium and message', *Journal of Modern History* 46 (pp. 87–8); Report of the Phrenological Society, *The Zoist* 1 (April 1843), p. 49. For Elliotson's involvement in penal reform, see Fred Kaplan (1975) *Dickens and Mesmerism: the Hidden Springs of Fiction*, Princeton, pp. 62–3, and Philip Collins (1962) *Dickens and Crime*, London, pp. 56–66. On the lunacy reform movement's involvement in phrenological societies, see Roger Cooter, 'Phrenology and the British alienists, ca 1825–1845', in Scull, *Madhouses, Mad-doctors and Madmen*, pp. 58–105. On the

cultural significance of the movement, see also Steven Shapin, 'The politics of observation: cerebral anatomy and social interests in the Edinburgh phrenology disputes', in *On the Margins of Science* (ed. Roy Wallis), pp. 139–79. Phrenology was still being actively discussed in the periodical press in the mid-nineteenth century, most notably in a series of articles by Bain, comprised of extracts from *The Senses and the Intellect* (1855), *The Emotions and the Will* (1859), and *On the Study of Character, Including an Estimate of Phrenology* (1861), in *Fraser's Magazine*: 'Phrenology and psychology', 61 (May 1860), pp. 692–708; and 'The propensities, according to phrenology', Part 1, 62 (September 1860), pp. 331–47; Part 2, 62 (November 1860), pp. 670–736; Part 3, 63 (February 1861), pp. 246–59; Part 4, 63 (June 1861), pp. 715–50.

92 For an analysis of the development of neurophysiology out of phrenology, see Young, *Mind, Brain and Adaptation*.

93 Locke had argued that all knowledge and experience sprang from the combination of sensations and perceptions triggered by external stimuli. But these only took on subjective meaning when combined or associated to produce complex ideas in different ways: by combination into one compound; by the juxtaposition of two ideas to connect them by resemblance without uniting them, and by separating ideas and perceptions and thus forming abstractions. In this he acknowledged that the association process took place to a large extent automatically, easily producing a bizarre or unexpected train of thought: 'This wrong connection in our Minds of Ideas in themselves, loose and independent of one another, has such an Influence, and is of so great force as to set awry in our Actions, as well as Moral and Natural Passions, Reasonings and Notions themselves, that there is not any one thing that deserves to be more looked after.' (1816) *An Essay Concerning the Human Understanding* (1st edn 1690), p. 422. Cited in Robert Hoeldtke (1967) 'The history of associationism and British medical psychology', *Medical History* 11, p. 47. See also, H. Warren (1921) *A History of Associationism*, New York, and Leslie Stephen (1876) *English Thought in the Eighteenth Century*, London.

94 In his *Observations on Man, His Frame, Duty and Expectations*, 2 vols (1749), David Hartley shifted the emphasis away from Locke's epistemological abstraction and introspection towards an analysis of the cognitive and moral faculties and the operation of physical vibrations along a continuum between the nerves and the brain. For Hartley, there was a relationship of repetitive association between ideas, sensations, muscular reflexes and motions which made sympathy, based on physiological correspondence, the basis of moral sense. For discussion of Hartley's role in the development of physiological psychology, see Robert Young, *Mind, Brain and Adaptation*, pp. 94–101, and Karl M. Figlio (1975) 'Theories of Perception and the Physiology of Mind in the Late Eighteenth Century', *History of Science*, 12, pp. 177–212.

95 S.T. Coleridge (1817) *Biographia Literaria*, 2 vols, ed George Watson, 1956. There is no space here to analyse Coleridge's psychological theory in detail; one of the best accounts of the philsophical and psychological undcrpinnings of Romantic aesthetic theory remains

M.H. Abrams's (1953) *The Mirror and the Lamp: Romantic Theory and the Critical Tradition*, Oxford. The fullest contemporary discussion of the development of the notion of the unconscious in German philosophy is Eduard von Hartmann's (1869) *Philosophy of the Unconscious: Speculative Results According to the Inductive Method of Physical Science*, trans. W.C. Coupland, 3 vols, 1884.

96 Thomas Brown (1820) *Lectures on the Philosophy of the Human Mind*, 4 vols, Edinburgh, I, p. 1.

97 ibid., II, pp. 339–40.

98 William Hamilton (eds H. L. Mansel and John Veitch) (1859) *Lectures on Metaphysics and Logic*, 4 vols, Edinburgh, I, p. 349. He goes on: 'Suppose, for instance, that A, B, C are three thoughts, – that A and C cannot immediately suggest each other, but that each is associated with B, so that A will naturally suggest B and B suggest C. Now it may happen that we are conscious of A, and immediately thereafter of C. How is the anomaly to be explained? It can only be explained on the principle of latent modification', I, p. 352.

99 John Abercrombie (1830) *Inquiries Concerning the Intellectual Powers and the Investigation of Truth*, Edinburgh, p. 3.

100 ibid., pp. 109 and 165.

101 p. 267. Abercrombie does not deny that dreams can have a cognitive function, although his analysis of what constitutes a thinking process in a dream is that which most closely corresponds to waking states. 'It appears then, that the mental operations which take place in dreaming, consist chiefly in old conceptions and old associations . . . But there are facts on record which show mental operations, in dreams of a much more intellectual character' (p. 288). He includes musical composition and the solving of mathematical problems in his cases.

102 Robert MacNish (1830) *The Philosophy of Sleep*, Glasgow, pp. 50 and 117. MacNish argues that preponderant organs influence dreaming as much as waking states: 'To speak phrenologically . . . an excess of *Cautiousness* will inspire [the dreamer] with terror; an excess of Self-esteem causes him to be placed in undignified situations . . . Secretiveness, a deceiver, Acquisitiveness, a thief . . .' (pp. 65–6). MacNish a leading exponent of phrenology, gives one of the fullest analyses of dreams here, and his general principles are echoed by Elliotson. See also Benjamin Brodie's *Psychological Inquiries*; John Sheppard, *On Dreams in their Mental or Moral Aspects*; Frank Seafield (1865) *The Literature and Curiosities of Dreams*, 2 vols.

103 Abercrombie, *Intellectual Powers*, pp. 262–89.

104 See *Dictionary of National Biography*, XIX, p. 272. Symonds's (1857) *The Principles of Beauty* argued that aesthetic qualities are objective features of works of art, and exist independently of the emotions of the observer. See also J.H. Buckley (1951) *The Victorian Temper, A Study in Literary Culture*, Cambridge, pp. 143–5 for details of this and a brief description of the Aesthetic Society.

105 (1851) *Sleep and Dreams*, p. 12.

106 ibid., p. 103.

107 ibid., p. 77.

108 'On Visions and Dreams', *Fraser's Magazine*, 7 (November 1862),

pp. 506–14 (p. 512). John Ferriar based his materialist theory of 'apparitions' on Erasmus Darwin's analysis of optical illusison. See also 'New Discoveries in Ghosts', *HW*, 17 January 1852, p. 403.

109 Symonds, *Sleep and Dreams*, p. 27; A.L. Wigan (1844) *The Duality of the Mind*, London.

110 Anton Mesmer (1779) *Mémoire sur la découverte du magnétisme animal*, Paris, trans. V.R. Meyers (1948), London, cited in Kaplan, *Dickens and Mesmerism*, p. 7; see also Robert Darnton (1968) *Mesmerism and the End of the Enlightenment in France*, Cambridge, Mass., pp. 3–7.

111 ibid., p. 4.

112 'What is mesmerism?', *Blackwood's Magazine* 70 (July 1851), p. 70. The article is a lengthy critique of mesmerism, concluding: 'Let it be announced from all authoritative quarters that the magnetic sensibility is only another name for an unsound condition of the mental and bodily functions' (p. 85).

113 *The Zoist* ran from 1843–1855. For a detailed description of Elliotson's career and an excellent accounts of the cultural impact of mesmerism in England, see Kaplan, *Dickens and Mesmerism*, pp. 3–74.

114 Puysegur developed the method of 'artificial somnambulism' in France in the early nineteenth-century. See H.F. Ellenburger (1970) *The Discovery of the Unconscious: the History and Evolution of Dynamic Psychiatry*, New York, pp. 70–4.

115 J. Elliotson (1840) *Human Physiology*, 5th edn, London, p. 674. Elliotson's quotation from Stewart is:

> That these pretensions (of mesmerism) involved much of ignorance, or of imposture, or both, in their author, has, I think been fully demonstrated . . . but does it follow from this that the *facts* witnessed and authenticated by those academicians should share in the disgrace incurred by the empirics who disguised or misrepresented them? For Mesmer's practice, with respect to the physical effects of the principle of imagination . . . are imcomparably more curious than if he had actually demonstrated the existence of his boasted science. (*Elements of the Philosophy of the Human Mind*, III, p. 221, cited in Elliotson, *Human Physiology*, p. 677)

116 Kaplan, *Dickens and Mesmerism*, pp. 46–52. Elliotson discusses the implications of the Okey sisters in *Human Physiology*:

> they exhibit perfect specimens of double consciousness. . . . In their ecstatic delirium, they know nothing of what has occurred in their natural state: they know not who they are, nor their ages, nor anything which they learnt in their healthy state; and in that natural state they are perfectly ignorant of all that has passed in their delirium. (p. 1165)

117 Kaplan's *Dickens and Mesmerism* is the most comprehensive study of Dickens's close and long-standing involvement with the movement. Bulwer-Lytton's involvement in mesmerism as one aspect of his 'occult' interests is discussed in Robert Lee Wolff (1971) 'Strange stories: the occult fiction of Bulwer-Lytton', in *Strange Stories and Other Explorations in Victorian Fiction*, Boston, pp. 143–322.

118 See Kaplan, *Dickens and Mesmerism*, pp. 99, 102; also Graham Storey and K.J. Fielding (eds) (1981) *The Letters of Charles Dickens*, vol. 5, 1847–9, Oxford, p. 254, note 3.

119 W.W.C. (1852) 'Magnetic evenings at home: to G.H. Lewes', Letter I, *The Leader*, 17 January 1852, pp. 64–5.

120 G.H. Lewes (1852) 'The fallacy of clairvoyance', *The Leader*, 28 March 1852, p. 305; 'The incredible not always impossible', *The Leader*, 3 April 1852, p. 328. See Introduction, Note 9 and Kirke H. Beet (1981) 'Wilkie Collins and *The Leader*', *Victorian Periodicals Review* 15, pp. 20–9. Beetz suggests that Collins dissented from *The Leader*'s religious agnosticism. Nine years later, too, Collins is described by George Eliot as entertaining G.H. Lewes, Spencer, and Pigott with a satirical story of Bulwer-Lytton's occultism while *A Strange Story* (1862) was being serialized in *All the Year Round*, Gordon S. Haight (ed.) (1954) Letter to Sara Henwell, 6 December 1861, *The Letters of George Eliot, III, 1859–1861*, Yale, p. 468. The evening described is 30 November 1861. *A Strange Story* was serialized in *All the Year Round* between 10 August 1861 and 8 March 1862, and is an explicit discussion of the possibilities of mesmerism.

121 See Henri F. Ellenburger (1970) *The Discovery of the Unconscious: the History and Evolution of Dynamic Psychiatry*, New York, pp. 70–6, and L.L. Whyte (1966) *The Unconscious Before Freud*, London.

122 William B. Carpenter (1877) *Mesmerism, Spiritualism, etc., Historically and Scientifically Considered*, London, p. 22.

123 For a description of Carpenter's career and development, see J. Estlin Carpenter's 'Memorial sketch', in William B. Carpenter (1888) *Nature and Man, Essays Scientific and Philosophical*, London, pp. 4–113. The Memoir mentions that Carpenter was a friend and neighbour of Wills, the co-editor of *Household Words* (p. 43).

124 G.H. Lewes (1874–9) *Problems of Life and Mind*, 5 vols. First Series, *The Foundations of a Creed*, 2 vols, I, p. 162.

125 William B. Carpenter (1874) *Principles of Mental Physiology, with their Application to the Training and Discipline of the Mind, and the Study of its Morbid Conditions*, London, pp. 429–30.

126 ibid., pp. 540–1.

127 ibid., pp. 454–5.

128 E.S. Dallas (1866) *The Gay Science*, 2 vols, London.

The first lesson of all is that art is for pleasure; the second is that the pleasure of art stands in no sort of opposition to truth. We in England have especial reason to bear this in mind, for we are most familiar with the doctrine that art is for pleasure, as it has been put by Coleridge; and it is not unlikely that some of the repugnance that the doctrine meets in minds of a certain order may be due to his ragged analysis and awkward statement. . . . Coleridge has defined science by reference to the external object with which it is engaged; but he has defined poetry with reference to the mental state which it produces. There is no comparison between the two. If he is to run the contrast fairly, he ought to deal with both alike, and to state either what is the outward object pursued by each, or what is the inward state produced by each. He would then find that, so much as the subject matter is concerned, there is no essential difference between poetry and science. (I, pp. 109–10)

129   ibid., I, pp. 43–4.
130   ibid., I, p. 181.
131   ibid., I, pp. 179–80.
132   ibid., I, pp. 193–4.
133   ibid., I, p. 205.
134   ibid., I, pp. 207–8.
135   ibid., I, pp. 222–3.
136   ibid., I, p. 316.
137   ibid., I, p. 192. Dallas criticizes both Spencer and Carpenter for their reductive conception of the 'play of thought'. Although he agrees with Carpenter that there is no clear boundary between reason and imagination, he argues that they cannot be differentiated by relating one to 'fact' and one to 'fiction' (I, pp. 187–8). See also James Sully (1874) *Sensation and Intuition, Essays in Psychology and Aesthetics*, London.
138   Pritchard, *A Treatise on Insanity*, pp. 156–70.
139   George Man Burrows (1828) *Commentaries on Insanity*, London, p. 41. He comments,

> Habitual luxury, and the vices of refinement, are peculiar to the rich, and consequently a greater degree of susceptibility and irritability is super-induced. The lower orders, who ought more generally to be exempt from the concomitant of wealth and indolence, that is, disease, unhappily provoke it by their excesses; and thus voluntarily graft onto themselves the evils which, from their condition, they might otherwise escape. (p.19)

140   Unsigned, probably Harriet Martineau (1854) 'Idiots again', *HW*, 15 April 1854, p. 197.
141   On the complex interaction between Darwin's work and mid-nineteenth-century culture, see Robert M. Young (1985) *Darwin's Metaphor: Nature's Place in Victorian Culture*, Cambridge; Beer, *Darwin's Plots*; Stephen Gould (1981) *Ever Since Darwin*, London; Lumilla Jordanova (1984) *Lamarck*, Oxford.
142   In the Preface to *First Principles* (1862), Spencer emphasized that his concept of the 'development hypothesis' had preceded Darwin's and was independent of it. For further analysis of Spencer's evolutionary ideas, their relation to associationism, see Young, *Mind, Brain and Adaptation*, pp. 150–90, and to Darwin, D. Freeman (1974) 'The evolutionary theories of Charles Darwin and Herbert Spencer', *Current Anthropology* 15, pp. 211–37.
143   Herbert Spencer (1859) 'Progress, its law and cause', reprinted *Essays: Scientific, Political and Speculative* (1858), p. 3. Spencer discovered Von Baer's formula that 'the development of every organism is a change from homogeneity to heterogeneity', from reviewing Carpenter's *Principles of Human Physiology* in 1851 (Young, *Mind, Brain and Adaptation*, p. 168).
144   Herbert Spencer (1855) *The Principles of Psychology*, London, p. 526.
145   Charles Bucknill and Daniel Hack Tuke's *A Manual of Psychological*

Medicine in 1858 argued that it was the methods of classification that had expanded rather than the numbers of insane themselves.

146 Wynter, 'Lunatic asylums', p. 392.

147 Henry Maudsley (1874) *Responsibility in Mental Disease*, London, p. 23. Maudsley was one of the most prolific and influential developers of psychiatric theory of the late nineteenth century. He was Fellow of the Royal College of Physicians and Professor of Medical Jurisprudence at University College, London. For a detailed analysis of the development and meaning of the term 'degeneration' in social and biological theory, and its impact on late-nineteenth-century novelists, see William Greenslade (1982) 'The concept of degeneration 1880–1910, with particular reference to the work of Hardy, Wells and Gissing' (unpublished Ph.D. dissertation, University of Warwick).

148 E. Ray Lancaster (1880) *Degeneration*, London, p. 33. Cited in Greenslade, 'The concept of degeneration', p. 14. The concept of the residuum, or the 'submerged tenth' of a criminalized class of casual poor, and the particular fears that they gave rise to, is analysed most thoroughly in Gareth Stedman Jones (1971) *Outcast London*, Oxford.

149 Cited in A. Ackerknecht (1959) *A Short History of Psychiatry*, New York, p. 49. See also Ian Dowbiggin 'Degeneration and hereditarianism in French mental medicine 1840–90: psychiatric theory as ideological adaptation', in Bynum, Porter, and Shepherd (eds) *The Anatomy of Madness*, I, pp. 188–232.

150 Henry Maudsley (1873) *Body and Mind*, London, pp. 44–5.

151 Morel, *On the Physical, Intellectual and Moral Degeneracy of the Human Race*, cited in Dowbiggin, 'Degeneration and hereditarianism', p. 192.

152 Maudsley, *Responsibility in Mental Disease*, p. 3.

153 ibid., p. 29.

154 Maudsley, *Body and Mind*, p. 63.

155 Elaine Showalter's *The Female Malady* includes a discussion of the role of degenerative theory in opposing the demands of feminism. Both socialist and feminist debates themselves were permeated with evolutionary assumptions, as witnessed particularly by, for example, Olive Schreiner (1911) *Woman and Labour* and Havelock Ellis's theory of homosexuality. See Ruth First and Anna Scott (1980) *Olive Schreiner*, London, and Jeffrey Weeks (1980) *Sex, Politics and Society*, London.

156 Hysteria had been established as a predominantly, but not exclusively, female disorder by classical medicine; it became to be seen specifically as a nervous disorder in the context of Whytt's general theory of the sympathetic structures of the nervous system in *Observations on the Nature and Causes of Those Disorders which have Commonly Been Called Nervous, Hypochondriac and Hysteric* in 1764. Thomas Laycock (1840) argued that while the nervous system was 'the seat of hysteric disease', there was a reciprocal action between the nerves, the sympathetic system, and the uterus, which has 'rather a directing than an exciting influence on nervous affectations' (*A Treatise on the Nervous Disorders of Women*, London, p. 144). See Veith, *Hysteria*, especially pp. 155–95.

157 'It is reasonable to expect that any emotion that is strongly felt by great numbers of people, but whose natural manifestations are completely repressed in compliance with the wages of society, will be the ones

whose morbid effects are most frequently noted' (Robert Carter (1853) *On the Pathology and Treatment of Hysteria*, London, p. 21; cited in Veith, *Hysteria*, p. 201). For an important reassessment of the simplistic 'repressive' conception of Victorian attitudes to sexuality, see Michel Foucault (1979) *The History of Sexuality*, vol. I, *An Introduction*, trans. Robert Hurley, London; Peter Gay (1984) *The Bourgeois Experience, Victorian to Freud*, vol. I, *The Education of the Senses*, Oxford; and M. Jeanne Peterson (1986) 'Dr Acton's enemy: medicine, sex and society in Victorian England', *Victorian Studies* 29 (Summer 1986), pp. 569–91.

158   F.C. Skey (1867) *Hysteria*, London, p. 55.
159   Henry Maudsley (1879) *The Pathology of Mind*, London, p. 466.
160   Henry Maudsley (1874) 'Sex in mind and education', *Fortnightly Review*, 21 (April 1874), pp. 466–83. Cf. also Herbert Spencer (1861): 'More or less of this constitutional disturbance will inevitably follow an exertion of the brain beyond the normal amount; and when not so excessive as to produce absolute illness, is sure to entail a slowly accumulating degeneracy of physique' (*Education, Intellectual, Moral and Physical*, London, p. 184).
161   Andrew Wynter (1875) *The Borderlands of Insanity*, London, p. 1.
162   Maudsley, *Responsibility in Mental Disease*, p. 63.
163   ibid., p. 40.

2   NERVOUS FANCIES OF HYPOCHONDRIACAL BACHELORS: *BASIL*, AND THE PROBLEMS OF MODERN LIFE

1   M. Bailey (ed.) (1951) *Boswell's Column*, London, pp. 42–3. Cited in Roy Porter, 'The Hunger of Imagination: Approaching Samuel Johnson's Melancholy', in *The Anatomy of Madness*, W.F. Bynum, Roy Porter, and Michael Shepherd (eds) (1985), vol. I, 'People and Ideas', pp. 63–89 (p. 66).
2   Wilkie Collins (1852) *Basil, A Story of Modern Life*, 3 vols, London, II, pp. 265–6.
3   ibid., I, p. 30.
4   (1852) '*Esmond* and *Basil*', *Bentley's Miscellany* 32 (November 1852), pp. 577, 586, and (1853) 'The progress of fiction as an art', *Westminster Review* 60 (October 1853), p. 358.
5   ibid., p. 372.
6   Dickens reiterated that it was his admiration for *Basil* that first made him take Collins seriously as a promising author, in a letter to Collins when he was writing *No Name*:

> I cannot tell you with what a dash of pride as well as pleasure I read the great results of your hard work. Because, as you know, I was certain from the *Basil* days that you were the Writer who would come ahead of all the Field – being the only one who combined invention and power, but humourous and pathetic, with that invicible determination to work, and that profound conviction that nothing is to be done without work, of which triflers and feigners have no conception. (Letter to Collins, 20 September 1862, in *The Letters of Charles Dickens to Wilkie Collins*, selected Georgina Hogarth, ed Lawrence Hutton, London, p. 124.)

7 *Basil*, Preface, I, pp. xi–xiv.
8 ibid., p. xi.
9 The 'hypochondria' was the region of the stomach immediately under the ribs, thought to be the seat of melancholy: Whytt (1767) uses the term hypochondriac primarily in this sense of melancholy in analysing it as a specifically nervous disorder in *Observations on the Nature, Causes and Cure of those Disorders which have been commonly called Nervous, Hypochondriac, or Hysteric, to which are prefixed some Remarks on the Sympathy of the Nerves* (Edinburgh, 1767). Following Hartley, Robert Whytt's work on nervous disorders attempted to narrow the vague use of the term down to 'hysteria' and 'hypochondria'. These were the products of the 'unnatural sensibility of the nerves' and the breakdown of the working of the delicate web of fibres between the nerves and the brain. This web formed a skein of sympathetic correspondences within the self in which 'nothing makes more surprising changes in the body than the several passions of the mind'. He noted that extreme physical sensation was thus often a subtle and complex form of emotional mediation, and often served 'the principle of preservation, without which we should cherish in our bodies such causes as would often end in our ruin'. Cited in I. Veith (1965) *Hysteria, the History of a Disease*, Chicago, pp. 160–1. In was in the latter half of the eighteenth century that 'nervous' shifted from meaning 'nervy' or 'of well strung nerves' to implying nervous weakness or debility, and to become increasingly associated with femininity. This overlaps with the changing primary meaning of 'hypochondria' – that it is a nervous disorder that takes the form of suffering from an imaginary disease. See W.F. Bynum, 'The nervous patient in late eighteenth and early nineteenth-century Britain: the psychiatric origins of British neurology', in W. Bynum, K. Porter, and M. Shepherd (eds) (1985) *The Anatomy of Madness*, I, pp. 89–103.
10 *Basil*, I, pp. 25–7. The 'morbid anatomy' metaphor is erased from the 1862 edition.
11 Compare the opening of *Basil* with the confessional openings of *Caleb Williams* and *The Confessions of a Justified Sinner*:

My life has for some time been a theatre of calamity. I have been a mark for the vigilance of tyranny, and I could not escape. My enemy has shown himself inaccessible to entreaties and untried in persecution. My fame, as well as my happiness, has become his victim. Everyone, as far as my story has been known, has refused to assist me in my distress and has execrated my name. I have not deserved this treatment. My own conscience witnesses in behalf of that innocence, my pretensions to which are regarded in the world as incredible. . . . I am incited to a penning of these memoirs only by a desire to divert my mind from the deplorableness of my situation, and by a faint idea that posterity may by their means be induced to render me a justice which my contemporaries refuse. My story will, at least, appear to have that consistency which is seldom attendant but upon truth. (William Godwin (1977) *Caleb Williams*, ed David Macracken, Oxford, p. 3 (1st edn 1794))

My life has been a life of trouble and turmoil; of change and vicissitude; of anger and exultation; of sorrow and of vengeance. My sorrows have all been for a slighted gospel, and my vengeance has been wreaked on its adversaries. Therefore, in the might of heaven will I sit down and write: I will let the wicked of this world know what I have done in the faith of the promises, and justification by grace, that they may read and tremble, and bless their gods of silver and gold, that the minister of heaven was removed from their sphere before their blood was mingled with their sacrifices. (James Hogg (1974) *The Private Memoirs and Confessions of a Justified Sinner*, ed John Carey, Oxford, p. 97 (1st edn 1824))

12 *Basil*, III, p. 296.
13 ibid., I, pp. 39–40.
14 ibid., I, p. 45.
15 ibid., I, p. 35.
16 ibid., I, p. 33.
17 ibid., I, pp. 46–7.
18 ibid., I, p. 291
19 ibid., I, p. 279.
20 ibid., I, p. 96.
21 ibid., I, pp. 120–1.
22 ibid., II, p. 4.
23 ibid., I, pp. 179–80.
24 ibid., I, pp. 199–200.
25 ibid., II, pp. 25–7.
26 ibid., II, pp. 28, 43.
27 ibid., II, p. 46.
28 ibid., I, p. 201.
29 ibid., I, pp. 235–6.
30 ibid., I, pp. 75–6.
31 ibid., I, pp. 77–8.
32 ibid., I, pp. 84–5.
33 ibid., I, p. 154.
34 ibid., I, pp. 158–9.
35 ibid., I, p. 149.
36 ibid., I, pp. 151–4.
37 John Abercrombie (1830) *Inquiries Concerning the Intellectual Powers and the Investigation of Truth*, Edinburgh, p. 267.
38 *Basil*, I, p. 160.
39 Thomas De Quincey (1821) *Confessions of an English Opium-Eater*, 1856 edition (1960), pp. 84–5 (note).
40 J.A. Symonds (1851) *Sleep and Dreams*, London, p. 78.
41 *Basil*, I, pp. 160–1.
42 Symonds, *Sleep and Dreams*, p. 24.
43 Audrey Peterson (1976) 'Brain fever in nineteenth-century literature: fact and fiction', *Victorian Studies* 19 (June 1976) in a discussion of the medical and fictional development of the concept of brain fever during the nineteenth century, argues that the simultaneous vagueness and medical authenticity of the term made it an attractive device for many nineteenth-century novelists. The term was a colloquial development of

the classical 'phrensy' and was defined, at the end of the eighteenth century, as inflammation of the brain. She quotes James Copland who described brain fever as being characterized by:

> Acute pain in the head, with intolerance of light and sound; watchfulness, delirium; flushed countenance and redness of the conjunctiva, or a heavy diffused state of the eyes; quick pulse, heavy spasmodic twitchings or convulsions, passing into somnolency, coma, and a complete relaxation of the limbs. (James Copland (1857) *A Dictionary of Practical Medicine*, London, p. 228)

In general an attack of brain fever was described as developing abruptly and as a potentially contagious disease, though precipated by moral causes.

44 *Basil*, II, pp. 159–62.
45 ibid., II, p. 175.
46 ibid., II, pp. 168–70.
47 ibid., II, p. 175.
48 De Quincey, *Confessions*, pp. 233–5.
49 *Basil*, II, pp. 176–80. De Quincey describes his architectural visions – the result of looking at Piranesi's pictures:

> With the same power of endless growth and self-reproduction did my architecture proceed in dreams. In the early stages of the malady, the splendours of my dreams were indeed chiefly architectural; and I beheld such pomp of cities and palaces as never yet was beheld by the waking eye, unless in the clouds. . . . Now it was that upon the rocking waters of the ocean the human face began to reveal itself; the sea appeared paved with innumerable faces, upturned to the heavens. (*Confessions*, pp. 239, 249)

50 *Basil*, III, p. 245.
51 ibid., III, p. 258.
52 ibid., III, p. 262.
53 ibid., III, pp. 288–9.
54 ibid., III, p. 147.
55 ibid., III, pp. 25–6.
56 Kenneth Robinson (1951) *Wilkie Collins, a Biography*, London, p. 73; Kirk H. Beetz (1978) *Wilkie Collins: an Annotated Bibliography 1889–1976*, New Jersey, p. 2. Dickens rejected the story on the grounds that its treatment of hereditary insanity might cause distress 'among those numerous families in which there is such a taint' in 1852. 'The Monktons of Wincot Abbey' eventually appeared in *Fraser's Magazine* during November and December 1855 and was reprinted in *The Queen of Hearts* collection as 'Brother Griffith's story of Mad Monkton', *The Queen of Hearts*, 3 vols (1859).
57 Edgar Allan Poe (1971) 'The fall of the house of Usher', *Tales of Mystery and Imagination*, London, p. 130. (First published in *Graham's Magazine*, 1839.)
58 See note 9.
59 ibid., p. 133.
60 ibid., p. 131.

61 Wilkie Collins, 'Brother Griffith's story of Mad Monkton', *The Queen of Hearts*, II, p. 2.
62 ibid., II, pp. 85–6.
63 Wilkie Collins (1856) *A Rogue's Life, Written by Himself, Household Words*, 13 March 1856, p. 157. The story was not published in book form until 1879.

3 *THE WOMAN IN WHITE*: RESEMBLANCE AND DIFFERENCE – PATIENCE AND RESOLUTION

1 Wilkie Collins (1973) *The Woman in White*, 3 vols, ed H.P. Sucksmith, Oxford, p. 22 (1st edn 1860).
2 ibid., p. 22.
3 ibid., p. 400.
4 See Introduction, and John Sutherland (1976) *Victorian Novelists and Publishers*, London, pp. 171–81.
5 Margaret Oliphant (1862) 'Sensation novels', *Blackwood's Edinburgh Magazine* 91 (May 1862), pp. 565, 566. For a discussion of Collins's development of fictional conventions in *The Woman in White*, see Walter Kendrick (1977) 'The "sensationalism" of *The Woman in White*', *Nineteenth-Century Fiction* 32 (June 1977), pp. 18–35, and Mark Hennelly (1980) 'Reading detection in *The Woman in White*', *Texas Studies in Literature and Language* 22 (winter 1980), pp. 449–67. For an interesting recent reading of the novel which at times overlaps with the one offered here, particularly in its focus on the rhetoric of 'nerves' to undermine gender identity, see D.A. Miller (1986) '*Cage aux folles*: sensation and gender in Wilkie Collins's *The Woman in White*', in Jeremy Hawthorne (ed.) *The Nineteenth-Century British Novel*, London, pp. 95–127.
6 *The Woman in White*, p. 75.
7 John Conolly (1830) *An Inquiry Concerning the Indications of Insanity*, London, p. 17.
8 'M.D. and MAD', *All the Year Round*, 22 February 1862, pp. 511, 513. This article also picks up on the debate about the definition of 'moral insanity' and what constitutes criminal responsibility. See Chapter 1.
9 In the course of his evidence to the Parliamentary Select Committee, Perceval argued that no one should be committed as insane on the evidence of doctors alone, but on medical opinion in combination with that of magistrates or clergy. Patients should have the right to appeal against their confinement, and should be able to correspond freely with friends or relatives. They should also be allowed to wear their own clothes, and not have their hair or beards forcibly cut. See *Report of the Parliamentary Committee into the Care and Treatment of Lunatics and their Property* (April 1859), pp. 17–19. See also Barbara Fass Leavy (1982) 'Wilkie Collins's Cinderella: the history of psychology and *The Woman in White*', *Dickens Studies Annual* 10, pp. 91–141, for a discussion of the reference of the Select Committee Enquiry to the novel in relation to the figure of Anne Catherick.
10 John Perceval (1846) 'Letters to the Right Honourable Sir James Graham, Bart., and to other noblemen and gentlemen, upon the reform of the law affecting the treatment of persons alleged to be of unsound mind', p. 35.

11 *The Woman in White*, p. 380.
12 'No pauper Asylum', Mrs Catherick insists: 'I won't have her put in a pauper Asylum. A Private Establishment, if *you* please. I have my feelings as a mother, and my character to preserve in the town; and I will submit to nothing but a Private Establishment, of the sort which my genteel neighbours would choose for afflicted relatives of their own.' Those were my words. It is gratifying for me to reflect that I did my duty. Though never over-fond of my late daughter, I had a proper pride about her. No pauper stain – thanks to my firmness and resolution – ever rested on *my* child.' (p. 498)

This of course only emphasizes her cynical obsession with propriety. The fact that the asylum is in a London suburb might have given it 'madhouse' connotations, since Hoxton was one of the main areas specializing in private madhouses in the eighteenth and early nineteenth centuries. But the asylum itself does not bear this out. See W. Parry-Jones (1972) *The Trade in Lunacy: A Study of Private Madhouses in England in the Eighteenth and Nineteenth Centuries*, p. 36 and, for a description of Fox's establishments, pp. 112–27.

13 *The Woman in White*, p. 386.
14 Alexander Morison (1824) *Outlines of Lectures on Mental Diseases*, Edinburgh, p. 125. The ability of madness itself to shape the habitual expression and thus the meaning of the face was a basic assumption of the physiognomy of madness. Morison, whose *Physiognomy of Mental Diseases* (1843, London) was one of the most influential mid-nineteenth-century analyses, emphasized the importance of expression over structure. See Sander Gilman (1982) *Seeing the Insane*, New York, pp. 92–100.
15 Unsigned, probably Morley (1859) 'The cure of sick minds', *HW*, 2 April 1859, pp. 416–17.
16 *The Woman in White*, p. 15. Compare this also with Pritchard's (1835) analysis of female insanity: 'A female modest and circumspect becomes violent and abrupt in her manners, loquacious, impetuous, talks loudly and abusively against her relatives and friends, before perfect strangers' (*A Treatise on Insanity*, London, p. 19).
17 John Conolly (1847) *The Construction and Government of Lunatic Asylums and Hospitals for the Insane*, London, pp. 59–60. See Chapter 1.
18 *The Woman in White*, p. 49. Conolly, like his contemporaries, stresses the importance of early education in establishing the correct associations, in *Indications of Insanity*, pp. 190–6. The article on idiots in *Household Words* also stresses that early education can modify inherited characteristics of the 'weak minded' ('Idiots again', *HW*, 15 April 1854, pp. 197–200).
19 *The Woman in White*, p. 85.
20 ibid., p. 90.
21 She is, however, described as briefly flashing the signs of mania when Percival Glyde's name is mentioned:

A most extraordinary and startling change passed over her. Her face, at all ordinary times so touching to look at, in its nervous sensitiveness, weakness and uncertainty, became suddenly darkened by an expression of maniacally-intense hatred and fear, which communicated a wild, unnatural force to every feature. Her eyes dilated in the dim evening light like the eyes of a wild animal. (p. 91)

It links the 'wildness' with Percival, though, as much as Anne.

22 ibid., p. 84.
23 ibid., p. 394.
24 ibid., p. 514. The biblical reference is to Exodus 34:7. Philip Fairlie is described as 'the spoilt darling of society, especially of the women – an easy, light-hearted, impulsive, affectionate man; generous to a fault, constitutionally lax in his principles, and notoriously thoughtless of his moral obligations where women were concerned' (p. 513).
25 ibid., p. 32.
26 ibid., p. 28.
27 ibid., pp. 54–5.
28 ibid., p. 381.
29 ibid., p. 445. The concept of 'nervous' as meaning resolute, or 'of well-strung nerves' refers back to the earlier eighteenth century usage of the term. See W.B. Bynum (1985) 'The nervous patient in eighteenth and nineteenth-century Britain: the psychiatric origins of British neurology', in W. Bynum, K. Porter, and M. Shepherd (eds) *Anatomy of Madness*, London, I, p. 90.
30 *The Woman in White*, pp. 1, 178.
31 ibid., p. 1.
32 ibid., p. 67.
33 ibid., p. 18.
34 ibid., p. 24. Conolly and Abercrombie both identify the loss of a coherent sense of time as one of the signs of derangement: John Conolly (1830) *An Enquiry Concerning the Indications of Insanity* (London), p. 177; N. Abercrombie (1830) *Inquiries Concerning the Intellectual Powers and the Investigation of Truth*, Edinburgh, pp. 99–101.
35 *The Woman in White*, p. 53.
36 John Barlow (1843) *On Man's Power Over Himself to Prevent and Control Insanity*, p. 27.
37 *The Woman in White*, pp. 65–6.
38 ibid., p. 66. Cf. J.C. Pritchard (1830) *A Treatise on Insanity*, London:

Mental defection, or melancholy, which extinguishes life and gives the mind up to fear and anticipation of evils, lays the foundation for many kinds of varieties of monomania. The most numerous and the worst instances are those in which the thoughts are directed towards the evils of a future life. (p. 30)

39 *The Woman in White*, p. 69.
40 ibid., p. 25.
41 ibid., p. 40.
42 ibid., pp. 41–2.
43 ibid., p. 42.
44 ibid., p. 166.
45 ibid., pp. 166, 145–6.
46 ibid., p. 158.
47 ibid., pp. 149–50.
48 ibid., pp. 167–78.

49 ibid., p. 172.
50 ibid., pp. 266–7.
51 ibid., p. 241. I owe this point to Mavis Daly.
52 ibid., p. 248.
53 ibid., p. 231.
54 ibid., p. 208.
55 ibid., p. 197.
56 ibid., p. 308.
57 ibid., p. 222. 'He laid his plump, yellow-white fingers . . . upon the formidable brute's head and looked him straight in the eyes' (p. 199).
58 ibid., p. 147.
59 ibid., pp. 194–5.
60 ibid., p. 195. Eleanor Fairlie never does break into mania though.
61 Pritchard, *A Treatise on Insanity*, p. 19. See also Conolly's treatment of the Nottridge case in Chapter 1.
62 *The Woman in White*, p. 195.
63 *The World*, 26 December 1877, p. 5. Reprinted as 'Mr Wilkie Collins in Gloucester Place' in Edmund Yates (1879) *Celebrities at Home*, third series, London, pp. 145–56.
64 *The Woman in White*, p. 211.
65 ibid., p. 213.
66 ibid., p. 560.
67 ibid., p. 558.
68 Cf. the point made by U.C. Knoepflmacher ((1975) in 'The counter-world of Victorian fiction and *The Woman in White*', in J.H. Buckley (ed.) *The Worlds of Victorian Fiction*, Cambridge, Mass.) that Fosco, like Frank Softly in *A Rogue's Life* and Captain Wragge in *No Name*, represents an anarchic and rebellious counterworld to the dominant order of 'respectability' represented by Hartright.
69 *The Woman in White*, p. 211.
70 ibid., p. 162. Thanks to Mavis Daly for this point about Marian's perception.
71 *The Woman in White*, p. 259.
72 ibid., pp. 305–7.
73 ibid., p. 17.
74 ibid., p. 471.
75 ibid., pp. 380, 379–80.
76 ibid., p. 379.
77 ibid., p. 381.
78 ibid., p. 423.
79 ibid., p. 438.
80 ibid., p. 413.
81 ibid., pp. 400–1.
82 ibid., p. 379.
83 ibid., p. 441.

4 SKINS TO JUMP INTO:
FEMININITY AS MASQUERADE IN *NO NAME*

1 Charles Dickens (1970) *Dombey and Son*, 3 vols, ed Peter Fairclough, Harmondsworth, p. 737 (1st edn 1848).

2 Wilkie Collins (1986) *No Name*, 3 vols, ed Virginia Blain, Oxford, p. 21 (1st edn 1862).
3 ibid., p. 7.
4 ibid., Preface, p. i.
5 See Norman Page (ed.) (1974) Introduction, *Wilkie Collins, the Critical Heritage*, London, p. 15, and Virginia Blain's introduction to the Oxford edition of *No Name*. *No Name* is generally considered the novel in which Collins was most influenced by Dickens's editorial interventions though Virginia Blain suggests that he extricated himself from Dickens's domination in her Introduction to the Oxford edition to the novel. Dickens suggested various names for the novel, none of which Collins chose, but which clearly suggest unconscious processes and pressures: 'Below the surface', 'Undercurrents', 'Behind the veil', 'Secret springs', 'Latent forces', 'Changed, or developed?', 'Nature's own daughter', *Letter to Collins*, 24 January 1862, *The Letters of Charles Dickens to Wilkie Collins*, selected by Georgina Hogarth, ed Laurence Hutton, London, p. 120. He also stressed in the same letter:

> It seems to be that great care is needed not to tell the story too severely. In exact proportion as you play around it here and there, and mitigate the severity of your own sticking to it, you will enhance and intensity the power with which Magdalen holds on to her purpose. (p. 121)

6 Review of *No Name*, *Blackwood's Edinburgh Magazine*, August 1863, p. 110. Cited in Page, *Wilkie Collins*, p. 143.
7 *North British Review*, February 1863, pp. 184–5. Cited in Page, *Wilkie Collins*, p. 141.
8 *No Name*, Preface, p. i.
9 ibid., p. 453.
10 ibid., p. 246.
11 ibid., p. 52.
12 ibid., p. 123.
13 ibid., p. 42.
14 Wragge's name for a series of roles based on characters whose history he has carefully researched, ibid., p. 235.
15 ibid., p. 361.
16 ibid., p. 232.
17 ibid., pp. 434–6.
18 ibid., p. 112.
19 This, as Gillian Beer points out, is one of the most important differences between Lamarck and Darwin. She argues that Lamarck's work 'follows the pattern of all stories of how things came to be the way they are: need brings about change or – in more admonitory versions – bad behaviour results in loss and degradation' (1983) *Darwin's Plots': Evolutionary Narrative, in Darwin, George Eliot and Nineteenth-Century Fiction*, London, p. 24.
20 *No Name*, p. 8.
21 ibid., p. 104.
22 ibid., pp. 104–5
23 ibid., p. 22. It should be 'Rochefoucauld'.

24 ibid., pp. 48–9.
25 Herbert Spencer (1858) 'Progress, its law and cause', *Essays: Scientific, Political and Speculative*, London, p. 3.
26 *No Name*, p. 4.
27 ibid., p. 26.
28 ibid., pp. 204–5.
29 ibid., p. 265.
30 ibid., p. 219.
31 ibid., pp. 188–9.
32 ibid., pp. 5–6.
33 ibid., p. 53.
34 ibid., p. 134.
35 ibid., p. 153.
36 ibid., p. 226.
37 ibid., p. 525.
38 ibid., p. 200.
39 Unsigned review, *Saturday Review*, 17 January 1863, p. 84.
40 *No Name*, p. 485, Cf. F.C. Skey's definition of hysterical patients in Chapter 1.
41 ibid., p. 357.
42 ibid., p. 521.
43 ibid., pp. 443–4.
44 ibid., p. 444.
45 ibid., pp. 239, 348–9.
46 ibid., p. 284.
47 ibid., pp. 275–6.
48 ibid., pp. 277–8.
49 John Abercrombie (1840) *Inquiries Concerning the Intellectual Powers and the Investigation of Truth*, Edinburgh, p. 102.

5 *ARMADALE*: THE SENSITIVE SUBJECT AS PALIMPSEST

1 G.H. Lewes (1874) *The Foundations of a Creed*, 2 vols, London, I, p. 162.
2 Wilkie Collins (1908) *Armadale*, 2 vols, pp. 39–40 (1st edn 1866).
3 ibid., pp. 20–1.
4 James Cowles Prichard (1835) *A Treatise on Insanity*, London, p. 14.
5 *Armadale*, p. 54.
6 J.A. Sutherland (1876) *Victorian Novelists and Publishers*, London, p. 105. As Sutherland points out, George Smith was an aggressive publisher who actively solicited his authors. He had made Collins the offer in 1861, but the writing of *Armadale* was delayed both by an attack of gout and by the sheer intricacy of its structure. See Sue Lonoff (1982) *Wilkie Collins and his Victorian Readers: a Study in the Rhetoric of Authorship*, New York, pp. 33–7, for Collins's working methods on *Armadale*.
7 *Armadale*, Preface. The Preface concludes: 'Estimated by the claptrap morality of the present day, this may be a very daring book. Judged by the Christian morality which is of all time, it is only a book that is daring enough to speak the truth.' For an excellent discussion of Collins's tone in his prefaces in relation to the critical establishment, see Lonoff,

Wilkie Collins and his Victorian Readers, pp. 55–66. Dickens's remarks to Collins on *Armadale* are also interesting:

> The plot is extraordinarily got together; its compactness is quite amazing . . . but insuperable and ineradicable from the whole piece is – *Danger*. Almost every situation in it is dangerous. I do not think any English audience would accept the scene in which Miss Gwilt in that widow's dress renounces Midwinter. And if you had got so far you would never have got to the last act in the Sanatorium. You would only carry those situations on a real hard wooden stage . . . and . . . *by the help of interest in some innocent person who they placed in peril, and that person a young woman* (Letter to Collins, 9 July 1866, *The Letters of Charles Dickens to Wilkie Collins*, selected by Georgina Hogarth, ed Laurence Hutton, 1892, p. 146)

The initial stage adaptation of *Armadale*, written in collaboration with Regnier, was produced in England; the final version, *Miss Gwilt*, was produced at the Globe Theatre in 1876.

8 *London Quarterly Review* (October 1866), pp. 107–9. In Norman Page (ed.) (1974) *Wilkie Collins: the Critical Heritage*, London, p. 156.

9 H.F. Chorley (a critic particularly hostile to Collins) *Athenaeum*, 2 June 1866, pp. 732–3.

10 *Saturday Review*, 16 June 1866, p. 726.

11 *The Woman in White*, p. 25.

12 *Armadale*, Appendix. This is followed, however, by another story of a bizarre coincidence concerning the name of the novel.

13 John Elliotson (1840) *Human Physiology*, London, p. 619.

14 J.A. Symonds (1851) *Sleep and Dreams*, London, p. 78.

15 Frank Seafield (1865) *The Literature and Curiosities of Dreams*, 2 vols, London, I, p. 61.

16 *Armadale*, pp. 136, 137.

17 ibid., p. 141.

18 John Abercrombie (1830) *Inquiries Concerning the Intellectual Powers and the Investigation of Truth*, Edinburgh, p. 267.

19 ibid.

20 *Armadale*, p. 142. Hawbury also explains the intervals of oblivion between the visions in strictly physiological terms:

> It means, in plain English, the momentary reassertion of the brain's intellectual action, while a deeper wave of sleep flows over it, just as the sense of being alone in the darkness, which follows, indicates the renewal of that action, previous to the reproduction of another set of impressions. (p. 139)

21 Abercrombie, *Intellectual Powers*, pp. 274, 280.

22 Seafield, *Literature and Curiosities of Dreams*, I, p. 272.

23 *Armadale*, p. 133.

24 Elliotson, *Human Physiology*, p. 676.

25 *Armadale*, pp. 134–5.

26 *The Woman in White*, p. 378.

27 For example, G.H. Lewes ((1859–60) *The Physiology of Common Life*, London, pp. 55–8) developed the concept of channels formed by culture directing and determining the flow of energy. See Sally Shuttleworth

(1986) 'Fairy tale or science? Physiological psychology in Silas Marner', in Ludmilla Jordanova (ed.) *Languages of Nature: Essays on Science and Literature*, London, p. 277.
28 E.S. Dallas (1866) *The Gay Science*, London, I, pp. 249, 250–1.
29 ibid., I, pp. 200, 207.
30 *Armadale*, p. 137.
31 ibid., p. 236.
32 Abercrombie, *Intellectual Powers*, p. 107.
33 *Armadale*, p. 44.
34 ibid., p. 81.
35 Herbert Spencer (1855) *Principles of Psychology*, London, p. 526.
36 Lewes, *The Foundations of a Creed*, I, p. 125.
37 *Armadale*, pp. 55–6.
38 ibid., p. 93.
39 ibid., p. 95.
40 ibid., pp. 213–17.
41 Abercrombie, *Intellectual Powers*, p. 421. Also Seafield:

> If our prevalent state and disposition of mind . . . determine and shape the complexions of our dreams it follows that those evil dreams are not innocent. . . . Our success in our efforts after self government may be estimated partly by our dream correctness. (*Literature and Curiosities of Dreams*, I, p. 71.)

42 *Armadale*, p. 284.
43 ibid., p. 218.
44 ibid., p. 357.
45 ibid., p. 258.
46 ibid., p. 373.
47 ibid., p. 480.
48 ibid., p. 334.
49 ibid., pp. 428–9.
50 ibid., p. 412.
51 ibid., p. 479.
52 ibid., p. 504.
53 ibid., p. 532.
54 ibid., pp. 621–2.
55 ibid., p. 330.
56 John Conolly (1856) *The Treatment of the Insane Without Mechanical Restraints*, London, p. 43.
57 *Armadale*, pp. 625–7.
58 ibid., p. 661.

6 LOST PARCEL OR HIDDEN SOUL? DETECTING THE UNCONSCIOUS IN *THE MOONSTONE*

1 Wilkie Collins (1982) *The Moonstone*, 3 vols, Oxford, p. 262 (1st edn 1868).
2 ibid., p. 227.
3 ibid., pp. 36–7.
4 ibid., p. 91.
5 ibid., p. 422.

6 Alethea Hayter ((1968) *Opium and the Romantic Imagination*, London, p. 259) notes this 'Chinese box' intricacy.

7 As William Tinsley, the novel's publisher, noted:

> During the run of *The Moonstone* as a serial there were scenes in Wellington Street that doubtless did the author and publisher's hearts good. And especially when the serial was nearing its ending, on publishing days there would be quite a crowd of anxious readers waiting for the new number, and I know of several bets that were laid as to where the moonstone would be found at last. Even the porters and boys were interested in the story and read the new numbers in sly corners, with packs on their backs. (*Random Recollections of an Old Publisher*, cited in Kenneth Robinson (1851) *Wilkie Collins – a Biography*, London, p. 216)

> Sue Lonoff (1982) *Wilkie Collins and His Victorian Readers: a Study in the Rhetoric of Authorship*, New York, offers an extensive analysis of the reader relations at work in *The Moonstone* and of the novel's sources and antecedents. See also her chapter on 'Collins at play' where she analyses how Collins invokes and plays with the expectations of his readers.

8 Albert D. Hutter (1975) 'Dreams, transformations and literature: the implications of detective fiction', *Victorian Studies* 19 (December 1975), pp. 181–209. However, *The Moonstone* cannot, *pace* T.S. Eliot, be described as the *first* English detective novel. An earlier novel, *The Notting Hill Mystery*, serialized in *Once a Week* in 1862 and 1863, and published in book form under the name Charles Felix in 1865, can according to Julian Symons (1974) *Bloody Murder: from the Detective Story to the Crime Novel: a History*, Harmondsworth, pp. 53–4, lay claim to this title.

9 For example, R. Ashley (1951) 'Wilkie Collins and the detective story', *Nineteenth-Century Fiction* 6 (June 1951), pp. 265–75; Ian Ousby (1976) *Bloodhounds of Heaven: the Detective in English Fiction from Godwin to Doyle*, Cambridge, Mass.; Gavin Lambert (1975) *The Dangerous Edge*, London; Stephen Knight (1980) *Form and Ideology in Detective Fiction*, London; Dennis Porter (1981) *The Pursuit of Crime: Art and Ideology in Detective Fiction*, Yale; D.A. Miller (1980) 'From *roman-policier* to *roman-police*: Wilkie Collins's *The Moonstone*', *Novel* 13 (Winter 1980) pp. 153–70.

10 Letter to W.H. Wills, 30 June 1867; Norman Page (ed.) (1974) *Wilkie Collins: the Critical Heritage*, London, p. 169.

11 *The Moonstone*, p. 395.

12 ibid., p. 7.

13 ibid., p. 513.

14 E.S. Dallas (1866) *The Gay Science*, London, I, p. 208.

15 ibid., I, pp. 207, 210.

16 William B. Carpenter (1874) *Principles of Mental Physiology*, London, p. 429.

17 *The Moonstone*, pp. 432–3. The passage from Elliotson is an exact quotation from *Human Physiology* (1840 edn); Jennings writes the Carpenter passage on a separate piece of paper rather than quoting directly from a text.

18 Preface to *The Moonstone*, p. xxxi.

19 ibid., pp. 432–3.
20 ibid., p. 433, and Elliotson (1840) *Human Physiology*, London, p. 646.
21 Carpenter, *Principles of Mental Physiology*, pp. 454–5.
22 ibid., pp. 542–3.
23 William B. Carpenter (1847) 'Dr Mayo on the relations of crime, insanity and punishment', cited in J. Estlin Carpenter (1888) 'Introductory memoir', *Nature and Man: Essays Scientific and Philosophical*, London, pp. 57–8.
24 Cited in J.E. Carpenter, 'Introductory memoir', *Nature and Man*, p. 56.
25 ibid., p. 58.
26 In the Preface to the 1871 edition of *The Moonstone*, Collins reported that he dictated sections of the novel crippled with the pain of gout and relieved by laudanum. Collins undoubtedly was addicted to the drug, but this account is probably exaggerated as Sue Lonoff suggests (*Wilkie Collins and His Victorian Readers*, p. 186). As Hayter notes in *Opium in the Romantic Imagination*, Collins was not unduly incapacitated by the use of opium in the 1860s. For an account of the widespread medical use of opium in the mid-nineteenth-century, see Terry M. Parssinen (1983) *Secret Passions, Secret Remedies: Narcotic Drugs in British Society 1820–1930*, Manchester, pp. 22–61; he argues that it was not until the 1870s that opium addiction came to be seen predominantly as a diseased appetite, or morbid craving.
27 Thomas De Quincey (1960) *Confessions of an English Opium-Eater*, London, p. 181. He goes on:

> Wine robs a man of his self-possession; opium sustains and reinforces it. Wine unsettles the judgment, and gives a preternatural brightness and a vivid exaltation to the contempts and the admirations, to the loves and the hatreds, of the drinker; opium, on the contrary, communicates serenity and equipoise to all the faculties.' (p. 181)

Parssinen argues that De Quincey's *Confessions* was widely cited as a medical as much as a literary source.
28 *The Moonstone*, p. 435.
29 ibid., p. 432.
30 Elliotson, *Human Physiology*, p. 677.
31 *The Moonstone*, p. 445.
32 ibid., pp. 317–18.
33 Dallas, *The Gay Science*, I, pp. 231, 235.
34 ibid., I, pp. 236–7.
35 *The Moonstone*, pp. 358–9.
36 ibid., p. 441.
37 ibid., p. 464.
38 ibid., p. 412. As Anthea Todd points out in the notes to the Oxford edition used here, Dr John Brown, a late-eighteenth-century Edinburgh doctor, the 'Scottish Paracelsus', gained an international reputation for advocating the stimulant method (p. 534).
39 Carpenter, *Principles of Mental Physiology*, pp. 429–30.
40 *The Moonstone*, p. 415.
41 ibid., p. 430.
42 ibid., p. 440.

43 ibid., pp. 510–11.
44 Dallas, *The Gay Science*, I, p. 250.
45 *The Moonstone*, p. 414.
46 The fullest analysis of the process of the psychic construction of the 'oriental other' in the western imagination that I have drawn on here is Edward W. Said (1978) *Orientalism*, London.
47 John Reed (1973) 'English imperialism and the unacknowledged crime of *The Moonstone*', *Clio* 2 (June 1973), pp. 281–90. Between December 1857 and June 1858 twenty-two articles on India appeared in *Household Words*, 'A sermon for Sepoy', *HW*, 27 February 1858, pp. 244–7, has been ascribed to Collins – an article that both reinforces and qualifies the dominant racism of the journal by pointing to the 'excellent moral lesson [the Indians] may learn from their own Oriental literature' (p. 244). See also William Oddie (1977) 'Dickens and the Indian Mutiny', *The Dickensian* 68 (January 1972), pp. 3–15.
48 *The Moonstone*, p. 4.
49 ibid., p. 34.
50 ibid., p. 321.
51 ibid., p. 227.
52 ibid., pp. 68–9.
53 Collins's notes from C.W. King (1865) *The Natural History, Ancient and Modern, of Precious Stones and of the Precious Metals*, London, p. 37. The other sources that Collins mentions in the Preface to the first edition of *The Moonstone*, the Orloff diamond, pillaged from India and adorning the Russian Imperial Diamond, and the Koh-i-noor, likewise of Indian extraction, are also taken from King, who mentions as well the diamond stolen from India by Governor Pitt (Lonoff, *Wilkie Collins and His Victorian Readers*, p. 176).
54 Dallas, *The Gay Science*, I, p. 200.
55 ibid., I, p. 273.
56 ibid., I, p. 274.
57 ibid., II, p. 138.
58 *The Moonstone*, p. 24.
59 ibid., pp. 24–5. The sexual connotations of the Shivering Sands have been emphasized by Albert D. Hutter in 'Dreams, transformations and literature'. His argument is interesting, but here I want to stress the specific use of magnetic references.
60 *The Moonstone*, p. 27.
61 ibid., p. 28.
62 ibid., p. 214. The way that the figure of Miss Clack corresponds to contemporary stereotypes and expectations is discussed by Lonoff, *Wilkie Collins and his Victorian Readers*, pp. 184–6, 204–6.
63 *The Moonstone*, p. 162.
64 ibid., p. 26.
65 ibid., p. 350.
66 ibid., pp. 349–50.
67 ibid., p. 194.
68 ibid., p. 58.
69 ibid., p. 91.
70 ibid., pp. 46–7.

71 ibid., pp. 347, 466.
72 ibid., pp. 9, 13.
73 ibid., p. 83.
74 ibid., p. 369.
75 ibid., p. 370.
76 ibid., p. 47.
77 ibid., pp. 398–9.
78 Dallas, *The Gay Science*, I, p. 117, II, p. 165.

7 RESISTLESS INFLUENCES: DEGENERATION AND ITS NEGATION IN THE LATER FICTION

1 Wilkie Collins (1879) *The Fallen Leaves*, First Series, 3 vols, London, I, p. 3.
2 Wilkie Collins (1893) *Man and Wife*, 3 vols, London, p. 174 (1st edn 1870).
3 Wilkie Collins (1880) *Jezebel's Daughter*, 3 vols, London, I, pp. 57–8.
4 The mould for this interpretation was set by A.C. Swinburne's couplet, 'What brought good Wilkie's genius nigh perdition?/Some demon whispered – "Wilkie! have a mission!"' which is repeatedly cited in subsequent critical discussions of Collins's later work. Swinburne goes on to argue that 'in some, but by no means all, of his later novels there is much of the peculiar and studious ability which distinguishes his best: but his original remarkable faculty for writing short stories had undergone a total and unaccountable decay' ((1894) 'Wilkie Collins', *Studies in Prose and Poetry*, London, p. 111). Kenneth Robinson (1951) *Wilkie Collins: a Biography*, London, suggests that Collins's later work is virtually marked by premature senility; Robert Ashley (1952) *Wilkie Collins*, London, presents a modified version of the same theme, arguing the poor health rather than turning to thesis novels contributed to Collins's decline. William Marshall (1970) *Wilkie Collins*, New York, gives a more positive account of his later fiction, as does Sue Lonoff (1982) *Wilkie Collins and His Victorian Readers*, New York, though she too lays stress on the 'detrimental' effect of Reade.
5 Bentley had published most of Collins's writing up until 1860; *Basil* was one of the novels chosen by him in an attempt to cut the price of first editions from 21s to 10s 6d. Collins wrote to Bentley that he was 'delighted to hear that your house is about to lead the way in lowering the present extravagantly absurd prices charged for works of fiction' (Berg Collection, cited in Guinivere Griest (1971) *Mudie's Circulating Library and the Victorian Novel*, Bloomington, Indiana, p. 68). See also Royal A. Gettmann (1960) *A Victorian Publisher, A Study of the Bentley Papers*, Cambridge. On the Chatto deal, see Robinson, *Wilkie Collins*, pp. 275–6; also the Chatto correspondence in the University of Reading library.
6 Chatto was also responding to developments in 'mass' publishing that had been established earlier, particularly to the railway bookstall publishing phenomenon as well as the sensation novel itself. See Richard Altick (1957) *The English Common Reader: a Social History of the Mass Reading Public 1800–1900*, Chicago, for an analysis of the complicated relationships between class patterns, literature and reading

habits. Also J.M.S. Tomkins (1932) *The Popular Novel in England*, London; Margaret Dalziel (1957) *Popular Fiction a Hundred Years Ago*, London; Louis James (1963) *Fiction for the Working Man 1830–1850*, Oxford; and, more recently, R.C. Terry (1983) *Victorian Popular Fiction 1860–1880*, London.

7 Letter to Bentley, 18 March 1873, cited in N.P. Davis (1956) *The Life of Wilkie Collins*, Urbana, Ill., p. 274. Collins's hopes for the cultural elevation of a mass lower-middle and working-class readership of 'penny novel journals', 'a public of three millions – a public unknown to the literary world . . . which lies right out of the pale of literary civilization', are expressed in *The Unknown Public*, which first appeared in *Household Words*, 21 August 1858, pp. 217–22, reprinted in *My Miscellanies*, 1875, 2nd edn, London (p. 261). See Introduction, note 53.

8 See Tomkins, *The Popular Novel in England*, for a discussion of the Minerva Press.

9 This sense of the need to appeal to a mass popular audience is one of the central arguments of *The Gay Science*: 'Now in art, the two seldom go together; the fit are not few and the few are not fit. The true judges of art are the despised many – the crowd – and no critic is worth his salt who does not feel with the many' E.S. Dallas (1866) *The Gay Science*, I, London, p. 127. See Introduction.

10 Letter of Dedication, *Jezebel's Daughter*, I, p. v.

11 One of the explicitly tendentious aspects of the novel is the attack on the anomalous marriage laws of Scotland and Ireland; Geoffrey avoids marrying Anne by attempting to use the Scottish ruling that public recognition of marriage is equivalent to marriage itself, to palm her off on his friend, compounding her 'illegitimate' position. However, the solution, Geoffrey's actual marriage to Anne, turns out to be a far greater source of danger, and this is reinforced by Hester's predicament of having her own property continually taken from her by her husband.

12 *Man and Wife*, preface, p. vi. Cf. Matthew Arnold:

> The Barbarians, again, had the passion for field-sports; and they have handed it down to our aristocratic class. . . . The case of the Barbarians for the body, and for all manly exercises; the vigour, good looks and fine complexion which they acquired and perpetuated in their families by these means, – all this may still be observed in our aristocratic class.' ((1969) *Culture and Anarchy*, ed J. Dover Wilson, Cambridge, pp. 102–3)

Arnold goes on to argue that the chief defect of the Barbarian class is 'insufficiency of light'.

13 *Man and Wife*, p. 46.

14 Henry Maudsley (1873) *Body and Mind*, London, p. 63.

15 *Man and Wife*, p. 32.

16 ibid., p. 435.

17 ibid., p. 437. An extremely interesting analysis of the contradictory representation of the pure fallen woman in women's reading of the mid-nineteenth century is Sally Mitchell (1981) *The Fallen Angel: Chastity,*

Class and Woman's Reading 1835–1880, Bowling Green, Ohio. See also Nina Auerbach (1982) *Woman and the Demon: The Life of a Victorian Myth*, Cambridge, Mass.

18 Wilkie Collins (1908) *The New Magdalen*, 2 vols, London, pp. 15–16 (1st edn 1873).
19 ibid., p. 171.
20 ibid., p. 96.
21 ibid., pp. 195–6.
22 ibid., p. 268.
23 ibid., p. 30.
24 ibid., p. 67.
25 ibid., p. 237.
26 ibid., pp. 371–2.
27 Wilkie Collins (1898) *The Law and the Lady*, 3 vols, London, 'Note addressed to the reader', p. 1 (1st edn 1875).
28 ibid., p. 84.
29 ibid., p. 177.
30 ibid., p. 175.
31 ibid., p. 203.
32 ibid., p. 210.
33 ibid., pp. 217–18.
34 ibid., p. 222.
35 ibid., p. 234.
36 ibid., p. 218.
37 ibid., p. 226.
38 ibid., p. 54.
39 ibid., pp. 289–90.
40 Henry Maudsley (1874) *Responsibility in Mental Disease*, London, p. 40.
41 Andrew Wynter (1875) *The Borderlands of Insanity*, London, p. 17.
42 *The Law and the Lady*, p. 214. Cf. Maudsley:

> When the insane temperament has been developed in its most marked form, we must acknowledge that the hereditary predisposition has assumed the character of degeneration of race, and that the individual represents the beginning of a degeneracy which, if not checked by favourable circumstances, will go on increasing from generation to generation and end finally in the extreme degeneration of idiocy. (*Responsibility in Mental Disease*, p. 46)

43 *The Law and the Lady*, p. 363.
44 *Jezebel's Daughter*, I, Letter of Dedication, p. vii.
45 ibid., I, p. 49.
46 He was calm [after his shackles were removed]; his attention appeared to be arrested by his new situation. He was invited to join in the repast, during which he behaved with total propriety. After it was concluded, the superintendent conducted him to his apartment and told him the circumstance on which his treatment would depend. . . . The maniac was sensible to the kindness of his treatment. He promised to restrain himself, and he so completely succeeded, that during his stay no coercive means were ever

employed towards him. (Samuel Tuke (1964) *A Description of the Retreat*, London, pp. 146–7).

47 *Jezebel's Daughter*, I, p. 47.
48 ibid., III, p. 299.
49 ibid., I, p. 255.
50 Wilkie Collins (1883) *Heart and Science: A Story of the Present Time*, 3 vols, London, I, Preface, p. xiv.
51 William Rutherford (1874) *Report of the Forty Third Meeting of the British Association for the Advancement of Science*, London, p. 122; cited in Robert M. Young (1970) *Mind, Brain and Adaptation: Cerebral Localisation from Gall to Ferrier*, Oxford, p. 239. Young gives a full account of Ferrier's *The Localisation of Brain Disease* (1878).
52 Unsigned review, *Spectator*, 15 May 1880, p. 627.
53 Preface, *Heart and Science*, I, p. ix and p. xiii. Cf. the Preface to the 1861 edition of *The Woman in White*: 'It may indeed be possible in novel-writing to present characters successfully without telling a story; but it is not possible to tell a story successfully without presenting characters' (p. xxxiii).
54 Preface to *Heart and Science*, I, p. xi.
55 *The Fallen Leaves*, I, p. 87.
56 ibid., I, p. 212.
57 Collins had visited the Brotherhood of the New Life during his American lecture tour in 1873, and had read Charles Nordoff's *The Communistic Societies of the United States* (1875) (Robinson, *Wilkie Collins*, p. 292).
58 Frederick Denison Maurice, Letter to Ludlow, 4 December 1848 in Frederick Maurice (ed.) (1884) *The Life of Frederick Denison Maurice, Chiefly Told in His Own Letters*, 2 vols, London, I, p. 484. F.D. Maurice and Charles Kingsley were founders of the English Christian Socialist movement in the late 1840s.
59 See Henry Pelling (1954) *The Origins of the Labour Party 1880–1900*, London, p. 126; Gareth Stedman Jones (1971) *Outcast London; a Study of the Relationship Between Classes in Victorian England*, Oxford.
60 *The Fallen Leaves*, II, pp. 95–6.
61 ibid., II, pp. 103–4.
62 ibid., III, pp. 180–1.
63 ibid., II, p. 159.
64 ibid., II, p. 167.
65 ibid., II, pp. 164–5.
66 This is most clearly stated in Max Nordau (1895) *Degeneration*, London, citing Morel and Maudsley: 'irregularities in the form and position of the teeth; pointed flat palates, webbed or supernumeracy fingers, etc.' (p. 17).
67 *The Fallen Leaves*, II, p. 169.
68 Wilkie Collins (1889) *The Legacy of Cain*, 3 vols, London, I, p. 150.
69 ibid., II, pp. 221–2.
70 ibid., III, p. 280.
71 'Recent novels', *Spectator*, 26 January 1889, p. 120.

72 *The Legacy of Cain*, II, p. 218.
73 Wilkie Collins (1848) *Memoirs of the Life of William Collins Esq. R.A.,
    with Selections from his Journals and Correspondence*, 2 vols, London, I,
    p. 43.

Wherever possible first editions of works are cited. The first reference will indicate editions used in the text.

MANUSCRIPT MATERIAL

Reading University Library, Chatto and Windus Archive.

WORKS BY WILKIE COLLINS

Books

Memoirs of the Life of William Collins, Esqu., R.A. with Selections from his Journals and Correspondence, 2 vols (1848), London.
Antonina, or the Fall of Rome, 3 vols (1850), London.
Rambles Beyond Railways, or Notes in Cornwall Taken Afoot (1851), London.
Basil, a Story of Modern Life, 3 vols (1852), London.
Mr Wray's Cash Box, or The Mask and the Mystery (1852), London.
Hide and Seek, 3 vols (1854), London.
After Dark, 2 vols (1856), London.
The Dead Secret, 2 vols (1857), London
The Queen of Hearts, 3 vols (1859), London.
The Woman in White (1973) ed H.P. Sucksmith, Oxford (1st edn 1860, 3 vols).
No Name (1986) Virginia Blain, Oxford (1st edn 1862, 3 vols).
My Miscellanies (1875), London (1st edn 1863).
Armadale (1908), London (1st edn 1866, 2 vols).
The Moonstone (1982) ed Anthea Trodd, Oxford (1st edn 1868, 3 vols).
Man and Wife (1893), London (1st edn 1870, 3 vols).
Poor Miss Finch, 3 vols (1872), London.
The New Magdalen (1891), London (1st edn 1873, 2 vols).
Miss or Mrs? and Other Stories in Outline (1873), London.
The Frozen Deep and Other Tales, 2 vols (1874), London.
The Law and the Lady, 3 vols (1875), London.
The Two Destinies, 2 vols (1876), London.
The Fallen Leaves, First Series, 3 vols (1879), London.
The Haunted Hotel, a Mystery of Modern Venice; to which is added My Lady's Money, 2 vols (1879), London.
Jezebel's Daughter, 3 vols (1880), London.
A Rogue's Life, From His Birth to His Marriage (1879), London.
The Black Robe, 3 vols (1881), London.
Heart and Science, a Story of the Present Time, 3 vols (1883), London.
I Say No (1884), London.

The Guilty River, a Story (1886), London.
The Evil Genius; a Dramatic Story, 3 vols (1886), London.
Little Novels, 3 vols (1887), London.
The Legacy of Cain, 3 vols (1889), London.
Blind Love, 3 vols (1890), London.
The Lazy Tour of Two Idle Apprentices; No Thoroughfare; The Perils of Certain English Prisoners (in collaboration with Charles Dickens) (1890), London.

Articles

'A plea for Sunday reform', *The Leader*, 27 September 1851: 925 (signed 'W.W.C.').
'Magnetic evenings at home – to G.H. Lewes', *The Leader*, 17 January–13 March 1852: 63–4, 160–1, 183–4, 207–8, 231–3, 256–7 (signed 'W.W.C.').
'The unknown public', *Household Words*, 21 August 1858: 217–22.
'Books necessary for a liberal education', *Pall Mall Gazette*, 11 February 1886: 2.
'How I write my books; related in a letter to a friend', *The Globe*, 26 November 1887: 6.
'Reminiscences of a story teller', *Universal Review* 1 (May–August 1888): 182–92.

Other primary material: works to 1889

Abercrombie, John (1830) *Inquiries Concerning the Intellectual Powers and the Investigation of Truth*, Edinburgh.
(1833) *The Philosophy of the Moral Feelings*, Edinburgh.
Allen, M. (1831) *Cases of Insanity, with Medical, Moral and Philosophical Observations on Them*, London.
Anon. (1763) 'A case humbly offered to the consideration of Parliament', *Gentleman's Magazine* 33 (April 1763): 25–6.
(1816) 'Insanity and madhouses', *Quarterly Review* 15 (July 1816): 588–617.
(1821) *Inquiry into Certain Errors Relating to Insanity*, by G.M. Burrows', *Quarterly Review* 24 (October 1821): 169–93.
(1844) 'Report on the treatment of lunatics', *Quarterly Review* 74 (October 1844): 416–47.
(1845) 'Lunatic asylums', *Westminster Review* 43 (March 1845): 162–92.
(1850) '*Antonina, or The Fall of Rome* by W.W. Collins', *Gentleman's Magazine* 30 n.s. (April 1850): 408–9.
(1850) '*Antonina, or The Fall of Rome* by W.W. Collins', *Bentley's Miscellany* 27 (April 1850): 395–8.
(1851) 'What is mesmerism?', *Blackwood's Edinburgh Magazine* 70 (July 1851): 70–85.
(1851) 'Traveller's books for 1851', *Fraser's Magazine* 4 (August 1851): 219–36.
(1851) 'The treatment of the insane', *Household Words*, 6 September 1851: 572–6.
(1852) 'A curious dance round a curious tree', *Household Words*, 17 January 1852: 383–9.
(1852) 'New discoveries in ghosts', *Household Words*, 17 January 1852: 403–6.

(1852) '*Esmond* and *Basil*', *Bentley's Miscellany* 32 (November 1852) 576–86.

(1853) 'The progress of fiction as an art', *Westminster Review* 60 (October 1853): 342–74.

(1854) 'Idiots again', *Household Words*, 15 April 1854: 197–200.

(1854) '*Psychological Inquiries* by Sir Benjamin Brodie', *Quarterly Review* 96 (December 1854): 86–117.

(1857) 'Grand jury powers', *Household Words*, 15 August 1857: 457–63.

(1857) 'The star of Bethlehem', *Household Words*, 15 August 1857: 144–150.

(1857) 'Things within Dr Conolly's remembrance', *Household Words*, 28 November 1857: 518–23.

(1859) 'The cure of sick minds', *Household Words*, 2 April 1859: 415–19.

(1859) 'Insanity, its cause and cure', *English Woman's Journal* 4 (September 1859): 1–14.

(1860) 'Novels of the day; their writers and readers', *Fraser's Magazine* 62 (August 1860): 205–17.

(1860) *The Philosophy of Insanity*, London.

(1861) 'The enigma novel', *Spectator*, 28 December 1861: 1428.

(1861) 'Insanity, past and present', *English Woman's Journal* 6, Part I (January 1861): 305–20; Part II (February 1861): 383–97.

(1861) 'A lunatic village', *English Woman's Journal* 7, Part I (March 1861): 19–33; Part II (April 1861): 94–102.

(1862) 'M.D. and M.A.D.', *All the Year Round*, 22 February 1862: 510–13.

(1863) 'Not a new sensation', *All the Year Round*, 25 July 1863: 517–20.

(1863) 'Sensation novels', *Medical Critic and Psychological Journal* 3, 513-19.

(1866) 'Recent novel writing', *Macmillan's Magazine* 13 (January 1866): 202–9.

(1866) 'Madness in novels', *Spectator*, 3 February 1866: 134–5.

(1866) 'Novels', *Saturday Review*, 16 June 1866: 727.

(1866) 'Belles lettres', *Westminster Review* 30 (July 1866): 268–80.

Arlidge, John (1859) *On the State of Lunacy and the Legal Provision for the Insane*, London.

Arnold, Matthew (1969) *Culture and Anarchy*, ed J. Dover Wilson, Cambridge (1st edn 1869).

Bain, Alexander (1855) *The Senses and the Intellect*, London.

(1859) *The Emotions and the Will*, London.

(1860) 'Phrenology and psychology', *Fraser's Magazine* 61 (May 1860): 692–7.

(1860–1) 'The propensities, according to phrenology', *Fraser's Magazine*, 62 (September 1860), Part I: 331–47; (November 1860), Part II: 620–36; 63 (February 1861), Part III: 246–59; (June 1861), Part IV: 715–30.

(1861) *On the Study of Character, Including an Estimate on Phrenology*, London.

(1866) *English Composition and Rhetoric*, London.

(1868) 'Common errors on the mind', *Fortnightly Review* 10 (August 1868): 160–75.

(1868) 'Mystery, and other violations of relativity', *Fortnightly Review* 10 (October 1868): 383–95.

Barlow, John (1843) *Man's Power Over Himself to Prevent and Control Insanity*, London.

Bell, Charles (1816) *The Anatomy and Philosophy of Expression as Connected with the Fine Arts*, London.

Bentham, Jeremy (1789) *An Introduction to the Principles of Morals and Legislation*, Wilfred Harrison, Oxford, 1948.

Binet, Alfred and Fere, Charles (1888) *Animal Magnetism*, London.

Braddon, Mary Elizabeth (1862) *Lady Audley's Secret*, 3 vols, London.

(1863) *Aurora Floyd*, 3 vols, London.

Brodie, Benjamin (1854) *Psychological Inquiries: Being a Series of Essays Intended to Illustrate the Mutual Relations of the Physical Organs and the Mental Faculties*, London.

Brown, Thomas (1820) *Lectures on the Philosophy of the Human Mind*, 4 vols, Edinburgh.

Browne, W.A.F. (1837) *What Asylums Were, Are and Ought to Be*, Edinburgh.

Buchanan, Robert (1872) *The Fleshy School of Poetry, and Other Phenomena of Day*, London.

Bucknill, J.C. (1854) *Unsoundness of Mind in Relation to Criminal Insanity*, London.

(1859) *The Psychology of Shakespeare*, London.

Bucknill, J.C. and Tuke, D.H. (1858) *A Manual of Psychological Medicine*, London.

Bulwer-Lytton, E. (1862) *A Strange Story*, 3 vols, London.

Burrows, George Man (1828) *Commentaries on Insanity*, London.

Cantlie, James (1885) *Degeneration Amongst Londoners*, London.

Carpenter, William (1855) *Principles of Human Physiology*, 5th edn, London.

(1874) *Principles of Mental Physiology*, London.

(1877) *Mesmerism, Spiritualism, etc., Historically and Scientifically Considered*, London.

(1888) *Nature and Man: Essays Scientific and Philosophical*, London.

Carter, R. (1853) *On the Pathology and Treatment of Hysteria*, London.

Chapman, John (1852) 'The commerce of literature', *Westminster Review* 57 (April 1852): 511–54.

Cheyne, George (1733) *The English Malady: or, A Treatise on Nervous Disorders of all Kinds*, London.

Coleridge, Samuel Taylor (1817) *Biographia Literaria*, 2 vols, ed George Watson, London, 1956.

Combe, Andrew (1831) *Observations on Mental Derangement*, Edinburgh.

Combe, George (1827) *The Constitution of Man in Relation to External Objects*, Edinburgh.

(1845) *Elements of phrenology*, 6th edn, Edinburgh.

Conolly, John (1830) *An Inquiry Concerning the Indications of Insanity*, London, 1964.

(1847) *The Construction and Government of Lunatic Asylums and Hospitals for the Insane*, London, 1968.

(1856) *The Treatment of the Insane Without Mechanical Restraints*, London, 1973.

Cox, Joseph (1813) *Practical Observations on Insanity*, 3rd edn, London.

Dallas, E.S. (1852) *Poetics*, London.

(unsigned, 1860) '*The Woman in White* by Wilkie Collins', *The Times*, 30 October 1860: 6.

(1861) 'On physiognomy', *Cornhill Magazine* 4 (July 1861): 472–81.

(1866) *The Gay Science*, 2 vols, London.

Darwin, Charles (1859) *On the Origin of Species by Means of Natural Selection, or the Preservation of the Favoured Races in the Struggle for Life*, ed John Burrow, Harmondsworth.

(1872) *The Expression of Emotions in Man and Animals*, London.

De Quincey, T. (1856) *The Confessions of an English Opium-Eater*, London, 1960.

Dickens, Charles (unsigned, 1850) 'A preliminary word', *Household Words*, 30 March 1850: 1.

(unsigned, 1850) 'New lamps for old', *Household Words*, 15 June 1850: 265-7.

(unsigned, 1852) 'A curious dance round a curious tree', *Household Words*, 17 January 1852: pp. 383-9.

(unsigned, 1857) 'Something Shakespeare lost', *Household Words*, 17 January 1857: 49-52.

(unsigned, 1864) 'The sensational Williams', *All the Year Round*, 13 February 1864: 14-17.

Eliot, George (1851) 'Review of R.W. Mackay, *The Progress of the Intellect*', *Westminster Review* 54 (January 1851): 353-68.

(unsigned, 1856) 'Arts and belles lettres', *Westminster Review* 9 (April 1856): 625-50.

Elliotson, John (1840) *Human Physiology*, 5th edn, London.

Gissing, George (1889) *The Nether World*, 3 vols, Brighton, 1969.

Godwin, William (1794) *Caleb Williams*, ed David McCracken, Oxford, 1977.

Gregory, W. (1851) *Letters to a Candid Inquirer on Animal Magnetism*, London.

Hamilton, Walter (1862) *The Aesthetic Movement in England*, London.

Hamilton, Sir William (1859) *Lectures on Metaphysics and Logic*, ed H.C. Mansel and John Veitch, 4 vols, London.

Hartley, David (1749) *Observations on Man, His Frame, Duty and Expectations*, 2 vols, London.

Hartmann, E. Von (1884) *The Philosophy of the Unconscious: Speculative Results According to the Inductive Method of Physical Science*, trans. W.C. Coupland, 3 vols, London.

Haslam, John (1817) *Considerations on the Moral Management of the Insane*, London.

Hill, R. Gardiner (1838) *Total Abolition of Personal Restraint in the Treatment of the Insane*, London.

Hinton, James (1862) 'What are the nerves?', *Cornhill Magazine* 2 (February 1862): 153-66.

Hogg, James (1824) *The Private Memoirs and Confession of a Justified Sinner*, ed John Carey, Oxford, 1970.

James, Henry (1865) 'Miss Braddon', *The Nation*, 9 November 1865: 593-5.

Jordan, Furneaux (1886) *Character as Seen in Body and Parentage*, London.

Lancaster, E. Ray (1880) *Degeneration, a Chapter in Darwinism*, London.

Lavater, J.C. (n.d.) *Essays on Physiognomy*, trans. Thomas Holcroft, London.

Laycock, Thomas (1840) *A Treatise on the Nervous Diseases of Women*, London.

Lewes, G.H. (1852) 'The fallacy of clairvoyance', *The Leader*, 27 March 1852: 305.

'Realism in art: recent German fiction', *Westminster Review*, 70 (1858), 488–518.

(1859–60) *The Physiology of Common Life*, 2 vols, London.

(1865) 'Criticism in relation to novels', *Fortnightly Review* 3 (December 1865): 352–61.

(1865) 'The principles of success in literature', *Fortnightly Review* 1 (May–September 1865), Part I: 85–95; Part II: 185–96; Part III: 572–89; Part IV: 697–709; Part V: 257–68.

(1868) 'Mr Darwin's hypothesis', *Fortnightly Review* 9 (April–December 1868), Part I: 353–73; Part II: 611–28; Part III: 61–80; Part IV, 492–501.

(1874–5) *Problems of Life and Mind*, 5 vols, First Series, *The Foundations of a Creed*, 2 vols, London.

Locke, J. (1690) *An Essay Concerning the Human Understanding*, London, 1816 edn.

MacNish, R. (1830) *The Philosophy of Sleep*, Glasgow.

(1837) *An Introduction to Phrenology*, Glasgow.

MacVicar, J.G. (1855) *The Philosophy of the Beautiful*, Edinburgh.

Maddock, A.B. (1854) *Practical Observations on Mental and Nervous Disorders*, London.

Mansel, Henry (unsigned, 1863) 'Sensation novels', *Quarterly Review* 113 (April 1863): 482–514.

Masson, David (1859) *British Novelists and Their Styles*, London.

(1860) 'The three vices of current literature', *Macmillans Magazine* 2 (May 1860): 1–13.

Maudsley, Henry (1873) *Body and Mind: an Inquiry into their Connection and Mutual Influence, Specially with Reference to Mental Disorders* (enlarged edn), London.

(1874) *Responsibility in Mental Disease*, London.

(1874) 'Sex in mind and in education', *Fortnightly Review* 15 (April 1874): 466–83.

(1879) *The Pathology of Mind*, London.

(1886) *Natural Causes and Supernatural Seemings*, London.

Maurice, Frederick (ed.) (1884) *The Life of Frederick Denison Maurice. Chiefly Told in His Own Letters*, 2 vols, London.

Mearns, Andrew (1880) *The Bitter Cry of Outcast London*, London.

Mill, J.S. (1874) *Nature, the Utility of Religion and Theism*, London.

Mitford, John (1825) *The Crimes and Horrors of Warburton's Private Madhouses*, London.

Morison, Alexander (1824) *Outlines of Lectures on Mental Diseases*, Edinburgh.

(1843) *The Physiognomy of Mental Diseases*, London.

Noble, J.A. (unsigned, 1889) 'Recent novels', *Spectator*, 26 January 1889.

Nordau, Max (1895) *Degeneration*, 6th edn, London.

Oliphant, Margaret (unsigned, 1862) 'Sensation novels', *Blackwood's Edinburgh Magazine* 91 (May 1862): 564–84.

Paternoster, Richard (1841) *The Madhouse System*, London.

Perceval, John (1838 and 1840) *Perceval's Narrative*, ed Gregory Bateson, London, 1962 edn. *A Narrative of the Treatment Experienced by a Gentleman in a State of Mental Derangement, Designed to Explain the Causes* and the Nature of Insanity, and to Expose the Injudicious Conduct Pursued Towards Many Unfortunate Sufferers Under that Calamity.

Poe, Edgar Allen (1839) 'The fall of the house Usher', in *Tales of Mystery and Imagination*, London, 1971 edn.

Pritchard, James Cowles (1835) *A Treatise on Insanity and Other Disorders Affecting the Mind*, London.

(1842) *On the Different Forms of Insanity in Relation to Jurisprudence*, London.

Reade, Charles (1863) *Hard Cash, a Matter of Fact Romance*, 3 vols, London.

(1883) *Readiana*, London.

Report of the Parliamentary Select Committee on the Care and Treatment of Lunatics and Their Property, April 1859.

Seafield, F. (1865) *The Literature and Curiosities of Dreams*, 2 vols, London.

Skey, F.C. (1867) *Hysteria*, 2nd edn, London.

Spencer, Herbert (1855) *The Principles of Psychology*, London.

(1858) *Essays: Scientific, Political and Speculative*, First Series, London.

(1861) *Education, Intellectual, Moral and Physical*, London.

Stephen, Leslie (1876) *English Thought in the Eighteenth Century*, 2 vols, London.

Stewart, Dugald (1854) *Works* ed Sir William Hart, 11 vols, London.

Sully, James (1874) *Sensation and Intuition*, London.

Swinburne, A.C. (1889) 'Wilkie Collins', *Fortnightly Review* 2 (November 1889): 589–99.

Symonds, J.A. (1851) *Sleep and Dreams*, London.

(1857) *The Principles of Beauty*, London.

Trotter, Thomas (1807) *A View of the Nervous Temperament*, London.

Tuke, Daniel Hack (1878) *Insanity in Ancient and Modern Life*, London.

(1861) 'Insanity among woman', *English Woman's Journal* 7 (May 1861): 145–57.

Tuke, Samuel (1813) *A Description of the Retreat, an Institution Near York for Insane Persons of the Society of Friends*, London, 1964.

Weismann, Auguste (1882) *Studies in the Theory of Descent*, London.

Wollstonecraft, Mary (1798) *The Wrongs of Woman*, ed James Kingsley and Gary Kelly, Oxford, 1980.

Wood, Mrs Henry (1861) *East Lynne*, 3 vols, London.

(1866) *St Martins Eve*, 3 vols, London, 1885.

Wynter, Andrew (1875) *The Borderlands of Insanity*, London.

(unsigned, 1857) 'Lunatic asylums', *Quarterly Review* 101 (April 1857): 353–93.

(unsigned, 1870) 'Non-restraint in the treatment of the insane', *Edinburgh Review* 131 (April 1870): 418–49.

Whytt, R. (1767) *Observations on the Nature, Causes and Cures of those Diseases Which Have Commonly Been Called Nervous, Hypochondriac or Hysteric*, Edinburgh.

Yates, Edmund (ed.) (1857) *The Train*, London.

(1879) *Celebrities at Home*, Third Series, London.

Secondary material

Abrams, M.H. (1953) *The Mirror and the Lamp: Romantic Theory and the Critical Tradition*, Oxford.
Ackerknecht, E.A. (1959) *A Short History of Psychiatry*, New York.
Altick, R.D. (1957) *The English Common Reader: a Social History of the Mass Reading Public*, Chicago.
(1987) *Evil Encounters: Two Victorian Sensations*, London.
Andrew, R.V. (1979) *Wilkie Collins: a Critical Survey of His Prose Fiction*, New York.
Ashley, Robert P. (1951) 'Wilkie Collins and the detective story', *Nineteenth Century Fiction* 6 (June 1951): 265–73.
(1952) *Wilkie Collins*, London.
(1953) 'Wilkie Collins and the Dickensians', *The Dickensian* 49 (March 1953): 59–65.
Auden, W.H. (1965) *The Dyer's Hand*, London.
Auerbach, Nina (1982) *Woman and the Demon: the Life of a Victorian Myth*, Cambridge, Mass.
Bailey, P. (1978) *Leisure and Class in Victorian England*, London.
Baker, William (1980) 'Wilkie Collins, Dickens and *No Name*', *Dickens Studies Newsletter* 11 (June 1980): 49–52.
Barker-Benfield, G.J. (1976) *The Horrors of the Half-Known Life*, New York.
Barnes, Barry (1974) *Scientific Knowledge and Sociological Theory*, London.
Beard, Nathaniel (1894) 'Some recollections of yesterday', *Temple Bar* 102 (July 1894): 315–39.
Beer, Gillian (1983) *Darwin's Plots: Evolutionary Narrative in Darwin, George Eliot and Nineteenth-Century Fiction*, London.
Beetz, Kirk H. (1978) *Wilkie Collins: an Annotated Bibliography, 1889–1976*, New Jersey.
(1982) 'Wilkie Collins and *The Leader*', *Victorian Periodicals Review* 15, Part I (1982): 20–9.
Berridge, Virginia (1976) 'Concepts of narcotic addiction in Britain 1820–1926', *Annals of Science Journal* 36: 67–85.
Blair, David (1979) 'Wilkie Collins and the crisis in suspense', in Ian Gregor (ed.) *Reading the Victorian Novel: Detail into Form*, New York.
Bloch, Ernst (1980) 'A philosophical view of the detective novel', trans. R. Mueller and S. Thaman, *Discourse* 2 (summer 1980): 32–51.
Bolt, Christine (1971) *Victorian Attitudes to Race*, London.
Booth, Bradford A. (1951) 'Wilkie Collins and the art of fiction', *Nineteenth-Century Fiction* 6 (September 1951): 131–43.
Booth, Michael (1965) *English Melodrama*, London.
Brannan, R.L. (1966) *Under the Management of Mr Charles Dickens: His Production of 'The Frozen Deep'*, New York.
Brantlinger, Patrick (1982) 'What is "sensational" about the sensation novel?', *Nineteenth-Century Fiction* 37 (June 1982): 1–28.
Briggs, Julia (1977) *Night Visitors: the Rise and Fall of the English Ghost Story*, London.
Brooks, C. (1984) *Signs of the Times: Symbolic Realism in the Mid Victorian World*, London.

Select bibliography

Buckley, J.H. (1951) *The Victorian Temper: a Study of Literary Culture*, London.

(1967) *The Triumph of Time: a Study of Victorian Concepts of Time, History, Progress and Decadence*, London.

(ed.) (1977) *The Worlds of Victorian Fiction*, Cambridge, Mass.

Burns, Wayne (1961) *Charles Reade: a Study in Victorian Authorship*, New York.

Butt, John and Tillotson, K. (1957) *Dickens at Work*, London.

Bynum, William (1974) 'Rationales for therapy in British psychiatry 1780–1835', *Medical History* 18.

Bynum, W., Porter, K., and Shepherd, M. (eds) (1985) *The Anatomy of Madness*, vol. I, *People and Ideas*, vol. II, *Institutions and Society*, London.

Byrd, M. (1974) *Visits to Bedlam: Madness and Literature in the Eighteenth Century*, Columbia, South Carolina.

Caine, Hall (1908) *My Story*, London.

Cawelti, N.G. (1975) *Adventure, Mystery and Romance*, Chicago.

Carlson, Eric and Dain, Norman (1960) 'The psychotherapy that was moral treatment', *American Journal of Psychiatry* 117 (1960): 519–24.

(1970–1) 'The nerve weakness of the nineteenth century', *International Journal of Psychiatry*, 9: 50–6.

Chapman, Raymond (1968) *The Victorian Debate: English Literature and Society 1832–1890*, London.

Codell, Julie F. (1986) 'Expression over beauty: facial expression, body language and circumstantiality in the paintings of the Pre-Raphaelite Brotherhood', *Victorian Studies* 29 (winter 1986): 225–91.

Colby, V. and R.A. (1966) *The Equivocal Virtue: Mrs Oliphant and the Victorian Literary Market Place*, London.

Collins, Philip (1962) *Dickens and Crime*, London.

Cooter, Roger (1984) *The Cultural Meaning of Popular Science: Phrenology and the Organisation of Consent in Nineteenth-Century Britain*, Cambridge.

Cosslett, Tess (1982) *'The Scientific Movement' and Victorian Literature*, Brighton.

Cross, Nigel (1986) *The Common Writer: Life in Nineteenth-Century Grub Street*, London.

Cruse, Amy (1935) *The Victorian and Their Books*, London.

Cunningham, Hugh (1980) *Leisure in the Industrial Revolution*, London.

Dalziel, Margaret (1957) *Popular Fiction a Hundred Years Ago: an Unexplored Tract of Literary History*, London.

Darnton, Robert (1968) *Mesmerism and the End of the Enlightenment in France*, Harvard.

Davis, Nuel Pharr (1956) *The Life of Wilkie Collins*, Urbana, Ill.

Delamont, S. and Duffin, L. (eds) (1978) *The Nineteenth-Century Woman: Her Cultural and Physical World*, London.

Denman, Peter (1981) 'The supernatural referent: the presence and effect of supernatural terror in English fiction in the mid nineteenth century' (Unpublished Ph.D. thesis, University of Keele).

Digby, Anne (1986) *Madness, Morality and Medicine: a Study of the York Retreat 1796–1982*, London.

Donnelly, Michael (1983) *Managing the Mind: a Study of Medical Psychology in Early Nineteenth-Century Britain*, London.

Drinker, G.F. (1984) *The Birth of Neurosis. Myth, Malady and the Victorians*, London.

Drinkwater, John (1932) 'Eneas Sweetland Dallas', in John Drinkwater (ed.) *The Eighteen Sixties*, London.

Duffin, L. (1978) 'Prisoners of progress: woman and evolution' in S. Delamont and L. Duffin (eds) *The Nineteenth-Century Woman: Her Cultural and Physical World*, London.

Eliot, T.S. (1927) 'Wilkie Collins and Dickens', *Selected Essays 1917–1932*, London.

Ellegard, Alvan (1959) *The Reception of Darwin's Theories in the British Periodical Press*, Goteborg.

Ellenburger, Henri F. (1970) *The Discovery of the Unconscious: the History and Evolution of Dynamic Psychiatry*, New York.

Ellis, S.M. (1951) *Wilkie Collins, Le Fanu and Others*, London.

Elwin, Malcolm (1934) *Victorian Wallflowers*, London.

Fahnestock, Jeanne (1981) 'The heroine of irregular features: physiognomy and conventions of heroine description', *Victorian Studies* 24 (spring 1981): 325–50.

Figlio, Karl (1975) 'Theories of perception and the physiology of mind in the late eighteenth century', *History of Science* 12: 177–212.

Flint, Kate (1986) 'The woman reader and the 'opiate' of fiction 1855–1870', in Jeremy Hawthorn (ed.) *The Nineteenth-Century British Novel*, London.

Ford, George H. (1965) *Dickens and His Readers*, New York.

Foucault, Michel (1970) *The Order of Things: an Archaeology of the Human Sciences*, London.

—— (1973) *Madness and Civilization: a History of Insanity in the Age of Reason*, trans. Richard Howard, 2nd edn, New York.

—— (1975) *The Birth of the Clinic: an Archaeology of Medical Perception*, trans. A.M. Sheridan Smith, New York.

—— (1977) *Discipline and Punish: the Birth of the Prison*, trans. Alan Sheridan, Harmondsworth.

—— (1979) *The History of Sexuality*. Vol. 1, *An Introduction*, trans. Robert Hurley, London.

Freud, Sigmund (1955) 'The "uncanny"', Vol. XVII, *The Standard Edition of the Complete Psychological Words of Sigmund Freud*, trans. and ed James Strachey, London.

Gaunt, William (1942) *The Pre-Raphaelite Tragedy*, London.

Genette, Gerard (1980) *Narrative Discourse*, trans. Jane Lewin, Oxford.

Gettmann, Royal A. (1960) *A Victorian Publisher: a Study of the Bentley Papers*, Cambridge.

Gibbons, Tom (1973) *Rooms in the Darwin Hotel: Studies in English Literary Criticism and Ideas 1880–1920*, Nedlands, Australia.

Gilbert, Sandra and Gubar, Susan (1980) *The Madwoman in the Attic*, London.

Gilman, Sander (1982) *Seeing the Insane*, New York.

Ginsburg, Carlo (1980) 'Morelli, Freud and Sherlock Holmes: clues and scientific evidence', trans. Anna Davin, *History Workshop Journal* 9 (spring 1980): 5–37.

Gold, Milton (1960–1) 'The early psychiatrists on degeneracy and genius', *Psychoanalysis and the Psychoanalytic Review* 47: 37–55.

Select bibliography

Graham, John (1961) 'Lavater's Physiognomy in England', *Journal of the History of Ideas* 22: 561–72.

Greenslade, William (1982) 'The concept of degeneration 1880–1910, with particular reference to the work of Thomas Hardy, George Gissing and H.G. Wells' (Unpublished Ph.D. thesis, University of Warwick).

Griest, G. (1971) *Mudie's Circulating Library and the Victorian Novel*, Bloomington, Ind.

Grieve, Alistaire (1976) *'Found' and the Pre-Raphaelite Modern Life Subject*, London.

Gross, John (1973) *The Rise and Fall of the Man of Letters: Aspects of English Literary Life Since 1800*, 2nd edn, London.

Giustino, D. de (1975) *Conquest of Mind: Phrenology and Victorian Social Thought*, London.

Haight, Gordon S. (ed.) (1954) *The Letters of George Eliot*, III, 1859–1861, Yale.

Halevy, E. (1928) *The Growth of Philosophic Radicalism*, trans. Mary Morris, London.

Hall, Catherine (1979) 'The early formation of Victorian domestic ideology' in Sandra Burman (ed.) *Fit Work for Woman*, London.

Halperin, J. (1974) *The Theory of the Novel: New Essays*, 2nd edn, Oxford.

Hawthorn, Jeremy (ed.) (1986) *The Nineteenth-Century British Novel*, London.

Hayter, Alethea (1968) *Opium and the Romantic Imagination*, London.

Henkin, Leo J. (1940) *Darwinism in the English Novel*, New York.

Hennelly, Mark M. Jr (1980) 'Reading detection in *The Woman in White*', *Texas Studies in Literature and Language* 22 (winter 1980): 449–67.

Himmelfarb, Gertrude (1959) *Rooms in the Darwin Hotel*, London.

(1986) *Victorian Minds*, London.

Hoeldtke, R. (1967) 'The history of associationism and British medical psychology', *Medical History* 11: 46–65.

Houghton, Walter C. (1963) *The Victorian Frame of Mind, 1830–1870*, Yale.

Hughes, W. (1980) *The Maniac in the Cellar: the Sensation Novel of the 1860s*, Princeton.

Hunt, W. Holman (1905) *Pre-Raphaelitism and the Pre-Raphaelite Brotherhood*, 2 vols, London.

Hunter, R. and MacAlpine, I. (1961) 'Dickens and Conolly: an embarrassed editor's disclaimer', *Times Literary Supplement*, 11 August 1961: 534–5.

(1963) *Three Hundred Years of Psychiatry 1535–1860*, London.

Hutter, Albert D. (1975) 'Dreams, transformations and literature, the implications of detective fiction', *Victorian Studies* 19 (December 1975): 181–209.

Hutton, Lawrence (ed.) (1892) *The Letters of Charles Dickens to Wilkie Collins*, selected by Georgina Hogarth, London.

Hyder, Clyde, K. (1939) 'Wilkie Collins and *The Woman in White*', *PMLA*, 54 (March 1939): 297–303.

Jackson, Rosemary (1982) *Fantasy: The Literature of Subversion*, London.

James, Louis (1974) *Fiction for the Working Man 1830–1850*, Harmondsworth.

Jameson, Frederick (1981) *The Political Unconscious: Narrative as a Socially Symbolic Act*, London.

Jones, Greta (1980) *Social Darwinism and English Thought: the Interaction Between Biological and Social Theory*, Brighton.

Jones, Kathleen (1955) *Lunacy, Law and Conscience*, London.

—— (1971) 'Moral management and the therapeutic community', *Society for the Social History of Medicine* 5 (October 1971): 6–10.

—— (1972) *A History of the Mental Health Services*, London.

Jordanova, L. (1980) 'Natural traits: a historical perspective on science and sexuality', in C. Mackormick and M. Strathan (eds) *Nature, Culture and Gender*, Cambridge.

—— (1984) *Lamarck*, London.

—— (1986) *Languages of Nature: Critical Essays on Science and Literature*, London.

Kaplan, Fred (1975) *Dickens and Mesmerism: the Hidden Springs of Fiction*, Princeton.

Kendrick, Walter (1977) 'The sensationalism of *The Woman in White*', *Nineteenth-Century Fiction* 32 (June 1977): 18–35.

Knight, Stephen (1980) *Form and Ideology in Detective Fiction*, London.

Knoepflmacher, U.C. (1875) 'The counterworlds of Victorian fiction and *The Woman in White*', in J.K. Buckley (ed.) *The Worlds of Victorian Fiction*, Cambridge, Mass.

Knoepflmacher, U.C. and Tennyson, G.B. (eds) (1977) *Nature and the Victorian Imagination*, Berkeley, California.

Lambert, Gavin (1975) *The Dangerous Edge*, London.

Lang, C.Y. (1968) *The Pre-Raphaelites and Their Circle*, Boston.

Lawson, Louis A. (1963) 'Wilkie Collins and *The Moonstone*', *American Imago* 20 (1963): 61–79.

Leavis, Q.D. (1932) *Fiction and the Reading Public*, London.

Leavy, Barbara Fass (1982) 'Wilkie Collins's Cinderella: the history of psychology and *The Woman in White*', *Dickens Studies Annual* 10: 91–141.

Lehmann, R.C. (1908) *Memories of Half a Century*, London.

Lehmann, R.C. (ed.) (1912) *Charles Dickens as Editor*, London.

Levine, George (1981) *The Realistic Imagination*, Chicago.

Ley, J.W.T. (1918) *The Dickens Circle*, London.

Lohrli, Anne (ed.) (1973) *Household Words: A Weekly Journal 1850–1859, Conducted by Charles Dickens*, Toronto.

Lonoff, Sue (1980) 'Charles Dickens and Wilkie Collins', *Nineteenth Century Fiction* 35 (September 1980): 150–70.

—— (1982) *Wilkie Collins and His Victorian Readers: a Study in the Rhetoric of Authorship*, New York.

Lovejoy, A.O. (1942) *The Great Chain of Being*, Cambridge, Mass.

MacEachen, D. (1950) 'Wilkie Collins and British law', *Nineteenth-Century Fiction* 5 (September 1950): 121–36.

—— (1966) 'Wilkie Collins, *Heart and Science* and the vivisection controversy', *Victorian Newsletter* 29 (spring 1966): 22–5.

MacLaren, A. (1974) 'Phrenology, medium and message', *Journal of Modern History* 46: 86–97.

Marcus, Stephen (1969) *The Other Victorians*, London.

Mare, W. de la (1932) 'The early novels of Wilkie Collins', in John Drinkwater (ed.) *The Eighteen-Sixties*, Cambridge.

Marshall, William (1970) *Wilkie Collins*, New York.

Miller, D.A. (1980) 'From *roman-policier* to *roman-police*: Wilkie Collins's *The Moonstone*', *Novel*, 13 (winter 1980): 153–70.

(1986) '*Cages aux folles:* sensation and gender in Wilkie Collins's *The Woman in White*', in Jeremy Hawthorn (ed.) *The Nineteenth-Century British Novel*, London.

Miller, Karl (1985) *Doubles: Studies in Literary History*, Oxford.

Moretti, Franco (1983) *Signs Taken for Wonders: Essays in the Sociology of Literary Forms*, trans. Susan Fischer, David Forgacs, and David Millar, London.

Nochlin, Linda (1982) 'Once more the fallen woman', in N. Broud and M. Garrard (eds) *Feminism and Art History*, New York.

Ousby, Ian (1976) *Bloodhounds of Heaven: the Detective in English Fiction from Godwin to Doyle*, Cambridge, Mass.

Page, Norman (ed.) (1974) *Wilkie Collins, the Critical Heritage*, London.

Parry-Jones, William (1972) *The Trade in Lunacy: A Study of Private Madhouses in England in the Eighteenth and Nineteenth Centuries*, London.

Parssinen, Terry (1983) *Secret Passions, Secret Remedies: Narcotic Drugs in British Society 1820–1930*, Manchester.

Pelling, H. (1954) *The Origins of the Labour Party 1880–1900*, London.

Pedersen-Krag, G. (1957) 'Detective stories and the primal scene', *Psychoanalytic Quarterly* xxvi, 229–45.

Peterson, Audrey C. (1976) 'Brain fever in nineteenth century literature: fact and fiction', *Victorian Studies* 19 (June 1976): 438–64.

Phillips, Walter C. (1919) *Dickens, Reade and Collins – Sensation Novelists: A Study of the Conditions and Theories of Novel Writing in Victorian England*, New York.

Pinney, T. (ed.) (1963) *The Essays of George Eliot*, London.

Poovey, Mary (1984) *The Proper Lady and the Woman Writer*, Chicago.

Porter, Dennis (1981) *The Pursuit of Crime: Art and Ideology in Detective Fiction*, Yale.

Porter, Roy (1983) 'The rage of party: a glorious revolution in English psychiatry?', *Medical History* 73: 35–50.

Porter, Roy and Rousseau, G.S. (eds) (1980) *The Ferment of Knowledge: Studies in the Historiography of Eighteenth-Century Science*, Cambridge.

Prickett, Stephen (1979) *Victorian Fantasy*, Brighton.

Punter, David (1980) *The Literature of Terror*, London.

Rabkin, E. (1976) *The Fantastic in Literature*, Princeton.

Reed, John R. (1973) 'English imperialism and the unacknowledged crime of *The Moonstone*', *Clio* 2 (June 1973): 281–90.

(1975) *Victorian Conventions*, Athens, Ohio.

Reierstad, Keith Brown (1980–1) 'Innocent indecency: the questionable heroines of Wilkie Collins's sensation novels', *Victorian Institute Journal* 9: 57–69.

(1976) 'The demon in the house, or the domestication of gothic in the novels of Wilkie Collins (unpublished Ph.D. thesis, University of Pennsylvania).

Robinson, Kenneth (1951) *Wilkie Collins, a Biography*, London.

Rosen, George (1968) *Madness in Society*, New York.

Rycroft, Charles (1957) 'The analysis of a detective story', *Psychoanalytic Quarterly* 26: 229–45.

Sadleir, Michael (1944) *Things Past*, London.
Said, Edward (1978) *Orientalism*, London.
Sayers, Dorothy L. (1977) *Wilkie Collins: a Biographical and Critical Study*, Toledo.
Sayers, Janet (1981) *Biological Politics*, Toledo.
Scull, Andrew (1979) *Museums of Madness: the Social Organization of Insanity in Nineteenth Century England*, London.
—— (1981) *Madhouses, Mad-Doctors and Madmen: the History of Psychiatry in the Victorian Era*, London.
—— (1983) 'The domestication of madness', *Medical History* 27 (July 1983): 233–48.
Sedgwick, Eve Kosofsky (1986) *The Coherence of Gothic Conventions*, 2nd edn, London.
Sedgwick, Peter (1982) *Psycho-Politics*, London.
Shattock, J. and Wolff, M. (1982) *The Victorian Periodical Press: Samplings and Soundings*, Leicester.
Showalter, Elaine (1977) *A Literature of Their Own: British Women Novelists from Bronte to Lessing*, Princeton.
—— (1985) *The Female Malady: Women, Madness and English Culture, 1850–1980*, New York.
Shuttleworth, Sally (1984) *George Eliot and Nineteenth Century Science: the Make-Believe of a Beginning*, Cambridge.
Skultans, Vieda (1978) *Madness and Morals: Ideas on Insanity in the Nineteenth Century*, London.
—— (1978) *English Madness: Ideas on Insanity 1580–1880*, London.
Smith, Roger (1981) *Trial by Medicine: Insanity and Responsibility in Victorian Trials*, Edinburgh.
Stallybrass, P. and White, A. (1986) *The Politics and Poetics of Transgression*, London.
Stamford, Derek (ed.) (1973) *Pre-Raphaelite Writing*, London.
Stang, R. (1959) *The Theory of the Novel in England 1850–1870*, London.
Stedman-Jones, Gareth (1971) *Outcast London: a Study in the Relationship Between Classes in Victorian Society*, Oxford.
Sutherland, John (1976) *Victorian Novelists and Publishers*, London.
Swinburne, A.C. (1894) *Studies in Prose and Poetry*, London.
Taylor, Barbara (1983) *Eve and the New Jerusalem*, London.
Temple, Ruth (1955) *The Critics Alchemy*, New York.
Thomas, Deborah (1973) 'Contributions to the Christmas numbers of *Household Words* and *All the Year Round*', *The Dickensian* 69 (September 1973): 170–2.
Tillotson, G. and K. *Mid Victorian Studies*, 1965.
Tillotson, K. (1969) 'The lighter reading of the 1860s', Introduction to *The Woman in White*, Boston.
Todd, Janet (1986) *Sensibility: an Introduction*, London.
Todorov, T. *The Fantastic: a Structural Approach to a Literary Genre*, trans. Richard Howard, London.
—— (1977) 'The typology of detective fiction', in *The Poetry of Prose*, trans. Richard Howard, Oxford.
Tomkins, J.M.S. (1932) *The Popular Novel in England 1780–1800*, London.
Veith, Ilza (1965) *Hysteria: the History of a Disease*, Chicago.

Vicinus, M. (ed.) (1972) *Suffer and Be Still: Women in The Victorian Age*, Bloomington, Indiana.

(1977) *A Widening Sphere: the Changing Roles of Victorian Women*, Bloomington, Indiana.

Walkowitz, Judith (1980) *Prostitution and Victorian Society: Women, Class and the State*, Cambridge.

Wallis, Roy (ed.) (1979) *On the Margins of Science: the Social Construction of Rejected Knowledge*, Keele.

Warren, A.H. (1967) *English Poetic Theory 1825–1865*, London.

Warren, H. (1921) *The History of Associationism*, New York.

Webb, R.K. (1955) *The British Working Class Reader 1790–1848*, London.

Weeks, Jeffrey (1981) *Sex, Politics and Society*, London.

Whyte, L.L. (1966) *The Unconscious Before Freud*, London.

Williams, Raymond (1973) *The Country and the City*, London.

(1980) *Problems in Materialism and Culture*, London.

Wolff, Robert Lee (1971) *Strange Stories, and Other Explorations in Victorian Fiction*, Boston.

Yates, Edmund (1879) 'The novels of Wilkie Collins', *Temple Bar* 89 (August 1890): 528–32.

Young, Robert M. (1970) *Mind, Brain and Adaptation in the Nineteenth Century*, Oxford.

(1985) *Darwin's Metaphor: Nature's Place in Victorian Culture*, Cambridge.

INDEX